ISIS IN
AMERICA

TARCHER
SUPER-
NATURAL
LIBRARY

JEREMY P. TARCHER / PENGUIN
a member of Penguin Group (USA)
New York

ISIS IN AMERICA

THE CLASSIC EYEWITNESS ACCOUNT OF
MADAME BLAVATSKY'S JOURNEY TO AMERICA
AND THE OCCULT REVOLUTION SHE IGNITED

Henry Steel Olcott

Includes a Comprehensive Timeline
of the Life of Henry Steel Olcott

ORIGINALLY PUBLISHED AS
Old Diary Leaves, volume one

JEREMY P. TARCHER/PENGUIN
Published by the Penguin Group
Penguin Group (USA) LLC
375 Hudson Street
New York, New York 10014

USA · Canada · UK · Ireland · Australia
New Zealand · India · South Africa · China

penguin.com
A Penguin Random House Company

Isis in America was originally published as *Old Diary Leaves*,
volume one, in 1895. First Tarcher/Penguin edition published 2014.

Most Tarcher/Penguin books are available at special quantity discounts for bulk
purchase for sales promotions, premiums, fund-raising, and educational needs.
Special books or book excerpts also can be created to fit specific needs.
For details, write: Special.Markets@us.penguingroup.com.

Library of Congress Cataloging-in-Publication Data

Olcott, Henry Steel.
Isis in America: the classic eyewitness account of Madame Blavatsky's journey to
America and the occult revolution she ignited / Henry Steel Olcott.
p.   cm.—(Tarcher supernatural library)
ISBN 978-0-399-16923-6
1. Blavatsky, H. P. (Helena Petrovna), 1831–1891.   2. Theosophists—Biography.
3. Theosophical Society (Chennai, India)—History.   4. Theosophy—History.
I. Olcott, Henry Steel, 1832–1907. Old diary leaves.   II. Title.
BP585.B6O43   2014   2014006261
299′.934092—dc23
[B]

Printed in the United States of America
1   3   5   7   9   10   8   6   4   2

Book design by Meighan Cavanaugh

CONTENTS

FOREWORD

In the history of public bodies, the chapter which relates the origin and vicissitudes of the Theosophical Society should be unique. Whether viewed from the friendly or the unfriendly standpoint, it is equally strange that such a body should have come into existence when it did, and that it has not only been able to withstand the shocks it has had, but actually to have grown stronger proportionately with the bitter unfairness of its adversaries. One class of critics says that this fact strikingly proves a recrudescence of human credulity, and a religious unrest which is preliminary to a final subsidence upon Western conservative lines. The others see in the progress of the movement the sign of a world-wide acceptance of Eastern philosophical ideas, which must work for the reinvigoration and incalculable broadening of the spiritual sympathies of mankind. The patent, the undeniable fact, is that up to the close of the year 1894, as the result of but nineteen years of activity, charters had been granted for 394 branches of the Society, in almost all parts of the habitable globe; and that

those issued in that latest year outnumbered the yearly average since the foundation, in 1875, by 29.9 per cent. Statistically
viewed, the relentless and unfair attack which the Society for
Psychical Research and the Scottish Missionaries delivered
against it in 1884, and which it was hoped would destroy it,
merely resulted in very largely augmenting its prosperity and
usefulness. The latest assault—that through the *Westminster
Gazette*—must inevitably have the same ending. The simple
reason is that, however thoroughly the private faults and
shortcomings of its individual leaders may be exposed, the
excellence of the Society's ideas is not impugned in the least.
To kill the Theosophical Society, it is first necessary to prove
its declared objects hostile to the public welfare, the teachings
of its spokesmen pernicious and demoralising. It being impossible to do either the one or the other, the world takes the
Society as a great fact, a distinct individuality, which is neither
to be condemned nor applauded because of the merit or demerit
of its representative personalities. This truth begins to force
itself upon outsiders. One of the ablest among contemporary
journalists, Mr. W. T. Stead, said in *Borderland*, in the course
of a digest of these "Old Diary Leaves" as they originally
appeared in the *Theosophist*, that nobody now cares whether
the Coulomb and S. P. R. charges of trickery against Madame
Blavatsky were true or false; her worst enemies being unable
to deny her the credit of having affected modern philosophical thought to an extraordinary degree by popularising certain noble Eastern ideas. The same holds with respect to her
many colleagues, who, like herself, have spread these ancient
teachings through the medium of the Theosophical Society.

This wonderful organisation, which grew out of a common-place parlour gathering in a New York house, in the year 1875, has already made for itself such a record that it must be included in any veracious history of our times. Its development having gone on by virtue of an inherent force, rather than as the result of astute foresight and management; and having been so closely—for some years almost exclusively, connected with the personal efforts of its two founders, Madame Blavatsky and myself, it will perhaps help the future historian if the survivor sets down truthfully and succinctly the necessary facts. The series of chapters which now compose this book was begun nearly three years ago in the *Theosophist* magazine, and a second series, devoted to the history of the Society after the transfer to India, is now in progress. The controlling impulse to prepare these papers was a desire to combat a growing tendency within the Society to deify Mme. Blavatsky, and to give her commonest literary productions a quasi-inspirational character. Her transparent faults were being blindly ignored, and the pinchbeck screen of pretended authority drawn between her actions and legitimate criticism. Those who had least of her actual confidence, and hence knew least of her private character, were the greatest offenders in this direction. It was but too evident that unless I spoke out what I alone knew, the true history of our movement could never be written, nor the actual merit of my wonderful colleague become known. In these pages I have, therefore, told the truth about her and about the beginnings of the Society—truth which nobody can gainsay. Placing as little value upon the praise as upon the blame of third parties, and having all my life been accustomed to act according to what I have regarded as duty, I have not shrunk from facing the witless pleasantries of those who regard me as a dupe, a liar, or a traitor. The absolute unimportance of others' opinions as a factor in promoting individual development is so plain to my mind, that I have pursued my present task to its completion, despite the fact that some of my most influential colleagues have, from what I consider mistaken loyalty to "H. P. B.," secretly tried to destroy my influence, ruin my reputation, reduce the circulation of my magazine, and prevent the publication of my book. Confidential warnings have been circulated against me, and the current numbers of the *Theosophist* have been removed from Branch reading-room tables. This is child's play: the truth never yet harmed a good cause, nor has moral cowardice ever helped a bad one.

Mrs. Oliphant in her *Literary History of England* (iii., 263) says of Benthan just what may be said of H. P. B: "It is evident that he had an instinct like that of the Ancient Mariner, for the men who were born to hear and understand him, and great readiness in adopting into his affections every new notability whom he approved of, . . . he received an amount of service and devotion, which few of the greatest of mankind have gained from their fellow-creatures."

Where was there a human being of such a mixture as this mysterious, this fascinating, this light-bringing H. P. B.? Where can we find a personality so remarkable and so dramatic; one which so clearly presented at its opposite sides the divine and the human? Karma forbid that I should do her a feather-weight of injustice, but if there ever existed a person in history who was a greater conglomeration of good and bad, light and shadow, wisdom and indiscretion, spiritual insight and lack of common sense, I cannot recall the name, the circumstances or the epoch. To have known her was a liberal education, to have worked with her and enjoyed her intimacy, an experience of the most precious kind. She was too great an occultist for us to measure her moral stature. She compelled us to love her, however much we might know her faults; to forgive her, however much she might have broken her promises and destroyed our first belief in her infallibility. And the secret of this potent spell was her undeniable spiritual powers, her evident devotion to the Masters whom she depicted as almost super-natural personages, and her zeal for the spiritual uplifting of humanity by the power of the Eastern Wisdom. Shall we ever see her like again? Shall we see herself again within our time under some other guise? Time will show.

H. S. OLCOTT.
"Gulistan."
Ootacamund, 1895.

Chapter I.

FIRST MEETING OF
THE FOUNDERS

Since I am to tell the story of the birth and progress of the Theosophical Society, I must begin at the beginning, and tell how its two founders first met. It was a very prosaic incident: I said, *"Permettez-moi, Madame,"* and gave her a light for her cigarette; our acquaintance began in smoke, but it stirred up a great and permanent fire. The circumstances which brought us together were peculiar, as I shall presently explain. The facts have been partly published before.

One day, in the month of July 1874, I was sitting in my law-office thinking over a heavy case in which I had been retained by the Corporation of the City of New York, when it occurred to me that for years I had paid no attention to the Spiritualist movement. I do not know what association of ideas made my mind pass from the mechanical construction of water-metres to Modern Spiritualism, but, at all events, I went around the corner to a dealer's and bought a copy of the

Banner of Light. In it I read an account of certain incredible phenomena, *viz.*, the solidification of phantom forms, which were said to be occurring at a farm-house in the township of Chittenden, in the State of Vermont, several hundred miles distant from New York. I saw at once that, if it were true that visitors could see, even touch and converse with, deceased relatives who had found means to reconstruct their bodies and clothing so as to be temporarily solid, visible, and tangible, this was the most important fact in modern physical science. I determined to go and see for myself. I did so, found the story true, stopped three or four days, and then returned to New York. I wrote an account of my observations to the New York *Sun*, which was copied pretty much throughout the whole world, so grave and interesting were the facts. A proposal was then made to me by the Editor of the *New York Daily Graphic* to return to Chittenden in its interest, accompanied by an artist to sketch under my orders, and to make a thorough investigation of the affair. The matter so deeply interested me that I made the necessary disposition of office engagements, and on September 17th was back at the "Eddy Homestead," as it was called from the name of the family who owned and occupied it. I stopped in that house of mystery, surrounded by phantoms and having daily experiences of a most extra-ordinary character, for about twelve weeks—if my memory serves me. Meanwhile, twice a week there appeared in the *Daily Graphic* my letters about the "Eddy ghosts," each one illustrated with sketches of spectres actually seen by the artist, Mr. Kappes, and myself, as well as by every one of the persons—sometimes as many as forty—present in the "séance-room."* It was the publication of these letters which drew Madame Blavatsky to Chittenden, and so brought us together.

I remember our first day's acquaintance as if it were yesterday; besides which, I have recorded the main facts in my book (*People from the Other Woria*, pp. 293 *et seq*). It was a sunny day and even the gloomy old farm-house looked cheerful. It stands amid a lovely landscape, in a valley bounded by grassy slopes that rise into mountains covered to their very crests with leafy groves. This was the time of the "Indian Summer," when the whole country is covered with a faint bluish haze, like that which has given the "Nilgiri" mountains their name, and the foliage of the beeches, elms, and maples, touched by early frosts, has been turned from green into a mottling of gold and crimson that gives the landscape the appearance of being hung all over with royal tapestries. One must go to America to see this autumnal splendour in its full perfection.

The dinner hour at Eddy's was noon, and it was from the entrance door of the bare and comfortless dining-room that Kappes and I first saw H. P. B. She had arrived shortly before noon with a French Canadian lady, and they were at table as we entered. My eye was first attracted by a scarlet Garibaldian shirt the former wore, as in vivid contrast with the dull colours

---

* In *People from the Other World* I have described all these phenomena and the tests against fraud which I invented and employed.

around. Her hair was then a thick blond mop, worn shorter than the shoulders, and it stood out from her head, silken-soft and crinkled to the roots, like the fleece of a Cotswold ewe. This and the red shirt were what struck my attention before I took in the picture of her features. It was a massive Calmuck face, contrasting in its suggestion of power, culture, and imperiousness, as strangely with the commonplace visages about the room as her red garment did with the grey and white tones of the walls and woodwork and the dull costumes of the rest of the guests. All sorts of cranky people were continually coming and going at Eddy's to see the mediumistic phenomena, and it only struck me on seeing this eccentric lady that this was but one more of the sort. Pausing on the door-sill, I whispered to Kappes, "Good gracious! look at *that* specimen, will you." I went straight across and took a seat opposite her to indulge my favourite habit of character-study.* The two ladies conversed in French, making remarks of no consequence, but I saw at once from her accent and fluency of speech that, if not a Parisian, she must at least be a finished French scholar. Dinner over, the two went outside the house and Madame Blavatsky rolled herself a cigarette, for which I gave her a light as a pre-

---

* In a chain-shot hit at an American vituperator, she draws the following amusing portrait of herself: "An old woman—whether forty, fifty, sixty, or ninety years old, it matters not; an old woman whose Kalmuco-Buddhisto-Tartaric features, even in youth, never made her appear pretty; a woman, whose ungainly garb, uncouth manners, and masculine habits are enough to frighten any bustled and corseted fine lady of fashionable society out of her wits." [*Vide* her letter "The Knout" to the *R. P. Journal* of March 16, 1878.]

text to enter into conversation. My remark having been made in French, we fell at once into talk in that language. She asked me how long I had been there and what I thought of the phenomena; saying that she herself was greatly interested in such things, and had been drawn to Chittenden by reading the letters in the *Daily Graphic:* the public were growing so interested in these that it was sometimes impossible to find a copy of the paper on the book-stalls an hour after publication, and she had paid a dollar for a copy of the last issue. "I hesitated before coming here," she said, "because I was afraid of meeting that Colonel Olcott." "Why should you be afraid of him, Madame?" I rejoined. "Oh! because I fear he might write about me in his paper." I told her that she might make herself perfectly easy on that score, for I felt quite sure Col. Olcott would not mention her in his letters unless she wished it. And I introduced myself. We became friends at once. Each of us felt as if we were of the same social world, cosmopolitans, free-thinkers, and in closer touch than with the rest of the company, intelligent and very worthy as some of them were. It was the voice of common sympathy with the higher occult side of man and nature; the attraction of soul to soul, not that of sex to sex. Neither then, at the commencement, nor ever afterwards had either of us the sense of the other being of the opposite sex. We were simply chums; so regarded each other, so called each other. Some base people from time to time, dared to suggest that a closer tie bound us together, as they had that that poor, mal-formed, persecuted H. P. B. had been the mistress of various other men, but no pure person could hold to such an opinion after passing any time in her company, and seeing how her every look, word, and action proclaimed her sexlessness.*

Strolling along with my new acquaintance, we talked together about the Eddy phenomena and those of other lands. I found she had been a great traveller and seen many occult things and adepts in occult science, but at first she did not give me any hint as to the existence of the Himalayan Sages or of her own powers. She spoke of the materialistic tendency of American Spiritualism, which was a sort of debauch of phenomena accompanied by comparative indifference to philosophy. Her manner was gracious and captivating, her criticisms upon men and things original and witty. She was particularly interested in drawing me out as to my own ideas about spiritual things and expressed pleasure in finding that I had instinctively thought along the occult lines which she herself had pursued. It was not as an Eastern mystic, but rather as a refined Spiritualist that she talked. For my part I knew nothing then, or next to nothing, about Eastern philosophy, and at first she kept silent on that subject.

The séances of William Eddy, the chief medium of the family, were held every evening in a large upstairs hall, in a wing of the house, over the dining-room and kitchen. He and a brother, Horatio, were hard-working farmers; Horatio attending to the outdoor duties, and William, since visitors

---

* I hold to this same view despite the pretended confessions of early misconduct, contained in certain letters of hers to a Russian gentleman and recently published in a work entitled *A Modern Priestess of Isis*. In short, I believe my estimate of her sexual purity to be true and her pretended revelations false—mere bravado.

came pouring in upon them from all parts of the United States, doing the cooking for the household. They were poor, ill-educated, and prejudiced—sometimes surly to their unbidden guests. At the farther end of the séance-hall the deep chimney from the kitchen below passed through to the roof. Between it and the north wall was a narrow closet of the same width as the depth of the chimney, 2 feet 7 inches, in which William Eddy would seat himself to wait for the phenomena. He had no seeming control over them, but merely sat and waited for them to sporadically occur. A blanket being hung across the doorway, the closet would be in perfect darkness. Shortly after William had entered the cabinet, the blanket would be pulled aside and forth would step some figure of a dead man, woman or child—an animate statue so to say—temporarily solid and substantial, but the next minute resolved back into nothingness or invisibility. They would occasionally dissolve away while in full view of the spectators.

Up to the time of H. P. B.'s appearance on the scene, the figures which had shown themselves were either Red Indians, or Americans or Europeans akin to visitors. But on the first evening of her stay spooks of other nationalities came before us. There was a Georgian servant boy from the Caucasus; a Mussulman merchant from Tiflis; a Russian peasant girl, and others. Another evening there appeared a Kourdish cavalier armed with scimitar, pistols, and lance; a hideously ugly and devilish-looking negro sorcerer from Africa, wearing a coronet composed of four horns of the oryx with bells at their tips, attached to an embroidered, highly coloured fillet which was tied around his head; and a European gentleman wearing the cross and collar of St. Anne, who was recognised by Madame Blavatsky as her uncle. The advent of such figures in the séance-room of those poor, almost illiterate Vermont farmers, who had neither the money to buy theatrical properties, the experience to employ such if they had had them, nor the room where they could have availed of them, was to every eye-witness a convincing proof that the apparitions were genuine. At the same time they show that a strange attraction to call out these images from what Asiatics call the Kama-loka at-tended Madame Blavatsky. It was long afterwards that I was informed that she had evoked them by her own developed and masterful power. She even affirms the fact in a written note, in our *T. S. Scrap-book*, Vol. I., appended to a cutting from the (London) *Spiritualist* of January, 1875.

While she was at Chittenden she told me many incidents of her past life, among others, her having been present as a volunteer, with a number of other European ladies, with Garibaldi at the bloody battle of Mentana. In proof of her story she showed me where her left arm had been broken in two places by a saber-stroke, and made me feel in her right shoulder a musket-bullet, still imbedded in the muscle, and another in her leg. She also showed me a scar just below the heart where she had been stabbed with a stiletto. This wound reopened a little while she was at Chittenden, and it was to consult me about it that she was led to show it to me. She told me many curious tales of peril and adventure, among them the story of the phantom African sorcerer with the oryx-horn coronet, whom she had seen in life doing phenomena in Upper Egypt, many years before.

H. P. B. tried her best to make me suspect the value of William Eddy's phenomena as proofs of the intelligent control of a medium by spirits; telling me that, if genuine, they must be the double of the medium escaping from his body and clothing itself with other appearances; but I did not believe her. I contended that the forms were of too great diversities of height, bulk, and appearance to be a masquerade of William Eddy; they must be what they seemed, *viz.*, the spirits of the dead. Our disputes were quite warm on occasions, for at that time I had not gone deep enough into the question of the plastic nature of the human Double to see the force of her hints, while of the Eastern theory of Maya I did not know its least iota. The result, however, was, as she told me, to convince her of my disposition to accept nothing on trust and to cling pertinaciously to such facts as I had, or thought I had acquired. We became greater friends day by day, and by the time she was ready to leave Chittenden she had accepted from me the nick-name "Jack," and so signed herself in her letters to me from New York. When we parted it was as good friends likely to continue the acquaintance thus pleasantly begun.

In November, 1874, when my researches were finished, I returned to New York and called upon her at her lodgings at 16 Irving Place, where she gave me some séances of table-tipping and rapping, spelling out messages of sorts, principally from an invisible intelligence calling itself "John King." This pseudonym is one that has been familiar to frequenters of mediumistic séances these forty years past, all over the world. It was first heard of in 1850, in the "spirit room" of Jonathan Koons, of Ohio, where it pretended to be a ruler of a tribe or tribes of spirits. Later on, it said it was the earth-haunting soul of Sir Henry Morgan, the famous buccaneer, and as such it introduced itself to me. It showed its face and turban-wrapped head to me at Philadelphia, during the course of my investigations of the Holmes mediums, in association with the late respected Robert Dale Owen, General F. J. Lippitt and Madame Blavatsky (*vide People from the Other World*, Part II.), and both spoke and wrote to me, the latter frequently. It had a quaint handwriting, and used queer old English expressions. I thought it a veritable John King then, for its personality had been as convincingly proved to me, I fancied, as anybody could have asked. But now, after seeing what H. P. B. could do in the way of producing *mayavic* (*i.e.*, hypnotic) illusions and in the control of elementals, I am persuaded that "John King" was a humbugging elemental, worked by her like a marionette and used as a help towards my education. Understand me, the phenomena were real, but they were done by no disincarnate *human* spirit. Since writing the above, in fact, I have found the proof, in her own handwriting, pasted in our *Scrap-book*, Vol. I.

She kept up the illusion for months—just how many I cannot recollect at this distance of time—and I saw numbers of phenomena done as alleged by John King—as, for example, the whole remarkable series at the Philadelphia residence of the Holmeses and that of H. P. B. herself, above referred to. He was first, John King, an independent personality, then John King, messenger and servant—never the equal—of living adepts, and finally an elemental pure and simple, employed by H. P. B. and a certain other expert in the doing of wonders.

It is useless to deny that, throughout the early part of her American residence, she called herself a spiritualist and warmly defended Spiritualism and its mediums from their sciolistic and other bitter traducers. Her letters and articles in various American and English journals contain many evidences of her occupying that position. Among other examples, I will simply quote the following:

"As it is, I have only done my duty; first, towards Spiritualism, that I have defended as well as I could from the attacks of imposture under the too transparent mask of science; then towards two helpless, slandered mediums. . . . But I am obliged to confess that I really do not believe in having done any good—to Spiritualism itself. . . . It is with a profound sadness in my heart that I acknowledge this fact, for I begin to think there is no help for it. For over fifteen years have I fought my battle for the blessed truth; have travelled and preached it—though I never was born for a lecturer—from the snow-covered tops of the Caucasian Mountains, as well as from the sandy valleys of the Nile. I have proved the truth of it practically and by persuasion. For the sake of Spiritualism I have left my home, an easy life amongst a civilised society, and have become a wanderer upon the face of the earth. I had already seen my hopes realised, beyond my most sanguine expectations, when my unlucky star brought me to America. Knowing this country to be the cradle of Modern Spiritualism, I came over here from France with feelings not unlike those of a Mohammedan approaching the birthplace of his Prophet," etc., etc. (Letter of H. P. B. to the *Spiritualist* of December 13, 1874.)

The two "helpless mediums" alluded to were the Holmeses, of whose moral quality I have always had the poorest opinion. Yet, *in H. P. B.'s presence* I witnessed, under my own test conditions, along with the late Robert Dale Owen and General Lippitt, a series of most convincing and satisfactory mediumistic phenomena. I half suspected then that the power that produced them came from *H. P. B.*, and that if the Holmeses alone had been concerned, I should either have seen tricks or nothing. Now, in hunting over the old scrap-books, I find in H. P. B.'s MSS. the following memorandum, which she evidently meant to be published after her death:

"IMPORTANT NOTE."

"Yes, I am sorry to say that I *had* to identify myself, during that shameful exposure of the Holmes mediums, with the Spiritualists. I had to save the situation, for *I was sent from Paris to America on purpose to prove the phenomena and their reality, and show the fallacy of the spiritualistic theory of spirits.* But how could I do it best? I did not want people at large to know that I could *produce the same things* AT WILL. I had received orders to the contrary, and yet I had to keep alive the reality, the genuineness and *possibility* of such phenomena, in the hearts of those who from Materialists had turned Spiritualists, but now, owing to the exposure of several mediums, fell back again, returned to their scepticism. This is why, selecting a few of the faithful, I went to the Holmeses, and, helped by M. and his *power*, brought out the faces of John King and Katie King from the Astral Light, produced the phenomena of materialisation, and allowed the spiritualists at large to believe it was done through the medium of Mrs. Holmes. She was terribly frightened herself, for she knew that *this once* the apparition was real. Did I do wrong? The world is not prepared yet to understand the philosophy of Occult Science; let them first assure themselves that there are beings in an invisible world, whether 'Spirits' of the dead or elementals; and that there are hidden powers in man which are capable of making a *god* of him on earth.

"When I am dead and gone people will, perhaps, appreciate my disinterested motives. I have pledged my word to help people on to *Truth* while living, and I will keep my word. Let them abuse and revile me; let some call me a medium and a Spiritualist, others an impostor. The day will come when posterity will learn to know me better. Oh, poor, foolish, credulous, wicked world!"

The whole thing is here made plain: the Spiritualism she was sent to America to profess and ultimately bring to replace the cruder Western mediumism, was Eastern Spiritualism, or Brahma Vidya. The West not being prepared to accept it, her first assigned work was to defend the real phenomena of the "circle" from that prejudiced and militant enemy of spiritual belief—materialistic, sciolistic, physical science, with its votaries and leaders. The one necessary thing for the age was to check materialistic scepticism and strengthen the spiritual basis of the religious yearning. Therefore, the battle being joined, she took her stand beside the American Spiritualists, and for the moment made common cause with them. Yes, posterity *will* do her justice.

I wish I could recall to memory the first phenomenon done by her confessedly as by an exercise of her own will power, but I cannot. It must have been just after she began writing *Isis Unveiled* and possibly it was the following: After leaving 16 Irving Place and making a visit to friends in the country, she occupied rooms for a time in another house in Irving Place, a few doors from the Lotos Club and on the same side of the street. It was there that, later, the informal gathering of friends was held at which I proposed the formation of what afterwards became the Theosophical Society. Among her callers was an Italian artist, a Signor B., formerly a Carbonaro. I was sitting alone with her in her drawing-room when he made his first visit. They talked of Italian affairs, and he suddenly pronounced the name of one of the greatest of the Adepts. She started as if she had received an electric shock; looked him straight in the eyes, and said (in Italian), "What is it? I am ready." He passed it off carelessly, but thenceforward the talk was all about Magic, Magicians, and Adepts. Signor B. went and opened one of the French windows, made some beckoning passes towards the outer air, and presently a pure white butterfly came into the room and went flying about near the ceiling. H. P. B. laughed in a cheerful way and said: "That is pretty, but I can also do it!" She, too, opened the window, made similar beckoning passes, and presently a second white butterfly came fluttering in. It mounted to the ceiling, chased the other around the room, played with it now and then, with it flew to a corner, and, presto! both disappeared at once while we were looking at them. "What does that mean?" I asked. "Only this, that Signor B. can make an elemental turn itself into a butterfly, and so can I." The insects were not real but illusionary ones.

I recall other instances of her control of elementals or, as Hindus would term it, Yakshini Vidya. An early one is the following: On a cold winter's night, when several inches of snow lay upon the ground, she and I were working upon her book until a late hour at her rooms in Thirty-fourth Street. I had eaten some saltish food for dinner, and at about 1 A.M., feeling very thirsty, said to her: "Would it not be nice to have some hothouse grapes?" "So it would," she replied, "let us have some." "But the shops have been closed for hours, and we can buy none," I said. "No matter, we shall have them, all the same," was her reply. "But how?" "I will show you, if you will just turn down that gas-light on the table in front of us." I turned the cock unintentionally so far around as to extinguish the light. "You need not have done that," she said. "I only wanted you to make the light dim. However, light it again quickly." A box of matches lay just at hand, and in a moment I had relit the lamp. "See!" she exclaimed, pointing to a hanging book-shelf on the wall before us. To my amazement there hung from the knobs at the two ends of one of the shelves two large bunches of ripe black Hamburgh grapes, which we proceeded to eat. To my question as to the agency employed, she said it was done by certain elementals under her control, and twice later on, when we were living in the so-called "Lamasery," she repeated the phenomenon of bringing fruits for our refreshment while at work on *Isis*.

Little by little, H. P. B. let me know of the existence of Eastern adepts and their powers, and gave me by a multitude of phenomena the proofs of her own control over the occult forces of nature. At first, as I have remarked, she ascribed them to "John King," and it was through his alleged friendliness that I first came into personal correspondence with the Masters. Many of their letters I have preserved, with my own endorsement of the dates of their reception. For years, and until shortly before I left New York for India, I was connected in pupilage with the African section of the Occult Brotherhood; but, later, when a certain wonderful psycho-physiological change happened to H. P. B. that I am not at liberty to speak about, and that nobody has up to the present suspected, although enjoying her intimacy and full confidence, as they fancy, I was transferred to the Indian section and a different group of Masters. For, it may be stated, there is and ever was but one altruistic alliance, or fraternity, of these Elder Brothers of humanity, the world over; but it is divided into sections according to the needs of the human race in its successive stages of evolution. In one age the focal centre of this world-helping force will be in one place, in another elsewhere. Unseen, unsuspected as the vivifying spiritual currents of the Akash, yet as indispensable for the spiritual welfare of mankind, their combined divine energy is maintained from age to age and forever refreshes the pilgrim of Earth, who struggles on towards the Divine Reality. The sceptic denies the existence of these adepts because he has not seen or talked with them, nor read in history of their visible intermeddling in national events. But their being has been known to thousands of self-illuminate mystics and philanthropists in succeeding generations, whose purified souls have lifted them up out of the muck of physical into the brightness of spiritual consciousness; and at many epochs they have come into personal relations with the persons who are devoting or inclined to devote themselves to altruistic labour for bringing about the brotherhood of mankind. Some of this class, very humble and apparently very unworthy—like us leaders of the Theosophical Society movement—have been blessed with their sympathy and partaken of their instruction. Some, like Damodar and H. P. B., have first seen them in visions while young; some have encountered them under strange guises in most unlikely places; I was introduced to them by H. P. B. through the agency that my previous experiences would make most comprehensible, a pretended medium-overshadowing "spirit." John King brought four of the Masters to my attention, of whom one was a Copt, one a representative of the Neo Platonist Alexandrian school, one—a very high one, a Master of the Masters, so to say—a Venetian, and one an English philosopher, gone from men's sight, yet not dead. The first of these became my first Guru, and a stern disciplinarian he was, indeed, a man of splendid masculinity of character.

In time I came to know from themselves that H. P. B. was a faithful servant of theirs, though her peculiar temperament and idiosyncracies made her too antipathetic to some of them to permit of their working with her. This will not seem strange if one remembers that each individual man, whether adept or laic, has evolved along a particular ray of the Logos, and is in spiritual sympathy with his associate souls of that ray, and may be in antagonism, on this physical plane, with entities of another ray when clothed in flesh. This is probably the *ultima ratio* of what is called magnetic, auric, or psychical sympathy and antipathy. Whatever the reason may be some of the Masters could not and did not work with H. P. B. Several did, among them some whose names have never as yet been given out, but whom I had much intercourse with in those early years of the Theosophical Society movement.

Among other things about herself H. P. B. told me, when I had got along far enough to know of the Brotherhood and her relation with it, that she had come to Paris the previous year (1873) intending to settle down for some time under the protection of a relative of hers, residing in the Rue de l'Université, but one day received from the "Brothers" a peremptory order to go to New York to await further orders.

The next day she had sailed with little more than money enough to pay her passage. She wrote to her father for funds to be sent her in care of the Russian Consul in New York, but this could not arrive for some time, and as the Consul refused her a loan, she had to set to work to earn her daily bread. She told me she had taken lodgings in one of the poorest quarters in New York—Madison Street—and supported herself by making cravats or artificial flowers—I forget which now—for a kind-hearted Hebrew shop-keeper. She always spoke to me with gratitude about this little man. As yet she had received no intimation as to the future, it was a sealed book. But the following year, in October, 1874, she was ordered to go to Chittenden and find the man who, as it turned out, was to be her future colleague in a great work—myself.

Her intimate friends will recollect her telling this story about her sudden departure under orders from Paris to New York. Mr. Sinnett mentions it in his *Incidents in the Life of*

Madame Blavatsky (page 175), and it has been elsewhere published. But these acquaintances had it from her later on, and her enemies may say it was an afterthought of hers, a falsehood concocted to fit in with a little farce she subsequently invented. Accident, however—if it be an accident—has just now, while I am writing these pages, brought me a valuable bit of corroborative proof. We have had staying at Adyar an American lady, Miss Anna Ballard, a veteran journalist, a life member of the New York Press Club, who, in the course of professional duty, met H. P. B. in the first week after her arrival at New York. In the course of conversation, amid a variety of less important facts, Miss Ballard casually mentioned to me two, that I at once begged her to put in writing, *viz.*: that H. P. B., whom she found living in a squalid lodging-house, said that she had suddenly and unexpectedly left Paris at one day's notice, and, secondly, that she had visited Tibet. Here is Miss Ballard's own version of the affair:

"Adyar, *17th January, 1892.*

"Dear Col. Olcott:—My acquaintanceship with Mme. Blavatsky dates even further back than you suppose. I met her in July, 1873, at New York, not more than a week after she landed. I was then a reporter on the staff of the New York *Sun*, and had been detailed to write an article upon a Russian subject. In the course of my search after facts the arrival of this Russian lady was reported to me by a friend, and I called upon her; thus beginning an

acquaintance that lasted several years. At our first
interview she told me she had had no idea of leaving
Paris for America until the very evening before she
sailed, but why she came or who hurried her off she
did not say. I remember perfectly well her saying with
an air of exultation, 'I have been in Tibet.' Why she
should think that a great matter, more remarkable
than any other of the travels in Egypt, India, and
other countries she told me about, I could not make
out, but she said it with special emphasis and
animation. I now know, of course, what it means.
ANNA BALLARD."

Unless prepared to concede to H. P. B. the power of foreseeing
that I should be getting this written statement from Miss Ballard
in India, nineteen years later, the fair-minded reader will admit
that the statements she made to her first friend in New York, in
1873, strongly corroborate the assertions she has ever since
made to a large number of people about the two most important
incidents in the history of her connection with the Theosophical
movement, (a) her preparation in Tibet, and (b) her journey to
America in search of the person whose Karma linked him to her
as the co-agent to set this social wave in motion.

She made an abortive attempt to found a sort of Spiritual Society at Cairo, in 1871 [vide Peebles' Around the World,
p. 215, and Sinnett's Incidents in the Life of Mme. Blavatsky,
p. 158], upon a basis of phenomena. Not having the right persons to organise and direct it, it was a lamentable fiasco and

brought upon her much ridicule. Yet the magical phenomena
she wrought with the help of the self-same Copt and another
adept whom I subsequently came into relations with, were
most startling.* It was apparently a reckless waste of psychic

---

* See an article in *Frank Leslie's Popular Magazine* for February 1892, illustrated by mendacious engravings, yet containing a few facts along with
much falsehood. The author, Dr. A. L. Rawson, mentions the Cairo failure
of the "attempt to form a society for occult research," and says that "Paulos
Metamon, a celebrated Coptic magician, who had several very curious
books full of astrological formulas, magical incantations and horoscopes
which he delighted in showing his visitors, *after a proper introduction*"
advised delay. Dr. Rawson says that she (H. P. B.) had told the Countess
Kazinoff "that she had solved at least one of the mysteries of Egypt, and
proved it by letting a live serpent loose from a bag she had concealed in the
folds of her dress." From an eye-witness I had it that while H. P. B. was in
Cairo the most extraordinary phenomena would occur in any room she
might be sitting in; for example, the table lamp would quit its place on one
table and pass through the air to another, just as if carried in some one's
hand; this same mysterious Copt would suddenly vanish from the sofa
where he was sitting, and many such marvels. Miracles no longer, since we
have had the scientists prove to us the possibility of inhibition of the senses
of sight, hearing, touch, and smell by mere hypnotic suggestion. Undoubtedly this inhibition was provoked in the company present, who were made
to see the Copt vanish, and the lamp moving through space, but not the
person whose hand was carrying it. It was what H. P. B. called a "psychological trick," yet all the same a fact and one of moment to science. Scientists attest the fact of inhibition yet confess ignorance as to its rationale.
"How"—say Drs. Binet and Féré, in their celebrated work *Le Magnetisme
Animal*—"has the experimentalist produced this curious phenomenon?
We know nothing about it. We only grasp the external fact, to know that
when one affirms to a sensitive subject that an object present does not
exist, this suggestion has the effect, direct or indirect, to dig in the brain of
the hypnotic an anesthesia corresponding to the designated object. But
what happens between the verbal affirmation, which is the means, and the
systematised anesthesia, which is the end? . . . Here the laws of association,
which are so great a help in solving psychological problems, abandon us
completely." Poor beginners! They do not see that the inhibition is *upon
the astral man*, and Eastern magicians excel them in "psychological tricks"

energy, and indicated anything but either personal infallibility or divine guidance. I could never understand it. And as regards the Theosophical Society every circumstance tends to show that it has been a gradual evolution, controlled by circumstances and the resultant of opposite forces, now running into smooth, now into rough grooves, and prosperous or checked proportionately with the wisdom or unwisdom of its management. The general direction has always been kept, its guiding motive ever identical, but its programme has been variously modified, enlarged, and improved as our knowledge increased and experience from time to time suggested. All things show me that the movement as such was planned out beforehand by the watching Sages, but all details were left for us to conquer as best we might. If we had failed, others would have had the chance that fell to our Karma, as I fell heir to the wasted chances of her Cairo group of 1871. Speaking of growth of knowledge, I can look back and trace a constant enlargement of my own ideas, deeper perception of truth, and capacity to assimilate and impart ideas. My published articles and letters between 1875 and 1878 prove this distinctly. When I was a child (in Occultism) I spoke as a child; often dogmatically, after the fashion of comparative tyros.

I never heard anything from H. P. B. in the early days to make me think that she had the least intimation, until sent to Chittenden to me, about any future relationship between us

---

simply because they know more about psychology, and can reach the Watcher who peers out upon the foolish world of illusion through the windows of the body: the telephonic nerves being inhibited, the telegraphic wires are cut, and no message passes in.

in work, nor even then that the Theosophical Society was to be. We have it on her own authority, as quoted above, that she was sent from Paris to New York in the interest of Spiritualism, in the best sense of that word, and before we met she had attended séances and consorted with mediums, but never came under public notice. In May, 1875, I was engaged in trying to organise at New York with her concurrence a private investigating committee under the title of the "Miracle Club." In the *Scrap-book* (Vol. I.) she writes about it:

"An attempt in consequence of orders received from T* B* (a Master) through P. (an Elemental) personating John King. Ordered to begin telling the public the truth about the phenomena and their mediums. And now my martyrdom will begin! I shall have all the Spiritualists against me, in addition to the Christians and the Sceptics. Thy will, oh M., be done. H. P. B."

The plan was to keep closed doors to all save the members of the Club, who were forbidden to divulge even the place of meeting. "All the manifestations, including materialisations, to occur in the light, and without a cabinet." [*Spiritual Scientist*, May 19, 1876.] Taking H. P. B.'s remark above, as written, it looks as though there would have been no Theosophical Society—it looks so, I say—if her intended medium for the Miracle Club had not utterly failed us and so precluded my completing the organisation.

I notice in Mr. Sinnett's book the coincidence that she arrived at New York on the 7th of July, 1873—that is to say on the *seventh* day of the *seventh* month of her forty-second year (6x7), and that our meeting was postponed until I should have attained my forty-second year. And, to anticipate, it must also be remarked that she died in the seventh month of the seventeenth year of our Theosophical relationship. Add to this the further fact, recently published by me in the *Theosophist*, that Mrs. Annie Besant came to H. P. B. as an applicant for membership in the seventh month of the seventeenth year after her final withdrawal from the Christian communion, and we have here a pretty set of coincidences to bear in mind.

Chapter II.

MADAME BLAVATSKY
IN AMERICA

I have found a letter to myself from an older acquaintance of Madame Blavatsky's than even Miss Ballard, the existence of which I had forgotten. The last-named lady met her at New York within the first week after her arrival from France, but Dr. Marquette knew her in Paris, before she started on that long and brilliant career which led, *per aspera ad astra*, to end at the Woking crematory for the moment, in 1891, and then keep on and ever onward. The innuendoes about her having led a wild life at the French capital in 1873, are answered by this frank statement of an educated lady physician, whom I personally knew at New York, but who, I understand, is now deceased. She says:

"NEW YORK, *December 26, 1875.*

"DEAR SIR:

"In reply to your inquiries, I have to say that I made Madame Blavatsky's acquaintance in Paris in the year 1873. She was living in the Rue du Palais, in an apartment* with her brother, M. Hahn, and his intimate friend M. Lequeux. I was with her almost daily, and, in fact, spent a good part of my time with her when I was not in the hospitals or attending the lectures. I am, therefore, able to state from positive knowledge, what her behaviour was. It gives me great pleasure to say that that behaviour was *unexceptionable*, and such as to entitle her to every respect. She passed her time in painting and writing, seldom going out of her room. She had few acquaintances, but among the number were M. and Mme. Leymarie. Mme. Blavatsky I esteem as one of the most estimable and interesting ladies I ever met, and since my return from France, our acquaintance and friendship have been renewed.

"Yours respectfully,
(Sd.) "L. M. Marquette, M.D."

In the preceding chapter it was mentioned that she had left Paris for New York, by order of the Masters, on a day's notice, and with barely enough money to pay her way out. I recall a circumstance of the journey which, as she told it, brings into high relief one trait of her many-angled character—her

---

* An "*appartement*" does not mean, as with us, a single chamber, but a suite of rooms, comprising reception, dining and bed-rooms, with a kitchen and servants' quarters.—O.

impulsive generosity. She had bought a first-class ticket from Havre to New York, and had gone to the quay to either see or embark on the steamer, when her attention was attracted by a peasant woman, sitting on the ground with a child or two beside her, and weeping bitterly. Drawing near, H. P. B. found she was from Germany on her way to America to rejoin her husband, but a swindling emigrant runner at Hamburgh had sold her bogus steamer tickets, and there she was, penniless and helpless: the steamship company could do nothing, of course, and she had neither relative nor acquaintance in Havre. The heart of our kind H. P. B. was so touched that she said: "No matter, good woman, I will see if something cannot be done." She first vainly tried her powers of persuasion (and objurgation) upon the blameless agent of the company, and then, as a last expedient—her own funds being insufficient for the purpose—had her saloon ticket changed for a steerage berth for herself, and for the difference got steerage tickets for the poor woman and her children! Many "proper" and "respectable" people have often expressed horror at H. P. B.'s coarse eccentricities, including profanity, yet I think that a generous deed like this would cause whole pages of recorded solecisms in society manners to be washed away from the Book of Human Accounts! If any doubt it, let them try the steerage of an emigrant ship.

We have seen how Miss Ballard found H. P. B. living in a wretched tenement-house in an East-end New York street, pending the arrival of money from home, and honestly supporting herself by sewing cravats. This was in July, 1873. In the following October her ever-indulgent, forbearing, and beloved father, died, and, on the 29th of the month, she received a cable dispatch from Stavropol, from her sister "Elise," conveying the news and informing her as to the amount of her heritage: adding that a draft for 1000 roubles had been sent her. [I have the original dispatch before me as I write.] In due course of post she received all the money, and then shifted her quarters to better neighbourhoods in New York city—Union Square, East Sixteenth St., Irving Place, etc., and it was in the last-named I found her domiciled upon returning from the Eddy Homestead. Her money did not stay with her long, however, for, as it is recorded in Mr. Sinnett's book, while she could endure with perfect patience the miseries of poverty if compelled, no sooner did money fall into her lap than she seemed to be unhappy unless she was throwing it away with both hands in the most imprudent fashion. A document in my possession illustrates this so well that I must quote from it. It is an agreement entitled "Articles of co-partnership entered into this twenty-second day of June, in the year One thousand eight hundred and seventy-four, by and between C. . . . . G. . . . . , party of the first part and Helen Blavatsky, party of the second part, to wit:" Clause 1 recites that the co-partnership is "for the purpose of working the land and farm at N——, in the County of——, Long Island," the property of C. G.; Clause 2 says, "the said co-partnership shall commence on the first day of July, 1874, and shall continue for the period of three years." Clause 3 states that C. G. puts the use of the farm into the co-partnership as an off-set against the sum of one thousand dollars paid in by H. P. B. By Clause

4 "all proceeds for crops, poultry, produce, and other products raised on the said farm shall be divided equally, and all expenses" equally shared. Clause 5, and last, reserves the title of the land to C. G. The document is duly signed and sealed by the parties, witnessed and recorded.

What anybody might have expected happened: H. P. B. went to live on the farm; got no profits, had a row, acquired debts and a neat little lawsuit which friends helped her to settle long afterward. That was the last of her bucolic dream of profits from sales of garden-truck, poultry, eggs, etc.: three months later she met me in the Vermont ghostland, and the wheels of our war chariot began rumbling prophetically through the lowest levels of the Akash!

In November, 1874, signing her letter "Jack the Pappoose," she wrote to ask me to get her an engagement to write weird stories for a certain journal, as she would soon be "hard up," and gave me a rollicking account of her family pedigree and connexions on both sides; talking like a democrat, yet showing but too plainly that she felt that she, if any one, had reason to be proud of her lineage. She writes me how the *Daily Graphic* people had interviewed her about her travels and asked for her portrait. Considering how many thousand copies of her likeness have since been circulated, the world over, it will amuse if I quote a sentence or two about this first experience of the sort:

"Don't you know, the fellows of the *Graphic* bored my life out of me to give them my portrait? Mr. F. was sent to get me into conversation after I came out [for the Eddys, she means], and wanted them to insert my article against . . . Beard. I suppose they wanted to create a sensation and so got hold of my beautiful nostrils and splendid mouth . . . I told them that nature has endowed and gifted me with a potato nose, but I did not mean to allow them to make fun of it, vegetable though it is. They very seriously denied the fact, and so made me laugh, and you know '*celui qui rit est desarmé*.'"

A well-known physician of New York, a Dr. Beard, attracted to Chittenden by my *Graphic* letters, had come out with a bombastic and foolish explanation of the Eddy ghosts as mere trickery, and she had flayed him alive in a reply, dated October 27th and published in the *Graphic* of October 30th. Her letter was so brave and sparkling a defence of the Eddy mediums, and her testimony as to the seven "spirit-forms" she herself had recognised so convincing, that she at once came into the blaze of a publicity which never afterwards left her. This was the first time her name had been heard of in America in connection with psychological mysteries, my own mention in the *Graphic*, of her arrival at Chittenden appearing, if I am not mistaken, a little later. However, be that as it may, her tilt with Dr. Beard was the primary cause of her notoriety.

She carried a tone of breeziness, defiant brusqueness, and *camaraderie* throughout all her talk and writing in those days, fascinating everybody by her bright wit, her contempt for social hypocrisies, and all "caddishness," and astounding them with her psychical powers. The erudition of *Isis Unveiled* had not yet overshadowed her, but she constantly drew upon a memory stored with a wealth of recollections of personal perils and adventures, and of knowledge of occult science, not merely unparalleled but not even approached by any other person who had ever appeared in America, so far as I have heard. She was a totally different personage then from what she was later on, when people saw her settled down to the serious life-work for which her whole past had been a preparatory school. Yes, the H. P. B. I am now writing about, in whose intimate comradeship I lived, with whom I was on terms of perfect personal equality, who overflowed with exuberant spirits and enjoyed nothing more than a comic song or story, was not the H. P. B. of India or London, nor recognisable in the mental colossus of the latter days. She changed in many things, yet in one thing she never improved, *viz.*, the choice of friends and confidants. It almost seems as though she were always dealing with *inner selves* of men and women, and had been blind to the weakness or corruption of their visible, bodily shells. Just as she flung her money to every specious wretch who came and lied to her, so she made close friends of the passing hour with people the most unworthy. She trusted one after another, and, for the time being, there seemed nobody like them in her eyes; but usually the morrow brought disillusion and disgust, without the prudence to avoid doing it all over again. I mentioned above the attempt to form a Miracle Club, for the study of practical psychology. The intended medium belonged to a most respectable family, and talked so honestly that we thought we had secured a prize. He proved to be penniless, and as H. P. B. in his hour of greatest need had no money to spare, she pawned her long gold chain and gave him the proceeds. That wretch not only failed utterly as a medium, but was also reported to us as having spread calumnies against the one who had done him kindness. And such was her experience to the end of her life; the ingratitude and cruel malice of the Coulombs being but one of a long series of sorrows.

The subsequent history of that gold chain is interesting. It was, of course, redeemed from pawn, and, later, she wore it in Bombay and Madras. When, in the Ninth Annual Convention of the Society, held at Adyar, a subscription was started to create the Permanent Fund, H. P. B. put her chain up at private auction, and it was bought by Mr. E. D. Ezekiel, and the money handed over to the Treasurer of the T. S. for the Fund in question.

Before my series of Chittenden letters to the *Daily Graphic* was finished, I had arranged for their publication in book form at Hartford, Conn., and about the same time H. P. B. removed to Philadelphia. A blight fell upon Spiritualism in those days, in consequence of Mr. Dale Owen's public denunciation of the Holmes mediums as cheats. The journals of that movement lost heavily in subscribers, the most popular books lay unsold on the publishers' shelves. My own publishers were so alarmed that I arranged, through Mr. Owen, with Mrs. Holmes for a course of test-séances under my own conditions, and went there and carried out my plan, with the colleagues before mentioned. Thence I proceeded to Havana, N. Y., and saw the truly marvellous mediumistic phenomena of Mrs. Compton. Both sets of experiences were embodied in my book, and it was published.

H. P. B. was still at Philadelphia, so I accepted her urgent invitation to come and take a few days' holiday after my long term of work. Expecting to be absent from New York only two or three days, I left no instructions at my office or club about forwarding my letters, but, finding upon arrival that she was not likely to let me go so soon, I went on the second day to the General Post-Office, gave the address of my lodgings, and asked that any letters coming for me might be delivered there by carrier. I expected none, but fancied that the people in my office, not hearing from me, might address me at the Philadelphia Post-Office on the chance of my getting their letter. Then happened something that astonished me—knowing so little as I did of the psychical resources of H. P. B. and her Masters—and which even now, despite so long an experience of phenomena, remains a world-wonder. To understand what follows, let the reader examine any letter he has received by post, and he will find two office stamps upon it; the one on the face, that of the office at which it was posted, the one on the back, that of the office to which it was addressed; if it has been sent on after him from the latter office, it will at least bear those two stamps, and, in addition, those of any series of post-offices to which it was re-addressed until it finally reached his hand. Now, on the evening of the very day on which I had left my address at the Philadelphia General Post-Office, the local postman brought me letters coming from widely distant places—one, I think, from South America, or at any rate, some foreign country—addressed to me at New York, bearing the stamps of the respective offices of posting, *but not that of the New York Post-Office*. Despite all post-office rules and customs, they had come straight to me to Philadelphia without passing through the New York Post-Office at all. *And nobody in New York knew my Philadelphia address*, for I did not myself know what it would be when I left home. I took these letters myself from the postman's hand, being just on the point of going out for a walk when he arrived. So the letters were not tampered with by H. P. B. *Upon opening them, I found inside each, something written in the same handwriting as that in letters I had received in New York from the Masters, the writing having been made either in the margins or any other blank space left by the writers.* The things written were, either some comments upon the character or motives of the writers, or matter of general purport as regards my occult studies. These were the precursors of a whole series of those phenomenal surprises during the fortnight or so that I spent in Philadelphia. I had many, and no letter of the lot bore the New York stamp, although all were addressed to me at my office in that city.

The accompanying fac-simile of one of the covers—a letter from Prof. J. R. Buchanan—will show that although addressed to me at New York, it was delivered by the Philadelphia carrier without having been re-addressed to that city. The house number—H. P. B.'s residence—was written in the City Delivery Department of the Philadelphia Post-Office. The New York stamp is not on the back.

When we come to analyse the psychical phenomena of or connected with Mme. Blavatsky, we find that they may be classified as follows:

1. Those whose production requires a knowledge of the ultimate properties of matter, of the cohesive force which agglomerates the atoms; especially a knowledge of Akash, its composition, contents, and potentialities.

2. Those which relate to the powers of the elementals when made subservient to human will.

3. Those where hypnotic suggestion through the medium of thought-transference creates illusive sensations of sight, sound, and touch.

4. Those which involve the art of making objective images, pictorial or scriptory—which are first purposely created in the adept-operator's mind; for instance, the precipitation of a picture or writing upon paper or other material surface, or of a letter, image, or other mark upon the human skin.

5. Those pertaining to thought-reading and retrospective and prospective clairvoyance.

6. Those of the intercourse at will between her mind and the minds of other living persons equally or more perfectly gifted, psychically, than herself. Or, sometimes, the subordination of her will and whole personality to the will of another entity.

7. Those, of the highest class, where by spiritual insight, or intuition, or inspiration—as indifferently called; there being no real difference in the condition, but only in names—she reached the amassed stores of human knowledge laid up in the registry of the Astral Light.

Recalling my observations for the past twenty years as well as I can, I think that all the tales I have ever told or shall henceforth tell, will drop into one or other of these classes.

The sceptic will certainly say that my groups are arbitrary and my hypotheses fanciful. He will ask me to prove that

there are elemental spirits; that there is such a thing as clairvoyance; that material objects called for can be brought from
a distance; that anybody really knows the nature of the attraction of cohesion, etc. I shall, for my sole answer, tell what I and
others have seen, and then challenge the doubter to find in
nature any thinkable laws, outside those above enumerated,
which explain the facts—the hard undeniable facts. If the theory of miracle, or diabolism, be propounded, then I shall be
dumb, for that cuts off argument. I do not pretend to be able
to explain the rationale of all of H. P. B.'s phenomena, for to do
that one would need to be as well informed as herself; which I
never pretended to be.

Chapter III.

PHILADELPHIA PHENOMENA

An experiment, made by H. P. B., with myself as a passive agent, shortly after my coming to her house in Philadelphia, narrows the phenomena of letter-transport, with precipitation of writing inside sealed covers, to very close limits. The facts were these: she was tipping tables for me, with and without the contact between her hands and the table; making loud and tiny raps—sometimes while holding her hand six inches above the wood, and sometimes while resting her hand upon mine as it lay flat upon the table; and spelling out messages to me from the pretended John King which, as rapped out by the alphabet, I recorded on scraps of paper that were subsequently torn up and thrown away. At last some of these messages relating to third parties seemed worth keeping, so one day, on my way home, I bought a reporter's note-book, and, on getting to the house, showed it to her and explained its intended use. She was seated at the time and I standing. Without touching the book or making any mystical pass or sign, she told me to put it in my bosom. I did so, and after a moment's pause she bade me take it out and look within. This is what I found: inside the first cover, written and drawn on the white lining paper in lead pencil:—

"JOHN KING,
HENRY DE MORGAN,

his book.

4th of the Fourth month in A.D. 1875."

Underneath this, the drawing of a Rosicrucian jewel; over the arch of the jewelled crown, the word FATE; beneath which is her name, "Helen," followed by what looks, after the rubbing of these seventeen years, like 99, something smudged out, and then a simple +. At the narrowest point, where the head of the compasses enters the crown, are the initials I. S. F.; beneath that a monogram, blending the capital letters A, T, D, and R, the T much larger than the others. At one foot of the compasses is my name, at the other the name of another man, a resident of Philadelphia; and along the segment of the arch connecting the two points of the pair of compasses run the words "Ways of Providence." I have the book on my table as I write, and my description is taken from the drawing itself. One striking feature of this example of psycho-dynamics is the fact that no one but myself had touched the book after it was purchased: I had had it in my pocket until it was shown to H. P. B., from the distance of two or three feet, had myself held it in my bosom, removed it a moment later when bidden, and the precipitation of the lead-pencil writing and drawing had been done while the book was inside my waistcoat. Now the writing inside the cover of my notebook is very peculiar; the e's being all like the Greek *epsilon*, and the n's something like the Greek *pi*: it is a quaint and quite individual handwriting, not like H. P. B.'s, but identical with that in all the written messages I had from first to last from "John King." H. P. B. having, then, the power of precipitation, must have transferred from her mind to the paper the images of words traced in this special style of script; or, if not she, but some other expert in this art did it, then that other person must have done it in that same way— *i.e.*, have first pictured to himself mentally the images of those words and that drawing, and then precipitated; that is, made them visible on the paper, as though written with a lead pencil. After seventeen years this psychograph remains legible, and some—not all—of the characters have the shine of plumbago: those that have not seem as though the lines had been sunken into the fabric of the paper. I have records of precipitations made in crayon, water colors, blue, red, and green pencils, ink and gold paint, as well as the formation of solid substances, but one scientific principle underlies them all, *viz.*, the objectivation of images, previously "visualised," or formed in the mind of the expert, by the employment of cosmic force and the diffused matter of space. The imagination is the creative hidden deity; force and matter its working tools.

The days and evenings of my Philadelphia visit were symposia of occult reading, teaching, and phenomena. Among H. P. B.'s most pleasant and sympathetic friends were Mr. and Mrs. Amer, and Messrs. M. D. Evans and J. Pusey, in whose presence a variety of phenomena were wrought. I remember, among others, that one afternoon she caused a photograph on the wall to suddenly disappear from its frame and give place to a sketch portrait of John King while a person present was actually looking at it. By degrees my mind was taking in the Eastern theories of spirit and spirits, of matter and materialism. Without being asked by H. P. B. to give up the spiritualistic hypothesis, I was made to see and to feel that, as a true science, Spiritualism could only be said to exist in the East, and its only proficients were pupils and teachers of the Oriental schools of occultism. With the sincerest desire to be fair to the Spiritualists, I must say that up to the present moment no scientific theory of mediumistic phenomena that covers the ground and is generally accepted among them, has been put forward, nor have I seen convincing proof that among Western adherents to the movement there has been discovered a system by which spirits may be evoked or physical phenomena compelled at will. Not a medium that I have ever met or heard of possesses a mantram or Vidya (scientific method) for those purposes, such as are common and have been known for ages in all Eastern countries. See, for example, the article "An Evocation by Sorcery," in the *Theosophist* for May, 1892. Thus for instance, while I and H. P. B.'s other friends were made to believe the John King (almost daily) phenomena were done by a disembodied man, once the famed buccaneer, Sir H. Morgan, and that she was serving him as medium, or, at least, contented helper, H. P. B. did things which implied a knowledge of magic. Let me give a homely example while at the same time remarking that great scientific inductions have been reached by the chance observation of equally commonplace facts—*e.g.,* the falling of an apple, the jumping of the lid of a boiling kettle. One day, bethinking me that a sufficiency of towels was but too evidently lacking in her house, I bought some and brought them home with me in a parcel. We cut them apart, and she was for putting them into immediate use without hemming, but, as I protested against such bad house-keeping, she good-naturedly set to plying her needle. She had hardly commenced when she gave an angry kick beneath the work-table at which she sat, and said, "Get out, you fool!" "What is the matter?" I asked. "Oh," she replied, "it is only a little beast of an elemental that pulled my dress and wants something to do." "Capital!" I said; "here is just the thing; make it hem these towels. Why should you bother about them, and you such an atrocious nee-dlewoman as that very hem proves you to be?" She laughed, and abused me for my uncomplimentary speech, but at first would not gratify the poor little bond-slave under the table that was ready to play the kindly leprachaun if given the chance. I, however, persuaded her at last: she told me to lock up the towels, the needles and thread, in a bookcase with glass doors lined with thick green silk, that stood at the farther side of the room. I did so and resumed my seat near her, and we fell to talking on the inexhaustible and unique theme that occu-pied our thoughts—occult science. After perhaps a quarter of an hour or twenty minutes, I heard a little squeaky sound, like a mouse's pipe, beneath the table, whereupon H. P. B. told me that "that nuisance" had finished the towels. So I unlocked the bookcase door, and found the dozen towels were actually hemmed, though after a clumsy fashion that would disgrace the youngest child in an infant-school sewing-class. Hemmed they were, beyond the possibility of doubt, and inside a locked bookcase which H. P. B. never approached while the thing was going on. The time was about 4 P.M., and, of course, it was broad daylight. We were the only persons in the room, and no third person entered it until all was finished.

Her house in Philadelphia was built on the usual local plan, with a front building and a wing at the back which contained the dining-room below and sitting or bedrooms above. H. P. B.'s bedroom was the front one on the first floor (the second, it is called in America) of the main building; at the turn of the staircase was the sitting-room where the towels were hemmed, and from its open door one could look straight along the passage into H. P. B.'s room if her door also stood open. She had been sitting in the former apartment conversing with me, but left to get something from her bedroom. I saw her mount the few steps to her floor, enter her room and leave the door open. Time passed, but she did not return. I waited and waited until, fearing she might have fainted, I called her name. There was no reply, so now, being a little anxious and knowing she could not be engaged privately, since the door had not been closed, I went there, called again, and looked in; she was not visible, though I even opened the closet and looked under the bed. She had vanished, without the chance of having walked out in the normal way, for, save the door giving upon the landing, there was no other means of exit; the room was a *cul de sac*. I was a cool one about phenomena after my long course of experiences, but this puzzled and worried me. I went back to the sitting-room, lit a pipe, and tried to puzzle out the mystery.

This was in 1875, it must be remembered, many years before the Salpétrière school's experiments in hypnotism had been vulgarised, so it never occurred to me that I was the subject of a neat experiment in mental suggestion, and that H. P. B. had simply inhibited my organs of sight from perceiving her presence, perhaps within two paces of me in the room. After awhile she calmly came out of her room into the passage and returned to the sitting-room to me. When I asked where she had been, she laughed and said she had had some occult business to attend to, and had made herself invisible. But how, she would not explain. She played me and others the same trick at other times, before and after our going to India, but even the latest instance happened long before the easy hypnotic solution of the problem would have occurred to me. As explained in the first chapter of this series, the superior neatness of Oriental over Western hypnotic suggestion is that in such cases as this, the inhibitory effect upon the subject's perceptive organs results from mental, not spoken, command or suggestion. The subject is not put on his guard to resist the illusion, and it is done before he has the least suspicion that any experiment is being made at his expense.

Since I took no measurement at the time, I must concede that the following also may have been a case of suggested illusion. H. P. B. was wearing her hair at that time in a bushy mop, without comb or pins or twists, and in length it might have been about to the lobes of her ears. I came home to tiffin one day, and, her bedroom door standing open as usual, stopped for a minute's chat, before mounting to my own room on the floor above. She was standing near one of the windows, and her head being in high light, I noticed particularly the mass of her hair and its tousled appearance. I also observed the shine of the daylight upon the glossy, pale grey paper with which the ceiling was covered. After a few words together I ran up stairs, but had not been there a minute before I heard her calling me to come down. I did so at once, saw her standing in the same place, but her hair was now so much longer that it almost touched her shoulders. She said nothing about that, but pointed to the ceiling over her head and said: "Here is something that John has drawn for you." My recollection is now very dim as to what it was, but, as I remember it, it was a huge sketch of a man's head, with some writing or symbols near it; all done in lead-pencil, at the spot where I had noticed the blank surface to be when I passed up stairs. I then took hold of her lengthened hair, and asked her, laughing, where she bought her pommade, as it was certainly very efficacious if it could cause hair to grow two inches within three minutes. She made some merry rejoinder, and said I should not meddle with things that were of no consequence; such freaks of nature sometimes happened to her; it was not to see that she had called me, but only to show me what John King had done on the ceiling. Considering the time that had elapsed from my leaving to my re-entering the room, and the fact that the ceiling was too high for her to reach, even by standing on a chair or table, my present inference is that the drawing was done in one of two ways, *viz.*, either by herself at her leisure, while I was out, by mounting upon a step-ladder, and inhibiting me from seeing the work until she chose; or by the process of instantaneous precipitation while I was ascending and descending one short flight of stairs. That it was not visible to me when I was first in the room, I can positively aver, and if the reader chooses to speculate as to the rationale of the matter, he must take my statement as made for what it is worth. What makes me suspect that the apparent lengthening of H. P. B.'s hair was illusory, is the fact that, try as I may, I cannot remember whether it continued to seem long or apparently resumed its previous length that day or the next. People in India, and others subsequently, in Europe, saw her hair twisted up into a knot and confined by a comb, but it was years after we met before she would let it grow long enough for that purpose; I am not sure that it was not when we went to visit the Sinnetts at Simla; so I am probably right in suspecting that the apparent sudden lengthening was a Maya done by way of a joke. But very, very strange things happened with her hair on several occasions, to be hereafter narrated. And strangest of all, was that which happened to my beard one night, as we shall see in good time. Speaking of her jokes, it may be said that, throughout all our years of intimacy, she wasted enough psychic force on useless phenomena to have sufficed to convince the whole Royal Society if it had been judiciously employed. I have heard her ring astral bells that were drowned in the noise of conversation, make raps that nobody heard save myself, and do other phenomena that passed unnoticed, but which would have greatly strengthened her credit as a thaumaturgist if she had but chosen the favourable moment and given the right chances for observation. However, all that is past and gone, and my task is to record, as remembered, the psychical experiments which satisfied my critical reason as to the reality of the science of Eastern Magic.

In doing which, shall I not be acting as a true friend to H. P. B., whose character has been vilified and whose occult powers denied because she fed rogues at her table and warmed traitors in her bosom? These days and events of which I write were in the pre-*Coulombian* era, when real adepts taught eager pupils and genuine phenomena happened. And they were days when I knew my colleague as a human being, before she had been half-deified by friends who had known nothing of her human failings, hence of her humanity. As I shall present her, the now fading ideal image of the writer of *Isis* and the S. D., will become clothed in flesh and blood; a real (masculinised) woman; living like other people when awake, but going into another world and dealing with nobler people, when asleep or in waking clairvoyance; a personality inhabiting an enfeebled female body, "in which . . . a vital cyclone is raging much of the time"—to quote the words of a Master. So fitful, so capricious, so unreliable, so exacting, so tempestuous as to call for heroic forbearance and self-control if one would live and work with her in an unselfish spirit. These phenomena of hers that I saw, the manifold proofs she gave of the existence behind her of teachers whose feet she felt she was scarce worthy to dust, and the later *epistasis*, when the turbulent and exasperating woman became a writing and teaching sage and a benefactress to the soul-seeker—all these, and the books she left behind her, combine to prove her exceptional greatness and make her eccentricities forgotten, even by those to whom they caused most mental suffering. In showing us the Path, she laid us all under such a weight of obligation that it is impossible to harbour any feeling save gratitude for her.

Chapter IV.

MADAME BLAVATSKY'S
SECOND MARRIAGE

In giving anything like a consecutive account of early Theo-sophic days—by which term I mean to include all days of intercourse between H. P. B. and myself, so far as I can recall them—I must briefly allude to the cases of precipitation of manuscript by her which are mentioned in my *People from the Other World* (pp. 455-6-7 and 8). Ostensibly, as above stated, they were given me by John King, of Kamaloca, whilom buc-caneer, knighted by His Britannic Majesty Charles II., but now apparently a mere pseudonym of H. P. B.'s elementals. At a séance at her hotel in Philadelphia, on the evening of Janu-ary 6, 1875, the alleged J. K. doing phenomena, I said: "If you are in reality a spirit, as you pretend, give me some exhibition of your power. Make me, for example, a copy of the last note from E. W. to Mr. Owen that I have in the portfolio in my pocket." No notice was taken of the request that evening, but on the next but one after it, while H. P. B. was writing and I reading at the same table, loud raps sounded, and, upon my calling the English alphabet, spelt out, "Hand me your dictionary under the table, will you?" The only dictionary there, was a Russian-English one of H. P. B.'s which was handed (not dropped, but *handed*, as if to a something or invisible somebody down there, that could take the bulky volume) beneath as requested. The raps then called for a mucilage bottle, and then for a pen-knife. These also having been passed under the table, there was momentary silence, after which was rapped the word "Look!" We took up the book, knife, and bottle, and upon a fly-leaf of the dictionary I found a precipitated copy of the note in question. The call for the knife was explained to me thus: a certain infinitesimal quantity of the metal composing the blades was disintegrated from the mass and used in precipitation of the black writing from the state of metallic vapour. The gum-arabic lent some of its particles—also vaporised for the purpose—as a cohesive aid in the experiment. The portfolio containing the duplicated note had been in my pocket continuously since my coming to Philadelphia, until half an hour prior to the experiment, when I had laid it on the mantel-shelf, and had had it in full view whenever I raised my eyes from my book. H. P. B. was all the time within two feet of me, at her table writing, and no person save ourselves was or had been in the room since I laid it upon the shelf. Upon comparing the original writing and the duplicate, by superposition, it was evident that they were not facsimiles, which made it the more interesting.

The next evening, H. P. B. and I being again alone, the raps called for a piece of Bristol-board drawing-paper to be handed beneath the table. Showing me first that both sides were blank, my colleague passed it down to "John King," whereupon the raps bade me look at my watch and note how long the experiment would require. With my watch in hand, I glanced under the table-cloth and satisfied myself that there was but the one sheet of paper there which I had handled the moment before. At the end of just thirty seconds the raps spelt out "Done." I looked at the paper and felt disappointed upon seeing that the exposed surface was as blank as before, but upon the under face, the one next to the carpet, was found a second and even better copy of the original E. W. letter. This time the portfolio containing the letter was in the inside breast-pocket of my coat, where it had been continuously since the previous evening's experiment in precipitation. A Mr. B——, who entered the room at this moment, assisted me in making a very careful scrutiny of the documents, placing one over the other as I had already done, and becoming, like myself, entirely convinced of the genuineness of the phenomenon. I may say, in parenthesis, that this gentleman received in his carpet-bag while travelling by railway train, a letter from "John King" conveying instructions as to something of a personal nature. He told me the story himself, showed me the letter, and stated upon honour, that it had come into his bag while in a train and miles distant from Philadelphia and H. P. B. This incident recalls similar experiences of my own while travelling by train, in France, with Babu Mohini M. Chatterji, and in Germany with Dr. Huebbe Schleiden, both in the year 1884.

The mention of this gentleman (Mr. B.) reminds me of the duty I owe to the memory of H. P. B. to state her exact relations with him. It has been insinuated that they were not altogether creditable, and that there was a mystery concealed which would not bear probing. This is of a piece with the multitudinous cruel reports that were spread about her. She is dead and gone now from the world's sight and beyond the reach of the slanderer, but, judging from my own feelings, I am sure that all who love her memory will be glad to know the facts from one of the half dozen who are able to give them. They are these: One of my Chittenden letters in the *Daily Graphic* aroused the interest of this Mr. B.—a Russian subject—and led him to write me from Philadelphia expressing his strong desire to meet my colleague and talk over Spiritualism. No objections being made by her, he came over to New York towards the end of 1875, and they met. It turned out that he fell at once into a state of profound admiration, which he expressed verbally, and later, by letter, to her and to me. She persistently rebuffed him when she saw that he was matrimonially inclined, and grew very angry at his persistence. The only effect was to deepen his devotion, and he finally threatened to take his life unless she would accept his hand. Meanwhile, before this crisis arrived, she had gone to Philadelphia, put up at the same hotel, and received his daily visits. He declared that he would ask nothing but the privilege of watching over her, that his feeling was one of unselfish adoration for her intellectual grandeur, and that he would make no claim to any of the privileges of wedded life. He so besieged her that—in what seemed to me a freak of madness—she finally consented to take him at his word and be nominally his wife; but with the stipulation that she should retain her own name, and be as free and independent of all disciplinary restraint as she then was. So they were lawfully married by a most respectable

Unitarian clergyman of Philadelphia, and set up their *lares* and *penates* in a small house in Sansom Street, where they entertained me as guest on my second visit to that city—after my book was finished and brought out. The ceremony took place, in fact, while I was stopping in the house, although I was not present as a witness. But I saw them when they returned from the clergyman's residence after the celebration of the rite.

When I privately expressed to her my amazement at what I conceived to be her act of folly in marrying a man younger than herself, and inexpressibly her inferior in mental capacity; one, moreover, who could never be even an agreeable companion to her, and with very little means—his mercantile business not being as yet established—she said it was a misfortune that she could not escape. Her fate and his were temporarily linked together by an inexorable Karma, and the union was to her in the nature of a punishment for her awful pride and combativeness, which impeded her spiritual evolution, while no lasting harm would result to the young man. The inevitable result was that this ill-starred couple dwelt together but a few months. The husband forgot his vows of unselfishness, and, to her ineffable disgust, became an importunate lover. She fell dangerously ill in June from a bruise on one knee caused by a fall the previous winter in New York upon the stone flagging of a sidewalk, which ended in violent inflammation of the periosteum and partial mortification of the leg; and as soon as she got better (which she did in one night, by one of her quasi-miraculous cures, after an eminent surgeon had declared that she would die unless the leg was instantly amputated), she left him and would not go back. When, after many months of separation, he saw her determination unchangeable, and that his business, through his mismanagement, was going to the dogs, he engaged counsel and sued for a divorce on the ground of desertion. The summonses were served upon her in New York, Mr. Judge acted as her counsel, and on the 25th May, 1878, the divorce was granted. The original documents have ever since been in my custody. That is the whole story, and it will be seen that it shows no criminality nor illegality on her part, nor any evidence that she derived the slightest worldly advantage from the marriage beyond a very modest maintenance, without a single luxury, for a few months.

Before dismissing Mr. B. from the scene, I might mention a variant of her precipitation phenomena which I personally witnessed. He talked continually of a deceased grandmother, whom he professed to have loved very dearly, and begged H. P. B. to get him, if possible, her portrait, the family having none. Wearied by his importunities, she, one day when we three were together, took a sheet of writing-paper, went to the window, held it against the glass with the palms of her two hands, and in a couple of minutes handed him the paper, upon which I saw the portrait, in black and white, of a queer little old woman, with a dark complexion, black hair, many wrinkles, and a large wart on her nose! Mr. B. enthusiastically declared the likeness to be perfect.

Her time during this period was fully engrossed with writing for the public press, upon Western Spiritualism at first, and later upon that of the East. Her "first occult shot," as she terms it in a note to the cutting pasted into our scrap-book, will be found in the (Boston) *Spiritual Scientist*, vol. i., July 15, 1875, comment upon which will be made in the next chapter.

The publication of my book led to important results; among others, to interminable discussions in the American and English organs of Spiritualism and in the secular press, in which both H. P. B. and I engaged, and to the formation of lasting friendships with several most excellent correspondents, with whom we threshed out the whole subject of Eastern and Western occultism. Almost immediately we found ourselves addressed by enquirers in both hemispheres and attacked or defended by opponents and sympathisers. The well-known Hon. Alexandre Aksakof, Russian Imperial Privy Councillor and a fervid Spiritualist, engaged H. P. B. to translate my book into Russian, offering to bring it out at his own expense. She complied, and shortly there appeared in St. Petersburgh a very kind and appreciative pamphlet by Professor N. A. Wagner, of the Imperial University, in which he (himself a scientific authority of the first rank) was good enough to say that in conducting my researches I "had complied with all the requirements of cautious scientific enquiry"; a testimonial of which I naturally felt very proud. Mr. Crookes, F. R. S., and Mr. Alfred R. Wallace, F. R. S., of England, and M. Camille Flammarion of France, the world-famous astronomer, were also very kind and sympathetic in their expressions. Some months later, Mr. C. C. Massey, of London, came over to America expressly to verify, by personal observation on the spot, the accuracy of my account of the Eddy phenomena. We saw much of each other, and were so mutually satisfied that a close, almost brotherly friendship sprang up between us; one that has lasted to this day unbroken and unclouded even by a single misunderstanding. I had already been brought into the most sympathetic relations with the late Hon. R. D. Owen and Mr. Epes Sargent, of Boston. The latter gentleman and scholar had been the channel for my gaining both a precious correspondent and the dearest of friends, in the late Mr. W. Stainton Moses,* M.A. (Oxon), teacher of Classics and English, in University College, London, and the most honoured and brilliant writer among British Spiritualists. A copy of my book was sent him and reviewed in the *Psychological Magazine* or *Human Nature*—I forget which—and little by little we drifted into an almost weekly interchange of letters for several years. His first one, now before me, is dated April 27, 1875, and is devoted to discussion of the conditions and results of "circle" mediumistic phenomena. He draws my attention to a fact, sneered at by Professor Tyndall in his well-known letter to the old London Dialectical Society, yet only too palpable to all experienced enquirers into this class of natural phenomena, *viz.*, that "as a matter of fact certain people by their mere presence do seriously interface with, and by their mere contiguity paralyse the phenomena: and that from no fault of their own, nor from any mental attitude (as want of faith, etc.), but from the atmosphere which surrounds them. The more sensitive the medium the more perceptible this is." Mr. Stainton Moses continues: "There are

---

* Moses is not the real name but Moseyn or Mostyn, as he told me. The other is a corruption.

many personal friends of mine in whose presence phenomena with me cease, to my great chagrin, nor have I the least power to alter the result." Alluding to the phenomenon of the apparent de-materialisation of the medium (*e.g.*, the case of Mrs. Compton, as described in my book), he declares it to be most astounding of all, and says he cannot account for it, though he believes "it is not unknown to the Oriental Magicians." What I have said in a previous chapter as regards the power of deluding the sight by the now scientific process of hypnotic inhibition of the nerves, solves this mystery and does away with a lot of superstitious beliefs and alleged diabolism. It was worth all the trouble of writing that book to have made two such life-long friends as Stainton Moses and Massey: but it did much more, it changed my life and made an epoch. While Mr. Massey was in America we together visited several mediums, and he was one of those who joined H. P. B. and myself in forming the Theosophical Society toward the close of that year (1875). I introduced him to H. P. B. and he frequently visited her rooms, became her close friend and constant correspondent until the intimacy was broken, several years later, by a circumstance known as the "Kiddle incident." When he returned to London I gave him an introductory letter to Mr. Stainton Moses, and thus began that intimacy between us three which has only been interrupted by the death of "M. A. Oxon."

Mention has been made of one Signor B——, an Italian artist possessed of occult powers, who visited H. P. B. in New York. I witnessed, one autumn evening, in 1875, just after the T. S. was formed, the extraordinary phenomenon of rain-making effected by him by—as he said—the control of spirits of the air. The moon was at the full and not a cloud floated in the clear blue sky. He called H. P. B. and myself out upon the balcony of her back drawing-room, and, bidding me keep perfectly silent and cool, whatever might happen, he drew from the breast of his coat and held up towards the moon a pasteboard card, perhaps 6310 inches in size, upon one face of which were painted in water-colors a number of squares, each containing a strange mathematical figure, but which he would not let me handle or examine. I stood close behind him, and could feel his body stiffen as though it were responding to an intense concentration of will. Presently he pointed at the moon and we saw dense black vapours, like thunder-clouds, or, I should rather say, like the tumbling mass of black smoke that streams away to leeward from the funnel of a moving steamer, pouring out of the shining eastern rim of the brilliant satellite, and floating away towards the horizon. Involuntarily I uttered an exclamation, but the sorcerer gripped my arm with a clutch of steel and motioned me to be silent. More and more rapidly the black pall of cloud rushed out, and longer and longer it stretched away towards the distance, like a monstrous jetty plume. It spread into a fan-shape and soon other dark rain-clouds appeared in the sky, now here, now there, and formed into masses rolling, drifting, and scudding exactly like a natural water metre. Rapidly the heavens became overcast, the moon disappeared from view, and a shower of rain-drops drove us into the house. There was no thunder or lightning, no wind, just simply a smart shower, produced within the space of a quarter-hour by this man of mystery. When we came into the light of the chandelier, I saw that his face had that look of iron firmness and that clenching of the teeth that one sees on the faces of comrades in battle. And truly for good reason, for he had just been battling against and conquering the unseen hosts of the elements, a thing that brings out every spark of virile force in man. Signor B. did not linger with us but hastily took his leave, and, as the hour was late, I followed his example within the next few minutes. The pavement was wet with rain, the air damp and cool. My rooms were but a few steps off, and I had barely reached them and settled myself for a smoke when the bell rang, and, upon opening the front door, upon the threshold I found Signor B., pale and partly exhausted. He excused himself for troubling me but asked for a glass of water. I made him enter, and after he had drunk the water and rested awhile, we went to conversing about occult subjects and kept it up for a long time. I found him ready to talk about art, literature or science, but extremely reticent about occult science and his personal experience in psychical development. He explained, however, that all the races of elemental spirits are controllable by man when his innate divine potencies are developed: his will then becoming an irresistible force before which all inferior, that is every elemental force, whether organised as entities or brute, blind cosmic agents, are compelled to yield. I had seen no black smoke actually pouring out of the moon, that was a simple illusion produced by the concentration of his thought upon her surface, but I had certainly seen clouds form out of the moonlit sky and rain fall, and he commended the fact to me for reflection. But now he gave me a bit of advice which

fairly astonished me. I had seen him on the best of terms with
H. P. B., talking in the most friendly and unreserved way
about Italy, Garibaldi, Mazzini, the Carbonari, the Eastern
and Western adepts, etc., and matching phenomena, like the
trick of the white butterflies, and I certainly had reason to be
amazed when, putting on an air of mystery, he warned me to
break off my intimacy with her. He said she was a very wicked
and dangerous woman, and would bring some terrible calamity upon me if I allowed myself to fall under her malign spell.
This—he said—he was ordered by the great Master, whose
name I had heard him pronounce to H. P. B., to tell me. I
looked at the man to see if I could detect the concealed meaning of this preposterous speech, and finally said: "Well, Signor,
I know that the Personage you mention exists; I have every
reason, after seeing your phenomena, to suspect that you have
relations with him or with the Brotherhood; I am ready, even
to the sacrifice of my life, to obey his behests; and now I
demand that you give me a certain sign by which I shall know,
positively and without room for the least doubt, that Madame
Blavatsky is the devil you depict, and that the Master's will is
that my acquaintance with her shall cease." The Italian hesitated, stammered out something incoherent, and turned the
conversation. Though he could draw inky clouds out of the
moon, he could not throw black doubt into my heart about my
friend and guide through the mazy intricacies of occult science. The next time I saw H. P. B. I told her about B.'s warning,
whereupon she smiled, said I had nicely passed through that
little test, and wrote a note to Signor B. to "forget the way to
her door." Which he did.

Chapter V.

SPIRITUALISM

O ut of the sea of controversy into which H. P. B. and I were plunged by my *Graphic* letters and my book; Mr. Owen's article on Katie King and his interleaved disclaimer, in the January (1875) *Atlantic Monthly*; General Lippitt's contributions to the *Galaxy* (December, 1874) and the *Banner of Light*; the attacks upon and defences of the Holmes mediums; and the universal discussion of Spiritualism in the American and European press—were churned certain precious things: among them, the forcing of Eastern occult ideas upon Western attention, and the birth of the Theosophical Society.

To refute the mendacious stories of Mahâtma meddlings and attendant phenomena, and show the natural stages by which the Society came into being, we must glance at the earlier letters written to the press by its two actual pioneers and parents (of which I have an incomplete set of copies). The details may be dry, but they are important as historical data.

As already explained, the self-advertising attack of the late Dr. George M. Beard—an electropathic physician of New

York city—upon the Eddys, and his wild and false assertion that he could imitate the form-apparitions with "three dollars' worth of drapery," lashed H. P. B. into a Berserker writing-rage and made her send the *Graphic* that caustic reply, covering a bet of $500 that he could not make good his boast, which first acquainted the American public with her existence and name. Naturally, people took sides; the friends of Spiritualism and the mediums siding with H. P. B., while the opponents, especially the materialistically inclined scientists, ranged themselves in the cohort of Dr. Beard's supporters. The one who profited by the dispute was Beard, whose *ruse*—worthy of Pears, Beecham, or Siegel—advertised him and his electricity beyond his expectations. Profiting by the chance, he gave a thoroughly well advertised lecture on this subject, and another, if I remember aright, upon Mesmerism and Thought-reading, at the New York Academy of Music. The *Banner of Light*, the *R. P. Journal* and other papers, commenting upon H. P. B.'s anti-Beard letter, she replied, and so, very speedily found herself with her hands full of controversy. As I said before, she took up the position of an out-and-out Spiritualist, who not only believed but *knew* that the powers behind the mediums, which wrote, produced physical phenomena, talked in air-formed voices, and even showed their entire forms and disconnected faces, hands, feet or other members, were the earth-haunting spirits of the dead; neither more nor less. In a previous chapter I quoted passages from her published letters and articles going to prove this, and in her very first letter to me, written from New York within a week after she left me at Chittenden (October, 1864) addressing me as "Dear Friend" and signing herself "Jack," and in her second one, dated six days later and signed "Jack Blavatsky," she entreats me not to praise the mediumistic musical performance of one Jesse Sheppard, whose pretence to having sung before the Czar, and other boasts she had discovered to be absolutely false; as such a course on my part would "injure Spiritualism more than anything else in the world."* "I speak to you," she tells me, "as a true friend to yourself and (as a) Spiritualist anxious to save Spiritualism from a danger." In the same letter, referring to a promise given her by "Mayflower" and "George Dix," two of the alleged spirit-controls of Horatio Eddy, that they would help her by influencing the judge before whom was pending her lawsuit to recover the money put into the Long Island market-garden copartnership—she says: "Mayflower was right, Judge—came in with another decision in my favour." Did she believe, then, that medium-controlling spirits could and would influence justices? If not, what does her language imply? Either she was a Spiritualist, or so represented herself for the time being, with the ulterior design of gradually shift-ing Spiritualists from the Western to the Eastern platform of belief in regard to the mediumistic phenomena. In her anti-Beard letter (*N.Y. Daily Graphic*, Nov. 13, 1874), she

---

* Led by his unlucky star, Sheppard—she writes—had brought her [[adot]] lot of his St. Petersburgh credentials, in Russian, to translate. Among them she found a Police license to sing at the Salle Koch, a low lager-bier saloon and dance hall, resorted to by dissipated characters of both sexes, and a music-master's bills for 32 roubles, for teaching him certain Russian songs—which we heard him sing at Eddy's, *in a dark séance when he was ostensibly under the control of Grisi and Lablache!* I give the facts on her authority without prejudice.

says—speaking of the incident of the bringing to her by the "spirits" of Horatio Eddy, of a decoration-buckle that had been buried with her father's body, at Stavropol—"I deem it my duty as a Spiritualist to," etc., etc. Later on, she told me that the outburst of mediumistic phenomena had been caused by the Brotherhood of Adepts as an evolutionary agency, and I embodied this idea in a phrase in my book (*P.O.W.*, p. 454, top), suggesting the thinkable hypothesis that such might be the fact. But then, in that case, the spiritualistic outbreak could not be regarded as absolutely maleficent, as some Theosophical extremists have depicted it; for it is inconceivable— at least to me, who knew them—that those Elder Brothers of Humanity would ever employ, even for the good of the race, an agency in itself absolutely bad. The Jesuit motto, *Finis coronat opus*, is *not* written on the temple walls of the Fraternity.

In the same number of the *Daily Graphic* to which she contributed her anti-Beard letter, was published her biography, from notes furnished by herself. She says, "In 1858, I returned to Paris and made the acquaintance of Daniel Home, the Spiritualist . . . Home converted me to Spiritualism . . . After this I went to Russia. I converted my father to Spiritualism." In an article defending the Holmes mediums from the treacherous attack of their ex-partner and show-manager, Dr. Child, she speaks of Spiritualism as "*our* belief" and "*our* cause"; and again, "the whole belief of *us* Spiritualists"; still further, "if we Spiritualists are to be laughed at, and scoffed, and ridiculed, and sneered at, we ought to know at least the reason why." Certainly; and some of her surviving colleagues might profitably keep it in mind. In the *Spiritual Scientist* of March 8,

1875, she says that a certain thing would "go towards showing that, notwithstanding the divine truth of our faith (Spiritualism) and the teachings of our invisible guardians (the spirits of the circles), some Spiritualists have not profited by them, to learn impartiality and justice."

This was both courageous and magnanimous on her part; thoroughly characteristic of the way in which she flung herself in the fore-front of battle for any cause that she took up. Her sympathies for liberty and free-thought led her to follow, with several other ladies, the victory-bringing flag of Garibaldi, the Liberator, and to plunge into the thick of the carnage at Mentana; and so now, when she saw the Spiritual Idea battling against Materialistic Science, no fear of contamination by contact with fraudulent mediums, evil spirits, or cliques of Spiritualists who preached and practised free-love and the breaking of healthy social bonds, made her hesitate for one moment about taking her stand on the side of Spiritualism. Her policy may be condemned by some, her language—as seen in the few specimens, out of many, above quoted—be regarded as a full endorsement of the very Spiritualism she afterwards so mercilessly criticised; but to judge her fairly, one must try and put himself beside her under the then existing conditions; he must try to realise how much she knew, both in theory and practise, about psychical phenomena that the world need to know before casting itself into the lethal stream of Materialism. Many of us would have used much more guarded language, and thus avoided leaving behind us such a tangle of contradictions and confusion; but then she was exceptional in every respect—in mental and psychical powers, in temperament and in method of controversy. One object of this narrative is to show that, with all human frailties and eccentricities that may be ascribed to her, she was a great, high-towering personage, who did a great altruistic work for the world, and was rewarded with savage ingratitude and blinded depreciation.

Her instructions to me about the existence of the elemental spirit world went on—as before noted—apace with our private intercourse with (alleged) rapping spirits, and so, long before I had adopted the Eastern theory of Pisachas and Bhûtas, called by us elementaries,* I had come to distinguish the two unlike classes of phenomena-working agents, the sub-human nature-spirits, and the earth-bound, ex-human elementaries. Towards the close of the winter season of 1874–5, while at Hartford seeing my book through the press, but too late to re-write it, I had the rare chance of consulting the superb collection of books on the occult sciences in the Watkinson Library of Reference, made for it by Dr. H. C. Trumbull, the erudite Librarian. I was thus pretty well prepared to understand H. P. B.'s verbal explanations, and her many surprising psychical phenomena in illustration of them. This course of preparatory reading, lectures, and phenomena also stood me in good stead when she addressed herself to the laborious task of writing *Isis Unveiled*, and enlisted me as her helper.

---

* In point of fact, both of us used to call the spirits of the elements "elementaries," thus causing much confusion, but when *Isis* was being written, I suggested that we should employ the distinctive terms "elemental" and "elementary" in the connections they have ever since had. It is too late to change them now, else I should do it.

It was in the first quarter of the year 1875, that we became interested in the *Spiritual Scientist*, a small but bright and independent journal, published and edited in Boston, by Mr. E. Gerry Brown. The crying need of the hour was a paper which, while recognised as an organ of Spiritualism, could be induced to help in bringing Spiritualists to scrutinise more closely the behaviour and pretended psychical gifts of their mediums, and to patiently listen to the theories of spirit being and intercourse with the living. The older journals of that class were, what might be termed too orthodox, while Mr. Brown's specialty seemed to be to win his way by fearless criticism of abuses. Our relations with him were brought about by a letter to him (*Spi. Sci.*, March 8, 1875), and within the next month he had been taken under the favour of the powers behind H. P. B. In the number of the journal in question for April 17th, appeared a very notable circular headed "Important to Spiritualists." The importance of it to Mr. Gerry Brown was in the promise (fairly redeemed)* it embodied of literary and pecuniary help to be given him, while to the public which concerned itself in the question of Spiritualism, it held out the profitable idea that the paper would be used as the organ of the new movement for placing American Spiritualism on a more philosophical and intellectual basis. The circular stated that the leading Spiritualist papers were "compelled to devote

---

* Professor Buchanan, Epes Sargent, Charles Sotheran and other known writers, not to mention our two selves, began contributing to his columns, and H. P. B. and I gave him several hundred dollars towards current expenses. The latter form of help was acknowledged in his "leader" of June 1, 1875, entitled "Rock Bottom."

most of their space to communications of a trivial and purely personal character, interesting only to the friends of the spirits sending them . . ." and to beginners. The London *Spiritualist* and Paris *Revue Spirite* were cited as "examples of the kind of paper that should have been established in this country (U.S.A.) long ago—papers which devote more space to the discussion of principles, the teaching of philosophy, and the display of conservative critical ability, than to the mere publication of the thousand-and-one minor occurrences of . . . circles." The third paragraph read as follows:

"It is the standing reproach of American Spiritualism that it teaches so few things worthy of a thoughtful man's attention: that so few of its phenomena occur under conditions satisfactory to men of scientific training; that the propagation of its doctrines is in the hands of so many ignorant, if not positively vicious, persons; and that it offers, in exchange for the orderly arrangements of prevailing religious creeds, nothing but an undigested system of present and future moral and social relations and accountability."*

---

* I was then and have since often been reproached by Spiritualists for the severity of my strictures upon the prevalent large admixture of immoral views and behaviour among mediums and whole groups of pretended Spiritualists, but I never wrote more caustic things about them than are to be found in the newspaper articles and books of leading writers among themselves. To say nothing of the sweeping and savage depreciation of the whole company of his brother mediums and psychics, by that peacock medium, Home, Mrs. Hardinge Britten says (*Nineteenth Century Miracles*, p. 426), that her spirit guides had told her that "the worst foes of Spiritualism would be of its own household, and the cruellest stabs directed against it would be dealt by the hands of Spiritualists themselves." In another place she says: "and thus this great cause, like many another of the world's purest Messiahs, has been lifted up on the cross of martyrdom between the

I wrote every word of this circular myself, alone corrected the printer's proofs, and paid for the printing. That is to say, nobody dictated a word that I should say, nor interpolated any words or sentences, nor controlled my action in any visible way. I wrote it to carry out the expressed wishes of the Masters that we—H. P. B. and I—should help the Editor of the *Scientist* at what was to him, a difficult crisis, and used my best judgment as to the language most suitable for the purpose. When the circular was in type at the printer's and I had corrected the proofs, and changed the arrangement of the matter into its final paragraphs, I enquired of H. P. B. (by letter) if she thought I had better issue it anonymously or append my name. She replied that it was the wish of the Masters that it should be signed thus: "*For the Committee of Seven*, BROTHERHOOD of LUXOR." And so it was signed and published. She subsequently explained that our work, and much more of the same kind, was

---

thieves of licentiousness and cupidity" if it had not died out, "it is not for lack of every available effort on the part of humanity to sap its integrity by internal corruption, as well as by external antagonism. . ." Free-love "had expanded from an incipient germ to the full maturity of a widespread movement . . . The monstrous flow of licentious doctrine, often illustrated by monstrous licentiousness of life and conduct, which for a certain period of time spread like an evil contagion throughout the United States. . . . cast a most unjust and ruinous ill-odour over the reputation and belief of tens of thousands of innocent persons," etc. I never wrote anything as strong as that: though even Mrs. Britten has not exaggerated the unsavoury condition of affairs produced by the unrestricted encouragement of intercourse between the living and the dead. To regulate this intercourse, to announce its perils, and to show what was true spiritualism, and how man can develop true spirituality, was true plainly H. P. B.'s design and her motive for declaring herself a Spiritualist. This will be evident. I think, to those who follow her course throughout to the day of her death.

being supervised by a Committee of seven Adepts belonging to the Egyptian group of the Universal Mystic Brotherhood.* Up to this time she had not even seen the circular, but now I took one to her myself and she began to read it attentively. Presently she laughed, and told me to read the acrostic made by the initials of the six paragraphs. To my amazement, I found that they spelt the name under which I knew the (Egyptian) adept under whose orders I was then studying and working. Later, I received a certificate, written in gold ink, on a thick green paper, to the effect that I was attached to this "Observatory," and that three (named) Masters had me under scrutiny. This title, Brotherhood of Luxor, was pilfered by the schemers who started, several years later, the gudgeontrap called "The H. B. of L." The existence of the real Lodge is mentioned in Kenneth Mackenzie's *Royal Masonic Cyclopaedia* (p. 461).

Nothing in my early occult experience during this H. P. B. epoch, made a deeper impression on my mind than the above acrostic. It proved to me that space was no bar to the transmission of thought-suggestions from the teacher's to the pupil's brain; and it supported the theory that, in the doing of world-work, the agent may often be actually led by overseeing directors to do things which they choose to have done, without his being at all conscious that his mind is not functioning under the sole impulse of its controlling Ego. Applying this not unreasonable or unscientific theory to the whole history of the Theosophical Society, who can say in what proportion

---

* It has been already explained that I first worked under the Egyptian part of the African section and later under the Indian section.

of cases any of us has been unconsciously doing what had to be done, but might not have been done if no external influence had given us the push? And how many of the wretched mistakes, missteps, and injurious eccentricities that have occurred, or been shown, by either of us, were due to our just being left to follow our own wrong impulses, the result of our temperaments, ignorance, moral weakness or bigoted prejudices? People often wonder why the various scandals, such as the Coulomb and lesser ones which we have had to suffer from, were not foreseen and prevented by the Masters; why H. P. B. was not forewarned of what traitors would do; and why, in the seemingly most serious crisis, no help came, no spiritual guide appeared. Of course, such questions imply the absurdity that Mahatmas, who implicilty believe in and govern their own actions by the strict rules of Karma, would take us, like so many puppets on wires, or so many poodles being taught tricks, and put us through set motions, to the meddling with our Karma, and the consequent interference with our rights. What the evolution of society needs at a particular juncture is, perhaps, that a certain person should do, write, or say a certain thing which, once done, brings after it a whole train of consequences. If that necessary thing involves no Karmic wrong to the individual, the mental impulse to do it may be given him, and so the sequences of cause and effect be begotten. The destinies of Europe, for example, are under the control of three or four men, who might meet together in a boating party and in the same boat. If some certain trifle should occur, then such a kingdom would ultimately be destroyed, such a dynasty develop into a scourge of the race, or such an era of peace and progress be entered upon. If either the one or the other be demanded at that juncture by the interests of all mankind, and *no other means are available* for precipitating the crisis, then I could conceive it as lawful for the mental suggestion to be made from without: or, take a simpler case, which is also historical. A point had been reached in the progress of Egyptology where the world needed a better clue than it had for reading the hieroglyphics: in the literature of that ancient civilisation lay great and precious truths—truths, the time to republish which had arrived. All other means failing, an Arab labourer is simply moved to dig at a certain sarcophagus; he finds an engraved stone or an inscribed papyrus; which he sells to Mr. Grey, at Thebes, in 1820, or to Signor Casati, at Karnak or Luxor; who, in turn, transmit it to Champollion, or Young, or Ebers; who find the missing clue, and with it decipher very important old writings. It is the helping, not the fratricidal, hand that these hidden benefactors of ours hold out to humanity. Or, to cite a case much nearer home: I am moved to buy a paper on a certain day; I read a certain thing in it; which prompts me to take a natural step; which, later, brings H. P. B. and myself together; which, after a while, evolves the Theosophical Society and its consequences. For taking the initial step, I reap no merit; but if the effect is a good one, and I merge myself into it, and work for it with unselfish fervour, then I *do* share in the *whole* benefit that that effect imparts to humanity. I saw some poor people at Galle, once, reaching up their hands to touch the baskets of food which richer neighbours had procured for and were bearing on their heads to a company of Buddhist monks.

Upon inquiry I was told that, by feeling a true sympathy for the deed of charity, they partook of the merit it involved. It meant more than a long sermon to me, and I embodied the idea in my *Buddhist Catechism*.

I found among my papers last week an old letter from the Hon. Alexander Aksakoff, of St. Petersburgh, which though probably not one of those which were so phenomenally abstracted from the mailbags en route to New York and delivered to me in Philadelphia, since it is dated in St. Petersburgh the 4–16th April, 1875, and must have reached me after my visit to H. P. B. was finished, contains a lead-pencil postscript on the fourth page in the quaint handwriting of "John King." He tells me that my correspondent "is a truly good man and a learned one, too"—facts which are now acknowledged universally. Having lost or given away the envelope, I cannot fix the exact date of the letter's arrival. In it, M. Aksakoff informs me that, after reading my *Graphic* letters and noting their effect in the two hemispheres, he is convinced of the absolute necessity for an exhaustive inquiry into the phenomena, by the best men of science. He asks me if I cannot organise such a committee, and tells me what has been done in Russia. There are four professors of eminence, in as many different Universities, who have, in committee, gone thoroughly into the matter and satisfied themselves of the reality of the phenomena; if I choose, these scientific gentlemen will send me a joint appeal to their American colleagues, to do as they have done, and thus settle, once and for all, the most important problem that man has to solve for his own sake and for the welfare of the race. Of course, this was exactly the motive which had prompted my undertaking the Eddy researches, but I found the obstacles presented, in the ignorant and brutish obstinacy of the mediums and their whole corps of "guides," insurmountable, and recorded the fact in my book. I was a little amused to read, in a Postscript written two days later than his letter, that M. Aksakoff, who had meanwhile finished reading H. P. B.'s Russian translation of my book, said it was plain that an orderly scientific search with such people as mediums was impossible, and begged me to consider his plan as cancelled. The matter did not drop there, however, for our correspondence was kept up, and resulted in H. P. B. and I being asked to serve as a committee to select a trustworthy medium to be sent over to St. Petersburgh, for trial and testing by a Special Committee of Professors of the St. Petersburgh Imperial University. We accepted the commission, and our joint card announcing the fact to the public appeared in the *Spiritual Scientist* of July 8, 1875—as far as I can make out from the confused way in which the newspaper-cuttings are pasted in our Scrap-Book, Vol. I. At all events, in the journal of that day was published a translation of Mr. Aksakoff's letter to H. P. B. broaching the subject, thus:

"My prayer to you and Col. Olcott is as follows: Will you be so kind as to translate into English the enclosed 'Appeal to Mediums' . . . consult together and report to us [the Imperial Society of Experimentalists in Physics] whom, of American mediums we had better invite to St. Petersburgh in the best interests of the Cause? For our first experiments we should prefer having mediums for simple but strong physical manifestations *in the light*. Use all your influence to get us good mediums, begin the work at once and advise me without loss of time. Bear in mind that money is no object with us," etc.

Naturally enough this letter drew out a good many applications, and we personally tested the mediumship of several of the parties, seeing some extremely surprising phenomena, and some really beautiful. Its appearance was seized upon by certain impudent impostors to give a public show of pretended mediumship at the Boston Theatre, on a Sunday evening in the same July, advertising themselves as engaged to go to Russia. We exposed and repudiated them in a card sent, July 19, 1875, to all the Boston papers.

Chapter VI

ORIENTAL DISAPPROBATION

By common consent the Western public have assumed that professional mediums, whose food and lodging depend upon their constant ability to produce psychical phenomena when patrons come to see the same, are greatly tempted in emergencies to supplement real ones with fraudulent imitations. Poor, almost without an exception; often invalids, yet obliged to support children and perhaps lazy or disabled husbands; their incomes extremely precarious, at best, because the mediumistic state depends upon psycho-physiological as well as atmospheric conditions beyond their control, it is not strange that, under the pressure of quarter-day or some other dire necessity, their moral sense should become blunted. Naturally they yield to the temptation flung at them by credulous visitors, who, apparently, ask nothing better than to pay to be duped. At any rate, that is how professional mediums have explained it to me. They have told me their miserable life-histories, how the fatal gift of mediumship embittered their childhood, made them shunned and persecuted by their schoolmates, sought after and run down by the curious, caused them to be used as a drawing sensation by travelling showmen, to the profit of their own parents (*vide* the tragical story of the Eddy children as told by them to me, in *P. O. W.*, chapter II.), and developed the seeds of hysteria, phthisis, or scrofula, to the ruin of their health. Mrs. Hardinge Britten, than whom nobody has known more of mediums and mediumship, told me in New York, in 1875, that she had seldom or ever known a medium who was not of a scrofulous or phthisical temperament, and medical observation shows, I believe, that derangements of the reproductive organs are quite common among them. Genuine mediumship, promiscuously practised, is, I fear, a serious physical danger, to say nothing as regards its effect morally. Every physician tells us that to sleep in an ill-ventilated room in company with a mixed company of persons, some perhaps diseased, is most dangerous and may prove fatal. But this risk is nothing as compared with that run by the poor public medium, who has to tolerate the presence and be soaked in the magnetic aura of all comers, be they morally or physically diseased or healthy: gross, sensual, irreligious, unspiritual, brutish in habitual thought, word, or deed, or the opposite. Alas! poor things, theirs is a psychical prostitution. Thrice happy such as can develop and practise their psychical gifts in the pure surroundings of a select and superior company: so were Temple seeresses guarded in the ancient times.

The above remarks are pertinent to the line of inquiry that H. P. B. and I had undertaken, at M. Aksakoff's request, on behalf of the St. Petersburgh scientific committee. While we realised that we should have to choose among professionals, it not being likely that any private medium would consent to the publicity and annoyance of such an ordeal, we determined that we should be thoroughly satisfied of the real and reasonably available psychical powers of the male or female medium we should ultimately recommend. M. Aksakoff's desire that preference should be given to those whose phenomena could be shown "in the light," was most reasonable, for thus the chance of successful trickery is minimised; yet there were then—and are now, for that matter—few mediums who could count upon anything of a very striking character happening at their séances by daylight. Our choice would have been narrowed down to two or three like C. H. Foster, or Dr. Slade, who were equally indifferent whether they sat by day or night since their successes in giving "tests of spirit identity" were tolerably certain. We decided, therefore, to find a good medium at any rate, whether he or she came quite up to M. Aksakoff's ideal or not. Our inquiries extended over several months, to the May of 1876, if I am not mistaken, and as I may as well finish with this episode, now that it is taken up, even though it breaks in upon the chronological sequence of events in T. S. history, I shall recall the successive stages of the St. Petersburgh mediumistic inquiry as best I can.

In the summer of 1875, a woman named Youngs was practising mediumship for a livelihood at New York. She was, as I dimly recall her, a largely built person, of obstreperous manners and strong physical as well as psychical powers. Her tone of bullying towards her "guides in Spirit Land" was in amusing contrast with the honeyed accents commonly used by most mediums towards the invisibles. "Now, then, spirits," she would say, "don't be lazy; hurry up; what are you about? Move the piano, or do this or that. Come, we are all waiting!" *And do it they did*, as though obedient to her will. Her chief phenomenon was the causing of the spirits to raise a full-sized, heavy piano and making it tilt forward and backward in time to her playing of airs upon it. I heard of her and thought I would get H. P. B. to go with me and see what she could do. She consented, so I put into my pocket three things, to be used as new tests of her mediumship, a raw egg and two English walnuts, the experimental value of which will be presently seen. Fortunately I am not obliged to rely wholly upon memory, since I find a cutting from the New York *Sun* of September 4, 1875, giving an accurate account of the séance and of my tests. Fifteen persons were present. The *Sun* reporter says:

"The performance began with the lifting of the piano by invisible powers, three times for 'yes' and once for 'no,' in answer to questions put by Mrs. Youngs, she resting her hands lightly on top of the music-rack. She then sat down and played various airs, and the instrument rose and fell and beat the time. She then went to one end of the piano and called up Colonel Olcott, and as many more of the others as chose to make the experiment, and, causing each to place his left hand underneath the case, laid one of her hands lightly under it, whereupon, at her demand, the end of the heavy instrument [He says elsewhere that he, the reporter, 'could not lift one end of it,' so great was its weight] was lifted off the floor without the slightest effort on her part. The Colonel here asked to be permitted to make a single test which should not injure the medium at all. Mrs. Youngs consenting, he produced a hen's egg from a box, and asked her to hold it in her hand against the under side of the piano, and then request the spirits to raise it. The medium said that, in the course of her mediumship, such a test had never been suggested, and she could not say it would be successful, but she would try. She took the egg and held it as desired, and then rapping upon the case with her other hand, asked the spirits to see what they could do. Instantly the piano rose as before, and was held for a moment suspended in the air. The novel and striking experiment was a complete success.

"Mrs. Youngs then asked as many of the heaviest persons in the room as could sit on the instrument to mount it, and the invitation being accepted by seven ladies and gentlemen, she played a march, and the instrument, persons and all, were lifted easily. Colonel Olcott now produced a couple of English walnuts, and asked the spirits to crack the shells under the piano legs without crushing the kernels, the idea being to show that some power beyond the one woman herself, and a power governed by intelligence, was exerting itself. The spirits were willing, but as the piano legs rested upon rolling casters the test was abandoned. He then asked to be permitted to hold an egg in his own hand against the under side of the piano, and have Mrs. Youngs lay her hand beneath and against his, so that he might have a perfect demonstration of the fact that no muscular force whatever was being exerted by her. This test was also agreed to and immediately tried. The piano rose the same as before. The manifestations of the evening were then brought to a close with the *lifting of the instrument without the medium's hands touching it at all.*"

This was certainly a very striking manifestation of psycho-dynamical power. Not only was a seven-and-a-half-octave piano, too heavy for one man to lift endwise, raised without the least expenditure of muscular force by the medium or any other living person present, and in a fully lighted room, but an *intelligent comprehension of requests and compliance with them* was demonstrated. Let us admit that the medium's intelligence was alone in play, still we have the problem of how she could transform her thought, first into will and then into active force. The final test of making her lay her hand beneath mine, which held the egg, and then cause the ponderous instrument to rise as lightly as a feather, contrary to the law of gravity, was to me, as well as to H. P. B., conclusive proof of her mediumistic gift, and we made her a conditional offer to recommend her to M. Aksakoff. The condition was that she should subject herself to a series of harmless yet convincing tests, the successful passing of which would warrant us in thoroughly endorsing her. She, however, declined the offer on account of the long voyage and her unwillingness to leave her country to go among foreigners. I do not know what became of her, but I heard that she adopted my egg test as her stock demonstration of her true mediumship. There was very little spirituality about it, but a good deal of revolutionising physics, that I thought might stagger Professor Mendeleyeff and his brother scientists.

A very much prettier and more poetical phase of mediumship was that of Mrs. Mary Baker Thayer, of Boston, Mass., to the examination of whose phenomena I devoted some five weeks of the same summer season. She is, or was, what is called a "flower medium," *viz.*, a pyschic in whose presence rain showers of flowers, growing bushes, vines and grasses, and leaves and branches freshly torn from trees, perhaps of a kind that are exotics and to be found only in hot-houses in that cold country. When I knew her she was a middle-aged woman of winsome manners, very obliging as to tests, and always cheerful and friendly. Like many other public mediums, however, she drank to some extent; she said—and I can quite believe it—to make up for the terrible drain of the phenomena upon her nervous power. That she was a real medium I am fully convinced, but that she also supplemented by trickery her genuine phenomena, I also *know*. I know, because I caught her at it one evening in the year 1878, shortly before our leaving for India, when she was trying to convince me of her ability to "pass matter through matter," in imitation of Professor Zöllner's celebrated experiments at Leipzig with the help of the medium Slade. I was very sorry that she tried the game with me, for until then I had had nothing but good to say of her. It is sad, I repeat, to know that these poor mediumistic martyrs to human selfishness and inquisitiveness are so often, not to say invariably, driven by necessity to practising on credulity for the lack of reasonable maintenance and surveillance, by properly constituted spiritualistic societies and committees, in command of adequate funds for the purpose. I have always pitied rather than blamed the wretched mediums, while laying the responsibility upon the Spiritualists as a body, where it solely belongs. Let those who think differently try starvation and selfish neglect for a while, and see if they will then be so quick to condemn tricking psychics.

A long summarised report of my Thayer investigations—in part of which H. P. B. assisted—appeared in the New York *Sun* of August 18, 1875, and was extensively copied throughout America and Europe, and translated into various languages.

The method of procedure at Mrs. Thayer's séances was this: The company being assembled, some respectable visitor agreeable to all was asked to examine the room and furniture, to fasten and, if he liked, seal the windows, lock the doors and take charge of the keys. The medium would also, if asked (provided that she meditated no trickery), suffer her dress to be searched for hidden flowers or other objects. She permitted me to do this whenever I liked, and willingly suffered me to tie and seal her up in a bag, a test I first employed with Mrs. Holmes. All present would then seat themselves about a large dining-table, join hands (the medium as well as the rest), the lights would be put out, and in perfect darkness phenomena would be waited for. After some delay one could hear a pattering on the bare tabletop, the air would be filled with fragrance, and Mrs. Thayer would call for a light. Upon the room being illuminated, the surface of the table would be seen, sometimes, quite covered with flowers and plants, and sometimes they would be found thrust into the dress of the sitters or into their hair. Occasionally butterflies would come, or a rush of flying birds would be heard overhead and there might be a dove, a canary, a linnet, or some other bird, fluttering to the four corners of the room; or a gold-fish would be flopping about on the table, wet, as if just taken from the water. Sometimes people present would cry out in pleased wonder on finding between their hands some flower or plant they had mentally asked might be brought them. One evening I saw in front of a Scottish gentleman a full-grown heather plant of his native country, roots and all, and with the soil clinging to them as if it had just been uprooted. There were even three angle worms wriggling in the dirt. It was quite a common thing for smilax and other vines, seemingly just torn from their pots or beds, and with the soil amidst their roots, to be brought: I had them myself. But I had a better thing than that. One afternoon, I visited Forest Hills Cemetery, situated in a suburb of Boston, and, passing through the green-houses, my attention was struck by a curious plant with long, narrow leaves, striped with white and pale green, known in botany as the *Dracana Regina*. With my blue pencil I drew underneath one of the leaves the six-pointed star and mentally asked the spirits to bring it to me in Mrs. Thayer's next circle, on the following evening. On that occasion I sat beside her and held her hands to make sure of her good faith. In the dark, I felt some cool and moist object drop upon one of my hands which, when the room was again lit up, proved to be my marked *Dracana* leaf! To make assurance doubly sure, I revisited the green-house and found that my leaf had actually been detached from the stalk and the one I had in my pocket fitted the fracture! A number of similar facts, which I lack space to even cursorily mention, convinced me that Mrs. Thayer was a real psychic; there was, moreover, a certain physiological phenomenon which not only strengthened my belief, but cast much light upon the whole problem of mediumship. Holding both her hands in mine, I noticed that just at the moment when the falling plants began to patter on the table, she would shudder as if chilly, sigh, and her hands instantly turned deathly cold, as though a flush of iced water had suddenly run through her veins. The next moment the hands would resume the normal temperature of health. I challenge all the doubting scientists in the world to imitate this phenomenon *in themselves*. It seems indicative of a total change of "vital polarity," in the making of phenomena, to use a necessary expression. When H. P. B. evoked the full-length spirit-form out of Mrs. Holmes's cabinet (*P. O. W.*, 477) she clutched my hand convulsively and her hand grew icy cold; the hand of Signor B., the Italian sorcerer was like ice after his rain-compelling phenomenon; and the passage of the hysteriac into the cataleptic trance and other deeper stages of physical unconsciousness, is attended with abnormal lowering of bodily temperature. Dr. A. Moll says (*Hypnotism*, 113) that the "particularly surprising" experiments of Kraft-Ebing prove that "we must assume an astonishing capacity for regulating the temperature of the body" by hypnotic suggestion. It is fair to infer, therefore, that such a very marked change in animal heat as we have seen occurring in Mrs. Thayer and others at the moment when psychical phenomena are happening, indicates *bona fides*—the pathological change could not be simulated. Not to dwell too long on this medium's case, highly interesting though it is, I will merely mention that at one of her public séances I counted and identified eighty-four species of plants; at another, given under my own test-conditions, saw birds appear, caught and *kept* them; at another, at a private house and in broad daylight, saw flowers and a branch torn from a tree in the compound, brought; and at still another, in the same friend's house—where H. P. B. and I were both guests, she having come there from Philadelphia and I from New York, to follow out these investigations for M. Aksakoff—saw big stones and a quaint old table-knife of an ancient pattern, dropped on the table. But one particular rose given me by Mrs. Thayer's benevolent Pushpa Yakshini (See Art. "Fire Elementals," *Theosophist*, vol. xii., 259) was the vehicle for a phenomenon by H. P. B. that excelled all that I had ever seen a medium do.

Our kind hostess, Mrs. Charles Houghton, wife of a well-known lawyer of Boston, living in the suburb of Roxbury, drove into town with me one evening to attend Mrs. Thayer's public séance. H. P. B. declined to go, so we left her talking with Mr. Houghton in the drawing-room. The carriage had been ordered to come for us at a certain hour, but the séance had proved a short one and all the assistants had left save Mrs. Houghton, another lady, and myself. As we had nothing better to occupy ourselves with, I asked Mrs. Thayer to give us three a private séance, to which she obligingly agreed. So we took places at the table. I held the medium's two hands and placed a foot upon her two feet, one of the ladies fastened the doors and saw that the windows were secure, and the other took charge of the light. This being extinguished, we waited in darkness for some time, but there was no sound of plant-dropping. Presently we heard the carriage drive up to the door, and at the same moment I felt a cool, moist flower lightly dropped, as though it might have been a snow-flake, upon the back of my hand. I said nothing until the candle was lighted, and even then continued holding Mrs. Thayer's hands, and called the ladies' attention to the fact. The flower on my hand was a lovely, half-opened double moss-rose bud, glistening with drops of dew. The medium, starting as though some one had addressed her from behind, said: "The spirits say, Colonel, that that is a present for Madame Blavatsky." I thereupon handed it to Mrs. Houghton, and she gave it over to H. P. B. on reaching home, where we found her smoking cigarettes and still talking with our host. Mrs. Houghton left the room to go and lay off her bonnet and wrap, and I seated myself with the others. H. P. B. was holding the rose in her hand, smelling its fragrance and with a peculiar far-away look in her face, that her intimates always associated with the doing of her phenomena. Her reverie was interrupted by Mr. Houghton's saying, "What an exquisite flower, Madame; will you kindly let me see it?" She handed it to him with the same dreamy look and as if mechanically. He sniffed its odour, but suddenly exclaimed: "How heavy it is! I never saw a flower like this. See, its weight actually makes it bend over towards the stalk!" "What are you talking about?" I remarked, "There is nothing unusual about it; certainly there was not a while ago when it fell on my hand. Let me see it." I took it from him with my left hand, and lo! it weighed certainly very heavy. "Take care; don't break it!" exclaimed H. P. B. Tenderly I lifted the bud with the thumb and finger of my right hand and looked at it. Nothing visible to the eye accounted for the phenomenal weight. But presently there sparkled a pin-point of yellow light in its very heart, and before I could take a second look, a heavy plain gold ring leaped out, as though impelled by an interior spring, and fell on the floor between my feet. The rose instantly resumed its natural erect position and its unusual weight had gone. Mr. Houghton and I, both lawyers, moved by the professional instinct of caution, then carefully examined the flower, but detected not the slightest sign of its petals having been tampered with; they were so closely packed and overlaid that there was no possibility of forcing the ring under cover without mutilating the bud. And, in fact, how could H. P. B. have played the trick, right before our two pairs of eyes, in the full glare of three gas-jets, and while holding the rose in her right hand for not above a couple of minutes before she gave it to Mr. Houghton? Well, certainly, there is an explanation possible in Occult Science: the matter in the gold ring and that in the rose petals could have been raised from the third to the fourth dimension, and restored back to the third at the instant when the ring leaped out of the flower. And that, doubtless, is what did happen; and open-minded physicists should kindly note the fact that matter may have weight without physical bulk, as this charming experiment proves. The ring has been found to weigh a half ounce. I am wearing it at this moment. It was not a creation out of nothing, only an *apport;* it belonged to H. P. B., I think, and it is "hall-marked," or otherwise stamped to indicate its quality. It was a great ring for phenomena, certainly, to judge from what happened to it a year and a half later. The Theosophical Society was a year old then, and H. P. B. and I were living in two apartment suites in the same house. One evening my married sister, Mrs. W. H. Mitchell,* came with her husband to visit H. P. B. and myself,

---

* If any one chooses to ask her she will corroborate my narrative, no doubt. Her address is Orange, New Jersey, U. S. A.

and, in the course of conversation, asked me to see the ring and bade me tell its history. She looked at it and put it on her finger while I was talking, after which she held it towards H. P. B. in the palm of her left hand for her to take it. But H. P. B. leaving it lying as it was without touching it, closed my sister's fingers on it, held the hand for a moment, then let go, and told my sister to look at it. It was no longer a plain gold ring, for we found three small diamonds imbedded in the metal, "gipsy" fashion, and set so as to form a triangle. How was it done? The least miraculous theory is that H. P. B. had had a jeweller insert the diamonds previously, and concealed them from us by inhibiting our sense of perception until the spell was removed at the moment my sister's hand opened. As a hypnotic experiment this is perfectly comprehensible; I have seen such things done and can do them myself. One can not only cover a little diamond with the mask of invisibility, but a man, a roomful of people, a house, a tree, rock, road, mountain—anything, in short: hypnotic suggestion includes seemingly limitless possibilities. Well, let this particular experiment be explained as it may, it was a very perfect success.

To return to Mrs. Thayer: we were so pleased with her phase of mediumship that we offered her the chance to go to Russia, but, like Mrs. Youngs and for the same reasons, she declined. Similar offers were conditionally made to Mrs. Huntoon, a sister of the Eddys, and to Mrs. Andrews and Dr. Slade, but all declined. So the affair dragged on until the Winter of 1875, by which time the Theosophical Society had come into existence; M. Aksakoff's committee had broken the original compact framed to secure a thorough investigation of the phenomena, and, with Prof. Mendeleyeff, an iron-clad materialist, at their head, had published a condemnatory report, framed on baseless conjecture, not on evidence; whereupon M. Aksakoff, with noble unselfishness and from sheer love of the truth, had determined to carry out the original programme at his own cost and risk. He writes to the London *Spiritualist* about that time:

"When I resolved to search after mediums to visit St. Petersburgh . . . I decided upon a line of action which I communicated to Colonel Olcott, whom I deputed to select mediums in America. I told him that I wanted our committee to have the means of proving the abnormal movement of solid objects in the light without contact with any living person. I further wished to find mediums who could get the movement of solid objects in the dark behind curtains, while they were seated in front thereof in full view of the sitters," etc.

This will give my Indian readers an idea of the extraordinary physical phenomena which were going on at the time in the Western countries. In the East, similar displacements of solid things, such as household furniture, cooking utensils, articles of clothing, etc., are occasionally heard of, but always with horror, and the eye-witnesses have scarcely ever dreamt of making them the subjects of scientific research: on the contrary, they are looked upon as misfortunes, the work of evil spirits, often of earth-bound souls of near relatives and intimate friends, and their greatest desire is to abate them as unqualified nuisances. I only repeat what has often been explained before by all theosophical writers, in saying that intercourse between the living and their deceased friends and connections is, to the Asiatic, an abhorrent proof that the dead are not happily dissevered from earthly concerns, and thus are hampered in their normal evolution towards the condition of pure spirit. The West, as a whole, despite its religious creed, is grossly materialistic, imagining the future life as but an extension of this in time—and in space too, if one comes to consider its physical conceptions of heaven and hell—and can only grasp the actuality of post-mortem conscious existence through such concrete physical phenomena as M. Aksakoff enumerates, and the many others which astonish the visitors to mediums.* The East, on the other hand, is spiritual and philosophical in its conceptions, and phenomena of the above kind are to Asiatics but evidences of the possession of a low order of psychical powers by those who show them. The incident of my flower-born ring, of Mrs. Thayer's showers of plants, flowers, and birds, and of Mrs. Youngs's lifting of pianos on eggs, strike the Western materialist's imagination, not as horrors but simply as interesting lies, too scientifically revolutionary to be true, yet vastly important if so. I suppose I must have heard a hundred times if once, in India, that it was a great pity that H. P. B. showed phenomena, for it went to prove that she had not reached a high stage of Yoga. True, the Yogi is warned by Patanjali, as the contemporary *bhikshus* were by Gautama Buddha, to beware of vainly showing their wonders

---

* In drafting the much-discussed "Third Object" of the Theosophical Society, at New York, my mind was influenced by the knowledge of this fact, and, at the same time, by my ignorance of the full scope of Oriental Science. Had I known what evils were to come upon us through the pretended development of psychical powers, I should have worded it otherwise.

when they found the *Siddhis* had developed themselves in the course of their psychical evolution. Yet the Buddha himself sometimes displayed his transcendent powers of this kind, but improved the occasion to preach the noble doctrines of his Arya Dharma, and spur his hearers to the noblest efforts to spiritualise, after de-brutifying themselves. And so with most other religious teachers. Did not H. P. B. adopt the like policy? Did she not, even while doing her wonders, warn us all that they were a very subordinate and insignificant part of Theosophy—some, mere hypnotic suggestions, others physical marvels in the handling of matter and force, by knowledge of their secrets and an acquired control over the elemental races concerned with cosmic phenomena? Nobody can deny this; nobody can truthfully aver that she did not invariably teach that the psychical experiment has the same relation to spiritual philosophy that the chemical experiment has to the science of chemistry. She, no doubt, erred in wasting power to astonish unimportant observers, that could have been far more profitably employed in breaching the walls of incredulous and despotic Western science: yet she did thereby convince some who were thus influenced to do good work for this great movement of ours; and some of the most tireless of that class among us came into Eastern out of Western Spiritualism over the bridge of psychical phenomena. For my part, I can say, that the great range of marvels of educated will-potency which she showed me, made it easy for me to understand the Oriental theories of spiritual science. My greatest sorrow is that others, especially those of my Eastern colleagues whose minds were thoroughly prepared, did not have the same chance.

Chapter VII.

DR. SLADE

Our search for mediums resulted in our selection of Dr. Henry Slade for the St. Petersburgh test. Mr. Aksakoff sent me $1,000 in gold for his expenses, and in due course he departed on his mission. But, through greediness, or vanity, perhaps, certainly most unadvisably, he stopped in London, gave séances, created a great public excitement, and was arrested on the complaint of Professor Lankester and Dr. Donkin on the pretence of trickery. C. C. Massey was his counsel, and saved him on a technical point, on appeal. Slade subsequently gave at Leipzig the famous tests by which Professor Zöllner proved his theory of the Fourth Dimension, and visited The Hague and other places before going to St. Petersburgh. Before we sent him abroad he submitted his mediumistic powers to the scrutiny of a special committee of the Theosophical Society, which with one dissentient, who made a most unfair minority report, certified to Mr. Aksakoff its belief in his genuineness. A most instructive account, showing long and intimate familiarity with his powers, was supplied by his former business partner, Mr. James Simmons, to the issue of the *Theosophist* for November, 1893.

I had quite forgotten until I came to write the present chapter, at what period in the year 1875 the Eastern theory of sub-human and earth-bound spirits was brought to public attention, but I now find in our Scrap Books that the term "Elementary Spirits" was first used by myself in a letter to the *Spiritual Scientist* of June 3, 1875, reference being made to the sub-human spirits of the elements, or what we now call, "the elementals." It was but a bare reference, without the giving of any explanatory details, and intended as a caution to Spiritualists against swallowing, as they had been doing previously, without proper sifting and analysis, the messages of real or pretended mediums as trustworthy communications from departed spirits. The publication of the "Luxor" circular (in the *Spiritual Scientist*, April 17, 1875) provoked some private correspondence and public comment, the most important example of the latter being a scholarly and interesting article by a young barrister named Failes, writing under the pseudonym of "Hiraf," which appeared in the *Spiritual Scientist* for 1875, p. 202, and was continued in the next week's issue. It is full of theosophical ideas interpreted in terms of Rosicrucianism and under that title. The writer presents the Eastern philosophy of Unity and Evolution; and shows how it anticipated by many centuries the modern theories of force-correlation and conservation of energy. Its major importance, however, was the fact that it drew from H. P. B. a reply, which, in our Scrap-book, she calls "My first occult shot," and which, in fact, laid open the whole field of thought since ploughed up by the members, friends, and adversaries of the Theosophical Society.

In tracing up H. P. B.'s literary history from that point until the close of her life, one important fact should be borne in mind by such as are willing to do her simple justice. She was not a "learned" woman, in the literary sense, when she came to America. When, long after *Isis Unveiled* was begun, I inquired of her ever-be-loved aunt Mdlle. N. A. Fadeyef, where her niece had acquired all this varied knowledge of recondite philosophies, metaphysics, and sciences, this prodigiously intuitive comprehension of ethnical evolution, the migrations of ideas, the occult forces of nature, etc., she wrote me frankly that up to their last meeting, some four or five years previously, Helena had "not even thought of such things in her dreams," that her education had been simply that of any young lady of good family. She had learnt, besides her native Russian, French, a little English, a smattering of Italian, and music: she was astounded at my accounts of her erudition, and could only attribute it to the same sort of inspiration as had been enjoyed by the Apostles, who, on the Day of Pentecost, spoke in strange tongues of which they had previously been ignorant. She added that from her childhood her niece had been a medium, more extraordinary for psychical power and variety of phenomena than any of whom she had read in the whole course of a lifelong study of the subject.* I had a better chance than any of her friends to know what were her actual literary attainments, having helped her in her correspondence

---

* Letter dated Odessa, 8/20 May, 1877.

and labours of authorship and corrected almost every page of her MSS. for years: besides which I had her confidence in a greater degree, from 1874 to 1885, than any other person. I can affirm, then, that in those early days she was not, in her normal state, a learned woman, and was never an accurate writer. This is *à propos* of her reply to "Hiraf," in which she went into particulars about Occultism and explained the nature of elementary spirits. A learned but blindly vindictive critic of hers, stigmatises this article as "simply a rehash of the writings upon Magic of Eliphas Levi, and Des Mousseaux, and Hargrave Jennings' "Rosicrucians." In it, he says, "the Madame (*sic*) disclaims any authority as a teacher, calling herself 'poor, ignorant me,' and states that she desired simply to tell a little of the little she picked up in her long travels in the East. The statement that she derived any of this article from 'the East' is untrue; the whole of it was taken from European books."

And whence did their authors get their knowledge, unless from other authors? And whence these authors? From the East, always from the East: not one of those mentioned was a practical occultist, an adept in practical psychology; not even Eliphas Levi, save to the minor extent of being able (taking himself as the authority) to evoke spirits by the formularies of Ceremonial Magic. He was too much addicted to the pleasures of the table to be anything higher in Magic. Des Mousseaux was simply a most industrious and successful compiler for the Jesuits and Theatins, whose complimentary certificates he publishes in his works; and as for the late Mr. Hargrave Jennings, we all knew him for an estimable little gentleman, a London *littérateur*, with a book knowledge of occult subjects and not conspicuously accurate in his deductions. Whether H. P. B. did or did not acquire her practical psychical knowledge or powers in the East, it is undeniable that she *had* them, could practise them whenever she liked, and that her explanations of them were identical with those which are given in the teachings of every Eastern school of Occult Science. I, personally, can further testify that she was in relations with Eastern adepts, and that not only she, but even I, was visited by them, conversed with them and was taught by them, before leaving America and after reaching India. To her, the books of Levi, Des Mousseaux, and all other modern and ancient writers were simply the toolboxes from which she could take the tools she needed in building the Western structure for the habitation of Eastern ideas: from one she could take one fact, from another, another. She found them but imperfect tools, at best, for those who knew, concealed, and those who did not, twisted and mutilated or misrepresented their facts. The Rosicrucian, Hermetic and Theosophical Western writers, producing their books in epochs of religious ignorance and cruel bigotry, wrote, so to say, with the headsman's axe suspended over their necks, or the executioner's fagots laid under their chairs, and hid their divine knowledge under quaint symbols and misleading metaphors. The world lacked an interpreter, and H. P. B. came to supply the need. Having the clues to the labyrinth in her own trained consciousness and full practical experience, she led the way, torch in hand, and bade the morally brave to follow

her.* An American critic said of *Isis* that she quoted indis-
criminately from the classical authors and from the current
newspapers of the day; and he was right, for it mattered not
what author or paragraphist she quoted from so long as his
writing suggested an idea illustrative of her present theme.
This answer to "Hiraf" was the first of her esoteric writings,
as her answer to Dr. Beard was the first of her defences of
mediumistic Spiritualism. The history of Literature furnishes
no more surprising spectacle than that of this fashionably
under-educated Russian noblewoman writing English at
times like an Englishman; French so pure that French authors
have told me her articles would serve as models of style in
French schools; and Russian so enticingly brilliant as to make
the conductor of the most important of their reviews actually
beseech her to write constantly for it, on terms as high as they
gave Tourguénief. She was not always at those high-water
marks, however; sometimes she wrote such bad English that
her MSS. had to be almost re-written. Nor, as said, was she an
orderly or accurate writer; her mind seemed to rush ahead at
such a pace, and streams of thought came pouring from both
sides in such force that confusion and want of method were
the result in her writing. She laughed once, but confessed the
justness of the comparison, when I told her that her mind was
like Dickens's image of Mugby Junction, with its ceaseless
trains screaming in and screaming out, backing and shunt-
ing, and from morning to night keeping up a bewildering

---

* I say this with a reservation as to the actual degree of her own independent agency in the affair, about which I do not feel willing to dogmatise.

confusion. But beginning with the "Hiraf" article, and coming down to the last line she wrote for type, one thing must honestly be said—her writing was always full of thought-suggestion, brilliant and virile in style, while her keen sense of humour often seasoned her most ponderous essays with mirth-provoking ideas. To the methodical scholar she was exasperating, yet never dull or uninteresting. Later on, I shall have occasion to speak of the phenomenal changes in her literary and conversational moods and styles. I have said, and shall always reiterate, that I learnt more from her than from any schoolmaster, professor, or author I ever had to do with. Her psychical greatness, however, so over-matched her early education and mental discipline that the critics who knew her only in literature have done her bitter and savage injustice. X. B. Saintine writes, in *Picciola*, that the penalty of greatness is isolation; her case proves the aphorism: she dwelt on spiritual heights whither only the eagles of mankind soar. Most of her adversaries have only seen the mud on her shoes; and, verily, sometimes she wiped them even on her friends who could not mount on wings as strong as her own.

The "Hiraf" letter has another historical value in that she therein proclaims unequivocally "from personal knowledge" the existencc of regular schools of occult training "in India, Asia Minor, *and other countries*." "As in the primitive days of Socrates and other sages of antiquity," she says, "so now, those who are willing to learn the Great Truth will ever find *the chance* if they only 'try' to meet someone to lead them to the door of 'one who knows when and how.'" She corrects "Hiraf's" too sweeping generalisation of calling all occultists

Rosicrucians; telling him that that fraternity was but one of many occult sects or groups. She now openly styles herself "a follower of Eastern Spiritualism," and foresees the time when American Spiritualism will "become a science and a thing of mathematical certitude." Again, reverting to the question of adepts, she says the real Kabbala, of which the Jewish version is but a fragment, is in possession of "but a few Oriental philosophers; where they are, who they are, is more than is given me to reveal. Perhaps I do not know it myself and have only dreamed it. Thousands will say it is all imagination: so be it. Time will show. The only thing I *can* say is that such a body exists, and that the location of their Brotherhoods will never be revealed to other countries until the day when Humanity shall awake, . . . Until then, the speculative theory of their existence will be supported by what people erroneously believed to be *supernal* facts." Her article conveys the warning that it is waste of time to seek to become a practical Kabbalist (or Rosicrucian, if you will) by acquiring a book knowledge of occult literature; it is as foolish, she says, "as to try to thread the famous labyrinth without the clue, or to open the ingenious locks of the mediæval ages without having possession of the keys." She defines the difference between White and Black Magic and warns against the latter. Finally, she says: "But say what you (the 'very orthodox priests and clergymen of various creeds and denominations, you who are so intolerant towards Spiritualism,' [mark what meaning her context gives the term now] 'the purest of the Children of Ancient Magic,') will, you cannot help that which was, is, and ever will be, namely, the direct communication between the two worlds. We term this intercourse modern Spiritualism with the same force and logic, as when we say the 'New World,' in speaking of America."

I am sure all earnest members of the Theosophical Society will be glad to know that as early as July, 1875, H. P. B. affirmed the existence of the Eastern Adepts, of the mystic Brotherhood, of the stores of divine knowledge in their keeping, and of her personal connection with them. She reaffirms this in a letter to the *Spi. Sci* (p. 64, but of what month of 1875 I cannot tell, as she has not dated the cutting in our Scrap-book; but she writes from Ithaca whither she went to visit Professor and Mrs. Corson, of Cornell University, in August or early September), and puts forth the important idea that "Spiritualism, in the hands of an adept, becomes Magic, for he is learned in the art of blending together the laws of the Universe, without breaking any of them and thereby violating Nature. In the hands of an inexperienced medium, Spiritualism becomes UNCONSCIOUS SORCERY; for . . . he opens, unknown to himself, a door of communication between the two worlds, through which emerge the blind forces of Nature lurking in the astral Light, as well as good and bad spirits."

The occult Idea was now fairly launched, and our published writings and private correspondence henceforth teemed with such allusions. My first extended contribution on those lines was a letter entitled "The Immortal Life," dated August 23, 1875, and published in the *New York Tribune* of the 30th of that month. I state in it that I had believed in the mediumistic phenomena for about a quarter of a century, but had discredited the assumed identification of the intelligences behind them. I affirm my belief in the reality of ancient occult science, and the fact that I had unexpectedly "been brought into contact with living persons who do, and had in my presence done the very marvels that Paracelsus, Albertus, and Apollonius are credited with." In saying this, I had in mind not only H. P. B.'s multifarious phenomena, not only the beginnings of my intercourse with the Mahâtmas, but also the disclosure to my own eyes, in my own bedroom, in a house where H. P. B. did *not* live, and when she was *not* present, of the spirits of the elements, by a stranger whom I casually met in New York, one day shortly before penning the letter.

The stranger came by appointment to my chambers. We opened the folding doors which separated the sitting from the small bedroom, sat on chairs facing the wide doorway, and by a wonderful process of Máya (I now suppose) I saw the bedroom converted, as it were, into a cube of empty space. The furniture had disappeared from my view, and there appeared alternately vivid scenes of water, cloudy atmosphere, subterranean caves, and an active volcano; each of the elements teeming with beings, and shapes, and faces, of which I caught more or less transient glimpses. Some of the forms were lovely, some malignant and fierce, some terrible. They would float into view as gently as bubbles on a smooth stream, or dart across the scene and disappear, or play and gambol together in flame or flood. Anon, a misshapen monster, as horrid to see as the pictures in Barrett's *Magus*, would glare at me and plunge forward, as though it wished to seize me as the wounded tiger does its victim, yet fading out on reaching the boundary of the cube of visualised *akásh*, where the two rooms joined. It was trying to one's nerves, but after my experiences at Eddy's I managed not to "weaken." My stranger friend declared himself satisfied with the result of the psychical test, and, on leaving, said we might meet again. But until now we have not. He seemed a fair-skinned Asiatic, but I could not exactly detect his nationality, though I then fancied him a Hindu. He talked English as fluently as myself.

Chapter VIII.

THEOSOPHICAL SOCIETY
PROPOSED

We may now take up the story of the formation of the Theosophical Society and show what led up to it, who were the people who formed it, and how its aims and objects were defined. For this, let it be remembered, is a complete history of the Society's beginnings, not a mere record of personal recollections of H. P. B.

The way had been prepared for the organisation of such a society by the active discussion, first, of Spiritualism and afterwards of some portions of Eastern spiritualistic ideas. This had been going on since my New York *Sun* report on the Eddys appeared, in August of the previous year (1874), and had been tenfold intensified since H. P. B. and I met at Chittenden, and used the press for the exposition of our heterodox views. Her piquant published letters, the stories that were afloat about her magical powers, and our several affirmations of the existence of non-human races of spiritual beings, drew into our acquaintanceship numbers of bright, clever people of occult leanings. Among these were scientific men, philologists, authors, antiquarians, broadminded clergymen, lawyers, and doctors, some very well known Spiritualists, and one or two gentlemen journalists attached to metropolitan papers, only too eager to make good "copy" out of the business. It was an audacious thing, certainly, to stand, defiant of public prejudice, and assert the scientific legitimacy of ancient Magic in this age of scientific scepticism. Its very boldness compelled public attention, and the inevitable result was that, in time, those whom the discussion had drawn together in sympathy should group themselves together as a society for occult research. The attempt of May, 1875, to form such a nucleus in a "Miracle Club" having failed, for the reason stated in Chapter I., the next opportunity presented itself when Mr. Felt lectured privately to a few friends of ours, in H. P. B.'s rooms at 46 Irving Place, New York, on the 7th of September of the same year. This time there was no failure: the tiny seed of what was to be a world-covering banyan tree was planted in fertile soil and germinated. I regret to say that, to my knowledge, no official memorandum exists of the persons actually present on that particular evening, though one of them, the Reverend J. H. Wiggin, an Unitarian clergyman, published in *The Liberal Christian* of Sept. 4th, a notice of a similar gathering during the previous week, at which the fact of Mr. Felt's promised lecture was, I think, announced for the evening of the 7th. He names H. P. B., myself, Signor Bruzzesi, a New Jersey judge and his wife, and Mr. Charles Sotheran (who had procured for him from H. P. B. an invitation to be present). He expresses his wonder at the range and depth of the conversation, remarking:

"It would be discourteous to detail the minutiae of a friendly conversation where there was no desire for publicity nor any magic display, or offer notions about it. The phallic element in religions; recent wonders among the mediums; history; the souls of flowers; Italian character; the strangeness of travel; chemistry; poetry; Nature's trinity; Romanism; gravitation; the Carbonari; jugglery; Crookes's new discoveries about the force of light; the literature of Magic—were among the topics of animated discussion lasting until after midnight. If Madame Blavatsky can indeed bring order out of the chaos of modern spiritism she will do the world a service."

On the evening of September 7th, Mr. Felt gave his lecture on "The Lost Canon of Proportion of the Egyptians." He was a remarkably clever draughtsman, and had prepared a number of exquisite drawings to illustrate his theory that the canon of architectural proportion, employed by the Egyptians, as well as by the great architects of Greece, was actually preserved in the temple hieroglyphics of the Land of Khemi. His contention was that, by following certain definite clues one could inscribe what he called the "Star of Perfection" upon a certain temple wall, within which the whole secret of the geometrical problem of proportion would be read; and that the hieroglyphs outside the inscribed figure were but mere blinds to deceive the profane curiosity-seeker; for, read consecutively with those within the geometrical figure, they either made undecipherable nonsense or ran into some quite trivial narrative.

This diagram consists of a circle with a square within and without, containing a common triangle, two Egyptian triangles and a pentagon. He applies it to the pictures, statues, doors, hieroglyphs, pyramids, planes, tombs and buildings of Ancient Egypt, and shows that they agree so perfectly with its proportions that they must have been made by its rule. He applies the same canon of proportion to the masterpieces of Greek art and finds that they were, or might have been, carved without models by this rule. It is, in fact, the true canon of Nature's architecture. The late Dr. Seth Pan-coast, M.D., of Philadelphia, a most erudite Kabbalist, being present, categorically questioned Mr. Felt as to whether he could practically prove his perfect knowledge of the occult powers possessed by the true ancient magician; among others, the evocation of spirits from the spatial deep. Mr. Felt replied as categorically that he had done and could do that with his chemical circle. "He could call into sight hundreds of shadowy forms resembling the human, but he had seen no signs of intelligence in these apparitions." I take these details from a contemporary cutting that I find in its proper place in our Scrap-book I., but to which the name of the paper is not attached. It looks as if it had been cut from Mr. Wiggin's paper, *The Liberal Christian*.

Felt's theory and drawings were so captivating that J. W. Bouton, the publisher of symbological books, had contracted with him to bring out his work in 1000 pages folio, with numberless illustrations, and had advanced a large sum for copper plates, graving tools, presses, etc., etc. But having to deal with a genius burdened with a large family and exasperatingly unpunctual, the thing dragged along until he lost all patience, and the final result was, I believe, a rupture between them and the grand work was never published.

Mr. Felt told us in his lecture that, while making his Egyptological studies, he had discovered that the old Egyptian priests were adepts in magical science, had the power to evoke and employ the spirits of the elements, and had left the formularies on record; he had deciphered and put them to the test, and had succeeded in evoking the elementals. He was willing to aid some persons of the right sort to test the system for themselves, and would exhibit the nature-spirits to us all in the course of a series of lectures, for which we were to pay him. Of course we passed an informal vote of hearty thanks for his highly interesting lecture, and an animated discussion followed. In the course of this, the idea occurred to me that it would be a good thing to form a society to pursue and promote such occult research, and, after turning it over in my mind, I wrote on a scrap of paper the following:

"*Would it not be a good thing to form a Society for this kind of study?*"

—and gave it to Mr. Judge, at the moment standing between me and H. P. B., sitting opposite, to pass over to her. She read it and nodded assent. Thereupon I rose and, with some prefatory remarks, broached the subject. It pleased the company and when Mr. Felt, replying to a question to that effect, said he would be willing to teach us how to evoke and control the elementals, it was unanimously agreed that the society should be formed. Upon motion of Mr. Judge, I was elected Chairman, and upon my motion Mr. Judge was elected Secretary of the meeting. The hour being late, an adjournment was had to the following evening, when formal action should be taken. Those present were requested to bring sympathisers who would like to join the proposed society.

As above stated, no official record by the Secretary of the attendance at this first meeting survives, but Mrs. Britten quotes, in her *Nineteenth Century Miracles,* (p. 296), a report which was published in a New York daily and copied into the *Spiritual Scientist,* and from her book I take the following extracts:

"One movement of great importance has just been inaugurated in New York, under the lead of Colonel Henry S. Olcott, in the organization of a society, to be known as the Theosophical Society. The suggestion was entirely unpremeditated, and was made on the evening of the 7th inst. in the parlors of Madame Blavatsky, where a company of seventeen ladies and gentlemen had assembled to meet Mr. George Henry Felt, whose discovery of the geometrical figures of the Egyptian Cabbala may be regarded as among the most surprising feats of the human intellect. The company included several persons of great learning and some of wide personal influence. The Managing Editors of two religious papers; the co-editors of two literary magazines; an Oxford LL.D.; a venerable Jewish scholar and traveller of repute; an editorial writer of one of the New York morning dailies; the President of the New York Society of Spiritualists; Mr. C. C. Massey, an English visitor [barrister-at-law]; Mrs. Emma Hardinge Britten and Dr. Britten; two New York lawyers besides Colonel Olcott; a partner in a Philadelphia publishing house; a well-known physician; and, most notable of all, Madame Blavatsky herself, comprised Mr. Felt's audience. . . . During a convenient pause in the conversation, Colonel Olcott rose, and after briefly sketching the present condition of the spiritualistic movement; the attitude of its antagonists, the Materialists; the irrepressible conflict between science and the religious sectaries; the philosophical character of the ancient theosophies and their sufficiency to reconcile all existing antagonism; and the apparently sublime achievement of Mr. Felt, in extracting the key to the architecture of Nature from the scanty fragments of ancient lore left us by the devastating hands of the Moslem and Christian fanatics of the early centuries, he proposed to form a nucleus around which might gather all the enlightened and brave souls who are willing to work together for the collection and diffusion of knowledge. His plan was to organise a society of Occultists and begin at once to collect a library; and to diffuse information concerning those secret laws of Nature which were so familiar to the Chaldeans and Egyptians, but are totally unknown by our modern world of science."

This being from an outside source and published within a few days of the meeting, is even more welcome than if official, as it shows conclusively what I had in mind when proposing the formation of our Society. It was to be a body for the collection and diffusion of knowledge; for occult research, and the study and dissemination of ancient philosophical and theosophical ideas: one of the first steps was to collect a library. The idea of Universal Brotherhood was not there, because the proposal for the Society sprang spontaneously out of the present topic of discussion. It was a plain, business-like affair, unaccompanied by phenomena or any unusual incident. Lastly, it was free of the least sectarian character and unquestionably anti-materialistic. The little group of founders were all of European blood, with no strong natural antagonism as to religions, and caste distinctions were to them non-existent. The Brotherhood plank in the Society's future platform was, therefore, not thought of: later on, however, when our sphere of influence extended so as to bring us into relations with Asiatics and their religions and social systems, it became a necessity, and, in fact, the corner-stone of our edifice. The Thesophical Society was an evolution, not—on the visible plane—a planned creation.

I have an official report of the meeting of September 8th, signed by myself, as Chairman, and W. Q. Judge, as Secretary, which I will quote from our Minute Book:

"In consequence of a proposal of Col. Henry S. Olcott, that a Society be formed for the study and elucidation of Occultism, the Cabbala, etc., the ladies and gentlemen then and there present, resolved themselves into a meeting, and, upon motion of Mr. William Q. Judge, it was

"*Resolved*, That Col. H. S. Olcott take the chair. Upon motion it was also

"*Resolved*, That Mr. W. Q. Judge act as Secretary. The chair then called for the names of the persons present, who would agree to found and belong to a Society such as had been mentioned. The following persons handed their names to the Secretary:

"Col. Olcott, Mme. H. P. Blavatsky, Chas. Sotheran, Dr. Chas. E. Simmons, H. D. Monachesi, C. C. Massey, of London, W. L. Alden, G. H. Felt, D. E. de Lara, Dr. W. Britten, Mrs. E. H. Britten, Henry J. Newton, John Storer Cobb, J. Hyslop, W. Q. Judge, H. M. Stevens (all present save one).

"Upon motion of Herbert D. Monachesi, it was

"*Resolved,* That a committee of three be appointed by the chair to draft a constitution and by-laws, and to report the same at the next meeting. Upon motion, it was

"*Resolved,* That the chair be added to the Committee.

"The chair then appointed Messrs. H. J. Newton, H. M. Stevens, and C. Sotheran to be such Committee.

"Upon motion, it was

"*Resolved,* That we now adjourn until Monday, September 13th, at the same place, at 8 P.M."

The Society, then, had sixteen *formers*—to use the most apposite term—not founders; for the stable founding was a result of hard work and self-sacrifice, of years, and during a part of that time H. P. B. and I worked quite alone in the trenches, laying the strong foundation. Our colleagues either went out entirely, or became listless, or were prevented by force of circumstances from devoting their time and efforts to the work. But I must not anticipate.

When this portion of my narrative appeared in the *Theosophist* (November, 1892), sketches were given of several of the officers of the Society, to which the interested reader is referred; the superabundance of material for the present volume compelling me to condense so far as practicable. I shall, however, preserve my note on Mr. Alden for the sake of the story of one of his occult experiences.

Mr. W. L. Alden, now so well known in London literary circles, was then an editorial writer on the *N. Y. Times*, of great repute for his caustic and humoristic criticisms upon current topics. I met him in Paris recently, after many years of separation, and learnt that he had been holding an important consular appointment under the American Government. He had an amusing adventure in New York, I recollect, at about the beginning of our acquaintance. He was then an editorial contributor to the *N. Y. Daily Graphic*, and I was writing for the paper my Chittenden letters. A host of eccentric people were attracted to the editorial rooms to ask idle questions, and they bored the editor, Mr. Croly, so much that at last he published a cartoon, representing himself standing at bay, with a revolver and huge pair of shears, to defend himself against an irruption of, "long-haired men and crop-haired women" Spiritualists. But one morning there came an aged man in Eastern garb, who carried a strange-looking, evidently very old book under his arm. Saluting the editorial staff with grave courtesy, he began talking about my letters, and about Western and Eastern Spiritualism. All left their writing-tables and clustered about him. When he spoke of Magic he turned quietly towards Alden, whose occult tastes nobody had until then suspected, and said: "Do you believe there is truth in Magic, Sir?" Taken aback, Alden replied: "Well, I have read *Zanoni* and think there may be something in it." By request, the stranger showed his queer book to the editors. It proved to be a treatise upon Magic, written in Arabic or some other Eastern tongue, with numerous illustrations interspersed with the text. All were very much interested, Alden especially, who, at parting, asked the old gentleman if he might have some further talk with him. The latter smilingly assented, and gave him an address at which to call. When Alden went there, however, *it proved to be a Roman Catholic image and book-shop;* my friend found himself tricked, and ever after, for months, fruitlessly kept a sharp eye upon the people he met, in the hope that he might once more see the mysterious Asiatic. I was told by Mr. Croly that the man never revisited the *Graphic* office; it was as if the earth had swallowed him. This unexpected appearance and sudden disappearance of mysterious people who bring rare books to the right man, or who impart useful hints that put him on the right path through the swamp of difficulties through which he is bravely floundering towards the truth, is not an uncommon experience. Many a case of the kind has been recorded in religious history. Sometimes the visit is made during the waking hours, sometimes in visions of the night. The revelations sometimes come in "flashes"— flashes of the *buddhi* in upon the *mânas*—begetting great discoveries in science; as the idea of the spectroscope flashed in upon the mind of Fraunhöfer, that of the nature of lightning upon Franklin's, that of the telephone upon that of Edison, and that of ten thousand other great facts or laws upon other minds open to suggestion. It would be deemed exaggeration to say that *every* aspirant to arcane knowledge has his chance to get it, once in his lifetime, yet it is true, I believe, that the percentage of those who have is a hundredfold greater than people imagine. It is the individual's misfortune if, through ignorant misconceptions as to how such a messenger should look, or with what phenomenal portents his message should be delivered, he "entertains an angel unawares" or elbows him in the street without feeling even a tremor to divert his attention from a passing cab. I speak of that which I know.

Chapter IX.

FORMATION OF THE
THEOSOPHICAL SOCIETY

At the adjourned meeting, on the evening of September 18th, 1875, Mr. Felt continued from the previous meeting, September 8th, the interesting description of his discoveries, which he illustrated by a number of colored diagrams. Some persons present thought they saw light quivering over the geometrical figures, but I incline to the belief that this was due to auto-suggestion, in part, and partly to what Felt said about their magical properties.* Certainly, I saw nothing of an occult nature nor did the others present, save a very incon-

---

* The following important draft of a letter signed by Mr. Felt was found by me a short time after this chapter was written. I cannot remember whether the letter was sent for publication or not, but incline to the latter opinion. The importance of the document lies in the fact that in it, Mr. Felt unreservedly affirms the existence of elemental spirits, his acquired control over them, their effect upon animals and their relations with humanity. I think the statements as to the influence of the Egyptian geometrical drawings upon Mr. Felt's hearers exaggerated. The would-be teachers who did not come to learn, as Mr. Felt describes them, were the Spiritualist members whose orthodoxy was unshakable.

siderable minority. The lecture finished, the order of the day was taken up; I acting as Chairman, and Mr. C. Sotheran as Secretary. The Minute Book says:

NEW YORK, June 19, 1878.

TO THE EDITOR OF THE "LONDON SPIRITUALIST."

My attention has but just now been called to certain articles, published in your city, and one of them in your paper, which reflect upon statements made by friends of mine, respecting the "Theosophical Society" and myself. One or more of the writers question whether such a person as myself actually exists, or is but "the creation of the brains of Mme. Blavatsky and others." Having very little in common with the public which supports your paper, I seldom see it, and would perhaps never have known of these statements, if they had not been pointed out to me. I am engaged in mathematical pursuits, and take little or no interest in anything that cannot be exactly demonstrated, for which reason Spiritualists and myself have very few bonds of sympathy. I have so little faith in their so-called manifestations that I have long since given up trying to keep track of them.

The Theosophical Society was started under the mistaken impression that a fraternity of that kind could be run on the modern mutual admiration plan for the benefit of the newspapers, but very soon everything was in confusion. There were no degrees of membership nor grades, but all were equal. Most members apparently came to teach, rather than to learn, and their views were thoroughly ventilated on the street corners. The propriety of making different degrees was at once apparent to the real Theosophists, and the absolute necessity of forming the Society into a secret body. This reorganization into a secret society, embracing different degrees, having been accomplished, all statements of what has transpired since the members were so bound in secrecy, are of course to be viewed with suspicion, as, even if such statements were true, things may have been done in the presence of the *illuminati*, of which many ex-members and novitiates had no knowledge. Of my own acts in and out of the society, before this bond of secrecy, I am at liberty to speak, but of my doings or the doing of others since that time, I have no right to give evidence. Mr. Olcott's statement about my experiments with elemental or elementary spirits, in his inaugural address, was made without consultation with me or my consent, and was not known to me until too long after its appearance for me to protest. Although substantially true, I looked upon it as premature, and as something that should have been kept within the knowledge of the Society.

"The Committee on Preamble and By-laws reported progress, and Mr. De Lara read a paper which he had been requested to write for the Committee.

"At the suggestion of the Committee it was, upon motion.

That these so-called elementals or intermediates, or elementary or original spirits were creatures that actually existed, I was convinced through my investigations in Egyptian archæology. While working at drawings of several Egyptian Zodiacs, in the endeavour to arrive at their mathematical correspondences, I had noticed that very curious and unaccountable effects were sometimes produced. My family observed that at certain times a pet terrier dog and a Maltese cat, which had been brought up together and were in the habit of frequenting' my study and sleeping on the foot of my bed, were acting very strangely, and at last called my attention to it. I then noticed that when I commenced certain investigations the cat would first appear to be uneasy and the dog for a short time would try to quiet him, but shortly the dog would also seem to be in dread of something happening. It was as though the perceptions of the cat were more acute, and they would both then insist on being let out of the room, trying to get out themselves, by running against the glass windows. Being released they would stop outside and mew and bark as though calling to me to come out. This behaviour was repeated until I was forced to the conclusion at last that they were susceptible to influences not perceptible to me.

I supposed at first that the hideous representations on the Zodiacs, etc., were "vain imaginations of a distempered brain," but afterwards thought that they were conventional representations of natural objects. After studying these effects on the animals, I reflected that as the spectrum gives rays, which though to our unaided sight invisible, had been declared by eminent scientists to be capable of supporting another creation than the one to us objective, and that this creation would probably also be invisible (Zöllner's theory), this phenomenon was one of its manifestations. As these invisible rays could be made apparent by chemical means, and as invisible chemical images could be reproduced, I commenced a series of experiments to see if this invisible creation delineated in a more or less precise manner, and interspersed with images of natural objects more or less conventionally drawn. I discovered that these appearances were intelligences, and that while some seemed to be malevolent and dreaded by the animals, others on the contrary were not obnoxious to them, but on the contrary they seemed to like them and to be satisfied when they were about.

"*Resolved*, That the name of the Society be 'The Theosophical Society.'

"The chair appointed the Rev. Mr. Wiggin and Mr. Sotheran

I was led to believe that they formed a series of creatures in a system of evolution running from inanimate nature through the animal kingdom to man, its highest development; that there were intelligences capable of being more or less perfectly controlled, as man was more or less thoroughly acquainted with them, as he was able to impress them as being higher or lower in the scale of creation, or as he was more or less in harmony with nature or nature's works. Recent researches showing that plants possess senses in greater or less perfection, having convinced me that this system can be still further extended. Purity of mind and body, I found to be very powerful, and smoking and chewing tobacco and other filthy habits, I observed to be especially distasteful to them.

I satisfied myself that the Egyptians had used these appearances in their initiations; in fact, I think I have established this beyond question. My original idea was to introduce into the Masonic fraternity a form of initiations such as prevailed among the ancient Egyptians, and tried to do so, but finding that only men pure in mind and body could control these appearances, I decided that I would have to find others than my whisky-soaked and tobacco-sodden countrymen, living in an atmosphere of fraud and trickery. to act in that direction. I found that when these appearances, or elementals could not be kept in perfect control, they grew malicious, and despising men whom their cunning taught them must be debased, they became dangerous, and capable of inflicting damage and harm.

With one of the members of the Society, a legal gentleman of a mathematical turn of mind. I accomplished the following, after the manner of Cornelius Agrippa, who claimed for himself and Trithemus, that "at a great distance, it is possible without any doubt to influence another person spiritually, even when their position and the distance is unknown." *De Occulta Phil.—lib.* III., p. 3. Several times, just before meeting me, he observed a bright light; and at last came to connect this light with my coming and questioned me about it. I told him to notice the hour and minute at which these lights would be seen, and when I met him afterwards I would tell him the exact time. I did this 30 or 40 times before his naturally sceptical mind was thoroughly convinced. These lights appeared to him at different times of the day, wherever he happened to be, in New York or Brooklyn, and we arranged that, in each case, about two hours from that time I should meet at his office.

a Committee to select suitable meeting rooms; and then several new members were nominated and, upon motion, it was

---

These phenomena differ essentially from any mesmeric, magnetic, or so-called spiritual manifestations that I am acquainted with, and are not referable thereto; this gentleman has never been influenced by me in either of these ways.

Once he came to my house, in the suburbs of this city, and examined some Kabbalistic drawings upon which I was working, with one of which he was much impressed. After leaving he saw, in bright day-light, in the cars, an appearance of a curious kind of animal, of which he then made a sketch from memory. He was so impressed with the circumstance and the vividness of the apparition, that he went at once to one of the *illuminati* of the Society, and showed his drawing. He was informed that though apparently an ideal figure, it was really a so-called elemental spirit which was represented by the Egyptians as next in the order of progression to a certain reptile, which was the figure he had seen at my house, and that it was employed by the Egyptians in making their Zodiacs, at initiations, etc., etc. He then returned to me, and without comment I showed him a drawing of the very figure seen by him, whereupon he told me that he had seen it and under what circumstances and produced his sketch. He was then convinced that I foresaw that he would see this appearance after having been impressed by my Kabbalistic drawing.

These phenomena are clearly not referable to any familiar form of manifestations.

At one of my lectures before the Theosophical Society, at which all degrees of members were present, lights were seen by the *illuminati* passing to and from one of my drawings, although they stood in the glare of several gas lights, a dark cloud was observed to settle upon it by others, and other phenomena, such as the apparent change of the Zodiacal figures into other forms or elemental representations, were observed.

Certain members of lower degree were impressed with a feeling of dread, as though something awful were about to happen; most of the probationers were rendered uncomfortable or uneasy; some became hypercritical and abusive; several of the novitiates left the room; and Mme. Blavatsky, who had seen unpleasant effects follow somewhat similar phenomena in the East, requested me to turn the drawings and change the subject. If there had previously been any doubt, the absolute necessity of forming the society into degrees was then apparent, and I have never since met others than the *illuminati* of the society, with similar manifestations.

"*Resolved*, That these persons be added to the list of founders."

"After which the meeting adjourned, subject to the call of the chair. The report is signed by me as Chairman and by Dr. John Storer Cobb, for C. Sotheran, Secretary."

The choice of a name for the Society was, of course, a question for grave discussion in Committee. Several were suggested, among them, if I recollect aright, the Egyptological, the Hermetic, the Rosicrucian, etc., but none seemed just the thing. At last, in turning over the leaves of the Dictionary, one of us came across the word "Theosophy," whereupon, after discussion, we unanimously agreed that that was the best of all; since it both expressed the esoteric truth we wished to reach and covered the ground of Felt's methods of occult scientific research. Some stupid story has gone about that, while the Committee were sitting, a strange Hindu walked into the room, threw a sealed packet upon the table and walked out again, or vanished, or something of the sort; the packet, when opened, being found to contain a complete draft of a Constitution and By-laws for the

---

The unfriendly tone of the article above referred to was entirely uncalled for, and there was no boasting on the part of any of the members in their remarks. Being a secret society we could not in any manner retaliate until permission to do so was given. Having now received permission, I here publicly state that I have lately performed what I agreed to do, and, unless the Council forbids, I hereby give permission to such of the *illuminati* as have seen it, to come forward. if they choose and bear evidence of the fact.

I do not know if you will think this worth the space it will occupy in your columns, but think that it is but just, after keeping an absolute silence for more than two years, I should now be heard in this matter. Modern Spiritualism need not weep with Alexander, for there is another world for it to discover and conquer.

GEORGE H. FELT.

Society, which we at once adopted. This is sheer nonsense; nothing whatever of the sort occurred. Several similarly absurd yarns have been set afloat about us from time to time; some of them very funny, some weird, some too childishly improbable to be worth even reading, but all misleading. An old journalist myself, I cared too little for such *canards* to take the least notice of them. While they create temporary confusion and misconceptions, in the long run they do no harm.

As regards the drafting of the original By-laws, we took much pains and drew up as good a set as any society could desire. The Rules of various corporate bodies were examined, but those of the American Geographical and Statistical Society and the American Institute were thought by us to be as good models as any to follow. All preliminaries being settled, we obtained permission from Mrs. Britten that the next meeting should be held at her private residence (no hall having as yet been taken), and I issued (on post-cards) the following notice:

The Theosophical Society.

NEW YORK, *October 13, 1875.*

The Committee on By-Laws having completed its work, a meeting of the Theosophical Society will be held at the private residence, No. 206 West 38th St., on Saturday, October 16, 1875, at 8 p.m., to organize and elect officers. If Mr. Felt should be in town, he will continue his intensely interesting account of his

Egyptological discoveries. Under the By-Laws proposed, new members cannot be elected until after thirty days' consideration of their application. A full attendance at this preliminary meeting is, therefore, desirable.

The undersigned issues this call in compliance with the order adopted by the meeting of September 13th ultimo.

(*Signed*) HENRY S. OLCOTT, *President, pro. tem.*

The copy of the original post-card sent by post by Sotheran to H. P. B. I have, framed, at "Gulistan," and my own copy is also in my possession.

Our Minute Book records the following persons as present at this meeting in question:

"Mme. Blavatsky, Mrs. E. H. Britten, Henry S. Olcott, Henry J. Newton, Chas. Sotheran, W. Q. Judge, J. Hyslop, Dr. Atkinson, Dr. H. Carlos, Dr. Simmons, Tudor Horton, Dr. Britten, C. C. Massey, John Storer Cobb, W. L. Alden, Edwin S. Ralphs, Herbert D. Monachesi, and Francisco Agromonte.

"On behalf of the Committee on Preamble and By-Laws, the Preamble was read by the chair, and the By-Laws by Mr. Chas. Sotheran."

Mr. Massey was then introduced by the chair and made some remarks; after which he was obliged to hurry away to the steamer on which he was to sail for England.

Discussions ensued and various motions were made on the adoption of the By-Laws; the final result being that the draft submitted by the Committee was laid on the table and order printed. The meeting then adjourned. H. S. Olcott was Chairman and J. S. Cobb Secretary of the meeting.

The next preliminary meeting was held at the same place on the 30th October. The Committee on rooms having reported, Mott Memorial Hall, 64 Madison Avenue (a few doors only from our recently purchased New York Headquarters), was selected as the Society's meeting-place. The By-Laws were read, discussed and finally adopted, but with the proviso that the Preamble should be revised by H. S. Olcott, C. Sotheran and J. S. Cobb, and then published as the Preamble of the Society.

Voting for officers was next proceeded with; and Tudor Horton and Dr. W. H. Atkinson being appointed tellers of the Election, the result was announced by Mr. Horton as follows:

President, HENRY S. OLCOTT; *Vice-Presidents*, DR. S. PANCOAST and G. H. FELT; *Corresponding Secretary*, MME. H. P. BLAVATSKY; *Recording Secretary*, JOHN STORER COBB; *Treasurer*, HENRY J. NEWTON; *Librarian*, CHARLES SOTHERAN; *Councillors*, REV. J. H. WIGGIN, R. B. WESTBROOK, LL.D., MRS. EMMA HARDINGE BRITTEN, C. E. SIMMONS, M.D., and HERBERT D. MONACHESI; *Counsel to the Society*, WILLIAM Q. JUDGE.

The meeting then adjourned over to the 17th November, 1875, when the perfected Preamble would be reported, the President Elect deliver his Inaugural Address, and the Society be thus fully constituted.

On the evening designated, the Society met in its own hired room; the minutes of the previous meeting were read and approved; the President's Inaugural Address was delivered and ordered printed; upon Mr. Newton's motion, thanks were voted to the President; and the Society, now constitutionally organised, adjourned over to the 15th December.

Thus the Theosophical Society, first conceived of on the 8th September and constitutionally perfected on the 17th November, 1875, after a gestatory period of seventy days, came into being and started on its marvellous career of altruistic endeavour *per angusta ad augusta*. Inadvertently, in our first published document, the *Preamble and By-Laws of The Theosophical Society*, the 30th October was given as the date of organisation, whereas, as seen above, it should properly have been November 17, 1875.

The foregoing narrative of the origin and birth of the Society is very prosaic and lacks all the sensational and imaginative features which have sometimes been ascribed to the event. It has, however, the merit of being historically exact; for, as I am writing history and not romance, I have stuck to the evidences of our certificated records and can prove every point. With an exaggeration of supposed loyalty which has bred injustice, as bigotry invariably does, many persons have been repeating to the echo the incorrect statement that H. P. B., and she alone, founded the Theosophical Society; what her colleagues did was less than nothing. The fact is that she herself vigorously repudiated the idea when put forward by Mr. J. L. O'Sullivan, in 1878. She says—answering a caustic critic:

"With crushing irony he speaks of us as 'our teachers.'

Now I remember having distinctly stated in a previous letter that we [she and I] have *not* offered ourselves as teachers, but, on the contrary, decline any such office—whatever may be the superlative panegyric of my esteemed friend, Mr. O'Sullivan, who not only sees in me a 'Buddhist priestess' (!) but, *without a shadow of warrant of fact, credits me with the foundation of the Theosophical Society and its Branches.*" [Letter of H. P. Blavatsky, in the *Spiritualist* of March 22, 1878.]

H. P. B. was quite wonderful enough as she actually was without the fulsome praise that has been lavished upon her; and the attempt to read into every word and action an occult value will only recoil upon its authors, by the inflexible general law of action and reaction observable in Nature. Her devotees ignore the fact, that the more previsionary power and infallible insight they ascribe to her, the more mercilessly will men hold her accountable for her every action, her mistakes in judgment, inaccuracies in statement, and other foibles which, in an ordinary—*i.e.*, an uninspired person, are often only mildly blamed because recognised as proofs of human infirmity. It is a most unfriendly act to try to make her a being above humanity, without a weakness, spot, or blemish, for her written public record, let alone her private correspondences, proves the thing impossible.

Though my Inaugural Address was applauded by my audience, and Mr. Newton, the orthodox Spiritualist, joined with Mr. Thomas Freethinker, and the Rev. Mr. Westbrook, to get a vote that it be printed and stereotyped—a good proof that they did not think its views and tone unreasonable—yet it reads a bit foolish after seventeen years of hard experience. A good deal of its forecast of results has been verified, much of it falsi-fied. What we counted on as its sound experimental basis, *viz.*, Felt's demonstration of the existence of the Elemental races, proved a complete and mortifying disappointment. Whatever he may have done by himself in that direction, he showed us nothing, not even the tip end of the tail of the tiniest Nature-spirit. He left us to be mocked by the Spiritualist and every other class of sceptic. He was a man of extraordinary acquire-ments, and had made what seemed a remarkable discovery. So probable, indeed, did it appear that—as I have above stated—Mr. Bouton, an experienced merchant, risked a very heavy sum on the speculation of getting out his book. For my part, I believe he had done what he claimed, and that, if he had but systematically followed up his beginnings, his name would have been among the most renowned of our epoch. Having so often seen H. P. B. employ the Elementals to do phenomena, Signor B. do the same on several occasions, and my mysteri-ous strangers show me them in my own rooms, what was eas-ier than for me to believe that Felt could do likewise; especially when H. P. B. assured me that he could? So, with the temerity of a born pioneer and the zeal of a congenital optimist and enthusiast, I gave rein to my imagination and depicted, in my Address, what was likely to result if Felt's promise was made good. Luckily for me, I put in the "if"; and it might have been better if it had been printed thus—IF. On the plea of his pecu-niary necessities, he got out of Treasurer Newton $100 to defray the costs of the promised experiments, but brought us no Elementals. In the Council meeting of March 29, 1876, a letter from him was read, in which he stated that "he was prepared to fulfil his promise to lecture before the Society upon the Kabbalah, and giving an outline of the different departments into which he would divide his subject."

Whereupon, Mr. Monachesi moved a Resolution, which was passed, that

"The Secretary be intrusted to have printed and circulated among the Fellows of the Society, either the letter of V. P. Felt, or a syllabus which Fellow Felt and himself would prepare." [Extract, "Minutes of the T. S.," p. 15.]

The circular was issued and helped somewhat to lessen the feeling of resentment that prevailed against Mr. Felt for his breach of promise. He actually delivered his second lecture on the 21st June, but then he again failed us, and I find that, in the Council meeting on the 11th October, on Treasurer Newton's motion, a Resolution was adopted, instructing Mr. Judge, the Society's Counsel, to demand that he should fulfil his legal obligation at an early date. But he never did. Finally, he went out of the Society; and, it having thus been proved that nothing was to be expected of him a number of persons also vanished from the Society, and left us others, who were not mere sensation-seekers, to toil on as best we might.

And it *was* toil, as all who were at all active in those days, very well recollect. Our object was to learn, experimentally, whatever was possible about the constitution of man, his intelligence, and his place in nature. Especially Mind, active as WILL, was a great problem for us. The Eastern magus uses it, the Western mesmerist and psychopath employ it; one man developes it, and becomes a hero, another paralyses it, and becomes a spirit medium. To its resistless sway the beings of all kingdoms and various planes of matter are obedient, and when imagination is simultaneously active, it *creates*, by giving objectivity to just-formed mind-images. So, though Felt had defaulted, and we could count on no sailing on smooth tides, yet we had still many fields left for research, and we explored them a little. The old records show that we tested mediums, tried experiments in psychometry, thought-reading and mesmerism, and wrote and listened to papers. But we made slow progress, for, though we all, by tacit consent, put the best face upon it, every one of us was secretly discouraged by Felt's fiasco, and there seemed no chance of finding a substitute: the rain-maker, Signor B., had been driven away by H. P. B., after his futile attempt to create a breach between her and myself; my swarthy, elemental-summoning visitor did not show his face again; and H. P. B., upon whose help everybody had—as we thought—not unreasonably counted, refused to do the slightest phenomenon at our meetings. So the membership dwindled by degrees, until, at the end of a year or so, there survived the following: the form of a good organisation, sound and strong in its platform; a clangorous notoriety; a few, more or less indolent, members; and an indestructible focus of vitality in the quenchless enthusiasm of the two friends, the Russian woman and American man, who were in deadly earnest; who never for a moment harboured a doubt as to the existence of their Masters, the excellence of their delegated work, or the ultimate complete success that would crown it. Judge was a loyal friend and willing helper, but he was so very much our junior that we could not regard him as an equal third party. He was more like the youngest son in a family. Many an evening after we had established our residential Headquarters, when our visitors had gone and H. P. B. and I stopped in the Library-room for a parting-smoke and chat, have we laughed to think how few we could count upon to stand by us through everything. The fair speeches and smiles of the evening's guests would be recalled, and the selfishness they often meant to mask detected. The one thing we felt more and more as time went on was, that we two could absolutely depend upon each other for Theosophy, though the sky itself should crack; beyond that, all depended upon circumstances. We used to speak of ourselves as the Theosophical Twins, and sometimes as a trinity; the chandelier hanging overhead making the third of the party! Frequent allusions to both these pleasantries occur in our Theosophical correspondence; and on the day when she and I were leaving our dismantled apartments in New York, to go aboard the steamer that was to take us towards India, the last thing we did was to say, with mock seriousness, "Farewell, old Chandelier; silent, light-giving, unchanging friend and confidant!"

The enemy have sometimes said that when we sailed away from America we left no Theosophical Society behind us; and to a certain extent that was true, for, owing to several causes, it did nothing to speak of during the next six years. The social nucleus—always the most powerful factor in movements of this kind—had been broken up; nobody was able to form a new one; another H. P. B. could not be created: and Mr. Judge, the then only potential future leader and organiser, was called away to Spanish countries by professional business, as above remarked.

It must be said, in justice to Mr. Judge, General Doubleday, and their associates in the original Theosophical Society, whom we left in charge on leaving for India, that the suspended animation was for two or three years mainly due to my own fault. There had been some talk of converting the Society into a high Masonic degree, and the project had been favourably viewed by some influential Masons. I shall have to recur to this subject later on. For the present it suffices to say that I was asked to draft an appropriate form of ritual, and when we left America this was one of the first things I was to do after reaching India. But instead of the quiet and leisure anticipated, we were instantly plunged into a confusion of daily work and excitement; I was forced on the lecturing platform; we made long journeys through India; the *Theosophist* was founded, and it was simply impossible to give any attention to the ritual; though I have several letters from General Doubleday and Judge complaining that it was not sent them, and saying they could do nothing without it. Moreover, our wider experience convinced us of the impracticability of the plan: our activity had taken a much wider extension, and our work a more serious and independent character. So, finally, I decided not to follow up the scheme. But by this time Judge had gone abroad and the others did nothing.

In a letter dated New York, October 17, 1879—a year after our departure—Mr. Judge writes: "We have taken in but few members and decided to wait for the ritual before taking in more, as that would make a serious change." For us two, however, there had been twelve months of heavy work. General Doubleday writes to the same effect under date of September

1, 1879, saying: "With regard to the T. S. in the United States we have been in *statu quo*, waiting for the promised ritual." On the 23d of June, 1880, he asks: "Why do you not send us that ritual?" And Mr. Judge, on April 10, 1880, tells me, "Everything here lags. No ritual yet. Why?" November 7, 1881, Judge being absent in South America, his brother, whom he had left in charge of T. S. affairs, writes me that nothing is doing, and that "the Society will not start working until W. Q. J., General Doubleday, and I [he] can find time and means to start it"; both of which were lacking. Finally—as it is useless to follow up the matter further—on January 7, 1882, Judge writes: "The Society is dormant, doing absolutely nothing. Your explanation about the ritual is satisfactory."

Yet throughout all these years, Mr. Judge's letters to H. P. B., myself, and Damodar show that his zeal for Theosophy and all mysticism was unquenchable. His greatest desire was that a day might come when he should be free to devote all his time and energies to the work of the Society. But as the clover seed, imbedded in the soil twenty feet below the surface, germinates when the well-diggers bring it up above ground, so the seed we planted in the American mind, between the years 1874 and 1878, fructified in its due time; and Judge was the husbandman predestined to reap our harvest. Thus, always, Karma evolves its pioneers, sowers, and reapers. The viability of our Society was proximately in us two founders, but ultimately in its basic idea and the transmitters, the August Ones, who taught us and shed into our hearts and minds the light of their benevolent goodwill. As both of us realised this, and as we were both permitted to work for it and with them, there was a closer bond between us two than any that the common social relationships could have forged. It made us put up with each other's weaknesses and bear all the grievous frictions incident to the collaboration of two such contrasting personalities. As for myself, it made me put behind me as things of no value all worldly ties, ambitions, and desires. Truly, from the bottom of my heart, I felt, and feel, that it is better to be a door-keeper, or even something more menial than that, in the house of the "Lord on High," than to dwell in any silken pavilion the selfish world could give me for the asking. So felt H. P. B., whose tireless enthusiasm for our work was a never-failing wellspring of encouragement to every one coming in contact with her. Feeling thus, and ready, as we were, to make every sacrifice for our cause, the extinction of the Theosophical Society was simply impossible.

Many things of interest to Theosophists are recorded in the early Society records. At the Council meeting of January 12, 1876, it was resolved, upon the motion of J. S. Cobb, "that William Q. Judge, Counsel to the Society, be invited to assist in the deliberations of the Council, at its meetings." At the same meeting, the withdrawal of Mr. Sotheran from the Society was noted and Mr. H. J. Newton appointed to fill the vacancy: and the Council ordered the Recording Secretary to lay before the Society, at its next regular meeting, the following Resolution, as upon the recommendation of the Council, for adoption:

"That in future this Society adopt the principle of secrecy in connection with its proceedings and transactions, and that a

Committee be appointed to draw up and report upon the details necessary to give effect to such a change."

So that, after an experience of barely three months—I had thought it was much longer—we were obliged in self-defence to become a secret body. At the Council meeting of March 8, 1876, on motion of H. P. Blavatsky, it was

"*Resolved*, That the Society adopt one or more signs of recognition, to be used among the Fellows of the Society, or for admissions to the meetings."

A Committee of three, of whom H. P. B. was one, was appointed by me to invent and recommend signs. The appropriate seal of the Society was partly designed after a very mystical one that a friend of H. P. B.'s had composed for her, to use on her letter-paper, and it was beautifully engraved for us by Mr. Tudor Harton. A little later Mr. Judge and I, with the concurrence of others, sketched a badge of membership, consisting of a serpent coiled about an Egyptian Tau. I had two made, for H. P. B. and myself, but we subsequently gave them away to friends. Quite recently, this very pretty and appropriate symbol has been revived in America.

But what little secrecy there ever was in the Society—as little, or even less than that so carefully guarded by the Tyler of a Masonic Lodge—has virtually passed away, after its brief period of use in our early days. In 1889, it was made the chief feature in the Esoteric Society which I chartered for H. P. B., and, I regret to say, has caused us much harm with much good.

Chapter X.

BARON DE PALM

The evolution of the Society up to its perfected organisation having been traced, we may now give attention to special incidents which occupied the attention of its founders and more or less affected its interests. If the details of early T. S. history were known to the majority of its members this historical retrospect might be left to some less busy person than myself to compile. In point of fact, however, no other living person knows them all so well as I; no one save H. P. B., and I assumed all the responsibilities, took all the hard knocks, organised all the successes: so, perforce, I must play the historian. If I do not, the truth will never be made known. The special incident to be dealt with in the present chapter is the story of Baron de Palm's connection with our Society, his antecedents, death, will, and funeral; his cremation will require a separate chapter. This is not Theosophy, but I am not writing Theosophy: it is history, one of several affairs which were mixed up in our Society's concerns, and which greatly occupied the time and thoughts of my colleague and myself. These affairs threw upon me, as President, in particular, very grave responsibilities. When I say that I carried through the De Palm funeral obsequies with the conviction that it would cost me a professional connection worth some £2,000 a year, my meaning will appear. The thing apprehended did happen, because I mortally offended the gentleman—a bigoted Christian—who controlled the matter in question, and who influenced its transfer to another friend of his. Of course, I should do it over again, and I only mention the circumstance to show that it cost something to be a worker with the Masters in those early days.

Joseph Henry Louis Charles, Baron de Palm, Grand Cross Commander of the Order of the Holy Sepulchre and Knight of various other orders, was born at Augsburg, May 10, 1809, in an ancient baronial family of Bavaria. Late in life he emigrated to America, lived a number of years in the Western States, and about December, 1875, came to me in New York with an introductory letter from the late Col. Bundy, editor of the *Religio Philosophical Journal*, commending him to my courtesy. Finding him a man of engaging manners, evidently familiar with the best society, and professing much interest in Spiritualism and a wish to learn something about our Oriental theories, I made him welcome, and at his request introduced him to H. P. B. The acquaintance was kept up, the Baron joined our Society and, a vacancy occurring soon after by the resignation of the Rev. J. H. Wiggin, he was elected a Member of Council on the 29th March, 1876. As he complained of feeble health, and of having no one in New York who cared whether he lived or died in the wretched boarding-house where he was put up, I invited him to come and occupy a room in my "apartment," looked after his comfort, and called in a physician to prescribe for him. Symptoms of pneumonia and nephritis showing themselves and the medical attendant pronouncing him in danger, he got me to send him Mr. Judge, the Society's Standing Counsel, and executed a will devising certain parcels of real estate at Chicago to two lady friends, making me residuary legatee, and appointing Mr. Newton, Treasurer of the T. S., and myself his executors, with full powers. Under medical advice and at his own earnest request, he was removed to the Roosevelt Hospital on Friday evening, May 19th, (1876), and died the next morning. The result of an autopsy was to show that he had for years been suffering from a complication of diseases of the lungs, kidneys, and other organs; a medical certificate that he had died of nephritis was given and filed, as prescribed by law, in the Health Bureau, and the body was conveyed to the receiving-vault of the Lutheran Cemetery pending the completion of arrangements for interment.

In religion Baron de Palm was a Voltairean with a gloss of Spiritualism. He particularly asked that no clergyman or priest should officiate at his funeral, but that I should perform the last offices in a fashion that would illustrate the Eastern notions of death and immortality. The recent agitation of the subject of cremation in Great Britain and America, caused by the incineration of the body of the first Lady Dilke, the scientific experiments of Sir Henry Thompson (*vide* his published essay *The Treatment of the Body after Death*, London, 1874), and the sensational articles and pamphlets of Rev. H. R.

Haweis upon the unspeakable horrors of the burial-grounds of London, led me to ask him how he would wish me to dispose of his remains. He asked for my opinion upon the relative superiority of the two modes of sepulture, concurred in my preference for cremation, expressed a horror of burial, some lady he had once known having been buried alive, and bade me do as I found most advisable. A dilettante sort of body calling itself the New York Cremation Society, had been formed in April, 1874, and I had enrolled myself as a member, and been elected a member of the Legal Advice Committee; but beyond passing resolutions and issuing pamphlets the members had done nothing to prove the faith that was in them. Here, at last, was the chance of having a body to burn, and thus inaugurating the very needed reform. I offered it to the Society in question and it was accepted. The weather being warm for the season, urgent haste was called for, and up to the evening before the day appointed for the public funeral of the Baron, it was understood that after the ceremonies I was to deliver over the body to the Society's agents for cremation. Meanwhile H. P. B. and the rest of us bestirred ourselves to organise an impressive "Pagan funeral"—as the press chose to call it—compose a litany, devise a ceremonial, write a couple of Orphic hymns for the occasion, and get them set to appropriate music. On the Saturday evening mentioned above we were rehearsing our programme for the last time when a note was brought me from the Secretary of the N. Y. Cremation Society, to say that they would have to give up the cremation because of the great noise that the papers had made about the funeral and their attacks upon the Theosophical Society. In other words, these respectable moral cowards dared not face the ridicule and animosity which had been excited against us innovators. The quandary we were in did not last longer than a half hour, for I finally offered to take the whole responsibility upon myself, and pledged my word that the body should be burnt if I had even to do it myself. The promise was fulfilled in due time, as the sequel will show.

Through the obliging courtesy of the Rev. O. B. Frothingham, whose congregation were worshipping in the great hall of the Masonic Temple, at the corner of Twenty-third Street and Sixth Avenue, New York City, we were enabled to hold the Baron's obsequies in that vast apartment. An hour before the appointed time the street was crowded by an eager, even somewhat obstreperous multitude, and a strong body of police had to be sent for to prevent the doors being forced. We had issued two kinds of admission tickets, both of triangular shape, one a black card printed in silver, for reserved seats, the other a drab one printed in black, for general admission; and the police were instructed to admit nobody without one or the other kind. But an American or British mob is hard to restrain, and there was such a rush when the doors were opened that the 1500 holders of tickets had to find seats as best they could. The great hall, which holds 2000 people, was crowded in every corner, the very passages and lobbies were blocked, and from the buzz of conversation and uneasiness prevailing it was easy to see that the multitude had come to gratify its curiosity, certainly not to evince either respect for the dead or sympathy with the Theosophical Society. It was just in that uncertain mood when the least unexpected and sensational incident might transform it into the wild beast that an excited crowd becomes at times. Through the whole of the previous week the leading papers had been lashing public curiosity into a frenzy, and one of the wittiest burlesques I ever read, that appeared in the *World* upon our anticipated ceremonial and public procession, set all New York laughing. For the benefit of our Theosophical grand-children I will quote the following fragment:

"'All right,' said the Colonel; 'go ahead and make out your programme, but leave everybody out but the members of the society, for the Masons won't have anything to do with it.'

"Two hours were then spent in making out an order of march and a programme of exercises after the procession reaches the Temple, and the following is the result. The procession will move in the following order:

"Colonel Olcott as high priest, wearing a leopard skin and carrying a roll of papyrus (brown card-board).

"Mr. Cobb as sacred scribe, with style and tablet.

"Egyptian mummy-case, borne upon a sledge drawn by four oxen. (Also a slave bearing a pot of lubricating oil.)

"Mme. Blavatsky as chief mourner and also bearer of the sistrum. (She will wear a long linen garment extending to the feet, and a girdle about the waist.)

"Colored boy carrying three Abyssinian geese (Philadelphia chickens) to place upon the bier.

"Vice-President Felt, with the eye of Osiris painted on his left breast, and carrying an asp (bought at a toy store on Eighth avenue).

"Dr. Pancoast, singing an ancient Theban dirge:

"'Isis and Nepthys, beginning and end;
  Ono more victim to Amenti we send.
  Pay we the fare, and let us not tarry,
  Cross the Styx by the Roosevelt Street ferry.'"

"Slaves in mourning gowns, carrying the offerings and libations, to consist of early potatoes, asparagus, roast beef, French pancakes, bock-beer, and New Jersey cider.

"Treasurer Newton, as chief of the musicians, playing the double pipe.

"Other musicians performing on eight-stringed harps, tom-toms, etc.

"Boys carrying a large lotus (sun-flower).

"Librarian Fassit, who will alternate with music by repeating the lines beginning:

"'Here Horus comes, I see the boat,
    Friends, stay your flowing tears;
  The soul of man goes through a goat
    In just 3,000 years.'

"At the Temple the ceremony will be short and simple. The oxen will be left standing on the sidewalk, with a boy near by to prevent them goring the passers by. Besides the Theurgic hymn, printed above in full, the Coptic national anthem will be sung, translated and adapted to the occasion as follows:

> "Sitting Cynocephalus, up in a tree,
>   I see you, and you see me.
>   River full of crocodile, see his long snout!
>   Hoist up the shadoof and pull him right out."

With this sort of thing going on for days together in advance, it may be imagined in what sort of dangerous mood was the crowded audience, only a handful of whom were members of the T. S. and most of whom were positively prejudiced against it. All went peacefully enough, however, until an excited Methodist, a relative of an F. T. S. who was assisting me in the ceremony, rising and wildly gesticulating, shouted "That's a lie!" just when I had pronounced the words "There is but one first cause, uncreated—." Instantly the audience sprang to their feet and some turned towards the door, as people will in such crises, not knowing whether the confused shout may not mean an alarm of fire: some of the rougher sort mounted the chairs, and, looking towards the stage, seemed ready to take part in fighting or skirmishing in case such should break out. It was one of those moments when the turn of events depends upon the speaker. As it happened, I had once seen the great Abolitionist orator, Wendell Philips, by imperturbable coolness quell a mob who were hooting and catcalling him, and as the memory flashed within me I adopted his tactics. Stepping quietly forward, I laid my left hand upon the Baron's coffin, faced the audience, stood motionless and said nothing. In an instant there was a dead silence of expectancy; whereupon, slowly raising my right hand, I said very slowly and solemnly: "We are in the presence of death!" and then waited. The psychological effect was very interesting and amusing to me, who have for so many years been a student of crowds. The excitement was quelled like magic, and then in the same voice as before, and without the appearance of even having been interrupted, I finished the sentence of the litany—"eternal, infinite, unknown."

The two Orphic hymns that we compiled for the occasion were sung by a volunteer choir of the New Yorker Sængerbund and the organ accompaniment was the music of an Italian Mass, 300 years old; "and"—says the *Sun*'s report—"as it swelled and then died softly away in the half gloom of the crowded but hushed room, with the symbolic fire flickering (on the triangular altar) and the ancient knightly decorations flashing on the coffin, the effect was very impressive."

After the singing of the first Orphic hymn, an invocation, or *mantram*, was made to "the Soul of the World, whose breath gives and withdraws the form of everything." "The universe," it went on to say, "is thy utterance and revelation. Thou, before whom the light of being is a shadow which changes and a vapor that passes away; thou breathest forth, and the endless spaces are peopled; thou drawest breath and all that went forth from thee returns again." Good Vedântism this and good Theosophy! The same thought ran throughout all the parts of the service—the hymns, invocation, litany, and my discourse. In the latter I gave such particulars about Baron de Palm as I had got from himself (and very misleading they were afterwards proved to be when I heard from the family solicitor). I explained the character and objects of the T. S.* and my view of the complete inefficacy of death-bed repentance for the forgiveness of sins. I am glad to see upon reading the newspaper reports after the lapse of many years that I preached the doctrine of Karma, pure and simple. There was an outburst of applause and hisses when I said that the Society "considered the ruffian who stood under the gallows a ruffian still though twenty prayers might have been uttered over him." I immediately commanded silence and continued my remarks—reported thus:

"He then went on to say that Theosophy could not conceive of bad going unpunished or good remaining unrewarded. I believe a man to be a responsible being, and it was a religion not of professions but of practices. It was utterly opposed to sensuousness and taught the subordination of the body to the spirit. There, in that coffin, lay (the body of) a Theosophist. Should his future be pronounced one of unalloyed happiness without respect to the course of his past life? No, but as he had acted so should he suffer or rejoice. If he had been a sensualist, a usurer, or a corrupter, then the divine first (and only) cause could not forgive him the least of

---

* "This Society," I said, "was neither a religious nor a charitable but a scientific body. Its object was to enquire, not to teach, and its members comprised men of various creeds and beliefs. 'Theology' meant the revealed will of God, 'Theosophy' the direct knowledge of 'God.' The one asked us to believe what some one else had seen and heard, the other told us to see and hear for ourselves. Theosophy taught that by cultivation of his powers a man may be inwardly illumined and get thereby a knowledge of his Godlike faculties."

his offences, for that would be to plunge the universe into chaos. There must be compensation, equilibrium, justice."

After the singing of the second Orphic hymn, Mrs. E. Hardinge Britten, the Spiritualist orator, addressed the audience for about ten minutes, in the capacity of a speaking medium, concluding with a strongly emotional apostrophe to the deceased Baron, bidding him farewell, declaring that he had "passed the golden gates wherein (*sic*) sorrow entereth not," and strewing his bier with flowers, "as symbols of full-blown life!" This closed the proceedings and the huge audience quietly dispersed.

The body of the deceased was given in charge of Mr. Buckhorst, the Society's undertaker, to be lodged in a receiving vault until I could arrange for its cremation. I was obliged to devise a better method of preserving it than the weak process of embalming that had been employed at the Hospital, which proved its inefficacy even within the fortnight. It gave me much anxiety, and no end of enquiry and research was involved, but I solved the difficulty at last by packing the cadaver in desiccated clay impregnated with the carbolic and other vapors of distilled coal tar. Decomposition had actually begun when the antiseptic was applied in the first week of June, but when we examined the corpse in the following December before removal for cremation, it was found completely mummified, all liquids absorbed and all decay arrested. It could have been kept thus, I am convinced, for many years, perhaps for a century, and I recommend the process as superior to any other cheap method of embalming that has ever come under my notice.

H. P. B. had no official part in the public celebration of the

De Palm obsequies, but made herself heard all the same. She sat with the non-officiating members of the Society among the audience, and when the excited Methodist interrupted our litany and a policeman was getting him in hand to escort him out of doors, she stood up and called out, "He's a bigot, that's what he is!" and set everybody around her laughing, in which she soon heartily joined. The members who took part in the ceremony were Messrs. Judge, Cobb, Thomas, Monachesi, Oliver, and three or four more whose names I cannot recall.

The Council of the T. S., at its meeting of June 14th, and the Society, in its session of 21st June (1876), passed Resolutions ratifying and confirming all that the officers had done in connection with the De Palm autopsy, obsequies, and enbalming. A Resolution was also adopted to the effect that,

> "The President and Treasurer of this Society, who are the executors under the last will and testament of our late fellow be, and hereby are, authorised and empowered to do in the name of this Society any and all further acts, which they may deem necessary to complete the disposal of the remains of our late fellow, according to his expressed wishes and direction."

The Baron's funeral being over, the next thing was to see what his estate was likely to realise for the Society (for although all was left to me individually there was an understanding between us that I should be free to hand over everything to the T. S.). Mr. Newton and I obtained probate of the will, and Mr. Judge was instructed to make the necessary inquiries. Our first shock came when we opened his trunk at the hospital: it contained two of my own shirts, *from which the stitched namemark had been picked out.* This looked very cloudy indeed, a bad beginning towards the supposed great bequest. There were also in the trunk a small bronze bust of a crying baby, some photographs and letters of actresses and prima donnas, some unreceipted bills, some gilt and enamelled duplicates of his orders of nobility, a flat, velvet-lined case containing the certificates of his birth, his passports and the several diplomatic and court appointments he had held, the draft of a former will, now cancelled, and a meagre lot of clothing. Beyond this, nothing; no money or jewelry, no documents, no manuscripts, no books, no evidences of a literary taste or habits. I give these details—in which Mr. Newton and Mr. Judge and others will corroborate me—for an excellent reason, to be presently stated.

The old will described him as Seignior of the castles of Old and New Wartensee, on Lake Constance, and his papers showed him to be the presumed owner of 20,000 acres of land in Wisconsin, forty town lots in Chicago, and some seven or eight mining properties in Western States. Upon the low estimate that the farming land was worth $5 per acre, the rumour spread that I had inherited at least £20,000, to say nothing of the two Swiss castles, the town lots, and the gold and silver mining claims. It ran through the whole American press, editorials were written upon it, and I received a shoal of letters, congratulatory and begging, from known and unknown persons in various countries. Mr. Judge communicated with the lady legatees, with public officials at home and abroad, and with a representative of the Baron's family. This took several months, but the final result was this: the ladies would not take the Chicago lots for a gift, the Wisconsin land had been sold for taxes years before, the mining shares were good only for papering walls, and the Swiss castles proved castles in the air; the whole estate would not yield even enough to reimburse Mr. Newton and myself for the moderate costs of the probate and funeral! The Baron was a broken-down noble, without means, credit, or expectations; a type of a large class who fly to republican America as a last resource when Europe will no longer support them. Their good breeding and their titles of nobility gain them an entrance into American society, sometimes chances of lucrative posts, oftener rich wives. I never knew exactly what our friend had been doing in the West, but through importunate creditors who turned up, I found out that he had at any rate been concerned in unprofitable attempts to form industrial companies of sorts.

Neither then nor since have I discovered one grain of proof that Baron de Palm had either literary talent, erudition, or scholastic tastes. His conversation with H. P. B. and myself was mainly upon superficial matters, the topics which interest society people. Even in Spiritualism he did not seem to have been a deep thinker, rather an interested observer of mediums and phenomena. He told us much about his experiences in diplomatic circles, and ascribed his present straitened circumstances (as regards the possession of ready cash) to his futile attempts, when an attaché, to vie with rich English diplomats in showy living and fashionable indulgences. He read little and wrote nothing: as I had ample opportunity of observing, since he was living with me as my guest.

It would be painful for me to dwell upon these personalities but for the necessity of my showing the man's character, and leaving my readers to judge for themselves whether he was fit to be a teacher or mentor to a person like the author of *Isis Unveiled* and *The Secret Doctrine*. For that is the disputed point. With an inconceivable malignity certain unprincipled foes of hers have spread the calumny that her *Isis Unveiled* is "nothing but a compilation from the manuscripts of Baron de Palm, and without acknowledgement." This will be found in a mendacious letter of Dr. Elliott Coues in the *New York Sun* of July 20, 1890, which the Editor of that influential paper more recently, in the most honorable spirit of justice, expressed regret for having published and declared unsupported by evidence. The falsehood has been circulated, as I am informed, by Mrs. Emma Hardinge Britten, by a learned calumniator in *The Carrier Dove*, and by other hostile newspaper writers: it has, moreover, been given a certain permanency of publication by an expelled French F. T. S., one Dr. G. Encausse (known by the pseudonym of *Papus*) in his work *Traité Methodique de Science Occulte*, which was reviewed in the *Theosophist* for August, 1892.

To those who knew H. P. B.'s mode of life while writing her book, who were acquainted with Baron de Palm at the West and in New York, and who were associated with him during his brief connection with the T. S., the above candid and easily proven details about his personality, habits, and acquirements will suffice. For others, I reluctantly append the scathing letter which Herr Consul Obermayer, of Augsburg, Bavaria, sent Mr. Judge in response to his official and professional enquiry as to M. de Palm's supposed European properties, and which has been translated for this publication from the original in my possession. From its date, the reader will see that we did not receive it, and consequently did not know the truth about the Baron's European antecedents, until a full year after his death, and five months after the world-famous cremation of his remains:

"CONSULATE OF THE ARGENTINE REPUBLIC,

AUGSBURG, *May* 16, 1877.

No. 1130.

TO WILLIAM Q. JUDGE,

Attorney and Counsellor at Law,

71 *Broadway, New York.*

"From your letter of the 7th ult., I gather that Baron Josef Heinrich Ludwig von Palm died in New York in the month of May, 1876.

"The undersigned, Consul Max Obermayer (late United States Consul at Augsburg from 1866 to 1873), happens by chance to be in a position to give you the information desired regarding the deceased in a thoroughly exhaustive manner, and is very willing to do so.

"Baron von Palm was in his youth an officer in the Bavarian army, but was forced on account of his many shady transactions and debts to leave the service. He then betook himself to other parts of Germany, but could not remain long anywhere, because his great frivolity, his love of good living and his debaucheries constantly led him to incur fresh debts and involve himself in shady transactions; so that he was even condemned by the courts and sent to jail.

"After it became impossible for him to remain longer in Germany, he went to Switzerland to enter on a new course of swindling, and he actually succeeded, by false promises and misrepresentations, in persuading the owner of Schloss (Castle) 'Wartensee' to sell him that property, which he forthwith occupied. His stay there, however, was short; not only was he unable to raise the purchase money, but he could not even pay the taxes, and in consequence the property was sold for the account of the creditors and Palm fled to America.

"Whether or not he supported himself in America by frauds is not known here.

"Of property in Europe he possesses not *one cent's* worth; all that may be found among his effects to that purport is *a pure swindle*.

"The only property on which he had any claim whatever, before he went to America, was a share in the Knebelisher inheritance in Trieste. When he left he had already taken much trouble to obtain immediate payment of this amount, but in vain.

"Towards the end of the year 1869, Palm addressed himself to the undersigned in his then capacity of United States Consul, with the request to arrange for the payment to him of his share in the Knebelisher estate mentioned above.

"This request was at once complied with, and, as appears from the enclosed copy of his receipt, the sum of 1,068 Thalers 4/6 = $3247.53 was placed at Palm's disposal by a consular letter of Jan. 21, 1870, and he availed himself thereof through the banking house of Greenbaum Bros. & Co., as appears from his letter to the consulate of Feb. 14, 1870.

"I can only repeat that Palm possessed in Europe neither a single dollar in money, nor a single foot of ground, and that everything which may be found among his papers to the contrary is based solely upon fraudulent representation.

"Palm's only known relatives are the two Baronesses Von T——domiciled in Augsburg, both families in every way most respectable, and to whom Palm in the last year of his residence in Europe caused much scandal and annoyance.

"The above gives all that is to be known about the deceased Palm in the most exhaustive manner, and probably more even than you may have expected.

(Signed) MAX OBERMAYER.

Consul Argentine Republic."

My compliments to M. Papus, Mrs. Britten and her "party."
Palmam qui meruit, ferat !

Chapter XI.

THE FIRST CREMATION
IN AMERICA

Baron de Palm's cremation is the theme of the present chapter. I have related above the circumstances which led to my taking it upon myself and, since it is historically important from having been the first public cremation in the United States and the first where a crematorium was employed, the details should be interesting.

The cremation took place December 6, 1876, at the small inland town of Washington, Washington County, Pennsylvania, more than six months after the body had been packed in carbolised dried clay at New York. It is very easy now to cremate a body, either in America or England, for efficient crematories are available and cremation societies exist, but then it was quite another thing. When I pledged myself to dispose of the Baron's remains as he wished, there were no facilities, no precedents in my country to follow, unless I wished to adopt the Eastern method of open-air burning, which had been once employed, and which, in the then state of public prejudice and the probable refusal of the Sanitary Board to issue a permit, would have been very difficult, not to say dangerous. My only practicable policy was to wait until the chance offered itself. In the year 1816, a Mr. Henry Laurens, a wealthy gentleman of South Carolina, ordered his executors to burn his corpse and compelled his family to acquiesce by the testamentary proviso that they should not inherit his estate unless his wishes were strictly carried out. Accordingly, his body was burnt on his own plantation in the Eastern fashion, on a funeral pyre and in the open air; his family and near relations being present. One other case of the kind is recorded, that of a Mr. Berry, the pyre being used in this instance also, if my memory serves me. But there had been no case of the disposal of human remains in a retort or crematorium constructed for the purpose, and so, as above said, I had no choice but to wait patiently the turn of events. I was not kept long in suspense, for one morning in July or August it was announced in the papers that Dr. F. Julius Le Moyne, an eccentric but very philanthropic physician of Western Pennsylvania, had begun erecting a crematorium for the burning of his own body. I immediately opened correspondence with him, with the result that (Letter of August 16, 1876) he consented that if he should survive the completion of his building, the Baron's corpse should be the first one disposed of. At the time of the funeral the possibility of there being a subsequent cremation was not publicly announced but only whispered about; now, however, it was openly declared, my purpose being to give the authorities fair warning, so that if any legal obstacle existed it might be brought to view. Mr. F. C. Bowman, Counsellor at Law (Barrister), and I were elected a legal Advisory Committee of the original N. Y. Cremation Society, to carefully examine the statutes and report whether or not a person had the right of choosing the way in which to dispose of his body. We found nothing to indicate the contrary; and, in fact, common sense itself would show that if a man has absolute ownership of anything belonging to him it must be of his physical body, and that he is free to say how it shall be disposed of after his death, provided that he chooses no method imperilling the rights or welfare of others. Under my private agreement with the N. Y. Cremation Society, and hence long before Dr. Le Moyne's crematorium was ready, we made formal application to the Brooklyn Board of Health for a permit of removal for cremation, and the Board took counsel's opinion.* It agreed with Mr. Bowman's and mine, and an application, couched in officially prescribed terms, being made later when the crematorium was finished, the permit was duly granted. Thus the first important point was made, and no legal impediment existing, the advocates of cremation had only to meet theological, economic, scientific, and sentimental objections. Dr. Le Moyne and I agreed upon the plan of arranging for a public meeting with addresses from representative men, to take place

---

* Following is the text of the note in question:

NEW YORK CITY, June 5, 1876.

GENTLEMEN:

The undersigned, Executors under the last Will and Testament of Joseph Henry Louis, Baron de Palm, hereby apply for the delivery to them of his body, now lying in the receiving vault of the Lutheran Cemetery: the said body to be removed to a convenient point beyond the city limits and cremated, agreeably to the request of the aforesaid De Palm.

(Signed) H. S. OLCOTT,
H. J. NEWTON.

immediately after the cremation, and for an evening meeting to discuss the merits and demerits of this mode of sepulture. We agreed that each public speaker should confine himself to a special branch of the subject, to avoid repetitions while covering the entire ground.

Owing to the neutral character of the T. S. upon all questions involving different religious opinions, it had been decided that my co-executor and I should carry out this affair in our personal capacities. It was also decided that there should be no further religious ceremonies. Both Dr. Le Moyne and I being strong advocates for cremation, we were fully convinced that the public interest demanded the giving of wide publicity to this event and the invitation of men of science and officers of Boards of Health, to be present and carefully scrutinise the process of reduction of the body by fire. "I agree with you," writes the good old Doctor, "that the addresses are to be confined to the subject of cremation without branching out on other topics, however proper and right they might be in themselves and in their own place. I have never intended or expected that our programme should include any kind of religious service, but should be a strictly scientific and sanitary experiment, looking to a reform in the disposition of a body." The American press, which had made fun of the T. S. for having too much religious ceremony at the Baron's funeral, now abused us for having none at all at his cremation. However, we cared nothing for that, the praise and the blame of the ignorant being equally valueless. Dr. Le Moyne and I wished to settle the following points: (*a*) Whether cremation was a really scientific method of sepulture; (*b*) Whether it was cheaper than burial; (*c*) Whether it offered any repugnant features; (*d*) How long it would take to incinerate a human body. In pursuance of the policy of bold publicity, Mr. Newton and I, as executors, and Dr. Le Moyne, as owner of the crematory, addressed the following invitation to Boards of Health, individual scientists, selected principals and professors of colleges, clergymen and editors:

New York, November, 1876.

Dear Sir: Upon the 6th of December, proximo, at Washington, Pa., will be cremated the body of the late
Joseph Henry Louis, Baron de Palm,
Grand Cross Commander of the Sovereign Order of the Holy Sepulchre at Jerusalem; Knight of St. John of Malta; Prince of the Roman Empire; late Chamberlain to His Majesty the King of Bavaria; Fellow of the Theosophical Society, etc., etc.,

in compliance with wishes expressed to his executors shortly before his decease. This ceremony you are respectfully invited, either in person or by proxy, to attend.

The cremation will be effected in a furnace specially designed for the purpose, and erected by F. Julius Le Moyne, M.D., as an earnest of his preference for this mode of sepulture.

The occasion being one of interest to Science, in its historical, sanitary, and other aspects, the Executors of Baron de Palm have consented that it shall have publicity. This invitation is accordingly sent you in the hope that you may find it convenient to be represented and, in case the general subject of cremation should be discussed, take part in the debate. The University of Pennsylvania, the Washington and Jefferson College, the New York College of Physicians and Surgeons, other institutions of learning, and the Health Boards of Boston, Philadelphia, Washington (D. C.), and other cities, have already signified their intention to send representatives. It is believed that the occasion will draw together a very large number of highly competent and influential scientific observers. Addresses appropriate to the occasion will be delivered.

Washington is a town in Washington County, in the State of Pennsylvania, twenty-five miles West of Pittsburgh, on the Chartiers Valley R. R., and about midway between the cities of Pittsburgh and Wheeling. Trains leave Pittsburgh and Wheeling for Washington at 9 o'clock A.M., and at 5 o'clock P.M., every day except Sunday. The running time is about two hours.

The audience room of the Crematory being quite small, it is necessary that the number intending to be present should be known in advance. You are therefore requested to signify your determination by mail or telegraph to either of the undersigned at your early convenience.

Henry S. Olcott,   }   *Executors under the last Will*

Henry J. Newton,   }   *and Testament of Baron de Palm.*

Address, Box 4335, N. Y. City.

Or, F. Julius Le Moyne, M.D.

Address, Washington, Washington Co., Pa.

. . .

The acceptances were numerous, the public interest being so thoroughly aroused that, as a gentleman (Mr. A. C. Simpson of Pittsburgh, Pa.), who had access to the exchanges of an influential journal, declares, "there is not a journal printed in the United States but has had more or less to say, not only about the Baron's burning, but also about his theosophical religious views" (see *Banner of Light, Jan. 6th, 1887*). One of the most amusing things written about the case was the expression used by Mr. Bromley in a *N. Y. Tribune* editorial, that "Baron de Palm had been principally famous as a corpse."

It was a great responsibility to take upon ourselves, for, if anything went wrong with Dr. Le Moyne's furnace, there would have been a tremendous clamour against us for exposing a human body to the chance of irreverential scientific maltreatment.* However, the object in view being so thoroughly humanitarian, we carried the affair through without flinching. To guard as far as possible against accident, the good Doctor first tested the furnace on a sheep's carcase and, in a letter dated October 26, 1876, he reports to me that it had been "a complete success. A carcase weighing 164 lbs. had

---

* There was one risk to be provided against, viz., the possibility of the corpse being carbonised in the still air of an incandescent clay retort heated up to a temperature of 1500° to 2000°. To obviate this, Dr. Le Moyne, against the protest of his contractor, drilled an air-hole in the iron door of the retort and fitted to it a revolving flap which permitted of the hole being opened or closed at pleasure. In the sheep-cremation experiment this proved so thoroughly efficacious that the contractor was converted to the Doctor's views.

been cremated in six hours and it could have been done in less time." He then had made a skeleton crate, or bier, composed of flat and round half-inch bars, the whole weighing about 40 lbs., in which to lay the corpse for putting it into the retort; and asked me to buy, if possible, a sheet of asbestos cloth to lay over it as a sort of fire-resisting shroud. This was not procurable at the time and I had to devise a substitute. Upon my arrival at the place, one peep into the heated retort showed me that any ordinary cerement about the corpse would be instantaneously consumed and the body be uncovered, so I soaked a bed-sheet with a saturated solution of alum and ventured that. It proved to be perfectly efficacious, and, I believe, has now come into general use.

I need not go into many details about the cremation, since they can all be found in the file of any American journal for the month of December, 1876: still, considering the historical interest which attaches to this first scientific cremation in the United States, a condensed narrative embodying the main facts had better be given by its responsible manager.

The Le Moyne crematorium is (for it still exists) in a small, one-storied brick structure divided into two rooms; the one to the left on entering, a reception-room, the other containing the furnace and retort. Exclusive of the value of the land, it cost Dr. Le Moyne about $1700, or say £340. Everything was very plain, repulsively so, one might say: there was no ornamentation within or without—just simply a practical corpse-incinerator, as unaesthetic as a back-oven. Yet results have shown that it is thoroughly practical and can do its intended work as well as if its walls had been of sculptured marble, its partitions of ornately carved wood, and its doors and furnace poems in modelled bronze. Dr. Le Moyne wrote me that his aim was to give the poor a method of sepulture that would be far cheaper than burial, and offer more safeguards against those violations of graves and those tragedies of premature burial which are unavoidable in the case of the prevailing fashion of sepulture. The theft of the corpses of the late Lord Crawford and Balcarres, of Scotland, and Mr. A. T. Stewart, of New York, not to mention the thousands of body-snatchings for dissectors, prove the reality of the former, while the alleged cutting up of poor Irving Bishop while entranced, and the instances where, upon re-opening a coffin, the body has been found turned and with the flesh of its arms gnawed by the hapless victim in his agony of starvation and suffocation, give a fearful weight to the last-named suggestion. The pecuniary and sanitary ends in view were attained with the Le Moyne furnace, for even this first cremation in America cost us only about ten dollars, and proved that a body could be disposed of without unpleasant concomitants.

Mr. Newton and I reached Washington, Pa., on the 5th December, 1876, with the Baron's remains enclosed in two envelopes—the coffin and an outer case of wood. Dr. Le Moyne and others met us at the station, and the corpse was taken in a hearse to the crematorium, where it lay until the next morning in charge of an attendant, the fireman who stoked the furnace. The fire (of coke) had been lighted at 2 A.M. that day and the retort was already at a dazzling white heat—"hot enough" the stoker said "to melt iron." The mechanical construction of the apparatus was simplicity itself. An arched retort of fire-clay, 8 ft. long by 3 ft. broad and the same in height, for receiving the corpse, was surrounded by a fire-flue communicating with a furnace beneath the retort; which had a tall chimney for making a draft and carrying off the smoke. An opening from the retort into the surrounding hot-air flue allowed the escape into it of the gases and other volatile products of cremation, where they were effectually consumed. A large iron door luted with fire-clay around the frame, was fitted into the front of the retort, and the swinging flap, above described, not only permitted of the introduction of cold air and the making of a slight draught through the retort at will, but also served as a peep-hole through which glimpses could be had of the progress of the cremation from time to time. As the corpse lay upon an open iron crate, swathed in its alum-saturated sheet, in a fire-clay box which effectually separated it from the furnace-fire beneath, it will be seen that there could be none of that horror of roasting human flesh and bursting entrails which makes one shudder at an open-air pyre-burning, while, as all the lighter products of cremation, the gaseous and watery components of a body, were burnt up in the heat-flue that encircled the white-hot retort, there was none of that unpleasant odour that sometimes sickens one who drives past an Indian burning-ghât. The corpse simply dries into nothing save the ashes of its skeleton. When the retort was opened, the morning after De Palm's cremation, there was nothing left of the once tall, stout body save a trail of white powder and some fragments of osseous articulations; the whole weighing but some 6 lbs.*

Our invitation to scientists and sanitary boards was accepted in many cases, and the following gentlemen attended the cremation: Dr. Otterson, of the Brooklyn Board of Health; Dr. Seinke, President of the Queen's County Board of Health; Dr. Richardson, Editor of the (Boston) *Medical Journal*; Dr. Folsom, Secretary of the Boston B. of H.; Prof. Parker, of the University of Pennsylvania; three physicians deputed by the Philadelphia B. of H.; one who represented Lehigh University;

---

* More fortunate than most innovators, I have lived to see several reforms that I helped in the cradle, become world-wide successes. Of these, cremation is one. Public opinion has now, after the lapse of seventeen years reached the point where a law-journal dares print the following praise of cremation:

"There is nothing surer than that in the not far distant future the cremation of dead bodies will be in universal vogue. It is now ascertained that earth-worms convey microbes of disease from cemeteries, and distribute them at their own sweet will. We have never yet been able to comprehend how about thirty thousand putrefying bodies in an acre or two of ground can be anything less than an unmitigated danger to those living within a few miles of their influence. Earth is a pretty good deodoriser, but there are limits to its capacity. If any one has studied the slow process of animal putrefaction; they know how revolting it is, and what a danger arises from the noisome gases which escape. Do the advocates of interment imagine that the gases from thousands of closely-packed corpses escape toward the centre of the earth? If so, they will have to learn that they easily permeate the few feet of earth, and have liberty to roam in the sunlight and poison those who happen to cross the path of their wanderings. Every malignant disease which curses mankind to-day is the admonition of law calling on us to improve our habits and live in accordance with reason, and the only hope of our ever being rid of epidemics is by the slow but sure process of education. The time will come when all putrefactive matter will be rendered harmless by the action of heat."—*Jury.*

Dr. Johnson, of the Wheeling, W. Va. B. of H.; Dr. Asdale, Secretary of the Pittsburgh B. of H.; a number of other medical men attending unofficially; and a swarm of reporters and special correspondents representing all the leading American and some foreign journals. I know it as a fact that the intention of the editors was to have the fullest details telegraphed to their papers, the *N.Y. Herald*, for instance, having ordered its reporter to wire at least three columns; but a tragedy occurred which changed their plans: the Brooklyn Theatre caught fire the same evening and some two hundred people were burnt alive. Thus, the greater cremation weakened the public interest in the lesser one.

The mummified corpse of the Baron being removed from the coffin and laid in the iron crate, enwrapped in my alum-soaked sheet, I sprinkled it with aromatic gums and showered it with choice roses, primroses, smilax, and dwarf palm leaves, and laid sprays of evergreens on the breast and about the head.* From the *N. Y. Times* report I quote the following:

"When all was ready the body was quietly and reverently slid into the retort. There were no religious services, no addresses, no music, no climax, such as would have thrown great solemnity over the occasion. There was not one iota of ceremony. Everything was as business-like as possible. At 8.20 o'clock Dr. Le Moyne, Col. Olcott, Mr. Newton, and Dr. Asdale

---

* Visitors to Adyar Headquarters may see framed and engraved pictures of this and other scenes and details of the cremation taken from the *N. Y. Daily Graphic*.

quietly took their stations on either side of the body, and raising the cradle from the catafalque bore it at once to the crematory retort, and slid it in with its unearthly burden head foremost.

"As the end of the cradle reached the further and hottest end of the furnace, the evergreens round the head burst into a blaze and were quickly consumed, but the flowers and evergreens on the other part of the body remained untouched. The flames formed, as it were, a crown of glory for the dead man."

The description is not quite complete, for as the head of the corpse passed into the superheated retort, the evergreens that surrounded it took fire and a plume of smoke drew out of the door, as if it were a bunch of ostrich feathers, such as a lady wears in her hair at a drawing-room, or a knight of old bore in the crest of his helmet. The iron door of the retort was closed at once after the crate had been thrust in, then bolted and screwed up tight. At first all was dark inside, owing to the steamy vapour from the soaked sheet and the disengagement of smoke from the incinerating gums and plants, but this passed off in a few minutes, and then we could see what is well described by the *Times* correspondent in these words:

"By this time the retort presented the appearance of a radiant solar disk of a very warm rather than brilliant color, and though every flower and evergreen was reduced to a red-hot ash condition, they retained their individual forms, the pointed branches of the evergreens arching over the body. At the same time I could see that the winding-sheet still enfolded the corpse, showing that the solution of alum had fully answered its purpose. This answers one of the avowed objections to cremation—the possibility of indecent exposure of the body. Half an hour later it was plainly evident that the sheet was charred. Around the head the material was blackened and ragged. This was easily accounted for. It appears that in saturating the sheet with the solution of alum, Col. Olcott began at the feet, and that by the time he reached the head the supply was exhausted. All were, however, rejoiced to see that the heat was increasing rapidly."

A REMARKABLE SCENE

"Just at this time a remarkable muscular action of the corpse, almost amounting to a phenomenon, occurred. The left hand, which had been lying by the side of the body, was gradually raised, and three of the fingers pointed upward. Although a little startling at the moment, this action was of course the mere result of intense burning heat producing muscular contraction. At 9.25 o'clock Dr. Otterson tested the draught in the retort by placing a piece of tissue paper over the peephole, some one having suggested that there was not a sufficient amount of oxygen in the retort to produce the necessary combustion. It was found that the draught was ample. At this time the left hand began to fall back slowly into its normal position, while a luminous rose-colored light surrounded the remains, and a slight aromatic odor found its way through the vent-hole of the furnace. An hour later the body presented the appearance of absolute incandescence. It looked red hot. This was the result of the extra firing, the heat of the furnace now being far more unpleasant than it was before, with the mouth of the retort wide open."

CURIOUS EFFECTS NOTICED

"As the retort became hotter the rosy mist I have spoken of assumed a golden tinge, and a very curious effect was noticed in the feet. The soles of the feet were, of course, fully exposed to any one looking through the peep-hole. They gradually assumed a certain transparency, similar in character to the appearance of the hand when the fingers are held between the eye and a brilliant light, but very much more luminous. At 10.40 o'clock Dr. Le Moyne, Col. Olcott, William Harding, and the health officers present entered the furnace-room and held a consultation with closed doors. On re-appearing they announced that the cremation of the body was practically complete. Any one looking into the retort at this moment would think it ought to have been.

"The fiery ordeal through which Shadrach, Meshach, and Abed-nego passed on account of Nebuchadnezzar's golden image must have been a trifling experience compared with what the body of the Baron de Palm had gone through. Some experiments with sheep were made by Dr. Le Moyne when the furnace was completed, but Mr. Dye, the builder of the furnace, says the body was more thoroughly cremated at the end of two hours and forty minutes than the sheep were in five or six hours. About this time I noticed that the body was beginning to subside, that, though incandescent to a degree, it was nevertheless a mere structure of powdery ashes, which the lungs of a child might blow away. The red-hot filmy shroud still covered the remains, and the twigs of evergreens still remained standing, though they had sunk with the subsidence of the body. The feet too had fallen, and all was rapidly becoming one glowing mass of a white light and an intense heat. . . . At 11.12 o'clock Dr. Folsom, Secretary of the Massachusetts Board of Health, made a careful examination, so far as possible, of the retort and its contents. His announcement that 'Incineration is complete beyond all question' was received with universal gratification. The last vestige of the form of a body had disappeared in the general mass."

I have given so much out of the scores of descriptions of the event that might have been quoted, because of the excellence of the narrative and its historical value. Another reason is that it shows how cleanly and esthetical this mode of sepulture is in contrast with that of burial. One feature of cremation must recommend it to the friends of those who die in far-distant lands, *viz.*, that the bodies can be converted into dust, and thus easily, unostentatiously, and unobjectionably be taken home and laid in the family vault or in the cemetery, alongside the remains of relatives—

"Those that he loved so long and sees no more, . . . not dead, but gone before."

On the afternoon of the same day, at the public meeting at the Town Hall, Dr. King, of Pittsburgh discoursed upon the deleterious and poisonous effects of crowded graveyards; Dr. Le Moyne upon the scriptural and practical issues of cremation; President Hays showed its unobjectionable character from the Biblical aspect; Mr. Crumrine expounded its legality; and I contributed a historical retrospect of the subject in ancient and modern times.

The furnace fire was, of course, drawn as soon as the body was thoroughly incinerated, and the draught-hole in the door stopped up, so as to give the retort time to cool down gradually as, if exposed to the cold air, it would inevitably have cracked. Dr. Asdale and I removed the ashes on the following morning and placed them in a Hindu urn that had been given me in New York for the purpose. I took them to town with me and kept them until shortly before our departure for India, when I scattered them over the waters of New York Harbour with an appropriate, yet simple, ceremonial.

And thus it came about that the Theosophical Society not only introduced Hindu philosophical ideas into the United States, but also the Hindu mode of sepulture. Since that first scientific cremation in America, many others, of men, women, and children, have occurred, other crematoriums have been built, and cremation societies have been originated in my country. British prejudice has been so far overcome that Parliament has legalised cremation, a society has been chartered, and it was in its crematorium at Working, near London, that the body of H. P. B. was burnt, agreeably to her verbal and written request.

In the abstract it matters not to me whether my "desire-body" be dropped through the salt sea to its amoebastrewn floor, or left in the snow-locked Himalayan passes, or on the hot sand of the desert; but, if I am to die at home and within reach of friends, I hope that, like those of the Baron de Palm and H. P. B., it may be reduced by fire to harmless dust, and not become a plague or a peril to the living after it has served the purpose of my present *prarâbdha karma*!

Chapter XII.

PUTATIVE AUTHOR OF
"ART MAGIC"

I shall now redeem my promise (See Chap. VIII.) to say something about Mrs. Hardinge Britten's *Art Magic*, and its production. It has been mentioned above that the book was launched almost coincidently with the formation of the Theosophical Society, and the circumstances are a little curious. Mrs. Britten was particularly struck by them, and testifies to her surprise in the following passages in a letter to the *Banner of Light*:

"So amazed and struck was I with the coincidence of *purposes* (*not ideas*), expressed in the inauguration of the Theosophic Society, at which I was present, with some of the purposes, though not the ideas put forth in my friend's work, that I felt it to be my duty to write to the President of that Society, enclose a copy of the still unpublished advertisement, and explain to him that the publication of the book in question anticipated, without concert of action or even personal acquaintance, with the parties concerned, whatever of Cabalistic lore the said Theosophic Society might hereafter evolve."

The coincidence consisted in the fact that the book and our Society simultaneously affirmed the dignity of ancient Occult Science, the existence of Adepts, the reality of, and contrast between, White and Black Magic, the existence of the Astral Light, the swarming of Elemental races in the regions of air, earth, etc., the existence of relations between them and ourselves, and the practicability of bringing them under subjection by certain methods long known and tested. It was, so to say, an attack from two sides simultaneously upon the entrenched camp of Western ignorance and prejudice.

Mrs. Britten affirmed that *Art Magic* had been written by an Adept of her acquaintance, "a life-long and highly honoured friend,"* whom she had first met in Europe, and for whom she was but acting as "Translator" and "Secretary." His name, she said, was Louis, and he was a Chevalier. A piquant Prospectus, calculated to switch the most jaded curiosity to the buying-point, was issued, and the bibliophile's cupidity excited by the announcement that the Author would only permit five hundred copies to be printed, and even then should reserve the right of refusing to sell to those whom he might find undeserving!† This right he seems to have exercised,

---

* *Nineteenth Century Miracles*, p. 437.

† "To prevent his recondite work from falling into the hands of such heterogeneous readers, as he felt confident would misunderstand or perhaps pervert its aims to evil uses." (*Nineteenth Century Miracles*, p. 437.) And in a letter to myself, of September 20, 1875, about her copy of *Cornelius Agrippa* that I wished to borrow, she calls Louis "The Author of the *book of books* (italics hers), just advertised in the *Banner*," and says, "This man would far sooner burn his book and die amidst its ashes than spare it even to a favoured 500."

since, in another published letter to "The Slanderers of *Art Magic*"—whom she calls "little pugs"—she tells us that "some twenty names have been struck off by the Author." The fact that some persons, more cavilling than well-informed, had hinted that her book had been hatched in the Theosophical Society, provoked her wrath to such a degree that, with a goodly show of capitals and italics, she warns all these "whisperers who dare not openly confront us," that she and her husband "had laid the case before an eminent New York legal gentleman," who had instructed them "to say publicly that, free as this country may be to do what each one pleases (*sic*), it is not free enough to allow the circulation of injurious libels"—and that they "had instructed him to proceed immediately against any one who hereafter shall assert, publicly or privately, that the work I have undertaken—namely, to become Secretary to the publication of *Art Magic*, or Mundane, Sub-Mundane and Super-Mundane Spiritualism—has anything to do with Col. Olcott, Madame Blavatsky, the New York Theosophic Society, or any thing or person belonging to either those persons or that Society" (*vide* her letter in *Banner of Light*, of about December, 1875; the cutting in our Scrap-Book being undated, I cannot be more exact).

This clattering of pans was kept up so persistently—she and her husband actually being all the while executive members of the Theosophical Society—that, despite the fancy price put upon the book—$5 for a volume of 467 pages, in pica type heavily leaded, or scarcely as much matter as is contained in a 7s. 6d. volume of the London publishers—her list was soon filled up. I, myself, paid her $10 for two copies, but the one now before me is inscribed, in Mrs. Britten's handwriting, "To Madame Blavatsky, in token of esteem from the Editor [herself] and the Author [?]." The Prospectus stated that, after the edition of 500 copies was run off, the "plates" were to be destroyed. The imprint shows the book to have been "Published by the Author, at New York, America," but it was copyrighted by William Britten, Mrs. Britten's husband, in the year 1876, in due form. The printers were Messrs. Wheat and Cornett, 8 Spruce St., N. Y.

I have given the above details for the following reasons: 1. The book marks a literary epoch in American literature and thought; 2. I suspect that good faith was not kept with the subscribers, myself included; since the work—for which we paid an extravagant price—was printed from type forms, not plates, and Mr. Wheat himself told me that his firm had printed, by Mr. or Mrs. Britten's orders, 1500 instead of 500 copies—the truth of which assertion his account-books should show. I only repeat what her printer told me, and give it for what it may be worth; 3. Because these and other circumstances, among others the internal evidence of the matter and execution of the work, make me doubt the story of the alleged adept authorship. Unquestionably there are fine, even brilliant, passages in it, and a deal that is both instructive and valuable. As a neophyte in this branch of literature, I was, at the time, deeply impressed with it, and so wrote to Mrs. Britten; but the effect of these upon me was afterwards marred by my discovery of the unacknowledged use of text and illustrations from Barrett, Pietro de Abano, Jennings, Layard, and even (see plates facing pp. 193 and 219) from *Frank Leslie's Illustrated Newspaper**; also by the unspiritual personification of God, "the eternal, uncreated, self-existent, and infinite realm of spirit" (p. 31), as a *globe*, that is to say, a limited sphere or central sun related to the universe as our sun is to our solar system; by much bad spelling and grammar; by such mistakes as the making of "Chrishna and Buddha Sakia" heroes of an episode identical with that told of Jesus, *viz.*, a "flight and concealment in Egypt and their return to work miracles," etc.;†

---

* The book-reviewer of *Woodhull and Claflin's Weekly*, a New York journal of the day, in noticing the appearance of *Art Magic* uses very severe language in regard to the reputed Author, whom he identifies, whether justly or unjustly, I cannot say, with Mrs. Britten. The book, he says, "is simply a rehash of books accessible to any student of even limited means, and (which) can be readily found in almost any book-store, or on the shelves of any public library. Ennemoser's *History of Magic*, Howitt's *Supernatural*, Salverte's *Philosophy of Magic*, Hargrave Jennings's *Rosicrucians*, Barrett's *Magus*, Agrippa's *Occult Philosophy*, and a few others are the real sources of this wretched compilation, which is full of bad grammar and worse assumptions. We unhesitatingly assert that there is not a single important statement in the book which cannot be discovered in already-printed books." This is exaggerated censure, for the book does contain passages worthy of Bulwer-Lytton; in fact, one would say they were written by him; and while the forced loans of illustrations and matter from the authors cited are palpable, there is much sound occult doctrine sententiously put, to reward the patient reader.

† But I really must quote, for the edification of the High Priest H. Sumangala, and other unenlightened Buddhist scholars, the whole passage: "The births of these Avatars through the motherhood of a pure Virgin, their lives in infancy threatened by a vengeful king, their flight and concealment in Egypt, their return to work miracles, save, heal and redeem the world, suffer persecution, a violent death, a descent into Hell, and a reappearance as a new-born Saviour, are all items of the Sun God's history, which have already been recited, etc. etc." (*Op. cit.*, p. 60). Fancy Buddha

also by the declaration, which contradicts every canon of Occult Science ever taught in any school, that for becoming a Magican, or Adept, the "first great pre-requisite is a prophetic or naturally *mediumistic organisation*" (p. 160); and that the sitting in "circles," mutual mesmerism, the cultivation of intercourse with spirits of the dead, and the acceptance of spirit guides and controls, are substantial and lawful aids to the development of Adept powers. Whatever Adept may have written this book, most assuredly it became in the process of "editing" and "translating" a panegyric upon mediumship, and upon those phases of it which Mrs. Britten's mediumistic history seems to illustrate. One has but to compare it with *Isis Unveiled*, to see the vast difference in favour of the latter as a trustworthy elucidation of the nature, history, and scientific conditions of magic and magicans, of both the Right and Left Hand paths. To affirm that mediumship and adeptship are compatible, and that any Adept would permit himself to be guided or commanded by departed spirits, is an absurdity

---

Gautama concealed in Egypt, suffering a violent death, and then descending into Hell! And this *Art Magic* is claimed to be the work of an Adept, who had studied in the East, and been initiated in its mystical lore! An Adept, moreover, who, when cholera was raging in London, "adjourned to an observatory"—in London—where he and "a select party—all distinguished for their scientific attainments," made "observations through an immense telescope, constructed under the direction of Lord Rosse" (*Ghost Land*, p. 134, by the same Author); which telescope happens to have never been nearer London than its site at Birr Castle near Parsons Town, Kings County, Ireland! The fact is that the Author of this book seems to have borrowed his (or her) alleged facts—even to the misspelling of the names of Krishna and Sakya Muni—from Chapter I. of Kersey Graves's veracious work, *The World's Sixteen Crucified Saviours*, which H. P. B. satirised so merrily in *Isis Unveiled*.

only equal to that of saying that the North and South Poles are in contact. I remember very well pointing this out to Mrs. Britten upon first reading her book, and that her explanation was not at all convincing. She makes one statement, however, which Spiritualists often deny, but which is doubtless true, nevertheless:

"It is also a significant fact, and one which should commend itself to the attention alike of the physiologist and psychologist, that persons afflicted with scrofula and glandular enlargements, often seem to supply the pabulum which enables spirits to produce manifestations of physical power. Frail, delicate women—persons, too, whose natures are refined, innocent, and pure, but whose glandular system has been attacked by the demon of scrofula, have frequently been found susceptible of becoming the most remarkable instruments for physical demonstrations by spirits."

The author had seen astounding phenomena exhibited by "rugged country girls and stout men of Ireland and North Germany," but careful scrutiny would often reveal in the mediums a tendency to epilepsy, chorea, and functual derangements of the pelvic viscera.

"It is a fact, which we may try to mask, or the acknowledgment of which we [Adepts?] may indignantly protest against, that the existence of remarkable medium powers augurs a want of balance in the system, etc."

Yet (p. 161), we are told that, "To be an 'Adept' was to be able to practise magic, and to do this was either to be a natural prophet [or medium, as above declared], cultured to the strength of a magician, or an individual who had acquired this prophetic [mediumistic?] power and magical strength through discipline." And this *soi-disant* Adept, says (p. 228) that if "the magic of the Orient combine with the magnetic spontaneity of Western Spiritism, we may have a religion, whose foundations laid in science and stretching away to the heavens in inspiration, will revolutionise the opinions of ages and establish on earth the reign of the true Spiritual Kingdom."

But this will suffice to show what manner of Adept is the reported Author of *Art Magic*, and what weight should be given to Mrs. Britten's current sarcasms and pifflings against H. P. B., her teachings, and the pretensions of the Theosophical Society which she helped us found. In the early days, she declared her acquaintanceship with us "a great privilege," her membership something to be proud of, and her office in the T. S. "a mark of distinction" [Letter on "The Slanderers of *Art Magic*" in *Spiritual Scientist*]; and, as late as the year 1881 or 1882, she calls herself, in a letter introducing Professor J. Smyth, of Sydney, to H. P. B., her unchanged friend, for whom she ever feels "the old time affection"; yet she has been anything but that of later years; and it is her attitude towards Theosophy which has created the necessity for my recording these several reminiscences, both in the interest of history, and for the profit of her friends and herself.

The author, we are told, had had "more than forty years" of occult experience (p. 166), after having "learned the truth" of magical science; so that he might reasonably be taken as at least fifty or sixty years of age when *Art Magic* was published; yet, from an alleged portrait of him, obligingly sent me by Mrs. Britten from Boston to New York, in 1876, for examination,* he seems a young man of about twenty-five. Moreover, all those years of profound study ought to have made his face embody the acquired masculine majesty one finds in the countenance of a true Yogi or Mahatma; whereas in this portrait, of a pretty man with mutton-chop whiskers, the face has the vapid weakness of a "sick sensitive," of a fashionable lady-killer, or, as many say who have seen it, that of a wax figure such as the Parisian barber sets in his shop window to display his wigs and whiskers upon. One who has ever been face to face with a real Adept, would be forced by this effeminate dawdler's countenance to suspect that either Mrs. Britten had, *faute de mieux*, shown a bogus portrait of the real author, or that the book was written by no "Chevalier Louis" at all.

The portrait is far less interesting in itself than in its relation to a remarkable phenomenon, which H. P. B. did upon the provocation of a French lady, a Spiritualist, then a guest at our New York Headquarters. Her name was Mlle. Pauline Liebert, and her place of residence at Leavenworth, in Kansas, a distant Western State. H. P. B. had known her in former years at Paris, where she took the deepest interest in "spirit photography." She believed herself to be under the spiritual guardianship of Napoleon Bonaparte, and that she possessed the power of conferring upon a photographer the mediumistic faculty of taking the portraits of the spirit-friends of living sitters! When she read in the papers H. P. B.'s first letters about

---

* Her conditions were that I was to show it only to those living in our house and then return it to her.

Dr. Beard and the phenomena of the Eddy family, she wrote to her and told about the wonderful success she had had in Kansas, St. Louis, and elsewhere among the photographers, in getting spirit portraits. Mr. H. J. Newton, the Treasurer of the T. S., was a distinguished and scientific amateur photographer, and had fitted up a very excellent experimental gallery in his own house. Upon hearing from me about Mlle. Liebert's pretensions, he asked us to invite her to pay us a visit and give him sittings, with a view to testing her claims in the interest of science. H. P. B. complied, and the eccentric lady came to New York at our expense, and was our guest during several months. The erudite calumniator of the *Carrier Dove*, whom I have above mentioned in another connection, published (*C. D.*, vol. viii., 298) an alleged assertion of Mlle. Liebert to himself, that H. P. B.'s phenomena were tricks to delude me along with others, that her pictures were bought or prepared in advance and foisted on us as instantaneous productions, etc., etc.; in short, a tissue of falsehoods. He parades her as an intelligent person, but the fact is that she was credulity personified, so far as her spiritualistic photographs were concerned. Upon her arrival at New York, she began a course of photographic sittings at Mr. Newton's house, confidently prognosticating that she should enable him to get genuine spirit portraits. Mr. Newton patiently went on with the trial, until, with the fiftieth sitting, and no result, his patience gave way and he stopped. Mlle. Liebert tried to account for her failure by saying that the "magnetism" of Mr. Newton's private gallery was not congenial to the spirits; notwithstanding the fact that he was the foremost Spiritualist of New York City, the president of the largest society of the kind. With Mr. Newton's obliging help, I then arranged for a fresh series of trials in the photographic gallery of Bellevue Hospital, the manager of which, Mr. Mason, was a man of scientific training, a member of the Photographic Section of the American Institute, and anxious to test Mlle. Liebert's pretensions in a sympathetic spirit. His success was no better than Mr. Newton's, despite seventy-five careful trials under the French lady's prescribed precautions against failure. All these weeks and months that the two series of experiments were going on, Mlle. Liebert lived with us, and almost every evening she used to bring out and lovingly con over a handful of so-called spirit photographs that she had collected in divers places. The ignominious collapse of her hopes as to the test trials in progress seemed to make her dote upon what the poor deluded creature regarded as past successes, and it was an amusing study to watch her face while handling her thumb-worn *pièces de conviction*. H. P. B. had naturally but small pity for intellectual weaklings, especially little for the stubborn dupes of mediumistic trickery, and she often poured out the vials of her wrath upon the—as she called her—purblind old maid. One cold evening (Dec. 1, 1875), after a fresh day of failures at Mr. Mason's laboratory, Mlle. Liebert was, as usual, shuffling over her grimy photographs, sighing and arching her eyebrows into a despairing expression, when H. P. B. burst out: "Why will you persist in this folly? Can't you see that all those photographs in your hand were swindles on you by photographers who did them to rob you of your money? You have had every possible chance now to prove your pretended power—more than one hundred chances have been given you, and you have not been able to do the least thing. Where is your pretended guide, Napoleon, and the other sweet angels of Summerland; why don't they come and help you? Pshaw! it makes me sick to see such credulity. Now see here: I can make a 'spirit picture' whenever I like and—of anybody I like. You don't believe it, eh? Well, I shall prove it on the spot!" She hunted up a piece of card-board, cut it to the size of a cabinet photograph, and then asked Mlle. Liebert whose portrait she wished. "Do you want me to make your Napoleon?" she asked. "No," said Mlle. L., "please make for me the picture of that beautiful M. Louis." H. P. B. burst into a scornful laugh, because, by Mrs. Britten's request, I had returned to her through the post the Louis portrait three days previously, and it being by that time in Boston, 250 miles away, the trap set by the French lady was but too evident. "Ah!" said H. P. B., "you thought you could catch me, but now see!" She laid the prepared card on the table before Mlle. Liebert and myself, rubbed the palm of her hand over it three or four times, turned it over, and lo! on the under side we saw (as we then thought) a fac-simile of the Louis portrait. In a cloudy background at both sides of the face were grinning elemental sprites, and above the head a shadowy hand with the index-finger pointing downward. I never saw amazement more strongly depicted on a human face than it was upon Mlle. Liebert's at that moment. She gazed in positive terror at the mysterious card, and presently burst into tears and hurried out of the room with it in her hand, while H. P. B. and I went into fits of laughter. After a half hour she returned, gave me the picture, and on retiring for the night I placed it as a book-mark in a volume I was reading in my own apartment. On the back I noted the date and the names of the three witnesses. The next morning I found that the picture had quite faded out, all save the name "Louis," written at the bottom in imitation of the original: the writing, a precipitation made simultaneously with the portrait and the elves in the background. That was a curious fact—that one part of a precipitated picture should remain visible, while all the rest had disappeared, and I cannot explain it. I locked it up in my drawer, and Mr. Judge, dropping in a day or two later, or, perhaps, the same evening, I told him the story and showed him the defaced card; whereupon he asked H. P. B. to cause the portrait to re-appear and to "fix" it. It needed but a moment for to lay the card again face down upon the table, cover it with her hand, and reproduce the picture as it had been. He took it by her permission, and kept it until we met him at Paris in 1884, when—as he had fortunately brought it with him—I begged it of him for the Adyar Library. From Paris I crossed over to London, and, going one evening to dine with my friend Stainton Moses, he showed me his collection of mediumistic curios, *among others, the very original of the Louis picture, which I had returned to Mrs. Britten by post from New York to Boston in 1876!* On the back was written "M. A. Oxon, March 1, 1877, from the Author of *Art Magic*, and *Ghostland*." The next day I brought and showed Stainton Moses the H. P. B. copy, and he kindly gave me the original. Thus, after the lapse of eight years, both came back to my hand. Upon comparing them, we found so many differences as to show conclusively that the one was not a duplicate of the other. To begin with the faces look in opposite directions, as though the one were the enlarged and somewhat deranged reflection of the other in a mirror. When I asked H. P. B. the reason for this, she said that all things on the objective plane have their images reversed in the astral light, and that she simply transferred to paper the astral reflection of the Louis picture *as she saw it*: the minuteness of its accuracy would depend upon the exactness of her clairvoyant perception. Applying this test to these two pictures, we find that there are material differences in horizontal and vertical measurements throughout, as well as in the curl of the hair and beard and the outlines of the dress: the "Louis" signatures also vary in all details while preserving a general resemblance. When the copy was precipitated, the tint was infused into the surface of the whole card as a sort of pigmentous blur, just as the background still remains, and H. P. B. touched up some of the main lines with a lead-pencil; to the artistic improvement of the picture, but to its detriment as an exhibit of occult photography.

I am fortunately able to cite an account, hitherto unpublished, by Mrs. Britten herself, of the incidents connected with the taking of the portrait. It is given in a letter to Lady Caithness, Duchesse de Pomar, who copied it out at my request:

"I now enclose you a faint shadow of our 'archimagus.' I deeply regret my inability to send you anything better, for, indeed, his face is wonderfully beautiful. He has raven hair, superb eyes, a very fine complexion, and the sweetest smile imaginable—you may judge therefore what a poor representation this picture forms of him. It only resembles him as he lay

fainting in the carriage* when we left the photographer's.
There was a very curious incident about this picture. When
the negative was finished, I insisted on the photographer
making me a proof, then and there, in order that I might judge
of its resemblance; that proof I took away with us, requesting
my friend, who is a fine artist, to make me an enlarged crayon
sketch for myself—this he agreed to do. I wondered why the
photographer did not send me any more pictures, and waited
for many days for them. I knew it only represented my poor
sufferer as he then was, not as he generally appears, still he
entreated me to send it as it was for his *Madonna*—as he calls
you—because he had made such a great exertion to have it
taken, and only for you. Still he did not come. The photographer might have been prevented from executing the pictures,
I thought, by bad weather. At last I called on him—when, with
a strange and singular air of reluctance, he acknowledged that
almost immediately after we had left, the picture on the negative FADED ENTIRELY OUT, leaving only some very faint
indications or marks, which looked like Cabalistic characters.
He was very angry about it, complained that these spiritualists were always playing tricks when they came for pictures,
and he could not bear to have anything to do with them. I
demanded to see the negative which he reluctantly showed
me. He then, at my request, developed the plate [Note above
that it had already been developed and printed from—H. S. O.],
but the figures or signs are so faint that they are scarcely

---

* A fainting adept would indeed be a novelty in the East!

perceptible. He added, in a frightened way, that he 'did not want the gentleman to come again, for he didn't think he was a mortal man anyway.'

"I was terribly disappointed, but had no resource but submission. I had half resolved to have my miniature copied, when I received from Cuba, where Louis went first, the chalk-drawing he has made from the proof. He added to it a statement that the proof he took with him *has most strangely faded out,* leaving nothing but a faint indication of some Cabalistic signs too faint to make out.

"Is not that very strange? Determined not to be balked, I have had the chalk-drawing photographed, and though it is somewhat inferior in softness to the proof, it is an equally good resemblance of our invalid. What momentous times we are living in!"

Momentous, indeed, when Adepts of forty years' experience are made to look like a school-girl's hero, and photographic negatives are twice developed, each time giving a different print!

Chapter XIII.

"ISIS UNVEILED"

Of the writing of *Isis Unveiled*, let us see what reminiscences memory can bring out of the darkroom where her imperishable negatives are kept.

If any book could ever have been said to make an epoch, this one could. Its effects have been as important in one way as those of Darwin's first great work have been in another: both were tidal waves in modern thought, and each tended to sweep away theological crudities and replace the belief in miracle with the belief in natural law. And yet nothing could have been more commonplace and unostentatious than the beginning of *Isis*. One day in the Summer of 1875, H. P. B. showed me some sheets of manuscript which she had written, and said: "I wrote this last night 'by order,' but what the deuce it is to be I don't know. Perhaps it is for a newspaper article, perhaps for a book, perhaps for nothing: anyhow, I did as I was ordered." And she put it away in a drawer, and nothing more was said about it for some time. But in the month of September—if my memory serves—she went to Syracuse

(N.Y.), on a visit to her new friends, Professor and Mrs. Corson, of Cornell University, and the work went on. She wrote me that it was to be a book on the history and philosophy of the Eastern Schools and their relations with those of our own times. She said she was writing about things she had never studied and making quotations from books she had never read in all her life: that, to test her accuracy, Prof. Corson had compared her quotations with classical works in the University Library, and had found her to be right. Upon her return to town, she was not very industrious in this affair, but wrote only spasmodically, and the same may be said as to the epoch of her Philadelphia residence, but a month or two after the formation of the Theosophical Society, she and I took two suites of rooms at 433 West 34th St., she on the first and I on the second floor, and thenceforward the writing of *Isis* went on without break or interruption until its completion in the year 1877. In her whole life she had not done a tithe of such literary labour, yet I never knew even a managing daily journalist who could be compared with her for dogged endurance or tireless working capacity. From morning till night she would be at her desk, and it was seldom that either of us got to bed before 2 o'clock A.M. During the daytime I had my professional duties to attend to, but always, after an early dinner we would settle down together to our big writing-table and work, as if for dear life, until bodily fatigue would compel us to stop. What an experience! The education of an ordinary life-time of reading and thinking was, for me, crowded and compressed into this period of less than two years. I did not merely serve her as an amanuensis or a proof-reader, but she made me a collaborator; she caused me to utilise—it almost seemed—everything I had ever read or thought, and stimulated my brain to think out new problems that she put me in respect to occultism and metaphysics, which my education had not led me up to, and which I only came to grasp as my intuition developed under this forcing process. She worked on no fixed plan, but ideas came streaming through her mind like a perennial spring which is ever overflowing its brim. Now she would be writing upon Brahma, anon upon Babinet's electrical "meteor-cat"; one moment she would be reverentially quoting from Porphyrios, the next from a daily newspaper or some modern pamphlet that I had just brought home; she would be adoring the perfections of the ideal Adept, but diverge for an instant to thwack Professor Tyndall or some other pet aversion of hers, with her critical cudgel. Higgledy-piggledy it came, in a ceaseless rivulet, each paragraph complete in itself and capable of being excised without harm to its predecessor or successor. Even as it stands now, and after all its numerous re-castings, an examination of the wondrous book will show this to be the case.

If she had no plan, despite all her knowledge, does not that go to prove that the work was not of her own conception; that she was but the channel through which this tide of fresh, vital essence was being poured into the stagnant pool of modern spiritual thought? As a part of my educational training she would ask me to write something about some special subject, perhaps suggesting the salient points that should be brought in, perhaps just leaving me to do the best I could with my own intuitions. When I had finished, if it did not suit her, she would usually resort to strong language, and call me some of the pet names that are apt to provoke the homicidal impulse; but if I prepared to tear up my unlucky composition, she would snatch it from me and lay it by for subsequent use elsewhere, after a bit of trimming, and I would try again. Her own manuscript was often a sight to behold; cut and patched, re-cut and re-pasted, until if one held a page of it to the light, it would be seen to consist of, perhaps, six, or eight, or ten slips cut from other pages, pasted together, and the text joined by interlined words or sentences. She became so dexterous in this work that she used often to humorously vaunt her skill to friends who might be present. Our books of reference sometimes suffered in the process, for her pasting was frequently done on their open pages, and volumes are not wanting in the Adyar Headquarters and London libraries which bear the marks to this day.

From the date of her first appearance in the *Daily Graphic*, in 1874, throughout her American career, she was besieged by visitors, and if among them there chanced to be any who had some special knowledge of any particular thing cognate to her field of work, she invariably drew him out, and, if possible, got him to write down his views or reminiscences for insertion in her book. Among examples of this sort are Mr. O'Sullivan's account of a magical séance in Paris, Mr. Rawson's interesting sketch of the secret initiations of the Lebanon Druses, Dr. Alexander Wilder's numerous notes and text paragraphs in the Introduction and throughout both volumes, and others which add so much to the value and interest of the work. I have known a Jewish Rabbi pass hours and whole evenings in

her company, discussing the Kabballa, and have heard him
say to her that, although he had studied the secret science of
his religion for thirty years, she had taught him things he had
not even dreamed of, and thrown a clear light upon passages
which not even his best teachers had understood. Whence did
she get this knowledge? That she had it, was unmistakable;
whence did she get it? Not from her governesses in Russia; not
from any source known to her family or most intimate friends;
not on the steamships or railways she had been haunting in
her world-rambles since her fifteenth year; not in any college
or university, for she never matriculated at either; not in the
huge libraries of the world. To judge from her conversation
and habits before she took up this monster literary task, she
had not learnt it at all, whether from one source or another;
but when she needed it she had it, and in her better moments
of inspiration—if the term be admissible—she astonished the
most erudite by her learning quite as much as she dazzled all
present by her eloquence and delighted them by her wit and
humorous raillery.

One might fancy, upon seeing the numerous quotations in
Isis Unveiled that she had written it in an alcove of the British
Museum or of the Astor Library in New York. The fact is,
however, that our whole working library scarcely comprised
one hundred books of reference. Now and again single vol-
umes would be brought her by Mr. Sotheran, Mr. Marble or
other friends, and, latterly, she borrowed a few of Mr. Bouton.
Of some books she made great use—for example, King's
Gnostics; Jennings' *Rosicrucians*; Dunlop's *Sod* and *Spirit
History of Man*; Moor's *Hindu Pantheon*; Des Mousseaux's

furious attacks on Magic, Mesmerism, Spiritualism, etc., all of which he denounced as the Devil; Eliphas Lévi's various works; Jacolliot's twenty-seven volumes; Max Muller's, Huxley's, Tyndall's, Herbert Spencer's works, and those of many other authors of greater or less repute: yet not to exceed the hundred, I should say. Then what books *did* she consult, and what library had she access to? Mr. W. H. Burr asked Dr. Wilder in an open letter to the *Truth-seeker* whether the rumour was true that *he* had written *Isis* for H. P. B.; to which our beloved old friend would truthfully reply that it was a false rumour, and that he had done as much for H. P. B. as I have above stated, had given her much excellent advice, and had, for a consideration, prepared the very copious Index of some fifty pages, from advanced plate-proofs sent him for the purpose. That is all. And equally baseless is the oft-repeated tale that I wrote the book and she touched it up: it was quite the other way about. I corrected every page of her manuscript several times, and every page of the proofs; wrote many paragraphs for her, often merely embodying her ideas that she could not then (some fifteen years before her death and anterior to almost her whole career as a writer of English literature) frame to her liking in English; helped her to find out quotations, and did other purely auxiliary work: the book is hers alone, so far as personalities on this plane of manifestation are concerned, and she must take all the praise and the blame that it deserves. She made the epoch with her book, and, in making it, made me—her pupil and auxiliary—as fit as I may have been found to do Theosophical work during these past twenty years. Then, whence did H. P. B. draw the materials which compose *Isis*, and which cannot be traced to accessible literary sources of quotation? *From the Astral Light*, and, by her soul-senses, from her Teachers—the "Brothers," "Adepts," "Sages," "Masters," as they have been variously called. How do I know it? By working two years with her on *Isis* and many more years on other literary work.

To watch her at work was a rare and never-to-be-forgotten experience. We sat at opposite sides of one big table usually, and I could see her every movement. Her pen would be flying over the page, when she would suddenly stop, look out into space with the vacant eye of the clairvoyant seer, shorten her vision as though to look at something held invisibly in the air before her, and begin copying on her paper what she saw. The quotation finished, her eyes would resume their natural expression, and she would go on writing until again stopped by a similar interruption. I remember well two instances when I, also, was able to see and even handle books from whose astral duplicates she had copied quotations into her manuscript, and which she was obliged to "materialise" for me, to refer to when reading the proofs, as I refused to pass the pages for the "strike-off" unless my doubts as to the accuracy of her copy were satisfactory. One of these was a French work on physiology and psychology; the other, also by a French author, upon some branch of neurology. The first was in two volumes, bound in half calf, the other in pamphlet wrapper. It was when we were living at 302 West 47th street— the once-famous "Lamasery," and the executive headquarters of the Theosophical Society. I said: "I cannot pass this quotation, for I am sure it cannot read as you have it." She said: "Oh don't bother; it's right; let it pass." I refused, until finally she said: "Well, keep still a minute and I'll try to get it." The far-away look came into her eyes, and presently she pointed to a far corner of the room, to an *étagère* on which were kept some curios, and in a hollow voice said: "There!" and then came to herself again. "There, there; go look for it over there!" I went, and found the two volumes wanted, which, to my knowledge, had not been in the house until that very moment. I compared the text with H. P. B.'s quotation, showed her that I was right in my suspicions as to the error, made the proof correction and then, at her request, returned the two volumes to the place on the *étagère* from which I had taken them. I resumed my seat and work, and when, after awhile, I looked again in that direction, the books had disappeared! After my telling this (absolutely true) story, ignorant sceptics are free to doubt my sanity; I hope it may do them good. The same thing happened in the case of the *apport* of the other book, but this one remained, and is in our possession at the present time.

The "copy" turned off by H. P. B. presented the most marked dissemblances at different times. While the handwriting bore one peculiar character throughout, so that one familiar with her writing would always be able to detect any given page as H. P. B.'s, yet, when examined carefully, one discovered at least three or four variations of the one style, and each of these persistent for pages together, when it would give place to some other of the caligraphic variants. That is to say, there would not often—never, as I now remember—be more than two of the styles on the same page, and even two only when the style which had been running through the work of, perhaps, a whole evening or half an evening, would suddenly give place to one of the other styles which would, in its turn, run through the rest of an evening, or the next whole evening, or the morning's "copy." One of these H. P. B. handwritings was very small, but plain; one bold and free; another plain, of medium size, and very legible; and one scratchy and hard to read, with its queer, foreign-shaped a's and x's and e's. There was also the greatest possible difference in the English of these various styles. Sometimes I would have to make several corrections in each line, while at others I could pass many pages with scarcely a fault of idiom or spelling to correct. Most perfect of all were the manuscripts which were written for her while she was sleeping. The beginning of the chapter on the civilisation of Ancient Egypt (vol. i., chap. xiv.) is an illustration. We had stopped work the evening before at about 2 A.M. as usual, both too tired to stop for our usual smoke and chat before parting; she almost fell asleep in her chair while I was bidding her good-night, so I hurried off to my bedroom. The next morning, when I came down after my breakfast, she showed me a pile of at least thirty or forty pages of beautifully written H. P. B. manuscript, which, she said, she had had written for her by——well, a Master, whose name has never yet been degraded like some others. It was perfect in every respect, and went to the printers without revision.

Now it was a curious fact that each change in the H. P. B. manuscript would be preceded, either by her leaving the room for a moment or two, or by her going off into the trance or abstracted state, when her lifeless eyes would be looking beyond me into space, as it were, and returning to the normal waking state almost immediately. And there would also be a distinct change of personality, or rather personal peculiarities, in gait, vocal expression, vivacity of manner, and, above all, in temper. The reader of her *Caves and Jungles of Hindustan* remembers how the whirling pythoness would rush out from time to time and return under the control, as alleged, of a different goddess? It was just like that—bar the sorcery and the vertiginous dancing—with H. P. B.: she would leave the room one person and anon return to it another. Not another as to visible change of physical body, but another as to tricks of motion, speech, and manners; with different mental brightness, different views of things, different command of English orthography, idiom, and grammar, and different—very, *very* different command over her temper; which, at its sunniest, was almost angelic, at its worst, the opposite. Sometimes my most stupid incapacity to frame in writing the ideas she wished me to put would be passed over with benevolent patience; at others, for perhaps the slightest of errors, she would seem ready to explode with rage and annihilate me on the spot! These accesses of violence were, no doubt, at times, explicable by her state of health, and hence quite normal; but this theory would not, in the least, suffice to account for some of her tantrums. Sinnett admirably describes her in a private letter as a mystic combination of a goddess and a Tartar, and in noticing her behaviour in these different moods, says:*

* *Incidents in the life of Madame Blavatsky*, p. 224.

"She certainly had none of the superficial attributes one might have expected in a spiritual teacher; and how she could, at the same time, be philosopher enough to have given up the world for the sake of spiritual advancement, and yet be capable of going into frenzies of passion about trivial annoyances, was a profound mystery to us for a long while, etc." Yet, upon the theory that when her body was occupied by a sage it would be forced to act with a sage's tranquillity, and when not, not, the puzzle is solved. Her ever-beloved aunt, Mme. N. A. F., who loved her, and whom she loved passionately to her dying day, wrote Mr. Sinnett that her strange excitability of temperament, still one of her most marked characteristics, was already manifest in her earliest youth. Even then she was liable to ungovernable fits of passion, and showed a deep-rooted disposition to rebel against every kind of authority or control. "... The slightest contradiction brought on an outburst of passion, often a fit of convulsions." She has herself described in a family letter (*Op. cit., p.* 205) her psychical experience while writing her book:

"When I wrote *Isis* I wrote it so easily, that it was certainly no labour, but a real pleasure. Why should I be praised for it? Whenever I am *told* to write, I sit down and obey, and then I can write easily upon almost anything—metaphysics, psychology, philosophy, ancient religions, zoology, natural sciences, or what not. I never put myself the question: 'Can I write on this subject?' ... or, 'am I equal to the task?' but I simply sit down and *write*. Why? Because *somebody who knows all* dictates to me. My *Master*, and occasionally others whom I knew on my travels years ago. Please do not imagine I have lost my senses. I have hinted to you before now about them . . . and I tell you candidly, that whenever I write upon a subject I know little or nothing of, I address myself to *them*, and one of them inspires me, *i.e.*, he allows me to simply copy what I write from manuscripts, and even printed matter that pass before my eyes, in the air, during which process I have never been *unconscious* one single instant."

She once wrote her sister Vera about the same subject—the manner of her writing:

"You may disbelieve me, but I tell you that in saying this I speak but the truth; I am solely occupied, not with writing *Isis*, but with Isis herself. I live in a kind of permanent enchantment, a life of visions and sights, with open eyes, and no chance whatever to deceive my senses! I sit and watch the fair goddess constantly. And as she displays before me the secret meaning of her long-lost *secrets*, and the veil becoming with every hour thinner and more transparent, gradually falls off before my eyes, I hold my breath and can hardly trust to my senses! . . . For several years, in order not to forget what I have learned elsewhere, I have been made to have permanently before my eyes all that I need to see. Thus, night and day, the images of the past are ever marshalled before my inner eye. Slowly, and gliding silently like images in an enchanted panorama, centuries after centuries appear before me . . . and I am made to connect these epochs with certain historical events, and I *know* there can be no mistake. Races and nations, countries and cities, emerge during some former century, then fade out and disappear during some other one, the precise date of which I am then told by . . . Hoary antiquity gives room to historical periods; myths are explained by real events and personages who have really existed; and every important, and often unimportant event, every revolution, a new leaf turned in the book of life of nations—with its incipient course and subsequent natural results—remains photographed in my mind as though impressed in indelible colours. . . . When I think and watch my thoughts, they appear to me as though they were like those little bits of wood of various shapes and colours, in the game known as the *casse-tête:* I pick them up one by one, and try to make them fit each other, first taking one, then putting it aside until I find its match, and finally there always comes out in the end something geometrically correct . . . *I certainly refuse point-blank to attribute it to my own knowledge or memory,* for I could never arrive alone at either such premises or conclusions . . . I tell you seriously *I am helped.* And he who helps me is my GURU." (*Op. cit.,* 207).

She tells her aunt that during her Master's absence on some other occupation—

"He awakens in me, his substitute in knowledge . . . At such times it is no more *I* who write, but my inner Ego, my *'luminous-self,'* who thinks and writes for me. Only see . . . you who know me. When was I ever so learned as to write such things? Whence was all this knowledge?"

Readers, whose taste leads them to probe such unique psychical problems as this to the bottom, should not fail to compare the above explanations that she gives of her states of consciousness, with a series of letters to her family that was begun in the *Path magazine* (N. Y. 144 Madison Ave.) for December, 1894. In those she plainly admits that her body

was occupied at such times, and the literary work done by foreign entities who taught me through her lips and gave out
knowledge of which she herself did not possess even a glim-
mering in her normal state.

Taken literally, as it reads, this explanation is hardly satisfactory; for, if the disjointed thought-bits of her psychical
casse-tête always fitted together so as to make her puzzle-map
strictly geometrical, then her literary work should be free
from errors, and her materials run together into an orderly
scheme of logical and literary sequence. Needless to say, the
opposite is the case; and that, even as *Isis Unveiled* came off
the press of Trow, after Bouton had spent above $600 for the
corrections and alterations that she had made in galley, page,
and electroplate proofs,* it was, and to this day is, without a
definite literary plan. Volume I. professes to be confined to
questions of Science, Volume II. to those of Religion, yet there
are many portions in each volume that belong in the other;
and Miss Kislingbury, who sketched out the Table of Contents
of Vol. II. on the evening when I was sketching out that of
Vol. I., can testify to the difficulty we had in tracing the features of a plan for each of our respective volumes.

---

* He writes me, May 17th, 1887, "the alterations have already cost $280.80,
and at that rate, by the time the book appears it will be handicapped with
such fearful expense that each copy of the first 1000 will cost a great deal
more than we shall get for it, a very discouraging state of affairs to begin
with. The cost of composition of the first volume alone (with stereotyping)
amounts to $1,359.69, and this for one volume alone, mind you, *without
paper, press work or binding!* Yours truly, J. W. Bouton." Not only did she
make endless corrections in the types, but even after the plates were cast,
she had them cut to transpose the old matter and insert new things that
occurred to her or that she had come across in her reading.

Then, again, when the publisher peremptorily refused to put any more capital into the venture, we had prepared almost enough additional MS. to make a third volume, and this was ruthlessly destroyed before we left America; H. P. B. not dreaming that she should ever want to utilise it in India, and the *Theosophist*, *Secret Doctrine*, and her other subsequent literary productions, not even being thought of. How often she and I mingled our regrets that all that valuable material had been so thoughtlessly wasted!

We had laboured at the book for several months and had turned out 870-odd pages of manuscript when, one evening, she put me the question whether, to oblige——(our "*Pârama-guru*"), I would consent to begin all over again! I well remember the shock it gave me to think that all those weeks of hard labour, of psychical thunder-storms and head-splitting archaeological conundrums, were to count—as I, in my blind-puppy ignorance, imagined—for nothing. However, as my love and reverence and gratitude to this Master, and all the Masters, for giving me the privilege of sharing in their work was without limits, I consented, and at it we went again. Well for me, was it, that I did; for, having proved my steadfastness of purpose and my loyalty to H. P. B., I got ample spiritual reward. Principles were explained to me, multifarious illustrations given in the way of psychical phenomena, I was helped to make experiments for myself, was made to know and to profit by acquaintance with various Adepts, and, generally, to fit myself—so far as my ingrained stubbornness and practical worldly self-sufficiency would permit—for the then unsuspected future of public work that has since become a matter of history. People have often thought it very strange, in fact incomprehensible, that, of all those who have helped in this Theosophical movement, often at the heaviest self-sacrifice, I should have been the only one so favoured with personal experiences of and with the Mahátmas that the fact of their existence is a matter of as actual knowledge as the existence of my own relatives or intimate friends. I cannot account for it myself. I know what I know, but not why many of my colleagues do not know as much. As it stands, many people have told me that they pin their faith in the Mahátmas upon my unchanging and unimpeached personal testimony, which supplements the statements of H. P. B. Probably I was so blessed because I had to launch the ship "Theosophy" with H. P. B. for H. P. B.'s Masters, and to steer it through many maelstroms and cyclones, when nothing short of actual knowledge of the sound basis of our movement would have influenced me to stick to my post.

Let us next attempt to analyse the mental state of H. P. B. while writing her book, and see if any known hypothesis will give us the clue to those marked differences in personality, handwriting, and mentality above mentioned. The task is one of so delicate and complicated a nature that I doubt if such a psychical problem, save Shakespeare's, has ever been presented before; and I think that, after reading what I have to say, my fellow-students in Theosophy and Occult Science will concur in this opinion.

Chapter XIV.

DIFFERENT HYPOTHESES

While I may well despair of proving the exact degree in which the complex personality, H. P. B., may be said to have written *Isis Unveiled*, yet I think it clear and beyond dispute that she digested and assimilated all the material, making it her own and fitting it into her book like bits of stone into a mosaic. As Prof. Wilder recently wrote me: "Few books are absolutely original. That these volumes were in her peculiar style is as plain as can well be. People only demand that Mr. Henry Ward Beecher's principle be applied: 'When I eat chicken, I do not become chicken; the chicken becomes me!'"

Nothing would be easier than to shirk the whole inquiry, and chime in with those who simply declare H. P. B. to have been, so to say, divinely inspired, and guiltless of errors, contradictions, exaggerations, or limitations; but I cannot do this, having so well known her, and the truth only will serve me. As for shrinking from the closest inquiry into her occult and mental gifts, it is not to be thought of. I, certainly, am not going to shut my eyes to facts, and thus abandon her and her work to those who would rejoice in destroying the pedestal upon which we ought to place her, and degrading her into the dangerous impostor which the leaders of the S. P. R. tried to show her to be. The very question of the alleged resemblances between her own handwriting and that of a Master—one of the counts in their indictment—properly comes within the lines of our present discussion of the MS. of *Isis Unveiled*.

One cannot fail to see, after reflection, that as regards the case in point, at least these several hypotheses must be considered:

1. Was the book written by H. P. B. entirely as an independent, conscientious amanuensis, from the dictation of a Master?
2. Or wholly or in part by her Higher Self while controlling her physical organism?
3. Or as a medium obsessed by other living persons?
4. Or partly under any two or more of these three conditions?
5. Or as an ordinary spiritual medium, controlled by intelligences disincarnate?
6. Or was it written by several alternately latent and active personalities of herself?
7. Or simply by her as the uninspired, uncontrolled and not obsessed Russian lady, H. P. B., in the usual state of waking consciousness, and differing in no way from any author doing a work of this class?

Let us begin with the last alternative. We shall discover very readily and unmistakably that H. P. B.'s education and training were quite incongruous with the idea that she was erudite, philosophical, or in the least degree, a book-worm. The memoirs of her life, as communicated by her family to Mr. Sinnett, her biographer, and to myself,* show that she was a rebellious pupil with no love of serious literature, no attraction for learned people, no tendency to haunting libraries: the terror of her governesses, the despair of her relatives, a passionate rebel against all restraint of custom or conventionality. Her early years were passed in the company of "hunchback goblins" and sprites, with whom she spent days and weeks together, and in playing disagreeable tricks upon, and clairvoyantly telling disagreeable secrets to, people. The only literature she loved was the folk-lore of Russia, and at no period of her life before she began to write *Isis*, not even during the year she lived in New York before being sent to hunt me up, did the family or any of her friends or acquaintances hear of her displaying bookish habits or tastes. Miss Ballard and other ladies who knew her in her several New York lodging-houses, and were familiar with her habits and mode of life, never knew her to have visited the Astor, the Society, the Mechanics', the Historical, the American Institute, the Brooklyn, or the Mercantile library: no one has ever come forward to recognise her as a frequenter of those alcoves of printed thought. She belonged to no scientific or otherwise learned society in any part of the

---

* Cf. Chapter VII.

world; she had published no book. She hunted up thaumaturgists in savage and semi-civilised countries, not to read their (non-existent) books, but to learn practical psychology. In short, she was not a literary person up to the time of writing *Isis*. This fact was equally clear to each of her New York intimates as it was to myself; and the opinion is confirmed by herself in the last *Lucifer* article, "My Books," that she wrote before her death.* In it she says that the following facts are "undeniable and not to be gainsaid:

> "(1). When I came to America in 1873, I had not spoken English—which I had learned in my childhood colloquially—for over thirty years. I could understand when I read it, but could hardly speak the language.

> "(2). I had never been at any College, and what I knew I had taught myself; I have never pretended to any scholarship in the sense of modern research; I had then hardly read any scientific European works, knew little of Western philosophy and sciences. The little which I had studied and learned of these disgusted me with its materialism, its limitations, narrow cut-and-dried spirit of dogmatism and air of superiority over the philosophies and sciences of antiquity.

---

* The article in question is very inaccurate, as was shown in this chapter as originally published in the *Theosophist*. May, 1893. Space does not permit its repetition here.

"(3). Until 1874, I had never written one word in English, nor had I published any work in any language. Therefore:

"(4). I had not the least idea of literary rules. The art of writing books, of preparing them for print and publication, reading and correcting proofs, were so many close secrets to me.

"(5). When I started to write that which developed later into *Isis Unveiled*, I had no more idea than the man in the moon what would come of it. I had no plan; did not know whether it would be an essay, a pamphlet, a book or an article. I knew that *I had to write it*, that was all. I began the work before I knew Colonel Olcott well, and some months before the formation of the Theosophical Society."

The last sentence is misleading, for she did not begin it until we were well acquainted and in fact, were close friends. In fact, the whole article ought to have been entirely rewritten if it was to have been her last.

The endless substitutions of new for old "copy" and transportations from one Chapter or one Volume to another, in *Isis Unveiled*, were confined to such portions of the work as, I should say, were done in her normal condition—if any such there was—and suggested the painful struggles of a "green hand" over a gigantic literary task. Unfamiliar with grammatical English and literary methods, and with her mind absolutely untrained for such sustained desk-work, yet endowed with a courage without bounds and a power of continuous mental concentration that has scarcely been equalled, she floundered on through weeks and months towards her goal, the fulfilment of her Master's orders. This literary feat of hers surpasses all her phenomena.

The glaring contrasts between the jumbled and the almost perfect portions of her MS. quite clearly prove that the same intelligence was not at work throughout: and the variations in handwriting, in mental method, in literary facility, and in personal idiosyncracies, bear out this idea. At this distance of time and with her MS. destroyed, it is impossible for me to say which of her shifting personalities is mainly responsible for her alleged unacknowledged use of quotations. Whatever came into my hands that seemed as if taken from another author I, of course, would put between inverted commas, and it is quite possible that their blending with some of her own original ideas is chargeable to me; the passages in question reading as if somebody's else. When she wrote other people's words into her current argument without break of the continuity, then, naturally enough—unless the passages were from books I had read, and that were familiar to me—I would go on correcting it as H. P. B.'s own "copy." I have said above that I got my occult education in the compilation of *Isis* and in H. P. B.'s teaching and experiments; I must now add that my previous literary life had taken me into other and much more practical fields of study than the literature which is synthesised in *Isis, viz.*, Agricultural Chemistry and Scientific Agriculture generally. So that she might have given me "copy" entirely made up of passages borrowed from Orientalists, Philologists, and Eastern Sages, without my being able to detect the fact. Personally I have never had plagiarisms in *Isis* pointed out to me, whether verbally or otherwise, nor do I know there are such; but if there are, two things are possible, (*a*) that the borrowing was done by the untrained, inexperienced literary beginner, H. P. B., who was ignorant of the literary sin she committed, or (*b*) that the passages had been so worked into the copy as not to draw my editorial attention to their incongruity with what preceded and succeeded them. Or—a third alternative—might it be that, while writing she was always half on this plane of consciousness, half on the other; and that she read her quotations clairvoyantly in the *Astral Light* and used them as they came *à propos*, without really knowing who were the authors or what the titles of their books? Surely her Eastern acquaintances will be prepared to think that a plausible theory, for if ever anyone lived in two worlds habitually, it was she. Often—as above stated—I have seen her in the very act of copying extracts out of phantom books, invisible to my senses, yet most undeniably visible to her.

Now let us consider the next hypothesis, the 6th, *viz.*, that the book was written by several different H. P. B. personalities, or several personal strata of her consciousness capable of coming *seriatim* into activity out of latency. Upon this point the researches of our contemporaries are not yet so far advanced as to unable us to dogmatise. In his *Incidents in the Life of Mme. Blavatsky* (p. 147), Mr. Sinnett quotes a written description of hers of a "double life" she led throughout a certain "mild fever," which was yet a wasting illness, that she had when a young lady in Mingrelia:

"Whenever I was called by name, I opened my eyes upon

hearing it, and was myself, my own personality in every particular. As soon as I was left alone, however, I relapsed into
my usual, half-dreamy condition, and became *somebody else*
(who, namely, Mme. B. will not tell) . . . . In cases when I was
interrupted, when in my other *self*, by the sound of my present
name being pronounced, and while I was conversing in my
dream-life—say at half a sentence either spoken by me or
those who were with my second *me* at the time—and opened
my eyes to answer the call, I used to answer very rationally,
and understood all, for I was never delirious. But no sooner
had I closed my eyes again than the sentence which had been
interrupted was completed by my other *self*, continued from
the word, or even the half word it had stopped at. When
awake, and *myself*, I remembered well *who I was* in my second
capacity, and what I had been and was doing. When *somebody
else, i.e.,* the personage I had become, I know I had no idea of
who was H. P. Blavatsky! I was in another far-off country, a
totally different individuality from myself, and had no connection with my actual life."

In view of what has since been seen, some might say that
the only H. P. B. was the conscious entity which inhabited her
physical body, and that the "somebody else" was not H. P. B.,
but another incarnate entity, having an inexplicable connection with H. P. B.'s body and H. P. B. True, there are cases
known where certain tastes and talents have been shown by
the second self which were foreign to the normal self. Prof.
Barrett, for instance, tells of a vicar's son in the North of London who, after a serious illness, became two distinct personalities. The abnormal self "did not know his parents, he had

no memory of the past, he called himself by another name, and, what is still more remarkable, he developed musical talent, of which *he had never shown a trace.*" So there are many cases where the second self, replacing the normal self, calls itself by a different name and has a special memory of its own experiences. In the well-known case of Lurancy Vennum, her body was completely obsessed by the disincarnate soul of another girl named Mary Roff, who had died twelve years before. Under this obsession her personality changed entirely; she remembered all that had ever happened to Mary Roff prior to her decease, but her own parents, connexions, and friends became total strangers. The obsession lasted nearly four months.* The body occupied seemed to Mary Roff "so natural that she could hardly feel it was not her original body born nearly thirty years ago." The Editor of the *Watseka Wonder* pamphlet copies from *Harper's Magazine* for May, 1860, the Rev. Dr. W. S. Plummer's account of a certain Mary Reynolds' double personality which lasted, with intervals of relapse to the normal state, from her eighteenth to her sixty-first year. During the last quarter century of her life, she *remained wholly in her second abnormal condition:* the normal self, that was the conscious owner of that body, had been wiped out, as it were. But, observe the strange fact that all she knew in the second self had been taught her in that state. She began that second life at eighteen (of the body's life) oblivious of Mary Reynolds, of all she had known or suffered; her second state was precisely that of a new-born infant. "All the past that

---

* See *The Watseka Wonder.* To be had of the Manager, *Theosophist* Office.

remained to her was the faculty of pronouncing a few words: until she was taught their significance, they were unmeaning sounds to her."—(*Watseka Wonder*, p. 42.)

In the *Incidents, etc.* (p. 146), is an explanation of the way in which H. P. B. would give the Gooriel and Mingrelian nobility, who came to consult her, answers to their questions about their private affairs. She would simply, while in full consciousness, clairvoyantly see their thoughts "as they evolved out of their heads in spiral luminous smoke, sometimes in jets of what might be taken for some radiant material, and settled in distinct pictures and images around them." The following is especially suggestive:

"Often such thoughts and answers to them *would find themselves impressed in her own brain, couched in words and sentences in the same way as original thoughts do.* But, so far as we are all able to understand, the former visions were always more trustworthy, as they are independent and distinct from the seer's own impressions, belonging to pure clairvoyance, not 'thought transference,' which is a process always liable to get mixed up with one's own more vivid mental impressions."

This seems to throw light upon the present problem, and to suggest that it is thinkable that H. P. B., while quite normal as to waking consciousness, saw clairvoyantly, or by thought-absorption—a better word than thought-transference in this connection—the stored-up wisdom of the branch of literature she was examining, and so took it into her own brain as to lose the idea that it was not original with herself. Practical Eastern psychologists will not regard this hypothesis so unreasonable as others may. True, after all, it is but a hypothesis, and her enemies will simply call her a cribber, a plagiarist. With the ignorant, insult is the line of least resistance.

The supporters of this theory should, however, recollect that H. P. B.'s most ardent and passionate wish was to gather together as many corroborations as possible, from all ancient and modern sources of the theosophical teachings she was giving out; and her interest all lay on the side of quoting respectable authorities, not in plagiarising from their works for her own greater glory.

I have read a good deal and known something about this question of multiple personality in man, but I do not remember a case where the awakened latent personalities, or second personality, was able to quote from books or talk languages with which the normal waking self had never had any connection. I know a scientific man in England who had quite forgotten his mother-tongue from having lived abroad from his eleventh year without speaking or even hearing it spoken, until his twenty-ninth year, when he began to re-learn it with the help of grammar and dictionary, yet while he was thus struggling through the rudiments of the language, spoke it correctly in his sleep. But the knowledge had in his case simply sunk into the realm of "sub-liminal" consciousness, *i.e.,* latent memory. And there is the familiar case of the illiterate house or kitchen-maid, who was overheard reciting in her somnambulic state Hebrew phrases and verses which—as afterwards proven—she heard declaimed by a former master, years before. But who brings forward proof that H. P. B. had ever in her life studied the authors quoted in *Isis Unveiled*? If she did not consciously plagiarise them, and had never read them, how could they have come to her on the theory that the book was written by an H. P. B. II. or H. P. B. III.? My readers in Western lands will have seen the unique case of Madame B., a French hysteriac and patient of Professor Janet, reported and commented upon by Prof. Richet, the eminent hypnotist. The case is quoted by Mr. Stead in his "Real Ghost Stories" number of the *Review of Reviews*, for Christmas, 1891. In her case the two personalities—we are told—"not only exist side by side, but in the case of the subconscious self, knowingly co-exist, while over or beneath both there is a third personality which is aware of both the other two, and apparently superior to both . . . Mme. B. can be put to sleep at almost any distance, and when hypnotised completely changes her character. There are two well-defined personalities in her, and a third of a more mysterious nature than either of the two first. The normal waking state of the woman is called Léonie I., the hypnotic state Léonie II. The third occult unconscious personality of the lowest depth is called Léonie III. Léonie I. is a 'serious and somewhat melancholy woman, calm and slow, very gentle and extremely timid.' Léonie II. is the opposite—'gay, noisy, and restless to an insupportable degree: she continues good-natured, but she has acquired a singular tendency to irony and bitter jests. In this state, she does not recognise her identity with her working self. "That good woman is not I," she says: "She is too stupid."' 'Léonie II. gets control of Léonie I.'s hand when she is in an abstracted mood; her face calm, her eyes looking into space with a certain fixity,' but not 'cataleptic, for she was humming a rustic tune; her right hand wrote quickly, and, as it were, surreptitiously.' When recalled to herself and the writing shown her, 'of the letter which she was writing she knew nothing whatever.' When Léonie I. (the waking self) was effaced and Léonie II., the second self, was aroused in the hypnotic condition, and rattling on with her usual volubility and obstreperousness, she suddenly showed signs of terror; hearing a voice as if from another part of the room, which scolded her and said: 'Enough, enough, be quiet, you are a nuisance.' This was a third personality, which awakened and took full possession of the patient's organism when she had been plunged into a deeper stage of lethargy. She unhesitatingly confessed that it was she who had spoken the words heard by Léonie II., and that she did it because she saw that the Professor was being annoyed by her babble. The imaginary voice which so terrified Léonie II. because it seemed super-natural, proceeded"—says Mr. Stead—"from a profound stratum of consciousness in the same individual."

Our present purpose being only to superficially examine the subject of multiple personality in connection with the hypothesis that H. P. B. might have had no other aid in writing *Isis* than her own several personalities, we need not go deeper into a problem to sound which one must turn to the Hindu philosophical and mystical authorities. The ancient theory is that the "KNOWER" is capable of seeing and knowing all when he has been disburthened of the last veil of the physical consciousness. And this knowledge comes to one progressively as the fleshly veils are raised. In common, I suppose, with most extemporaneous public speakers, I have by long practice acquired, in some degree, the habit of triplex mental action. When lecturing in India extemporaneously, in English, and being interpreted, sentence by sentence into some other tongue, I find one part of my mind following the translator and trying to guess from the behaviour of the audience, often aided by the hearing of familiar words, whether my thoughts are being correctly rendered; at the same time, another part of my mind will be observing individuals and making mental comments upon their peculiarities or capabilities—sometimes I may even address side remarks to some acquaintance sitting near me on the platform; the two mental activities are distinct and independent. The instant my interpreter has uttered his last word, I catch up the thread of my argument and proceed through another sentence. Simultaneously with the progress of these two functions, I have a third consciousness, as of an observant third, and higher self, which notes the other two trains of thought, yet without becoming entangled with them. This represents, of course, a rudimentary stage of psychical development, the higher degrees of which are indicated in some of the aspects of H. P. B.'s spiritual endowments; yet even so much experience as this helps one to comprehend the problem of her mental phenomena: it is a feeble, yet sure, sign that the Knower can observe and know.

If I were a Mussulman, I should probably affirm with Mahommed himself, that the writing of the Koran in such classical Arabic by so uneducated a man as himself was the greatest of psychical miracles, a proof that his spiritual Ego had burst through trammels of flesh and drawn knowledge directly from its heavenly source. If H. P. B. had been an ascetic, mistress of her physical self and her waking brain, able to write pure English without having acquired it, and to have formed and fashioned her book after a consistent plan, instead of messing up her materials as she did, I might believe the same thing of her, and ascribe that wonder-book of entrancing interest to her own developed individuality. As it is, I cannot; and I must pass on to discuss our other theories.

Chapter XV.

APPARENT POSSESSION BY
FOREIGN ENTITIES

O ur next question is, did she write *Isis* in the capacity of
an ordinary spiritual medium, *i.e.*, under the control
of spirits of the dead? I answer, Assuredly not. If she did, then
the power controlling her organism worked differently from
any that is recorded in books or that I, personally, ever saw
operating during the many years in which I was interested in
that movement. I have known mediums of all sorts—speaking,
trance, writing, phenomena-making, medical, clairvoyant,
and materialising; have seen them at work, attended their
séances and observed the signs of their obsession and possession. H. P. B.'s case resembled none of them. Nearly all they
did she could do; but at her own will and pleasure, by day or
by night, without forming "circles," choosing the witnesses, or
imposing the usual conditions. Then, again, I had ocular
proof that at least some of those who worked with us were
living men, from having seen them in the flesh in India after
having seen them in the astral body in America and Europe;
from having touched and talked with them. Instead of telling
me that they were spirits, they told me they were as much alive

as myself, and that each of them had his own peculiarities and capabilities; in short, his complete individuality. They told me that what they had attained to, I should, one day, myself acquire; how soon, would depend entirely upon myself; and that I might anticipate nothing whatever from favour; but, like them, must gain every step, every inch of progress by my own exertions.

One of the greatest of them, the Master of the two Masters about whom the public has heard a few facts and circulated much foul abuse, wrote me on June 22, 1875: "The time is come to let you know who I am. I am not a disembodied spirit, Brother, I am a living man; gifted with such powers by our Lodge as are in store for yourself some day. I cannot be with you otherwise than in spirit, for thousands of miles separate us at present. Be patient and of good cheer, untiring labourer of the sacred Brotherhood! Work on and toil too for yourself, for self-reliance is the most powerful factor of success. Help your needy brother and you shall be helped yourself in virtue of the never-failing and ever active Law of Compensation": the law of Karma, in short, which, as the reader perceives, was taught me from almost the beginning of my intercourse with H. P. B. and the Masters.

And yet, despite the above, I was made to believe that we worked in collaboration with at least one disincarnate entity—the pure soul of one of the wisest philosophers of modern times, one who was an ornament to our race, a glory to his country. He was a great Platonist, and I was told that, so absorbed was he in his life-study, he had become earth-bound, *i.e.*, he could not snap the ties which held him to the Earth, but sat in an astral library of his own mental creation, plunged in his philosophical reflections, oblivious to the lapse of time, and anxious to promote the turning of men's minds towards the solid philosophical basis of true religion. His desire did not draw him to taking a new birth among us, but made him seek out those who, like our Masters and their agents, wished to work for the spread of truth and the overthrow of superstition. I was told that he was so pure and so unselfish that all the Masters held him in profound respect, and, being forbidden to meddle with his Karma, they could only leave him to work his way out of his (Kámalokaic) illusions, and pass on to the goal of formless being and absolute spirituality according to the natural order of Evolution. His mind had been so intensely employed in purely intellectual speculation that his spirituality had been temporarily stifled. Meanwhile there he was, willing and eager to work with H. P. B. on this epoch-making book, towards the philosophical portion of which he contributed much. He did not materialise and sit with us, nor obsess H. P. B., medium-fashion; he would simply talk with her psychically, by the hour together, dictating copy, telling her what references to hunt up, answering my questions about details, instructing me as to principles, and, in fact, playing the part of a third person in our literary symposium. He gave me his portrait once—a rough sketch in colored crayons on flimsy paper—and sometimes would drop me a brief note about some personal matter, but from first to last his relation to us both was that of a mild, kind, extremely learned teacher and elder friend. He never dropped a word to indicate that he thought himself aught but a living man, and, in fact, I was told that he did not realise that he had died out of the body. Of the lapse of time, he seemed to have so little perception that, I remember, H. P. B. and I laughed, one morning at 2.30 A.M., when, after an unusually hard night's work, while we were taking a parting smoke, he quietly asked H. P. B., "Are you ready to begin?"; under the impression that we were at the beginning instead of the end of the evening! And I also recollect how she said: "For Heaven's sake don't laugh deep in your thought, else the 'old gentleman' will surely hear you and feel hurt!" That gave me an idea: to laugh superficially is ordinary laughter, but to laugh deeply is to shift your merriment to the plane of psychic perception! So emotions may, like beauty, be *sometimes* but skin-deep. Sins, also: think of that!

Except in the case of this old Platonist, I never had, with or without H. P. B.'s help, consciously to do with another disincarnate entity during the progress of our work; unless Paracelsus may be called one, about which in common with the Alsatians, I have grave doubts. I remember that one evening, at about twilight, while we lived in West Thirty-fourth Street, we had been talking about the greatness of Paracelsus and the ignominious treatment he had had to endure during his life and after his apparent death. H. P. B. and I were standing in the passage between the front and back rooms, when her manner and voice suddenly changed, she took my hand as if to express friendship, and asked, "Will you have Theophrastus for a friend, Henry?" I murmured a reply, when the strange mood passed away, H. P. B. was herself again, and we applied ourselves to our work. That evening I wrote the paragraphs about him that now stand on p. 500 of Vol. II. of *Isis*. As for his being dead, the odds are always against any given Adept's having actually died when to ordinary men he seemed to. With his knowledge of the science of mâyâvic illusion, even his seeming corpse screwed into a coffin and laid away in a tomb, would not be sufficient proof that he was really dead. Barring accidents, which may happen to him as well as to a common man if he be off his guard, an Adept chooses his own place to die in, and his body is so disposed of as to leave no trace behind. For example, what became of the gifted, the noble-souled Count St. Germain, the "adventurer" and "spy" of the encyclopaedias, who dazzled the courts of Europe a century ago, moved in the highest and the most erudite circles, was admitted to the intimacy of Louis XV., built hospitals and otherwise lavished vast sums in charities, took nothing for even the greatest personal services, retired to Holstein, and—disappeared as mysteriously as he had appeared?* *Après nous*

---

* No one ever knew his origin or his real name. The Maréchale de Belle Isle, who met him in Germany, induced him to come to Paris. He had a noble personal appearance and polished address, "considerable erudition and a wonderful memory, spoke English, German, Spanish, and Portuguese to perfection, and French with a slight Piedmontese accent. . . . He occupied for many years a remarkable social position at the French Court. . . . He was in the habit of telling the credulous that he had lived 350 years, *and some old men, who pretended to have known him in their youth, declared that in 60 or 70 years his appearance had in no wise changed.* Frederic the Great, having asked Voltaire for some particulars respecting this mysterious person, was told that he was 'a man who never dies and who knows everything.'" No one knowing his motives or the sources of his wealth, they settled it to their own satisfaction in the same way as that which Hodgson, the spy of the S. P. R., resorted to in the case of H. P. B. to explain her presence in India; he was alleged "to have been employed during the greater part of his life as a spy at the courts at which he resided"

le Deluge, said the King's mistress; after St. Germain came the French Revolution and the upheaval of mankind.

Rejecting the idea that H. P. B. wrote *Isis* as an ordinary spirit medium "under control," we have seen, however, that some portions of it were actually written to a spirit's dictation: a most extraordinary and exceptional entity, yet still a man out of the physical body. The method of work with him as above described tallies closely with that she described in a family letter, when explaining how she wrote her book without any previous training for such work.

"Whenever I am *told* to write, I sit down and obey, and then I can write easily upon almost anything—metaphysics, psychology, philosophy, ancient religions, zoölogy, natural sciences, or what not. . . . Why? Because *somebody who knows all* dictates to me. *My Masters*, and occasionally *others whom I knew on my travels years ago*." (*Incidents*, page 205.)

This is exactly what happened between her and the old Platonist, but he was not her "Master," nor could she have met him on her travels on this physical plane, since he died before she was born—this time. Then arises the question whether the Platonist was really a spirit disincarnate, or an Adept who

---

(*Am. Cyc.*, Ed. 1868, vol. xiv., pp. 266–7). But, all the same, no evidence whatever to support this calumny has ever been forthcoming. The *Encyclopædia Britannica* takes the same view of St. Germain, and the *Dictionnaire Universel d' Histoire et de Geographie* echoing the falsehood, says that "this will account for his riches and the mystery with which he enwrapped himself!" If Mme. de Fadeef—H. P. B.'s aunt—could only be induced to translate and publish certain documents in her famous library, the world would have a nearer approach to a true history of the preRevolutionary European mission of this Eastern Adept than has until now been available.

had lived in that philosopher's body and seemed to, but really did not, die out of it on September I, 1687. It is certainly a difficult problem to solve. Considering that the ordinary concomitants of spirit-possession and spirit-intercourse were wanting, and that H. P. B. served the Platonist in the most matter-of-fact way as amanuensis, their relation differing in nothing from that of any Private Secretary with his employer, save that the latter was invisible to me but visible to her, it does look more as if we were dealing with a living than with a disincarnate person. He seemed not quite a "Brother"—as we used to call the Adepts then—yet more that than anything else; and as far as the literary work itself was concerned, it went on exactly as the other parts of it did when the dictator, or writer, as the case might be, was professedly a Master (Cf. Theory I). The dictator or *writer*, I say, and this requires some explanation.

It is stated above that the H. P. B. manuscript varied at times, and that there were several variants of the one prevailing script; also that each change in the writing was accompanied by a marked alteration in the manner, motions, expression, and literary capacity of H. P. B. When she was left to her own devices, it was often not difficult to know it, for then the untrained literary apprentice became manifest and the cutting and pasting began; then the copy that was turned over to me for revision was terribly faulty, and after having been converted into a great smudge of interlineations, erasures, orthographic corrections and substitutions, would end in being dictated by me to her to re-write (Cf. Theory 7). Now often things were, after a while, said to me that would be more than hints that other intelligences than H. P. B.'s were at times using her body as a writing machine: it was never expressly said, for example, "I am so and so," or "Now this is A or B." It did not need that after we "twins" had been working together long enough for me to become familiar with her every peculiarity of speech, moods, and impulses. The change was as plain as day, and by and by after she had been out of the room and returned, a brief study of her features and actions enabled me to say to myself, "This is——, or——, or,——" and presently my suspicion would be confirmed by what happened. One of these *Alter Egos* of hers, one whom I have since personally met, wears a full beard and long moustache that are twisted, Rajput fashion, into his side whiskers. He has the habit of constantly pulling at his moustache when deeply pondering: he does it mechanically and unconsciously. Well, there were times when H. P. B.'s personality had melted away and she was "*Somebody else*," when I would sit and watch her hand as if pulling at and twisting a moustache that certainly was not growing visibly on H. P. B.'s upper lip, and the faraway look would be in the eyes, until presently resuming attention of passing things, the moustached Somebody would look up, catch me watching him, hastily remove the hand from the face, and go on with the work of writing. Then there was another Somebody, who disliked English so much that he never willingly talked with me in anything but French: he had a fine artistic talent and a passionate fondness for mechanical invention. Another one would now and then sit there, scrawling something with a pencil and reeling off for me dozens of poetical stanzas which embodied, now sublime, now humorous ideas. So each of the several Somebodies had his peculiarities distinctly marked, as recognisable as those of any of our ordinary acquaintances or friends. One was jovial, fond of good stories and witty to a degree; another, all dignity, reserve, and erudition. One would be calm, patient, and benevolently helpful, another testy and sometimes exasperating. One Somebody would always be willing to emphasise his philosophical or scientific explanations of the subjects I was to write upon, by doing phenomena for my edification, while to another Somebody I dared not even mention them. I got an awful rebuke one evening. I had brought home a while before two nice, soft pencils, just the thing for our desk work, and had given one to H. P. B. and kept one myself. She had the very bad habit of borrowing penknives, pencils, rubber, and other articles of stationery and forgetting to return them: once put into her drawer or writing-desk, there they would stay, no matter how much of a protest you might make over it. On this particular evening, the artistic Somebody was sketching a navvy's face on a sheet of common paper and chatting with me about something, when he asked me to lend him another pencil. The thought flashed into my mind, "If I once lend this nice pencil it will go into her drawer and I shall have none for my own use." I did not say this, I only thought it, but the Somebody gave me a mildly sarcastic look, reached out to the pen-tray between us, laid his pencil in it, handled it with his fingers of that hand for a moment, and lo! a dozen pencils of the identical make and quality! He said not a word, did not even give me a look, but the blood rushed to my temples and I felt more humble than I ever did in my life. All the same, I scarcely think I deserved the rebuke, considering what a stationery-*annexer* H. P. B. was!

Now when either of these Somebodies was "on guard," as I used to term it, the H. P. B. manuscript would present the identical peculiarities that it had on the last occasion when he had taken his turn at the literary work. He would, by preference, write about the class of subjects that were to his taste, and instead of H. P. B. playing the part of an amanuensis, she would then have become for the time being that other person (Cf. Theory 3). If you had given me in those days any page of *Isis* manuscript, I could almost certainly have told you by which Somebody it had been written. Where, then, was H. P. B.'s self at those times of replacement? Ah, that is the question; and that is one of the mysteries which are not given to the first comer.* As I understood it, she herself had loaned her body as one might one's type-writer, and had gone off on other occult business that she could transact in her astral body; a certain group of Adepts occupying and manœuvring the body by turns. When they knew that I could distinguish between them, so as to even have invented a name for each by which H. P. B. and I might designate them in our conversation in their absence, they would frequently give me a grave bow or a friendly farewell nod when about to leave the room and give place to the next relief guard. And they would sometimes talk to me of each other as friends do about absent third parties, by

---

* Nearly two years after the above was published H. P. B. explained to her relatives (cf. *Path* articles above cited) the secret; she was not in her body, but seemingly near it, with full consciousness watching its manipulation by third parties.

which means I came to know bits of their several personal histories; and would also speak about the absent H. P. B., distinguishing her from the physical body they had borrowed from her. One Mahâtma, writing me about some occult business, speaks of it—the H. P. B. body—as "the old appearance"; again, in 1876, he writes about "it and the Brother inside it"; another Master asks me—*à propos* of a terrific fit of anger to which I had (unintentionally) provoked H. P. B.—"Do you want to kill the body?"; and the same one, in a note of 1875, speaks of "those who represent us in the *shell*"—the underscoring of the word being his. Can any one understand my feelings upon discovering on a certain evening that I had unsuspiciously greeted the staid philosopher described in the next few sentences of the main-text, with an hilarious levity that quite upset his usual calm? Fancying that I was addressing only my "chum" H. P. B., I said: "Well, Old Horse, let us get to work!" The next minute I was blushing for shame, for the blended expression of surprise and startled dignity that came into the face, showed me with whom I had to deal. It was as bad a *gaucherie* as that committed by good old Peter Cooper at the New York Academy Ball to the Heir Apparent, when he slapped him on the shoulder and said: "Well, Wales, what do you think of this?" This was the one of them for whom I had the most filial reverence. It was not alone for his profound learning, lofty character and dignified demeanour, but also for his really paternal kindness and patience. It seemed as if he alone had read to the bottom of my heart, and wished to bring out every little spiritual germ that lay there as a latent potentiality. He was—I was told—a South Indian personage of long spiritual experience, a Teacher of Teachers; still living among men ostensibly as a landed proprietor, yet known for what he was by nobody around him. Oh, the evenings of high thinking I passed with him; how shall I ever compare with them any other experiences of my life! Most vividly of all I remember one evening when, by half hints more than anything else, he awakened my intuition so that it grasped the theory of the relationship of cosmic cycles with fixed points in stellar constellations, the attractive centre shifting from point to point in an orderly sequence. Recall your sensations the first time you ever looked through a large telescope at the starry heavens—the awe, the wonder, the instant mental expansion experienced in looking from the familiar and, by comparison, commonplace Earth to the measureless depths of space and the countless starry worlds that bestrew the azure infinity. That was a faint approach to my feeling at the moment when that majestic concept of cosmic order rushed into my consciousness; so over-powering was it, I actually gasped for breath. If there had previously been the least lingering hereditary leaning towards the geocentric theory, upon which men have built their paltry theologies, it was then swept away like a dried leaf before the hurricane. I was borne into a higher plane of thought, I was a free man.

It was this Master who dictated to H. P. B. the Replies to an English F. T. S. on questions suggested by a reading of "Esoteric Buddhism," which was published in the *Theosophist* for September, October, and November, 1883. It was at Ootacamund, at the house of Maj.-Gen. Morgan, when, shivering with the cold, and her lower limbs swaddled in rugs, she sat writing them. One morning I was in her room reading a book, when she turned her head and said: "I'll be hanged if I ever heard of the Iaphygians. Did you ever read of such a tribe, Olcott?" I said I had not, why did she ask? "Well," she replied, "the old gentleman tells me to write it down, but I'm afraid there is some mistake; what do you say?" I answered that if the Master in question gave her the name, she should write it without fear as he was always right. And she did. This is an example of multitudinous cases where she wrote from dictation things quite outside her personal knowledge. She never studied Hindî, nor, normally, could she speak or write it; yet I have a Hindî note in Devanágari characters that I saw her write and hand to Swami Dayánand Saraswati at the Viziana-gram garden-house at Benares, where we were guests in 1880. The Swami read it, wrote and signed his answer on the same sheet, and H. P. B. left it on the table, from which I took it.

But I wish to say again, as distinctly as possible, that, not even from the wisest and noblest of these H. P. B. Somebodies did I ever get the least encouragement to either regard them as infallible, omniscient, or omnipotent. There was never the least show of a wish on their part that I should worship them, mention them with bated breath, or regard as inspired what they either wrote with H. P. B.'s body, or dictated to her as their amanuensis. I was made simply to look upon them as men, my fellow-mortals; wiser, truly, infinitely more advanced than I, but only because of their having preceeded me in the normal path of human evolution. Slavishness and indiscrim-inate adulation they loathed, telling me that they were usually but the cloaks to selfishness, conceit, and moral limpness.

Their candid opinions were frequently vouchsafed to me after the departure of some of these flattering visitors, and it would have sent any of my readers into a fit of laughter if they had been there one evening after a gushing lady had bade us goodnight. Before leaving she petted H. P. B., sat on the arm of her chair, patted her hand and kissed her on the cheek; I standing near by and seeing the blank despair depicted in the (male) Somebody's face. I conducted the lady to the door, returned to the room, and almost exploded with merriment when the ascetic Somebody—a sexless *sadhoo* if there ever was one—turned his mournful eyes at me and in an accent of indescribable melancholy said, "She KISSED me!" It was too much; I had to sit down.

I have remarked above that the dictation and literary collaboration between the old Platonist and H. P. B. was identical with that between her and the actual Adepts; and that, as he delighted in one branch of work, so each of the others had their individual preferences. But there was the difference that while they at times would dictate to her and at others occupy her body and write through it as if it were their own (just as the spirit of Mary Roff utilised the body of Lurancy Vennum and felt it as natural as if she had been born in it), the Platonist never obsessed her: he only used her as his amanuensis. Then, again, I have spoken of the part of the *Isis* writing that was done by H. P. B. *in proprid persond*, which was inferior to that done for her by the Somebodies. This is perfectly comprehensible, for how could H. P. B., who had had no previous knowledge of this sort, write correctly about the multifarious subjects treated in her book? In her (seemingly) normal state, she would read a book, mark the portions that struck her, write about them, make mistakes, correct them, discuss them with me, set me to writing, help my intuitions, get friends to supply materials, and go on thus as best she might, so long as there were none of the teachers within call of her psychic appeals. And they were not with us always, by any means. She did a vast deal of splendid writing, for she was endowed with marvellous natural literary capacity; she was never dull or uninteresting, and, as I have elsewhere noted, she was equally brilliant in three languages when the full power was upon her. She writes her Aunt that when her Master was busy elsewhere he left his substitute with her, and then it was her "Luminous Self," her Augoeides, which thought and wrote for her (Cf. Theory 2). About this, I cannot venture an opinion, for I never observed her in this state: I only knew her in three capacities, *viz.*, her proper H. P. B. self; with her body possessed or over-shadowed by the Masters; and as an amanuensis taking down from dictation. It may be that her Augoeides, taking posses-sion of her physical brain, gave me the impression that it was one of the Masters that was at work: I cannot say. But what she omits telling her Aunt is that there were many, many times, when she was neither possessed, controlled nor dictated to by any superior intelligence, but was simply and palpably H. P. B., our familiar and beloved friend, latterly our teacher; who was trying as well as she could to carry out the object of her literary mission. Yet, despite the mixed agencies at work in producing *Isis*, there is an expression of individuality running throughout it and her other works—something peculiar to herself. Epes Sargent and other American literati expressed to me their wonder at the grasp she showed of our language, and one gentleman went to the length of publishing the opinion that we had no living author who could excel her in writing English. This, of course, is vague exaggeration, but happily her style has been made the subject of a close comparison with those of others by a philologist of scientific training.

In his work on the *Origin, Progress, and Destiny of the English Language and Literature*, the learned author, Dr. John A. Weisse, publishes a number of analytical tables which show the sources of the words used by English writers of renown. In the following excerpts will be seen the derivations of the English of *Isis Unveiled* in comparison with those of the words employed by some other authors. Dr. Weisse says the book is "a thesaurus of new phases and facts, so sprightfully related that even the uninitiated may read them with interest."

FOLLOWING IS THE ANALYSIS:

Which Author and Work Analysed.	Greco-Latin Words.	Gotho-Germanic Words.	Celtic Words.	Semitic Words.
Robert Burton, A.D. 1621, *Anatomy of Melancholy*. . . .	54	46	0	0
John Bunyan, 1682, *Pilgrim's Progress*	31	68	1	0
Sir Thomas Browne, 1682, *Hydriotaphia*	51	47	2	0

Sam. Johnson, 1784, (1780?) *Lives of the English Posts.*	47	51	2	0
R. C. Trench, *On the Study of Words*	30	68	2	0
George P. Marsh, *Lectures on the English Language,* p. 133	58	41	1	0
S. A. Allibone, 1872, *Crit. Dict. Eng. Literature, etc* . .	53	46	1	0
Darwin, *Origin of Species* . . .	53	46	1	0
H. P. Blavatsky, *Isis Unveiled*	46	51	1	2
Her Majesty the Queen, *Leaves of our four. High-lands*	36	63	0	1

It seems, therefore, that the English of Madame Blavatsky is practically identical with that of Dr. Samuel Johnson, which one might say is as nearly classically perfect as one could ask. The same test applied to her French writings would, doubtless, prove her to be as facile in the use of that beautiful language as the greatest of modern French authors.

Chapter XVI.

DEFINITION OF TERMS

Then how are we to regard the authorship of *Isis Unveiled*, and how H. P. B.? As to the former, it is unquestionably a collaborated work, the production of several distinct writers and not that of H. P. B. alone. My personal observations upon this point are fully borne out by what she herself admits in her explanatory letters to her family, as quoted by Mr. Sinnett, for she says that all the portions which deal with subjects previously unfamiliar to her were either dictated to her by some master or written by her higher self through the brain and hand of her physical body. The question is highly complex, and the exact truth will never be known as to the share which each of the participants had in it. The personality of H. P. B. was the mould in which all the matter was cast, and which, therefore, controlled its form, colouring, and expression, so to say, by its own idiosyncracies, mental as well as physical. For, just as the successive occupiers of the H. P. B. body only modified its habitual handwriting, but did not write their own,* so in using the H. P. B. brain, they were forced to allow

---

* A very curious fact is to be noticed in this connection, *viz.*, that the "Mahátmá M.'s" handwriting, which was so carefully scrutinised by the S. P. R., their experts and agents, and said to resemble that of H. P. B., was a coarse, rough script, something like a collection of chopped roots and brush-wood, while the handwriting of the same personage in the *Isis* MS. and in the notes he wrote me was totally different. It was a small, fine script, such as a lady might have written, and while generally resembling H. P. B.'s own handwriting, yet differing from it so as to present an appearance of distinct individuality, which enabled me to recognise it as that personage's MS. whenever I saw it. I do not pretend to account for this fact, I only state it as something which must be recorded. It should be considered hereafter by whatever psychological experimentalist may be studying the general phenomenon of psychic writing through mediums, or intermediaries of a similar kind, whether by precipitation, control of the hand, or occupancy of the body. I think that such an inquiry will result in proving that such writing, when as closely analysed as were the alleged Mahátmá's writings by the S. P. R., *always* resembles that of the intermediary to a greater or lesser extent, and without carrying the implication of bad faith on his or her part. Ignorance, or wilful disregard of this fact, caused the S. P. R.'s indictment against H. P. B. to lose almost all its point. The late W. Stainton Moses, M.A. (Oxon.), quotes in his work on *Psychography*, p. 125, from a letter to him from Mr. W. II. Harrison, formerly editor of *The Spiritualist*, and a very experienced observer of psychical phenomena, the following remarks about the messages through Dr. Slade: "I noticed that they were nearly always in the handwriting of the medium; and this, which, to an ignorant person, would have been indicative of imposture, was in favour of the genuineness of the phenomena to an expert. On leaving the room after the séance, I had a short talk with Mr. Simmons, and without telling him what I knew, but merely to test his integrity, I asked whether the handwriting on the slates bore any resemblance to that of Dr. Slade. Without hesitation, he replied that there was usually a strong resemblance. This shows the truthfulness and absence of exaggeration incidental to the statements of Mr. Simmons." Mr. Harrison adds that "before Dr. Slade came to London, years of observation at numerous séances had proved to me that the materialised hands common at séances were most frequently the duplicates of those of the medium, and produced nearly the same handwriting." And yet, in the presence of Slade, and another psychic,

it to colour their thoughts and arrange their words after a fixed personal fashion peculiar to it. Like as the daylight passing through cathedral windows becomes coloured to the tints of the stained glass, so the thoughts transmitted by them through H. P. B.'s peculiar brain would have to be modified into the literary style and habits of expression to which it had been by her developed. And even common sense teaches us that the closer the natural identity between the possessing intelligence and the intellectual and moral personality controlled, the easier should be the control, the more fluent the composition, the less involved the style. In point of fact what I noticed was this, that at times when the physical H. P. B. was in a state of supreme irascibility, the body was rarely occupied save by the Master whose own pupil and spiritual ward she was, and whose iron will was even stronger than her own; the gentler philosophers keeping aloof. Naturally, I asked why a permanent control was not put upon her fiery temper, and why she should not always be modified into the quiet, self-centred sage that she became under certain obsessions. The answer was that such a course would inevitably lead to her death from apoplexy; the body was vitalised by a fiery and imperious spirit, one which had from childhood brooked no restraint, and if vent were not allowed for the excessive corporeal energy, the result must be fatal. I was told to look into

---

named Watkins, alleged "spirit messages" were written in some twenty different languages, none of which were known to the mediums nor written by them in the usual way of writing, but all either by precipitation or the manipulation of a crumb of pencil or crayon laid on a slate, which their hands did not touch.

the history of her kinsfolk, the Russian Dolgoroukis, and I would understand what was meant. I did so and found that this princely and warlike family, tracing back to Rurik (ninth century A.D.), had been always distinguished by extreme courage, a daring equal to every emergency, a passionate love of personal independence, and a fearlessness of consequences in the carrying out of its wishes. Prince Yakob, a Senator of Peter the Great, was a type of the family character. Disliking an imperial ukase, he tore it to pieces in full council of the Senate, and when the Tsar threatened to kill him, he replied: "You have but to imitate Alexander, and you will find a Clitus in me." (*Am. Encyc.*, *VI.*, 551.) This was H. P. B.'s own character to the life, and she more than once told me that she would not be controlled by any power on earth or out of it. The only persons she actually reverenced were the Masters, yet even towards them, she was occasionally so combative that, as above said, in certain of her moods the gentler ones could not, or did not approach her. To get herself into the frame of mind when she could have open intercourse with them had—as she had pathetically assured me—cost her years of the most desperate self-restraint. I doubt if any person had ever entered the Path against greater obstacles or with more self-suppression.

Of course, a brain so liable to disturbance was not the best adapted to the supremely delicate business of the mission she had taken upon herself; but the Masters told me it was far and away the best now available, and they must get all they could out of it. She was to them loyalty and devotion personified, and ready to dare and suffer all for the sake of the Cause. Gifted beyond all other persons of her generation with innate psychical powers, and fired with an enthusiasm that ran into fanaticism, she supplied the element of fixity of purpose, which, conjoined with a phenomenal degree of bodily endurance, made her a most powerful, if not a very docile and equable agent. With less turbulence of spirit she would, probably, have turned out less faulty literary work, but instead of lasting seventeen years under the strain, she would, doubtless, have faded out of the body ten years earlier and her later writings have been lost to the world.

The fact that the psychic's personality distinctly modifies the extraneous writing that is done through her agency or intermediation, gives us, it seems to me, a test by which to judge of the genuineness of any communications alleged to have come from Mahátmás "M." or "K. H." since H. P. B.'s death. While she was alive their communications always, wherever received or by whomsoever apparently written, resembled her own handwriting to some extent. This is as true of the letters which I phenomenally received on a steamer on the high seas and in railway carriages, as of those which dropped out of space, or otherwise phenomenally reached the hands of Mr. Sinnett, Mr. Hume, and other favoured correspondents of our Eastern teachers. For, wherever she might be, she was the vortex-ring through which they had to work with us in the evolution of our galaxy out of the nebula of modern thought. It did not matter at all whether she were with them in Tibet, or with me in New York, or with Mr. Sinnett at Simla: their co-operative affinity was psychical, hence as unaffected as thought itself, by questions of time and space. We have seen in the phenomenon of letters which were arrested in postal transit, written in, and made to reach me at Philadelphia instead of New York, a striking illustration of this principle in psycho-dynamics (Cf. Chapter II.). Bearing this in mind, the important deduction follows that the probabilities are as an hundred to one that any written communication alleged to be from either of the Masters and received since H. P. B.'s death *is open to suspicion if the handwriting is the same as it used to be before that event.** Grant the premise, and the conclusion is inevitable. If all Mahátmá MSS. in her time had to, and did, resemble in some degree her own handwriting because they were transmitted through her psychical agency, then, of course, none coming to us since May, 1891, should resemble it or would be at all likely to, her agency having ceased and her modifying action upon it having been destroyed. Such writings should now resemble the manuscript of the new agent or agents. Of course, I pre-suppose that the evidence for the genuineness of the writing is satisfactory, as it was in the case of H. P. B., whose transmitted communications were often done by precipitation in one's presence, or made to come inside sealed covers, *which she had not handled*, or dropped out of space before one's eyes, or were otherwise phenomenally produced. The precipitated writings of Slade, Watkins, and various other mediums come under the same category. Neither a resemblance of a Master's handwriting, nor the fact that there was more or less likeness to that of the

---

* This Chapter was originally published in July, 1893. My deduction has been objected to by some for whose judgment I have great respect. It may be that I am wrong, but at least I can say that I have seen no proofs to the contrary, even up to the present time (August, 1895). The specimens of Mahátmá writing that have come to my notice since 1891 are, I fear, fraudulent imitations.

supposed intermediary, would be the least evidence, *primá facie*, of genuineness; quite the contrary. Unless every reasonable suspicion of bad faith had been eliminated, the mystical message would not be worth the paper it was written upon, nor the time required to read it. Even when the genuineness is beyond doubt, psychical messages are often commonplace and absolutely valueless, save as psychical facts. I, for one, can say that since 1853, when I first knew of these phenomena, I never attached the least importance to any psychical teaching on account of its reputed authorship, its only value being its subject-matter. I strongly advise all my readers to follow the same rule if they would be on the safe side: better far an enlightened scepticism than the most lauded credulity. For remember that probably no one has ever received a line in English from a Master in his own normal handwriting and written by him in the usual way, unless possibly we except the note which K. H. formed in my own hand when he visited me in his physical body, one night in my tent at Lahore, in 1883. I should not care to dogmatise even about that, as I did not see him write it, and he may have created the letter then and there through the H. P. B. aura that went everywhere with me. Besides K. H. and the old Platonist above mentioned, none of the Masters had learnt to write English, and when they did write it, they had to resort to the same abnormal method as that used by H. P. B. at Benares to write the Hindî note, in Devanâgari characters, to Swami Dayánand Saraswati, above alluded to. In this connection the two completely dissimilar handwritings of Mahátmá M. in the *Isis* MSS. of 1875–7 and the Indian letters to sundry persons after 1879, must be kept in mind. When H. P. B. wrote to the Masters or they to her, on business that was not to be communicated to third parties, it was in an archaic language, said to be "Senzar," which resembles Tibetan, and which she wrote as fluently as she did Russian, French, or English. In fact, I have preserved a note I received from one of the Masters while in New York, along the top of which is written, in pure Tibetan characters in a sort of gold ink, the word "Sems dpah." I had shown it to no one all these years, until quite recently at Calcutta, when Pandit Sarat Chandra Das, C. I. E., the Tibetan explorer and scholar, translated it for me as meaning "Of powerful heart"—an honorific title given in Tibet to a Bodhisattva.

There was another and supreme reason why the Masters dare not control and compel H. P. B.'s innate character to be softened and refined into the higher ideal of a benevolent and gentle Sage independently of her own volition. To do so would have been an unlawful interference with her personal Karma—as I may now express it. Like every other human being, she represented, as she then was, a certain personal equation, the fruit of a certain evolutionary progress of her entity. It was its Karma to have been born this time in just such a tumultuous female body and to have the chances thus offered to gain spiritual progress by a life-long combat against its hereditary passions. To have interfered with that by benumbing the violent temper and suppressing the other personal defects of character, would have been a grievous wrong to her without hastening her evolution one whit: it would have been something like the keeping of a hypnotic sensitive perpetually under the hypnotiser's will, or an invalid

permanently stupefied by a narcotic. There were intervals
when her body was not occupied by the writing Mahátmás,
nor her mind absorbed in taking down what was dictated to
her: at least I assume it to be so, although I have sometimes
been even tempted to suspect that none of us, her colleagues,
ever knew the normal H. P. B. at all, but that we just dealt with
an artificially animated body, a sort of perpetual psychical
mystery, from which the proper *jíva* was killed out at the battle of Mentana, when she received those five wounds and was
picked out of a ditch for dead. There is nothing intrinsically
impossible in this theory, since we have the historical fact that
the normal personality of the girl Mary Reynolds was thrust
aside or obliterated for the space of forty-two years, while her
body was occupied, energised and controlled by another personality, which had no knowledge of the eighteen years' experiences and reminiscences of the normal self prior to this
replacement. As regards H. P. B., I do not assert but only the-
orise, for I dare not say positively who this marvel of a woman,
or, as M. de Buffon would have classified her, this *homo
duplex*, was. She was such a bundle of contradictions, so
utterly incapable of being classified like any of us common
folk, that as a conscientious man I shrink from anything like
dogmatic assertion. Whatever she may have said to myself or
anybody else, counts with me for very, very little, for having
lived and travelled with her so long, and been present at so
very many of her interviews with third parties, I have heard
her tell the most conflicting stories about herself. To have been
open and communicative would have been to betray the resi-
dences and personalities of her Teachers to that multitude of

self-seekers whose egotistic importunities have ever driven the would-be Yogi to the seclusion of the cave or forest. She chose as the easiest way out of the difficulty to contradict herself and throw the minds of her friends into confusion. How easy it would have been for her, for example, to have told Mr. Sinnett that, when trying to enter Tibet in 1854, *viâ* Bhutan or Nepál, she was turned back by Capt. (now Maj.-Genl.) Murray, the military commandant of that part of the frontier, and kept in his house in his wife's company a whole month. Yet she never did, nor did any of her friends ever hear of the circumstance until Mr. Edge and I got the story from Major-General Murray himself, on the 3rd March last, in the train between Nalhati and Calcutta, and I had printed it. So as to her age, she told all sorts of stories, making herself twenty, forty, even sixty and seventy years older than she really was. We have in our scrap-books certain of these tales, reported by successive interviewers and correspondents to their journals, after personal interviews with her, and on sundry occasions when I was present myself.* She said to me in excuse that the

---

* Cf. an interviewer's report in the *Hartford Daily Times*, December 2, 1878. She had been making herself out a sort of Methusaleh, and the correspondent writes: "Very, very old? Impossible. And yet she declares it is so: sometimes indignantly, sometimes with a certain pride, sometimes with indifference or impatience. 'I came of a very long-lived race. All my people grow to be very old. . . . You doubt my age? I can show you my passports, my documents, my letters for years back. I can prove it by a thousand things.'" It was a large way she had of knocking the numerals about! Like that of the Sikh Akali (*vide* Mr. Maclagan's Punjab Census Report of 1891) who "dreams of armies and thinks in lakhs";—(a lakh is 100,000). "If he wishes to imply that five Akalis are present, he will say that five lakhs are before you."

Somebodies inside her body at these various times were of these various ages, and hence no real falsehood was told, although the auditor saw only the H. P. B. shell and thought what was said referred only to that!

I have used the word "obsession" above, but am well aware of its wretched insufficiency in this case. Both "obsession" and "possession" have been made to signify the troubling of a living person by evil spirits or demons: an obsessed person is one vexed or besieged, a possessed person one who is possessed, controlled, overshadowed, or occupied by them. Yet what other term is available in English? Why did not the early Fathers invent a more decent word to signify the possession, control, occupancy, or overshadowing of a person by good spirits than that of "filling," or even let obsession and possession stand for that also? "And they were all *filled* with the Holy Ghost, and began to speak with other tongues, as the spirit gave them utterance." But this will not help us unless we ignore the circumstance that H. P. B.'s body became, at times, occupied by other entities—how far let the following anecdote suggest. She and I were in our literary workroom in New York one summer day after dinner. It was early twilight, and the gas had not been lighted. She sat over by the South front window, I stood on the rug before the mantle-piece, thinking. I heard her say "Look and learn"; and glancing that way, saw a mist rising from her head and shoulders. Presently it defined itself

---

The *Phrenological Journal* for March, 1878, contains her portrait and character-sketch. The writer says: "In the course of her long life—for she is upward of eighty years old—etc." I myself heard her tell this yarn to the writer of the article.

into the likeness of one of the Mahátmás, the one who, later, gave me the historical turban, but the astral double of which he now wore on his mist-born head. Absorbed in watching the phenomenon, I stood silent and motionless. The shadowy shape only formed for itself the upper half of the torso, and then faded away and was gone; whether re-absorbed into H. P. B.'s body or not, I do not know. She sat statue-like for two or three minutes, after which she sighed, came to herself, and asked me if I had seen anything. When I asked her to explain the phenomenon she refused, saying that it was for me to develop my intuition so as to understand the phenomena of the world I lived in. All she could do was to help in showing me things and let me make what I could of them.

Numerous witnesses can testify to another phenomenon which may or may not go towards proving that other entities were sometimes occupying the H. P. B. body. On five different occasions—once to please Miss Emily Kislingbury, and once my sister, Mrs. Mitchell, I remember—she gathered up a lock of her fine, wavy auburn hair, and either pulled it out by the roots or cut it off with scissors, and gave it to one of us. But the lock would be *coarse, jet black, straight* and without the least curliness or waviness in it; in other words, Hindu or other Asiatic human hair, and not in the least like her own flossy, baby-like, light-brown locks. My Diary for 1878 shows that other two occasions were on July 9th, when she did the thing for Hon. J. L. O'Sullivan, ex-U. S. Minister to Portugal, and on November 19th, when she did it for Miss Rosa Bates in the presence of six other witnesses besides Miss Bates and H. P. B. and myself. The enemy may suggest that this was but a trick of simple "palming," but that is met by the statement that in the case of the lock given to Miss Kislingbury or my sister—I forget which—the recipient was allowed to take the scissors and cut out the lock herself. I have two locks taken from her head, both black as jet and far coarser than hers, but one distinctly coarser than the other. The former is Egyptian, and the latter Hindu hair. What better explanation of this phenomenon is there than that of supposing that the men to whom these black locks had belonged were actually occupying the mâyâvic H. P. B. body when they were removed from the head? But to return to our philological difficulty.

The word *epistasis* will not do for us; for that means "inspection, superintendence, command, management," which does not cover the case. Epiphany is not much better, *epiphaneia* being a shining upon, manifestation, etc., etc. We have no word; yet one is greatly needed at this stage of our psychical research, and for it we must go to the East.

This occupancy by living persons of another living person's body, though so outside our Western experience that we have no word for it is, like all else in psychological science, known and defined in India. *A'ves'a* (pronounced Ahveysha) is the act of possessing, i.e., entering and controlling, a human body belonging to a living being (*jîva*). It is of two kinds: when the Adept's own *ams'a* (*súkshma s'arîra*), or astral body, is withdrawn from his own physical body and introduced into the other person's body, it is then called *suarúpáves'a;* but when by his mere *sankalpa* (will-power) he influences, broods over, or controls that other person's (*jîva*) body to do that which would otherwise be beyond its power, *e.g.,* to speak an unlearnt foreign tongue, to understand unfamiliar branches of knowledge, to instantly disappear from the sight of bystanders, to transform itself into a terrifying shape, as of a serpent or a ferocious animal, etc., then the thing is called *saktyáves'a*. This gives us all we need, and so, as we took "Epiphany" from the Greek, why should we not all agree to adopt the easy word *A'ves'a* from the Sanskrit, since it is ready to our hand and means the very thing that we, toddling babes in the nursery of adeptship, must have to get on with in our studies? It applies only to the psychical commerce between two living persons or to the overshadowing and inspiration of a living person by a superior spiritual entity, and must not be degraded to signify the occupancy of a medium's body or its control for the production of phenomena, by a dead man's soul. That is called *gráhana,* and the elementary (dead man's soul) *gráham* (pronounced grah-hum). The same word is used to express the occupancy of a living body by an elemental, or Nature-spirit. Such occupancy may be (*a*) spontaneous, *i.e.,* effected by the attraction of the elemental towards a psychic; or (*b*) compulsory, *i.e.,* compelled by the will of a sorcerer or magician who has learnt the formulas for subjecting an elemental or elementary to his control. I got in Japan a photograph of a bronze group representing Ko-bo-dai-shi, the alleged Adept founder of the Shingon sect, with two little elementals crouched at his feet and awaiting his pleasure. A monk of the Yama-busi sect—that of the wonder-workers of Japan—gave me a scroll wall-painting of the Founder of his sect with attendant elemental servants. This picture now hangs in H. P. B.'s old room in London. She, herself, had also such servants obedient to her.

There is an old and amusing Indian story of how King Vikramádit`á conquered the obstinacy of the Princess Pés'ámadandé who had made a vow to keep silent and marry nobody who could not compel her to answer his questions. The mighty king magician got astride his favourite elementary—not elemental—the Brahmarákshás Bhetála, and made him transport him into the very chamber of the lady. Finding that she would not answer him in the natural way, he made Bhetála obsess all her ladies-in-waiting and set them to praising him, telling him a story, and reproaching their mistress for her silence. Thereupon she sent them out of the room. The Princess then drew a curtain between herself and the king, but the spirit was made to enter the curtain and set it talking. The Princess pushed the curtain aside; whereupon her petticoat took up the conversation, and she cast that aside. Then the robe was made to speak, then the undergarment, then the four legs of her *charpai* or lounge; but the stubborn damsel held her tongue. Finally Bhetála was made to show (materialise) himself as a parrot, was caught by the Princess's order and given to her, and it straightway went on to tell a story about the Princess being obsessed by S'ani, the god of Ill Luck. This was too much for her; she flung herself at Vikram's feet, confessed herself vanquished, and as he did not want her for wife, was given by him in marriage to a suitable Prince. The story is given in *Pés'ámadandé Kathai,* a Tamil story book.

The weighty subject of A'ves'a is treated of in the *Laghu Sabdârtha Sarvasva* of Mahámahopádhyáya Paravastu Vencatarungáchárya, Vol. I., p. 316, art. *Avatâra.* All intelligent

Western readers of theosophical literature have heard of the Hindu theory of Avatárs—the Avatárs of Vishnu, the visible manifestations of the protecting care of God over erring mankind, the proofs of his desire to keep them walking in the path of religious aspiration. Avatâras are of two kinds: *Prádur-bháva* and *A'ves'a*. The act of assuming a body which is not presided over, or rather animated by, a jîva, is called Prádur-bháva, of which Râma and Krishna are cited as examples. What A'ves'a is, has been shown above. We find in *Páncharátra Pádmasamhitá Charyápada*, Chapter XXIV., verses 131–140, full instructions for performing the A'ves'a:

"I now tell thee, O Lotus-born, the method by which to enter another's body (Pindam). . . . The corpse to be occupied should be fresh, pure, of middle age, endued with all good qualities and free from the awful diseases resulting from sin (*viz.*, syphilis, leprosy, etc.). The body should be that of a Brahmin or even of a Kshatriya. It should be laid out in some secluded place (where there is no risk of interruption during the ceremonial process), with its face turned towards the sky and its legs straightened out. Beside its legs, shouldst thou seat thyself in *Yogásana* (a posture of yoga), but previously, O four-faced one, shouldst thou with fixed and mental concentration, have long exercised this yoga power. The jîva is located in the *nábhichakra* (solar plexus), is of itself radiant as the sun and of the form of hamsa (a bird)* and it moves along

---

* Hamsa is "Soham" inverted, which means "That I am," referring to Parabrahm. Thus Parabrahm = Jívátma = Soham = Hamsa. But at the same time Hamsa being also the name of a divine bird supposed to possess the power of separating milk from water, it is made to esoterically represent

the Idâ and Pingala nâdis (two alleged channels of psychic circulation). Having been concentrated as hamsa (by yoga), it
will pass out through the nostrils, and, like a bird, dart
through space. Thou shouldst accustom thyself to this exercise, sending out the Prána to the height of a palm-tree, and
causing it to travel a mile, or five miles or more, and then
re-attracting it into thy body, which it must re-enter as it left
it, through the nostrils, and restore it to its natural centre in
the nâbhichakra. This must be practised daily until perfection be reached."

Then, having acquired the requisite skill, the Yogi may
attempt the experiment of psychical transfer and, seated as
above described, he will be able to withdraw his *Prána-jîva*
from his own body, and introduce it into the chosen corpse, by
the path of the nostrils, until it reaches the empty solar-plexus,
there establishes its residence, reanimates the deceased person,
and causes him to be seen as though "risen from the dead."

The story of the resuscitation of the body of the deceased
Rajah Amaraka of Amritapura by the Sage S'ankaráchárya,
given by Mádhava, one of his biographers, has been very
widely read. A *résumé* of it will be found in the article "Life of
S'ankaráchárya, etc.," contributed by Mr. (later Justice) K. T.
Telang, on page 69 of the number of the *Theosophist* for
January, 1880. The Sage had pledged himself, if granted one
month's respite, to answer questions propounded to him by

A'tmá. This is what is meant by the text "of the form of the bird Hamsa."
Hamsa is that "silvery spark in the brain," that starry spark which is "not
the soul, but the halo around the soul," so vividly described by Bulwer Lyt-
ton in the XXXI. chapter of *A Strange Story*.

the wife of Sage Mándana Misra upon the science of Love, with which he, a celibate from childhood, was totally unacquainted. Journeying with his disciples, he reached the vicinity of Amritapura and saw the Rajah's corpse lying at the foot of a tree, surrounded by mourners. This was his chance to acquire the desired knowledge practically, so leaving his body to the care of his disciples, he withdrew from it his *prána-jîva,* entered the body of the King, and amid the tumultuous joy of his subjects over the supposed resuscitation, went to the capital and for some months lived the usual Zenana life of a sovereign ruler, and finally answered the questions about love.* The details need not be given here, my object being merely to use the incident in connection with the problem of H. P. B., as an illustration of the recognised power of A'ves'a possessed by a Yogi. Mádhaváchárya's *S'ankaravijáya* thus describes it:

"Withdrawing the (Prána) *Váyu* from the extremities of the toes and emerging through the *brahmarándhra,* the knower of Yoga (S'ankara) entered, and, by slow degrees, occupied the whole body of the dead (King) down to its very feet."

By an interesting coincidence, I had just read this passage when a certain circumstance flashed into my memory, and I turned over my old New York files of letters and memoranda until I had found the following. It occurs in some notes I made at the time, of a conversation between myself and one of the Mahátmás, a Hungarian by birth, who, on that evening, occupied H. P. B.'s body:

"He shades his eyes and turns down the gas in the

---

* Vide "Káma Sutra."

standing burner on the table. Ask him why. Says that light is a physical force, and entering the eye of an unoccupied body, encounters—*i.e.*, strikes against—the astral soul of the temporary occupant, gives it a shock and such a push that the occupant might be pushed out. Paralysis of the occupied body is even possible. Extreme caution must be used in entering a body, and one cannot thoroughly fit oneself to it throughout until the automatic movements of the circulation, breathing, etc., adjust themselves to the automatism of the occupier's own body—with which, however far distant, his projected astral body is most intimately related. I then lit a burner of the chandelier overhead, but the occupier at once held a newspaper so as to shade the crown of the head from the light. Surprised, I asked for an explanation, and was told that it was even more dangerous to have a strong top light strike upon the crown of the head than to have light shine into the eyes."

I knew nothing then about the six vital centres (*shat chakramas*) of the body; nor was I aware that the most important of them, the *brahmarândhra,* was under the parietal bones; nor that it is the custom in India to break the skull of the burning corpse at that place to facilitate the withdrawal of the astral body of the deceased: moreover, I had not then read the story of S'ankaráchárya's leaving his own body and entering that of the deceased Rajah by that path of the soul. I simply saw what the Mahátmá did, and wondered over his explanation; but now, in the fulness of time, the mystery is cleared up and the cases of New York and Amritapura are mutually related. By the light of the latter and the teachings of Aryan occult science, one can more readily comprehend the mystery of the former. Whereas before all was dark, and we had not even a name at our disposal to explain the fact, we can now see that it is possible for any one versed in Yoga to occupy the body of another living person, when the astral body of its owner has been withdrawn and the empty house is placed at the disposal of visiting friends. The bearing which this matter has upon the problem of H. P. B. is most evident; as I shall try to show in the next chapter.

Chapter XVII.

RE-INCARNATION

The first effect of proving the collaborate nature of *Isis Unveiled*, is to confirm our critical view of its registered author: she remains a mental prodigy, yet drops out of the literary class which includes such giants of acquired knowledge as Aristotle, Longinus, Buddaghosha, Hiouen Thsang, Alberuni, Mádháváchárya, Nasireddin—the Persian philosopher and cyclopædist—and in modern times, Leibnitz, Voltaire, Spencer, etc. The justness of her self-estimate is shown, and, without, ranking as erudite, she becomes an almost unique problem among Western people. If the theory of Bacon's authorship of Shakespeare's plays be disproved, then Shakespeare's production of them, when his vagabond disposition and commonplace character are taken into account, rather supports than contradicts the theory that, like H. P. B., he was but an agent of greater, unseen, living intellects, who controlled his body and used it to write things far beyond his normal capacity. The comparison is to his advantage, because we find in his works a far deeper acquaintance with human nature

and wider grasp of intuitive knowledge than in hers. His natural mind (or that which was drawn from) seems to have contained from the beginning all that he would ever be obliged to
utilise; whereas she appears to have been the subject of a distinct mental evolution. Take, for instance, her teachings on
Re-incarnation, the strong foundation-stone of the ancient
occult philosophy, which was affirmed in the *Secret Doctrine*
and her other later writings. When we worked on *Isis* it was
neither taught us by the Mahátmás, nor supported by her in
literary controversies or private discussions of those earlier
days. She held to, and defended, the theory that human souls,
after death, passed on by a course of purificatory evolution to
other and more spiritualised planets. I have notes of a conversation between a Mahátmá and myself in which this same theory is affirmed. And this puzzles me most of all; for, while it
is quite conceivable that, either through imperfect cerebro-
psychic training, or otherwise, she, the pupil and psychic
agent, might not have known the solid philosophical basis of
the Re-incarnation theory, I can scarcely see how the like
ignorance could extend to the Adept and Teacher. Is it possible
that Re-incarnation was not taught this Adept by *his* Master,
and that he, as well as H. P. B., had to learn it subsequently?
There are said to be sixty-three stages of Adeptship, and it is
not impossible. There are, among them, I was told, men who
are great natural psychics yet almost illiterate; and at least one
who, like Buddha's favourite, Ananda, possesses no *Siddhis*,
yet is so intuitional as to be able to understand all esoteric
writings at sight. My notes report the Teacher as telling me
that "Souls go hence after death to other planets. Souls that are

to be born on this Earth are waiting in other invisible planets."
These two statements agree with the latest teachings of H. P. B.,
the planets in question at either end of the soul's earthly habitation being members of our "chain of globes." But there is left
a vast hiatus between the two extremes, that we now understand to be filled with the multitudinous evolutionary re-births
of the travelling entity. Let the note stand as it is, but H. P. B.,
in *Isis* (Vol. I., p. 351) says most unequivocally.

"We will now present a few fragments of this mysterious
doctrine of Re-incarnation—as distinct from transmigration—
which we have from an authority. Re-incarnation, *i.e.*, the
appearance of the same individual, or rather of his astral
monad, twice on the same planet, *is not a rule in nature; it is
an exception*, like the teratological phenomenon of a two-
headed infant."

The cause of it, when it does occur is, she says, that the
design of nature to produce a perfect human being has been
interfered with, and therefore she must make another attempt.
Such exceptional interferences, H. P. B. explains, are the cases
of abortion, of infants dying before a certain age, and of congenital and incurable idiocy. In such cases, the higher principles have not been able to untie themselves with the lower, and
hence a perfect being has not been born. But—

"If reason has been so far developed as to become active
and discriminative, *there is no Re-incarnation on this Earth*,
for the three parts of the triune man have been united together,
and he is capable of running the race. But when the new being
has not passed beyond the condition of monad, or when, as in
the idiot, the trinity has not been completed, the immortal

spark which illuminates it has to re-enter on the earthly plane, as it was frustrated in its first attempt. Otherwise, the mortal or astral, and the immortal, or divine, souls could not progress in unison and pass onward to *the sphere above*."

The italics are mine, and thus I was taught. My present belief is that of the Hindus and Buddhists. She told Mr. Walter R. Old—who is my informant—that she was not taught the doctrine of Re-incarnation until 1879—when we were in India. I willingly accept that statement, both because it tallies with our beliefs and writings in New York, and, because, if she knew it when we were writing *Isis*, there was no earthly reason why she should have misled me or others, even if she had so desired, which I do not believe.

She and I believed, and taught orally as well as wrote that man is a trinity of physical body, astral body (soul—the Greek *psuché*), and divine spirit. This will be found set forth in the first official communication made by us to the European reading public. It was an article entitled "The Views of the Theosophists," and appeared in the *Spiritualist* for December 7, 1877. In it, speaking for our whole party, I say:

"We believe that the man of flesh dies, decays, and goes to the crucible of evolution, to be worked over and over again; that the astral man (or *double*, or soul), freed from physical imprisonment, is followed by the consequences of his earthly deeds, thoughts and desires. He either becomes purged of the last traces of earthly grossness, and, finally, after an incalculable lapse of time, is joined to his divine spirit, and lives forever as an entity, or, having been completely debased on earth, he sinks deeper into matter and is annihilated."

I go on to say that "the man of pure life and spirituality of aspiration would be drawn towards a more spiritual realm than this earth of ours and repelled by its influence"; while, on the other hand, the vicious and thoroughly depraved person would have lost his spirit during life, be reduced to a duality instead of a trinity at the hour of death, and, upon passing out of the physical body, become disintegrated; *its grosser matter going into the ground* and its finer turning into *a bhut*, or "elementary," "wandering in and about the habitations of men, obsessing sensitives to glut vicariously its depraved appetites, until its life is burnt out by their very intensity and dissolution comes to crown the dreadful career."

This was the sum and substance of our teaching at that time about the nature and destiny of man, and shows how infinitely far away from believing in Re-incarnation H. P. B. and I were then. If any one should be disposed to say that this letter of mine in the *Spiritualist* represents only my personal views, and that neither the Masters nor H. P. B. are responsible for my crudities, I shall just refer them to the issue of the *Spiritualist* for February 8, 1878,* where appears a letter from H. P. B. herself upon the general subject of my letter; which had aroused a most animated discussion between the chief exponents of British Spiritualism on the one side, and C. C. Massey, John Storer Cobb, Prof. Alex. Wilder, Miss Kislingbury, Dr. C. Carter Blake, Gerald Massey and myself, on the other, and been called by M.A. (Oxon.) "a Theosophical rock

---

* Apparently the wrong date has been pasted above the cutting in our scrap-book. I think it must have been February 1.

hurled by the vigorous arm of the P. T. S. and creating a huge splash" in the unhealthy pool of trans-Atlantic Spiritualism. H. P. B.'s clarion, as usual, waked the echoes. She calls herself "the unattractive old party *superficially known* as H. P. Blavatsky"—a most significant phrase, says that "the Colonel corresponds directly with Hindu scholars, and has from them a good deal more than he can get from so clumsy a preceptor as myself;" and that she thinks I have "thrown out some hints worthy of the thoughtful consideration of the unprejudiced." A second letter from me in answer to M.A. (Oxon.) appeared in February, and a very long, very powerful, and very explicit one from H. P. B., of date N. Y., January 14, 1878, *did* appear in the *Spiritualist* of February 8, of the same year. This whole letter is well worth reading. In it she says, *á propos* of the necessity that an Ego which has failed to unite itself with the physico-psychical duality of a child who prematurely dies, should re-incarnate—"Man's cycle is not complete until he becomes individually immortal. No one stage of probation and experience can be skipped over. He must be a man before he can become a spirit. A dead child is a failure of nature—he must live again; and the same *psuché* re-enters the physical plane through another birth. *Such cases, together with those of congenital idiots are, as stated in "Isis Unveiled," the only instances of human re-incarnation."* Can anything be plainer?

Our party left New York for India on Dec. 17, 1878, and a few days previously H. P. B. wrote to the *Revue Spirite*, of Paris, an article which appeared in that magazine, Jan. 1, 1879; it was in answer to sundry critics. She now describes man as four-principled, a "tetraktis" or quaternary. I translate:

"Yes, 'for the Theosophists of New York, man is *a* trinity, and not a duality.' He is, however, more than that: for, by adding the physical body, man is a *Tetraktis*, or quaternary. But, however supported in this particular doctrine we may be by the greatest philosophers of ancient Greece, it is neither to Pythagoras, to Plato, nor, furthermore, to the celebrated *Theodidaktoi* of the school of Alexandria, that we owe it. We shall speak further on of our Masters."

After citing passages from various ancient authorities in support of the views presented, she says: "our Masters [meaning those from whom we learnt the doctrine] are Patanjali, Kapila, Kanada, all the systems and schools of A'ryavârta which served as inexhaustible mines for the Greek philosophers, from Pythagoras to Plato." Not all the Indian schools, certainly, for among them the old sects of Charvakas and Brihâspatis denied the survival of man after death, and were almost exact prototypes of our modern Materialists. It is also to be noted that Patanjali, Kapila, and the other Masters she names, taught that Re-incarnation is the rule in Nature, while she and I declared it to be the exception.

Ultimately, the doctrine of Re-incarnation was fully accepted and expounded, both in its exoteric sense and esoterically. Not publicly taught so early as 1879, however, for it is not to be found in the first two volumes of the *Theosophist*, but only appears in the third, and then in connection with the *Fragments of Occult Truth*, a series of essays, chiefly by Mr. A. P. Sinnett, and based upon instructions given him by the Masters and by H. P. B. In its plain exoteric, or orthodox form, I had got it in Ceylon and embodied it in the *Buddhist*

Catechism, of which the first edition, after passing through the ordeal of critical examination by the High Priest Sumán-gala Thero, appeared in July, 1881. The *Catechism*, of course, was only a synopsis of the doctrines of Southern Buddhism, not a proclamation of personal beliefs. The exposition of the Re-incarnation theory was rather meagre in the first edition; but it was given at much greater length in the revised edition of 1882, where I defined the relation of the re-incarnated being of this birth to that of the preceding ones, and answered the question why we have no memory of experiences in prior incarnations. A conversation with Sumángala Thero upon the morality of the theory of Karma, led me to frame the note defining the difference between Personality and Individuality, between physical memory, or the recollection of things which pertain to the ordinary waking consciousness, and spiritual memory, which has to do with the experiences of the Higher Self and its Individuality. The distinction had not previously been made, but it was at once accepted and has been propagated by all our chief Theosophical writers since that time. H. P. B. adopted it, and has introduced it in her *Key to Theosophy* (pp. 130 and 134), with enlargements and illustrations. These are historical facts, and their bearing upon the present discussion is evident.

H. P. B.'s first published declaration that Re-incarnation was an element in Theosophical belief occurs in the leading article of the first number ever issued of the *Theosophist* (*What is Theosophy?* Vol. I., p. 3, October, 1879). It was but a bare allusion to the subject and nothing more.

"Theosophy," she says, "believes also in *Anastasis*, or

continued existence, and in transmigration (evolution), or a series of changes in the soul, which can be defended and explained on strict philosophical principles; and only by making a distinction between *Paramátmá* (transcendental, supreme soul) and *fiuátmá* (animal, or conscious soul), of the Vedântins."* This is extremely vague, and does little towards solving the difficulty. In a foot-note to this passage, however, she promises a series of articles on *The World's Great Theosophists*, in which, says she, "we intend showing that from Pythagoras, who got his wisdom in India, down to our best known modern philosophers and Theosophists—David Hume and Shelley, the English poet, and the spiritists of France, included—many believed and yet believe in metempsychosis, or Re-incarnation of the soul, etc." But she does not clearly say what is her own belief. The promised series of articles most unfortunately never appeared, though it may have been the germ of her idea to devote one of the new volumes of *The Secret Doctrine* to an account of the Great Adepts.

Mr. Sinnett's famous series of essays entitled *Fragments of Occult Truth* was begun by H. P. B. in No. I, of Vol. III., of the *Theosophist*, as an answer to Mr. Terry, of Melbourne, who had taken exception to the anti-spiritualistic views of Theosophists. In the first *Fragment*, she reiterates the teaching of New York, that the soul at death passes into another world, "the so-called world of effects (in reality, a state and not a place), and there, purified of much of its material taints,

---

* *Anastasis* does not mean Re-incarnation, but a raising from the dead of the same person; and *fivátmá* is not the animal soul—as even all younger Theosophists are aware.

evolves out of itself a new Ego, to be re-born (after a brief period of freedom and enjoyment) *in the next higher world of causes, an objective world similar to this present globe of ours*, but higher in the spiritual scale, where matter and material tendencies play a far less important part than here." Re-incarnation is herein postulated, but not on this globe nor by the same Ego, but by another one which generates out of our present one in an interplanetary state. In *Fragment No. 3* (*Theosophist* for Sept., 1882), the new Ego is said after passing its normal time—according to its merit, which agrees with the doctrine taught by S'rî Krishna, in the *Bhagavadgíta*—in a state of felicity (Devachan) either to pass on to the "next superior planet," or return for re-birth on this globe "if it has not completed its appointed tale of earth-lives." Previously to this there had been nothing published about an appointed number of Re-incarnations, either on this globe or others, but only the outlines sketched of a psychic pilgrimage, or evolutionary progress from star to star, of a Divine Self which clothed itself with a new soul-body in each palingenesis.

In 1880, we two visited Simla, and Mr. A. O. Hume enjoyed the good fortune, which had previously fallen to Mr. Sinnett's lot, of getting into correspondence with our Mahátmás. H. P. B. revisited Simla without me in 1881, and the two friends above-named received in due time from the Masters the Re-incarnation theory. Mr. Sinnett expounded it in *Fragment No. 4* (*Theosophist*, Vol. IV., No. I, October, 1882), where he laid the basis of the doctrine of terrestrial Re-incarnations in a series of major and minor, or root and sub-races, and the extension of the process to the other planets of a chain to which the Earth belongs. Mr. Hume did the same in his *Hints on Esoteric Theosophy* (Calcutta, August, 1882), where he synthetically says that "man has many complete rounds to make of the entire cycle (chain, he means) of the planets. And in each planet, in each round, he has many lives to live. At a certain stage of his evolution, when certain portions of his less material elements are fully developed, he becomes morally responsible." (Op. cit., p. 52.)

Thus, six years after the date of my New York conversation with the Mahátmá, the fundamental and necessary idea of Re-incarnation was launched on the sea of modern Western thought from the congenial land of its primeval birth.

I have been obliged to trace its evolution within our lines at the risk of a small digression, as it was necessary for the future welfare of the Society to show the apparent baselessness of the theory that our present grand block of teaching had been in H. P. B.'s possession from the beginning. That theory I consider pernicious and without foundation. If I am wrong, I shall be most happy to be corrected. To admit it would involve the necessity of conceding that she had knowingly and wilfully lent herself to deception and the teaching of untruth in *Isis*, and later. I believe that she wrote then as she did later, exactly according to her lights, and that she was just as sincere in denying Re-incarnation in 1876–'78 as she was in affirming it after 1882. Why she and I were permitted to put the mis-statement into *Isis*, and, especially, why it was made to me by the Mahátmá, I cannot explain, unless I was the victim of glamour in believing that I talked with a Master on the evening in question. So let it pass. The Masters could give

H. P. B. whatever they chose by dictation, they could write it themselves with her hand by occupying her physical body, and they could enable me to write by giving me hints and outlines and then helping my intuitions. Yet, notwithstanding all this, they certainly did not teach us what we now accept as the truth about Re-incarnation; nor bid us keep silent about it; nor resort to any vague generalities capable of being now twisted into an apparent agreement with our present views; nor interpose to prevent us from writing and teaching the heretical and unscientific idea that, save in certain few cases, the human entity was not, and could not, be re-incarnated on one and the same planet.*

To return to the matter of the occupancy (*dves'a*) of H. P. B.'s body. There was one collateral proof continually thrusting ·itself upon one's notice, if one but paid attention to it. Let us say that the Master A or B had been "on guard" an hour or more, had been working on *Isis*, alone or jointly with me, and was at a given moment saying something to me or, if third parties were present, to one of them. Suddenly she (he?) stops speaking, rises and leaves the room, excusing herself for a moment on some pretext to strangers. She presently returns, looks around as any new arrival would upon entering a room where there was company, makes herself a fresh cigarette, and says something which has not the least reference to what had been talked about when she left the room. Some one present,

---

* Some valued friends have tried to persuade me to omit all the foregoing argument about the genesis of the Re-incarnation idea within our movement, but I cannot see it as my duty to do so. I will no more suppress important facts than I will make false statements.

wishing to keep her to the point, asks her kindly to explain. She shows embarrassment and inability to pick up the thread; perhaps expresses an opinion flatly contradicting what she had just affirmed, and when taken to task, becomes vexed and says strong things; or, when told that she had said so-and-so, appears to take an introspective glance and says, "Oh yes: excuse me," and goes on with her subject. She was sometimes as quick as lightning in these changes, and I myself, forgetting her multiplex personality, have often been very irritated for her seeming inability to keep to the same opinion, and her bold denial that she had not said what she had certainly said plainly enough, the moment before. In due time, it was explained to me that it takes time, after entering another's living body, to link on one's own consciousness with the brain memory of the preceding occupier, and that if one tries to continue a conversation before this adjustment is complete, just such mistakes as the above may occur. This accords with what the Mahátmá told me in New York about occupancy, and with the description of the way in which, we were told in *Shankaravijâya*,* Shankara entered the defunct Rajah Amaraká's body: "entered and *by slow degrees occupied* the whole body of the dead down to its very feet." The explanation of the gradual blending of the two *jîvas* in one steady heart and other bodily automatism (Cf. XVI.) extends to the matter of the two consciousnesses, and until this is perfected, there

---

* In a recent Calcutta lecture on "The Kinship between Hinduism and Buddhism" I show that the best Orientalists regard *Shankaravijâya* as an old spurious work. I quote it now merely for the sake of the description of the *dves'a* process.

must be just such a confusion of ideas, assertions, and recollections as I have above described, and as the majority of H. P. B.'s visitors must have been puzzled by. Sometimes, when we were alone, has either the departing Somebody said: "I must put this into the brain so that my successor may find it there," or the incoming Somebody after greeting me with a friendly word, asked me what was the subject of discussion before the "change."

I have noted above how various Mahátmás, in writing to me about H. P. B. and her body, spoke of the latter as a shell occupied by one of themselves. In my Diary of 1878, I find entered under date of October 12, and in the H. P. B. manuscript of Mahátmá "M," the following: "H. P. B. talked with W. alone until 2 after midnight. He confessed he saw *three* DISTINCT individualities in her. He *knows* it. Does not wish to say so to Olcott for fear H. S. O. will make fun of him!!!" The underscorings and points of exclamation are copied literally. The "W." mentioned was Mr. Wimbridge, who was then our guest. To account for an entry made by another person in my private Diary, I must explain that when I left New York on professional business, which I had to do several times in that year, the daily record was written up by "H. P. B.," the noun of multitude. In the entry of the following day (Oct. 13) the same hand, after specifying the seven visitors who called that evening, writes of one of them: "Dr. Pike, looking at H. P. B. several times, started and said that no one in the world impressed him so much. Once he sees in H. P. B. a girl of 16, at another an old woman of 100, and again a man with a beard!!" On Oct. 22, the same hand writes: "H. P. B. left them [our visitors of that evening] in the dining-room and retired with H. S. O. to the library to write letters. N——[a certain Mahátmá] left watch and in came S——[another adept]; the latter with orders from .˙. to complete all by the first day of December" [for our departure for India]. On November 9, in another modified H. P. B. script, is written: "Body sick and no hot-water to bathe it. Nice caboose." November 12, in the "M" script: "H. P. B. played a trick on me by suddenly *fainting*, to the great dismay of Bates and Wim. Used the greatest will-power to put up the body on its legs." November 14, in same handwriting: "N——decamped and M. walked in [from and into the H. P. B. body is meant]. Came with definite orders from .˙. *Have to go* at the latest from 15 to 20 Dec. [to India]." November 29, another Mahátmá writes that he had "answered the Russian Aunt"—*i.e.,* the beloved aunt of H. P. B. Finally, not to dwell upon one subject too long, on Nov. 30, a third Mahátmá writes: "Belle Mitchell came at 12 and took away the S——[Mahátmá M.] for a walk and drive. Went to Macy's. Had to materialise rupees. H. P. B. came home at 4, etc." I have also various letters from the Mahátmás alluding to H. P. B. in her own individual capacity, sometimes speaking very frankly about her peculiarities, good and bad, and was once sent, by the Masters, *with written instructions*, on a confidential mission to another city to bring about certain events necessary for her spiritual evolution. I have the document still. One quite long letter that I received in 1879, while in Rajputana, most strangely alters her sex, speaks of her in the male gender, and confounds her with Mahátmá M.—known as our Guru. It says—about a first draft of the letter itself which had been written but not sent me: "Owing to certain expressions therein, the letter was stopped on its way by order of our Brother H. P. B. As you are not under my direct guidance but his (hers), we have naught to say, either of us; etc." And again: "Our Brother H. P. B. rightly remarked at Jeypore that, etc." It is a noble communication throughout, and if it were pertinent to our present theme, I should feel tempted to publish it, so as to show the high quality of the correspondence that for years went on between my blessed Teachers and myself. It was in this particular letter that I was told, in answer to my expressed desire to retire from the world and go and live with them, that, "The only means available and at hand for you to reach us, is *through the Theosophical Society*," which I was abjured to consolidate, push forward and build up; I must learn to be unselfish. My correspondent adds: "None of us live for ourselves, we all live for humanity." This was the spirit of all my instructions, this is the idea inculcated throughout *Isis Unveiled*. Let the literary faults of that book be what they may; let its author be charged with plagiarism or not; the sum and substance of its argument is that man is of a complex nature, animal at one extreme, divine at the other; and that the only real and perfect existence, the only one that is free from illusions, pain and sorrow, because in it, their cause—Ignorance—does not exist, is that of the spirit, the Highest Self. The book incites to pure and high living, to expansion of mind and universality of tenderness and sympathy; it shows there is a Path upwards, and that it is accessible to the wise who are brave; it traces all modern knowledge and speculation to archaic sources; and, affirming the past and present existence of

Adepts and of occult science, affords us a stimulus to work and an ideal to work up to.

Upon its appearance the book made such a sensation that the first edition was exhausted within ten days.* The critics, on the whole, dealt kindly with it. Dr. Shelton Mackenzie, one of the most capable ones of the day, writes that "it is one of the most remarkable works for originality of thought, thoroughness of research, depth of philosophic exposition, and variety and extent of learning that has appeared for very many years" (*Phila. Press*, October 9, 1887). The literary critic of the *N. Y. Herald* (Sep. 30, 1877) says that independent minds "will welcome the new publication as a most valuable contribution to philosophical literature," and that it "will supplement the *Anacalypsis* of Godfrey Higgins. There is a great resemblance between the works. . . . With its striking peculiarities, its

---

* The *American Bookseller* (October, 1877), says: "The sale . . . is unprecedented for a work of its kind, the entire edition having been exhausted within ten days of the date of publication. In 1783, Godfrey Higgins published his *Anacalypsis*, a work of similar character, and although only 200 copies were printed, at the death of the author, a number of years after, many copies remained unsold, and were disposed of in bulk by his executors to a London bookseller. The work is now exceedingly rare and readily brings $100 per copy. The world has grown older since the days of Higgins, and Madame Blavatsky's book is of greater interest; but still the demand for it is quite remarkable, and far beyond the expectations of its publishers." Perfectly true; and so surprised and pleased was Mr. Bouton, that on Sunday, Feb. 10, 1878, in my presence, he offered her $5,000 as copyright on an edition of a book in one volume, if she would write it, which should a little more unveil *Isis*. He intended to print only 100 copies and make the price $100 per copy. Though she needed money badly enough, she refused the offer on the ground that she was not permitted at that time to divulge any more arcane secrets than she had done in *Isis*. Mr. Bouton is still living and can corroborate this statement.

audacity, its versatility and the prodigious variety of subjects which it notices and handles, it is one of the remarkable productions of the century." Dr. G. Bloede, an erudite German scholar, says that, "under all considerations, it will range among the most important contributions to the literature of the modern science of the spirit, and be worth the attention of every thinking student of this."

Some of the notices were flippant and prejudiced enough to make it clear that the critics had not read the book. For instance, the *Springfield Republican* said it was "a large dish of hash"; The *N. Y. Sun* classifies it with the similar works of past times as "discarded rubbish"; the Editor of the *N. Y. Times* wrote to Mr. Bouton that he was sorry they could not touch *Isis Unveiled*, as they "have a holy horror of Mme. Blavatsky and her letters"; the *N. Y. Tribune* says her learning is "crude and undigested" and "her incoherent account of Brahmanism and Buddhism, suggests a hint of the presumption rather than the information of the writer." And so on and so forth. The weighty fact, however, is that the book has become a classic—as Mr. Quaritch prophesied to Mr. Bouton that it would;* has gone through a number of editions; and now, after the lapse of seventeen years, is in demand all over the world. When it was ready for publication I, of course, did what I could to bring it to the notice of my personal acquaintance;

---

* Mr. Quaritch writes to Mr. Bouton from London, December 27, 1877, in a letter which the latter kindly gave us as an encouraging forecast: "The book will evidently make its way in England and become a classic. I am very glad to be the English agent." And, I may add, we were more glad that he should be; knowing his reputation for indomitable energy and high-mindedness.

and I remember shortly afterwards meeting one of them—a leading legal functionary—in the street, and having him shake his fist at me in a friendly way, and say, "I have a crow to pick with you." "And why?" I asked. "Why? Because you made me buy *Isis Unveiled*, and I found it so fascinating that my law cases are getting into arrears, and I have been sitting up nearly the whole of the past two nights to read it. Not only that, but she makes me feel what a lot of commonplace men we are in comparison with those Eastern mystics and philosophers she writes so charmingly about." The first money received for a copy of *Isis* was sent me by a lady of Styria with her order; we kept it "for luck," and it now hangs, framed, on the walls of the *Theosophist* office at Adyar.

The truest thing ever said about *Isis* was the expression of an American author that it is "a book with a revolution in it."

Chapter XVIII.

EARLY DAYS OF
THE SOCIETY

Among the public events which contributed to give notoriety to our Society in its early days, was the rescue of a party of pauper Arabs from threatened starvation, and their shipment to Tunis. It was theosophical only in the limited sense of being humanitarian, hence an act of altruism; and all altruistic endeavours are essentially theosophical. Moreover, in this case, the element of religion was a factor. The story, in brief, is as follows:

One Sunday morning, in July, 1876, H. P. B. and I, being alone in the "Lamasery," read in the morning papers that a party of nine ship-wrecked Mussulman Arabs had been landed from the schooner *Kate Foster*, just arrived from Trinidad. They were penniless and friendless, could not speak a word of English, and had wandered about the streets for two days without food, until the secretary of the Turkish Consul gave them some loaves of bread, and, by order of His Honor the Mayor of New York, temporary shelter had been given them at Bellevue Hospital. Unfortunately for them, certain

New Regulations about emigrants had been adopted in the March preceding by the Commissioners of Public Charities and the Emigration Board, which made both those public bodies powerless to deal with cases like the present. The papers stated that the Arabs had brought no documents with them to prove their nationality, and thereby fix upon some foreign Consul the responsibility for their custody and relief; in vain they had been taken to the consuls of Turkey and France; and, unless private relief were forthcoming, a bitter prospect was before them. How well I remember the scene when we had read the narrative! H. P. B. and I stood shoulder-to-shoulder, looking out of the south front window each deploring the lot of the poor cast-aways. The fact which appealed strongest to our feelings was that they were Mussulmans—Heathen, whose religion placed them outside the bounds of ready sympathy in a community of Christians, who, to say nothing about popular prejudice, had too frequent appeals to relieve the wants of their co-religionists. These unfortunates had a right, then, to the kind offices of fellow Heathen like ourselves, and then and there it was decided that I should go to work. The result was that I succeeded, under the favour of the Mayor of New York, in collecting some $2000, with which their necessities were supplied, and they were sent to Tunis under charge of a member of our Society. All the details will be found in the *Theosophist* for September, 1893.

As said in a previous chapter, among the most delightful reminiscences of those early theosophic years is our correspondence with thoughtful, cultured persons of both sexes, of whom two are most lovingly remembered. They are Charles Carleton Massey and William Stainton Moseyn (or, as corrupted, Moses). The general topic of our correspondence was mentioned above (Cf. Chapter IV.), and the names of these two loyal friends can never pass out of my memory. We, of course, represented the conservative party of Oriental Occultism; Stainton Moseyn (Moses) was a progressive, truth-seeking, highly-educated Spiritualist, taking him all-in-all the ablest man among them; and Massey was between the two extremes, a candid and convinced investigator of the phenomena, with a deeply metaphysical mental bias, ready to meet half-way any new facts or ideas we might put forward. The interchange of letters—some so long as to be rather essays—continued between us four during several years, and our discussions covered a very wide range of interesting, important, even vital questions relating to psychological subjects. The one most thoroughly threshed out was, I fancy, that of the Elemental Spirits, their place in nature, and their relations with humanity. I had lightly touched upon this question in our first European manifesto above alluded to, but it was now gone into in all its chief bearings. I deeply regret that those in charge of Stainton Moseyn's papers, have not yet sent me those which might have helped me in my present work, as I might have made it much more interesting by comparing H. P. B.'s and my letters with the replies of our friends, which I have preserved. S. M. had gone into the investigation of mediumistic phenomena with the sole purpose of satisfying himself whether they were real or not, but shortly found himself a medium despite himself, and the subject of phenomena of the

most extraordinary kind. By night and by day, whether alone
or in company, they would occur, and soon all the scientific
and philosophical ideas he had brought away from Oxford,
were scattered to the four winds, and he had to accept new
theories of matter and force, man and nature. His revered
friend and benefactress, Mrs. Speer, gave in *Light*, weekly
reports of the séances held by S. M. at Dr. Speer's house, and,
I venture to say, a more interesting record of mediumship has
never been written, for, in past ages or the present, there has
hardly ever been a more gifted medium than my heart-
brother, now dead and gone. His preeminence consisted in
the surprising variety of his phenomena, which were both
physical and psychical and all highly instructive, added to his
trained mental endowments, which reflected themselves in
the quality of the psychically transmitted intelligence, and his
dogged determination to believe nothing taught him by the
alleged spirits which he could not perfectly understand. The
major part of these teachings he received by automatic writing
through his own hand, just as Mr. Stead seems now to be getting his own spirit-teachings from *Julia*; he might give his
whole attention to reading a book or conversation, but his dis-
engaged hand would go on writing and writing by the half-
hour together, and when he turned his eyes upon the pages
thus covered, he would find original thoughts, conveying new
ideas foreign to his own beliefs, or successfully answering his
questions previously put, perhaps, on another occasion. He
was always convinced, and vehemently so declared in his letters to us, that the intelligence controlling his hand was not
his own; neither his waking or latent consciousness, but just

simply a spirit or spirits; he claimed to know them perfectly by sight (clairvoyant), speech (clairaudient), and writing, as unmistakably as he knew any living person. We, on the other hand, urged that the question was not yet proven, and that there was at least an even chance that his "Imperator," or chief spirit-teacher, was his latent self, and that his circle phenomena were produced by Elementals coming for the time being under the dominion of his own masterful will. It appeared upon comparing notes that several of his most striking mediumistic phenomena were almost identical with those with which H. P. B. was edifying us in New York, and, since hers were admittedly produced by her subject Elementals, I could not see why his might not be also. Among these were the ringing of sweet "fairy bells" in the air; the production of delicious scents in the air and as exudations from the psychic's body, which, with H. P. B., bedewed the palms of her hands, and in S. M.'s case the scalp of his head; lights floating through the air; precipitations of writing on surfaces beyond the operator's reach; *apports* of gems and other objects; air-born music; the possession by each of gems which changed colour and grew dull or black when the possessor fell ill; the disintegration of crayons or leads to be used in precipitated writings; identical Oriental perfumes perceived when certain invisible intelligences versed in occult science were present; Oxon's perceiving in the astral light glowing points of coloured light arranged in a triangle so as to form the mystic symbol of the Eastern Lodge of our Mahátmás; and, finally, the power of leaving the physical body in the "double," retaining consciousness and resuming bodily occupancy at the end of the soul-flight. So close a resemblance in experiences would naturally create a strong mutual interest between the two great psychics, and naturally enough S. M. was most eager to profit by any instructions or hints that H. P. B. could give him as to how he might improve his knowledge of the other world and gain that complete control over his psychical nature which the completed training for adeptship implies. What effect our interchange of views had upon S. M.'s mind and the teachings of "Imperator" to the Speer circle, will be considered in the next chapter. I shall also have something to say with respect to the view taken by educated Hindus as to the danger and puerility of psychical phenomena, whether produced by mediums or *mántrikas*—possessors of charms of power.

Chapter XIX.

CONFLICTING VIEWS

The poles are scarcely farther apart than the views of Western Spiritualists and Asiatics, with respect to communion with the dead. The former encourage it, often try to develop mediumship in themselves or their family members to enjoy it, support many journals and publish many books to tell about and discuss their phenomena, and cite the latter as proofs of the scientific basis of the doctrine of a future life. Asiatics, on the contrary, discourage these necromantic dabblings as soul-debaucheries, and affirm that they work incalculable evil both upon the dead and the living; obstructing the normal evolution of man's spirit and delaying the acquirement of *gnanám*, the highest knowledge. In Europe and America one often meets around the séance-table the noblest, purest, most learned, as well as their opposites; in the East, the mediums and sorcerers are patronised only by Pariahs and other degraded castes, as a general rule. At the West, in these latter days, families usually feel glad rather than sorry if a medium is discovered in their household, whereas in India it is thought a disgrace, a calamity, something to deplore and to abate as soon as possible.

The Hindu, the Buddhist, the Zoroastrian, the Mussulman, are of one mind in the above respect, all being influenced by ancestral tradition as well as by their sacred writings. Dealings with the dead are not alone discountenanced, but also the exhibition of one's own psychical powers, whether congenital or developed later by ascetic training. The Indian Brahmin would, therefore, look with disfavour both upon the phenomena of M. A. Oxon, the medium, and those of H. P. B., the educated thaumaturgist. Not caring for the problems of Western psychology as intellectual stimuli, and having forms of religion which start with the basic hypothesis of spirit, they place but a minimum stress upon the psychic phenomena as proofs of immortality, loathe the obsessed medium as spiritually impure, and hold in diminished respect those who, possessing *siddhis*, vulgarise them by display. The development of a long list of *siddhis* occurs naturally and spontaneously in the progress of Yogic training, of which only eight, *Anima, Mahima, Laghima*, etc.—the Ashta Siddhis, in short—relate to the higher spiritual state; the other eighteen or more pertain to the astral plane and our relations to it and to the plane of this life. Black magicians and beginners have to do with these; the progressed Adepts of White Magic with the nobler group. It is to be observed, then, that while H. P. B.'s phenomena commanded the adoring wonder of her Western pupils and other intimate friends, and caused the malignant scepticism of her opponents, they actually lowered her in the opinion of the orthodox pundits and ascetics of India and Ceylon,

as marking an inferior spiritual evolution. With them, there
was no question of the possible genuineness of the marvels,
for all such are recognised and catalogued in their Scriptures;
the mental aura of a Lankester would asphyxiate them. At the
same time, while the display of psychical phenomena in public or before the vulgar is condemned, the knowledge that a
religious teacher possesses them adds to his sancity, as being
signs of his interior development; but the rule is that they are
not to be shown by a teacher even to his pupils before they
have become so versed in spiritual philosophy as to be able to
understand them.

In the *Kullavagga*, v., 8, I., is related the story of the sandalwood bowl of the Setthi of Rágagaha. He had had a bowl
carved out of a block of sandalwood, and lifted it high up into
the air on the top of a bamboo tied to a succession of other
bamboos, and then offered it as a gift to any Sramaña or Brahman possessed of psychical powers (*Iddhi*) who could levitate
himself and get it down. A renowned monk named Pindala
Bháradvaga accepted the challenge, rose into the air and
brought down the bowl, after going "thrice round Rágagaha
in the air." The onlookers, a great concourse, fell to shouting
and doing him reverence, which noise coming to the ears of
the Buddha, he convened a private meeting of his disciples
and rebuked Pindala.

"This is improper," said he. "Not according to rule, unsuit-
able, unworthy of a Sramaña, unbecoming, and ought not to
be done. . . . Just like a woman who displays herself for the sake
of a miserable piece of money, have you, for the sake of a miserable wooden pot displayed before the laity the superhuman

quality of your miraculous power of Iddhi. This will not con-
duce either to the conversion of the unconverted, or to the
increase of the converted; but rather to those who have not
been converted remaining unconverted, and to the turning
back of those who have been converted." He then made this
imperative rule: "You are not, O Bhikkus, to display *before the
laity* the superhuman power of Iddhi." (*Vide Sacred Books of
the East*, Vol. xx., p. 79.)

In *Kullavagga*, vii., 4, 7, Devadutta is said to have "come to
a stop on his way (to Arahatship), because he had already
attained to some lesser thing" (pothugganiká iddhi, or psychical powers)—and *being satisfied that he had reached the sum-
mit of development.*

In Dr. Rájendralála Mitra's note to Aphorism xxviii., of
Patanjali's Yoga Sutras, speaking about the developed psychical powers (*siddhis*), he says:

"The perfections described are of the world, worldly,
required for worldly purposes, but useless for higher meditation, having isolation for its aim. Nor are they simply useless,
but positively obstructive, for they interfere with the even
tenor of calm meditation."

It is not widely understood that the developed psychical
powers, covering the whole range of sublimated degrees of
sight, hearing, touch, taste, smell, intuition (prophetic, retrospective, and contemporary), etc., bear to the awakened individuality a relation similar to that which the ordinary five
senses do to the physical self, or personality. Just as one must
learn to restrain one's perceptions of external things through
the avenues of sense, to concentrate one's whole thought upon

some deep problem of science or philosophy, so must the would-be *gnáni*, or sage, control the activity of his developed clairvoyance, clairaudience, etc., if he would not have his object defeated by the wandering of his thought into the bypaths they open up. I have never seen this point clearly stated before, yet it is most important to bear in mind. Through ignorance of this rule Swedenborg, Davis, the Catholic Saints and religious visionaries of all other sects have, as it were, staggered, clairvoyantly drunk, through the picture-galleries of the Astral Light; seeing some things that were and creating others that were not until they begot them; then giving out mangled prophecies, imagined revelations, bad counsel, false science, and misleading theology.

Asiatics throng to a possessor or reputed possessor of siddhis from the most selfish motives—to get sons from barren wives; cures for diseases, often the fruit of vice; recover lost valuables; influence the minds of masters to favour them; and to learn the future. They call this "asking the blessings of the Máhátma," but no one is deceived by the euphuism in the least, and in ninety-nine cases out of a hundred, the begging hypocrite is dismissed unsatisfied. Even I, in my humble experience, came to know the meanness of this class, for out of the thousands of clamorous sick persons that I healed or relieved in my experimental researches of 1881, I doubt if one hundred were really grateful; and before the year was up, I had practically learnt how a Yogi must feel about exhibiting his psychical powers. Truly, indeed, does the Sage declare in *Suta Samhita* that the true Guru is not he who teaches one the physical sciences, who confers worldly pleasures, who trains one's powers until he may reach the gandharvas or develop the siddhis, for all these are sources of trouble and sorrow: the real Teacher and Master is he who imparts the knowledge of Brahman. This is taught likewise in Chandogya, Brahadaranya, and other Upanishads, where it is said that while the Yogi can by will-power make or destroy worlds, call to him pitris, gandharvas, and other spiritual beings, enjoy the power of Ishwara in unalloyed sathwa, yet he should avoid all these vanities as tending to foster the sense of separateness and as being hostile to the acquisition of true *gnánam*. As for voluntarily consorting with the denizens of the astral spheres, invoking their favours and submitting to their behests, no right-minded, well-informed Asiatic would even dream of it. Sri Krishna sums it up most concisely in that famous verse of the *Gita* (Ch. IX.): "Those who worship (invoke, make *pujá* to) the Devatas (higher elementals) go to them (after death); those who worship the Pitris, go to the Pitris. The worshippers of the Bhútas (here defined by S'ankara as the lowest nature-spirits; but the word is also a synonym of Pisachas, meaning the souls of the dead or astral shells) go to the Bhútas. Only my worshippers (*i.e.,* the devotees of *gnánam*, the highest spiritual knowledge), come to me." To repeat, then H. P. B. would be respected as possessing *siddhis*, but blamed for showing phenomena; while M. A. Oxon would be looked down upon as the medium of Pisachas and Bhútas, gifted as he may have been in mind, highly educated as the University may have made him, pure and unselfish as may have been his motives.

So much for the Asiatic view of our case. As for myself, I

was through-and-through a Westerner in my way of looking at the wonders of H. P. B. and Stainton Moseyn. They were to me supremely important as psychical indications and as scientific problems. While I could not solve the riddle of her complex entity, I was convinced that the forces in and behind H. P. B. and her phenomena were skilfully handled by living persons who knew Psychology as a science, and by its practice had gained power over the elemental races. In Stainton Moseyn's case there was an equal obscurity. His rooted idea was that his teachers, "Imperator," "Kabbila" [Kapila?], "Mentor," "Magus," "Sade" [Sadi?], *et al*, were all disincarnate human spirits; some very ancient, some less so, but all wise and beneficent. They not only permitted but insisted that he should use his reason and work his own way upward; and with tireless patience answered his questions, solved his doubts, helped to develop his spiritual insight, aided him to project his astral body, and, by multifarious marvels, proved the nature of matter and force and the possibility of controlling natural phenomena: moreover, they taught him that a system of impartation of knowledge by teacher to pupil existed throughout the Cosmos, in ordinated stages of mental and spiritual development: like the classes in a school or college. In all these respects his teachings were identical with my own; and he never could convince me that, if not the same group, at least the same kind of Masters were occupying themselves in forming these two reformatory and evolutionary centres of New York and London. What a noble soul animated his body; how pure a heart, how high an aim, how deep a devotion to truth! At once a scholar, a gentleman, a clear thinker and writer, he became the most eminent of all the leaders of the Spiritualist party; or, at least so it seems to me, and I have had the personal friendship of Davis, Sargent, Owen, and many others. Before commencing this present chapter I have read and studied some seventy of his delightful letters to H. P. B. and myself—representing an interchange of above two hundred epistles; I have also consulted Mrs. Speer's "Records," and they have re-awakened the charm of our early intercourse. His close relation with us and the way in which our psychical experiences were interwoven, make it necessary that I should give more than a merely cursory glimpse of the man; and the best way to show what he was in thought, mind, and aspiration, will be to publish in this connection some portions of an autobiographical narrative contained in one of his letters to me. It is dated from University College, London, 29th April, 1876, and reads as follows:

"My life has been cut up into 'junks'—generally of about five years' duration—and the discipline of each is peculiar; but all tends to the same. Illness in some form pervades all, and I seldom am left at one form of work more than five or seven years. I inherited good property: but it was taken from me. I lost it all in one day by an incursion of the sea. I was doing well at College—a likely First and Fellowship to follow. Ten days before examination I broke down from overwork, and was not able to read or even write a letter for two years, or rather I was obliged to defer work for my degree for two years, and then to take an ordinary one. During that two years I went all over

Europe, and learned more really than I should have got from books. But it was a wreck of life's prospects.

"Then I had my five years, or six rather, at Theological work. I had a name in the Church, and was counted a preacher who would make a reputation, and get on. I was thoroughly orthodox, a more or less intelligent theologian who had really studied *all round*, and who had a knack of argument. I went to a wild country district, partly by doctor's advice, to have benefit by sea air and solitude to recruit my health shattered at Oxford, and then I read omnivorously, and worked hard. My people would do anything for me. I could lead them anywhere, and I got a reputation in Parish and Pulpit. I overdid myself again, and felt that I must get off the excessive work (30 square miles of district to work is no joke: and all in my hands). I came to the West of England, and was appointed to a grand position in the Diocese of Sarum—a sort of select preacher. I acted twice, and irreparably broke down. Doctors could make nothing of me. They said I was overwrought: that I must rest, etc. I did rest, and got no better. Physically I was not exactly ill, but I dare not try to do anything in public.

"Then I fell ill again, this time with a fever: and in a place where no good doctor was to be had. A visitor tended me—my life was barely snatched out of the fire, and he became my fast friend—Dr. Speer. I came to London, and he asked me to live in his house and coach his boy. My property was gone, my position, my health. He took me in and I lived with him. But I could do nothing in public. He could not understand it. I could not explain it: *but it was an awful, ever-present fact.* I felt my old life was done. Yet I had no doubts as to the faith I had always held, not one—not a bit of one.

"But by degrees I found the old landmarks getting fainter: the bread grew stale. Then one day a man broke down here [at the London Univ.] and the authorities wanted somebody to carry on lectures on Philology. Few could do it, for the thing requires preparation. I heard and offered. I have a way of pigeon-holing knowledge till it is wanted, and I had read Philology at Oxford. So I took up the thread, and they finally gave me a permanent appointment.

"Another change, you see. I could lecture well enough, but could not do my old clerical work. When friends found me at work again, they said, now you'll take a Church in London, or So and So will be delighted to have you preach for him: but I simply *could not.* Yet I never write a lecture, and can go a session through without a note.

"Queer, Eh?

"Well, Mrs. Speer fell ill with some serious ailment, and got hold of one of Dale Owen's books. As soon as she got down stairs she set at me. I pished and pshawed, but agreed to look into the thing. I went to Burns, got all I could, went to Herne and Williams, and in two months was in the thick of physical mediumship, such as is hardly credible. Our phenomena were far ahead of anything I have seen elsewhere. It went on for four years, and now it is dying out, and I am going into another phase—and there have been plenty more that I have passed over. Indeed, I have said too much of self. But you may as well know what sort of man I am.

"At the present I have lost all sectarian faith, *i.e.,* all distinctive dogmatism. You will see in *Spirit Teachings* how I fought for it. Now I have lost the body, and kept the spirit. I no longer count myself a member of any Church, but I have got all the good I could out of them all. I am a free man: with such knowledge as Theological systems can give. I have thrown the husks away. And now, as soon as I have been sufficiently purified, I humbly hope to be allowed to enter within the veil, hoping there to repeat a process which, with some modifications, will be unceasing. Endless progress, perpetual purification, the lifting of veil after veil until—Eh? where have I got to? God bless you.

> "Your friend and brother,
> "M. A. Oxon."

At this stage had he arrived when we were brought together; thenceforth to keep in perfect sympathy and lovingly work together along parallel lines: our aspirations the same, our views not radically divergent. Often and often does he in his letters bemoan the fact that we were not living in the same city, where we might continually exchange ideas. Several chapters were devoted in the *Theosophist* to the subject of Stainton Moseyn's mediumship and the resemblance between his phenomena and H. P. B.'s, which may be read with profit.

Our Western friends will be interested in knowing that the Hindu who would enter upon a course of meditation, *i.e.,* of concentration of all one's mental faculties upon spiritual problems, has a triple system to observe. There is, first of all, to make the *Sthalla S'uddhi*, or ceremony, with the object of purifying the ground upon which he is to sit: cutting himself off from astral connection with the astral body of the earth and with the elementals which inhabit it [*Vide Isis*, I., 379]. This isolation is helped by first purifying the ground by washing, and by the person sitting upon a spread of Kusa grass, one of the group of vegetables whose aura resists bad and attracts good elementals. In this category are also included the Neem (Margosa), Tulsi (sacred to Vishnu), and Bilwa (sacred to Shiva). Among trees infested with bad influences and which the "adversaries" of Imperator are believed to frequent, are the Tamarind and the Banyan: they also infest old wells, long-empty houses, cremation-grounds, cemeteries, battle-grounds, slaughtering places, sites of murders and all other places where blood has been spilt: this is the Hindu belief, and in this connection see *Isis*, Chaps. XII. and XIII., Vol. I. The ground having been purified and the operator isolated from terrene bad influences, he next makes the *Bhúta S'uddhi*, a recitation of verses having power to keep off the "adversaries" dwelling in the atmosphere, including both elementals and elementaries; assisting the operation by making circular (mesmeric) passes around his head with his hand. He thus creates a psychical barrier or wall about him. After having very carefully performed these two indispensable preliminaries—never to be forgotten or perfunctorily done—he then proceeds with the *A'tma S'uddhi*, or recitation of mantrams which assist in purifying his body and mind and in preparing the way for the awakening of the spiritual faculties, the absorption called "meditation," whose aim is the attainment of *gndnam*, knowledge. A pure spot, pure air, the absence of unclean persons, *i.e.,* the unwashed, the immoral, the unspiritually-minded, the over-fed, the unsympathetic—are all indispensable for the seeker after divine truth.

Imperator's admonitions to the Speer circle and, in fact, those which have been given to all really choice circles of spiritualistic investigators in all parts of the world, substantially accord with the Eastern rules. In short, the closer these precautions have been observed, the higher and nobler have been the teachings received. The revolting scenes and disgusting language and instructions which have attended so many séances where unprotected and unpurified mediums have given their services to mixed gatherings of foul and pure inquirers, are traceable to neglect of these protective conditions. Gradually, things have been changing for the better within these past seventeen years; physical mediums and physical phenomena are slowly beginning to give place to the higher forms of mediumship and manifestations.

The views of Imperator about the evils of mixed circles were reflected in Stainton Moseyn's published writings, and, if possible, more strongly in his private correspondence. He fully comprehended that the experiences of centuries must have taught the Asiatics this verity, that pure spiritual aura can no more be passed untainted through a vile medium and incongruous circle, than the water of a mountain spring be made to run pure through a foul filter. Hence their strict and stern rules for the isolation of the postulant for knowledge from all corrupting influences, and for the thorough purification of his own self. When one sees the blind ignorance and rash confidence with which Western people go themselves and take their sensitive children into the sin-sodden aura of many a séance room, one can feel how thoroughly just is the stricture of M. A. Oxon's chief guide, about the surprising fatuity shown with respect to dealings with the spirits of the departed. The most "orthodox" of the Spiritualist writers are now only, after forty-odd years' experience with mediumistic phenomena, partly realising this truth. Yet these same persons, yielding to a rooted hatred of Theosophy—which they excuse on the score of their detestation of H. P. B.—will not hearken to the voice of the ancients nor take the precautions which experience dictates against the perils of the open circle and the public medium. The improvement above noticed is due rather to the general interest created by our literature, and its reflex action upon mediums and circles, than to the direct influence of editors, speakers, and writers. Let us hope that before long the views of the Theosophists respecting elementals and elementaries will be accorded the full attention they merit.

Chapter XX.

CONFLICTING VIEWS
(CONTINUED)

I sat in the verandah at "Gulistan," my mountain cottage, one morning, looking northward above the sea of clouds that hid the Mysore plains from view. Presently, the vaporous ocean dissolved away, and the eye could distinctly see the Bilgirirangam Hills, seventy miles off: with a good glass the details could be easily made out. By association of ideas, the problem of the connection between Stainton Moses* and our two selves—H. P. B. and I—came to my mind. As I turned over the facts of our intercourse one by one, the confusing clouds of subsequent events rolled away, and in the distant past the glass of memory brought out his relationship to us and our Sages more distinctly than ever before. It is now clear to me that one directing Intelligence, pursuing a wide-reaching plan covering all nations and peoples, and acting through many agents besides ourselves, had in hand his development and mine, his body of psychical proofs and those

---

* I use the distorted name under protest.

given me by and through H. P. B. Who "Imperator," its agent, was, I know not—I do not even know who H. P. B. really was—but I have always been inclined to believe that he was either S. M.'s own Higher Self or an adept; and that "Magus" and others of S. M.'s *band* were adepts likewise. I had my *band* also—though not of "spirit controls." S. M. had an Arabian teacher, so had I; he an Italian philosopher, so had I; he had Egyptians, I had a Copt; he had a "Prudens," "versed in Alexandrian and Indian lore," so had I—several; he had Dr. Dee, an English mystic, I also had one—the one previously spoken of as "the Platonist"; and between his phenomena and H. P. B.'s there was a striking resemblance. Until Mrs. Speer's *Records* were published all these particulars were not known to me, but now everything is plain. No wonder that S. M. and I were so drawn together; it was inevitable. That he felt it too, his whole correspondence proves. He sums it up in these few words, in his letter of Jan. 24, 1876: "My strongest attraction lies to you two; and I would give anything to be able to come to you"—in the Double, he means. The saddening thing to me is that he could not have known his "band" for what they were—or what I think they were, if you like. Supposing my surmise to be correct, the obstacle was his peculiar mental bias. His intellectual history resembles Mrs. Besant's in certain respects: each fought desperately for old ideas and changed them only under the compulsion of cumulative proofs; each sought only truth, and each stood bravely for it. How pathetic the story of Mrs. Besant's struggle against reason in the interest of her old faith, and her final brave yielding to logic! So, the reader of Stainton Moses' published and unpublished personal narrative must see that Imperator and his colleagues had to contend against a combative incredulity in the mental man that would not loose its hold upon the medium's mind, until it had been swept out, so to say, by a tornado of psychical demonstrations.* He was, by temperament, a conscientious mule; but once brought to accept the new philosophy, he was courage and loyalty personified, a lion for fighting and bravery. The first portrait that he sent me represents him as a thin-faced curate, seemingly as mild as milk; and no one could have guessed that that inoffensive parson was destined to become a chief leader of the party of spiritualistic free-thinkers. So necessary is trained clairvoyance to show us what our neighbour is behind his *mdyd*.

It will be objected to my hypothesis about Imperator that he declared himself a spirit; and so he was as regards S. M., whether he still had connection with a physical body or not. Must not babes be fed with milk? See how ardently H. P. B. professed herself a Spiritualist in her first letters to the papers and her first interviews with reporters. See her at Philadelphia, doing phenomena in the Holmes séances, and allowing Gen. Lippitt, Mr. Owen, and myself to believe they were attributable to the mediumship of Mrs. Holmes whom, in our Scrap-Book, she brands as a common cheat. Was not I at first made to believe that I was dealing with disincarnate spirits; and was not a stalking-horse put forward to rap and write, and produce materialised forms for me, under the

---

* Among many corroborative passages, see what Imperator says in Mrs. Speer's Record, XX.: *Light*, July 30, 1892.

pseudonym of John King? That this delusion was shortly dropped and the truth told me, I attribute to the fact of my chronic indifference to theologies and to the identity of personalities behind the phenomena. My record is clear in this respect, as I had committed my opinions to print as far back as 1853.*

My bias of mind then was identical with my present one: which explains the fact why, with all my affection for H. P. B. and my reverence for our Masters—in neither of which do any of her disciples surpass me—I continually protest against the assertion that a fact or teaching is one whit better or weightier when associated with H. P. B. or one of our Masters or their chelas. No religion, philosophy, or expounder thereof is higher, greater, or more authoritative than Truth: for Truth and God are identical. Having no sectarian barriers to be pulled down, I was soon disabused about my teaching intelligences: whereas S. M. was obstinacy incarnate, and it is the greatest of wonders to me that his "band" were so patient, kind, and tolerant of what must have seemed to them the whimsies of a spoilt child. His health, never very robust, broke down from overwork, as he tells us, before the commencement of his medium-ship; but we also see that the powers which were already shaping his destiny caused him to break down whenever there was a good chance of his reverting to ministerial work. He was compelled to keep out of it, whether he would or not.

---

* *Vide* the old *Spiritual Telegraph* journal, S. B. Britten Editor, for 1853: articles of mine signed with my own name and the pseudonym "Amherst."

. . .

In view of all the above (*i.e.*, the facts and arguments given in the original version of this and the preceding chapter), am I far wrong in suspecting a close connection between the Intelligence behind Stainton Moses and that behind H. P. B.? He writes me, December 31, 1876: "I do not know whether I rightly conjecture from Imperator this morning that she (H. P. B.) is about me, working about me, I mean—for my good or enlightenment in some way. It is no use asking her; but *I believe she is*." October 10, 1876, he writes me that he had had.

"A splendid and perfectly complete 'vision'—or, as I prefer to call it, interview with Isis.* It was late, or rather near midnight—I have an accurate memo. at home—when I suddenly saw Isis in my sitting-room looking through the open door into my study, where C. C. M. was sitting and where I stood. I cried out and rushed into the next room, followed by M. He saw *nil*. I saw Isis as plain as possible, and talked with her for some time. I noticed my first *rush* into the room had the effect of 'dissipating' the form, but it soon reappeared and went into my study, where M. says I seemed to pass into a sort of 'trance' or abnormal state of some kind, and went through pantomimic gestures of masonic import."

Since copying this out, I find, endorsed in my handwriting on the back of a letter of M. A. Oxon's, the following:

---

* One of several nicknames H. P. B.'s intimate friends used to give her; others being "Sphinx," "Popess," and the "Old Lady."

"If between now and the 15th instant M. A. O. does not see H. P. B., she will not visit him any more. (Sgd.) H. S. O." And that very night he did see her, as described above. A year before (October 16, 1875), he thanks H. P. B. for her letter, and says it "throws a flood of light, not only on the phenomena of Spiritualism at large, but on many hints made to me which were not before clear." In short, she had helped him to understand his own spirit-teachings. Here is a beautiful passage from his letter of Oct. 7, 1876:

"One thing alone fills my eye—the search for Truth. I don't look for anything else; and though I may turn aside to examine what claims to be Truth, I soon leave the sham and return to the straight road. Life seems to me given for that alone, and all else is subordinate to that end. The present sphere of existence seems to be only a means to that end, and when it has served its purpose, it will give place to one adapted to secure progress. Whether I live, I live for Truth: If I die, when I die, I die to pursue it better."

There is a true man's heart opened out to the sunlight. He remarks farther on:

"It is because I dimly see—and far more because he (Imperator) tells me that in Occultism I shall find a phase of Truth not yet known to me, that I look to it and you (H. P. B.). Probably the time will never come during my stay on earth when I shall have penetrated the veil, probably my life will be spent in

searching for Truth, through means of which you are to me
the present exponent."

As regards "Magus," I have some very interesting data, and
have come to a much clearer opinion than I have as to Imperator. I am almost certain that he is a living adept; not only
that, but one that had to do with us. In March, 1876, I sent S. M.
a bit of cotton wool or muslin impregnated with a liquid perfume which H. P. B. could cause to exude from the palm of her
hand at will, asking him if he recognised it. On the 23d of that
month, he replies:

' "That sandalwood scent is so familiar to me. One of the most
persistent phenomena in our circle was the production of
scent, either in a liquid form, or in that of a scent-laden breeze.
The scent we always called 'The Spirit Scent' was this; and we
always had it under the best conditions. This for the past two
years. My friends always knew when our best séances would
be by the prevalence of that perfume in my atmosphere. The
house where we used to meet would be redolent of it for days;
and Dr. Speer's house in the Isle of Wight, when I was staying
there, got so permeated with it that when it was reopened
again six months after, the perfume was as strong as ever.
What a marvellous power is it that these Brothers wield . . .
I stayed in my rooms all day trying to ease my racking
cough. . . . At midnight I had a more than ordinarily severe

fit of coughing. When it was over, I saw by my bedside, distant about two yards, and at the height about 5 ft. 6 in. from
the floor, three small phosphorescent balls of light
about the size of a small orange. They were arranged
thus and formed an equilateral triangle, the base of
which would measure 18 in. First I thought it was an opti-
cal delusion caused by my violent cough. I fixed my gaze on
them, and they remained quiet, glowing with a steady phosphorescent light which cast no gleam beyond itself. Satisfied
that the phenomenon was objective, I reached a match-box
and struck a match. I could not see the balls through the
match-light; but when the match went out they came again
into view just as before. I repeated the match-striking six
times (seven in all) when they paled, and gradually went
out. It is the symbol that J. K. put at the back of your portrait. [While in transit through the post from me to him—
O.] Was it he again? It was not any of my own people,
I believe."

As I have elsewhere explained, the three luminous spheres
form the special symbol of the Lodge of our Adepts; and better proof of their proximity to Stainton Moses no one of us
who have been their pupils would desire. He, too, says:

"Certainly all doubt as to the Brotherhood and their work is
gone. I have no shred remaining. I believe, simply, and I

labour so far as in me lies to fit myself for such work as they may design me for."

"Do you know anything of my friend Magus?"—he writes in another letter. "He is powerful, and is working on me *occultly*." In another one—May 18, 1877—he says to H. P. B.:

"Some of your friends have paid me a visit of late rather often, if I may judge by the atmosphere of sandalwood—the Lodge scent, O. calls it—which pervades my rooms and myself. I taste it, I exhale it, everything belonging to me smells of it, and there has recurred the old and inexplicable phenomenon which I have not seen for many months—more than a year—and *which used to obtain with me in respect of other odours.* From a well-defined spot just round the crown of the head [over the Brahmarândhra?—O.], quite small (the size of a half-crown piece), exudes a most powerful odour. It is now, this Lodge scent, so strong as to be almost unbearable. It used to be rose, or indeed that of any fresh flower in my neighbourhood.... A friend gave me a Gardinia the other evening at a party. In a few minutes it gave an overpowering odour of the Lodge perfume, turned a mahogany-brown before our eyes, till the whole flower was of that colour, and it now remains dead and saturated with the odour.... I feel myself in a transition state, and wait what turns up. 'Magus' seems the presiding genius in many ways now."

Not at all strange, one would say, with S. M. saturated and all but stifled with the Lodge's scented atmosphere! It is a most persistent odour. In 1877, I sent him a lock of H. P. B.'s natural hair, and with it a lock of the Hindu jet-black that I have spoken of above as having been cut from her head when she was the subject of an A'ves'am. I cut this lock myself to send S. M. He acknowledged its receipt in his letter to H. P. B. of March 25, 1877. Wishing to photograph the different kinds of hair for an illustration for this book, to show the actual contrasts in fibre and color, I asked C. C. M. to return these two specimens to me out of S. M.'s collection, and quite recently they reached my hand. The Lodge scent lingers still in the black tress after the lapse of sixteen years. Readers of Church history will recall the fact that in mediæval times this odoriferous phenomenon was frequently observed among really pious and ascetic monks, nuns, and other recluses of the cloister, the cave, and the desert. It was then called "the odour of Sanctity"; although this was a misnomer, for otherwise all saintly personages would have smelt sweet, whereas we know too well that it was more often the opposite! Sometimes from the mouth of an ecstatic, while lying in her trance, would trickle a sweet and fragrant liquor—the nectar of the Greek gods; and in the case of Marie Ange it was caught and preserved in bottles. Des Mousseaux,* the demonophobe, ascribes this product of psychical chemistry to the Devil. Poor fanatic!

---

* *Hauts Phénomènes de la Magie*, p. 377.

Chapter XXI.

NEW YORK HEADQUARTERS

The early story of the Theosophical Society is almost told. Little remains for me but to complete my first series of reminiscences, with some sketches of our social life in New York, up to the time of our embarkation for India.

From the close of 1876 to that of 1878, the Theosophical Society as a body was comparatively inactive: its By-laws became a dead letter, its meetings almost ceased. Its few public appearances have been described above, and the signs of its growing influence are found in the increase of the Founders' home and foreign correspondence, their controversial articles in the press, the establishment of Branch societies at London and Corfu, and the opening up of relations with sympathisers in India and Ceylon.

The influential Spiritualists who joined us at first had all withdrawn; our meetings in a hired room—the Mott Memorial Hall, in Madison Avenue, New York—were discontinued; the fees formerly exacted upon entrance of members were abolished, and the Society's maintenance devolved entirely upon us two. Yet the idea was never more vigorous, nor the movement more full of vitality, than when it was divested of its external corporateness, and its spirit was compressed into our brains, hearts, and souls. Our Headquarters' life was ideal throughout those closing years. United in devotion to a common cause, in daily intercourse with our Masters, absorbed in altruistic thoughts, dreams, and deeds, we two existed in that roaring metropolis as untouched by its selfish rivalries and ignoble ambitions as though we occupied a cabin by the seaside, or a cave in the primeval forest. I am not exaggerating when I say that a more unworldly tone would not be found in any other home in New York. The social distinctions of our visitors were left outside our threshold; and rich or poor, Christian, Jew, or Infidel, learned or unlearned, our visitors received the same hearty welcome and patient attention to their questions upon religious and other subjects. H. P. B. was born so great an aristocrat as to be at ease in the highest society, and so thorough a democratic altruist as to give cordial hospitality to the humblest caller.

One of the best read of our guests in Greek philosophy was a working house-painter, and I well remember how gladly H. P. B. and I signed his application-form as his sponsors and welcomed him into membership. Without a single exception those who published accounts of their visits to "The Lamasery"—as we humorously called our humble suite of rooms—declared that their experience had been novel and out of the usual course. Most of them wrote about H. P. B. in terms of exaggerated praise or wonder. In appearance there was not a shade of the ascetic about her: she neither meditated in seclusion, practised austerities in regimen, denied herself to the frivolous and worldly-minded, nor selected her company. Her door was open to all, even to those whom she knew meant to write about her with pens over which she could have no control. Often they lampooned her, but if the articles were witty, she used to enjoy them with me to the fullest extent.

Among our constant visitors was Mr. Curtis, one of the cleverest reporters on the New York press, and later, a member of our Society. He made yards of good "copy" out of the Lamasery, sometimes sober, sometimes farcical, but always bright and smart. He led us into a nice trap one evening: taking us off to a circus where, he said, two Egyptian jugglers were exhibiting certain marvels that might be ascribed to a knowledge of sorcery, but which, at any rate, he wished us to see and pronounce upon as experts in the uncanny. We listened to the voice of the syren and went. The show proved to be commonplace and the Egyptians *bonâ-fide* Frenchmen, with whom we had a long talk in the Manager's office between "acts." They had not even seen an Egyptian magician of the real sort described by Mr. Lane in his well-known work. On leaving the place I condoled with Curtis on the barrenness of his experiment, but he sent us into fits of laughter by replying that, on the contrary, he now had a free hand and could supply all needed facts to make a sensational article. He did. The next day's *World* contained an account headed "Theosophs at the Circus," in which our stale talk with the two Frenchmen was converted into a highly mystical interview, accompanied by no end of weird phenomena, of spectral apparitions, *apports*, and disappearances; the whole description proving, if not the reporter's veracity, at least, his fertile fancy. Another time he brought us a paper giving an account of the night-walking of the ghost of a defunct night-watchman, along the wharves of a certain district on the East side of the city, and begged us to go and see the phantom: the police, he said, were all agog, and the inspector of that district had made all preparations to have it seized that night. Forgetting our circus experience, again we accepted. It was a rather bleak starlit night, and we sat for hours well wrapped, on a pile of lumber, by the river side, beguiling the time with smoking and chaff with a score of newspaper reporters detailed to describe the events of the night. But "Old Shep" did not manifest his disreputable *eidôlon* that time, and in due course we returned to our Lamasery vexed at the waste of a whole evening. The next day's papers, to our ineffable disgust, paraded us as a couple of crack-brained persons who had expected the impossible, and half conveying the idea that we had kept "Old Shep" away to cheat the reporters of their lawful prey! We even got into the illustrated papers, and I have preserved in our Scrap-Book a picture representing us two, and the worshipful company of reporters as "Members of the Theosophical Society watching for Old Shep's ghost." Fortunately, the portraits of H. P. B. and myself looked no more like us than like the Man in the Moon.

One evening Curtis was present when the Countess Paschkoff was relating an adventure she had with H. P. B. in the Libanus, she speaking in French and I translating into English. The tale was so weird and interesting that he asked permission to print it, and this being granted, it duly appeared in his paper. As it exemplifies the theory of the latency in the A'kâs'a of pictures of human events and the power of calling them out which may be attained, I will quote a portion of it in this place, leaving the responsibility for the facts with the fair narrator:

"The Countess Paschkoff spoke again, and again Colonel Olcott translated for the reporter. . . . I was once travelling between Baalbec and the river Orontes, and in the desert I saw a caravan. It was Mme. Blavatsky's. We camped together. There was a great monument standing there near the village of El Marsum. It was between the Libanus and the Anti-Libanus. On the monument were inscriptions that no one could ever read. Mme. Blavatsky could do strange things with the spirits, as I knew, and I asked her to find out what the monument was. We waited until night. She drew a circle and we went in it. We built a fire and put much incense on it. Then she said many spells. Then we put on more incense. Then she pointed with her wand at the monument and we saw a great ball of white flame on it. There was a sycamore tree near by; we saw many little flames on it. The jackals came and howled in the darkness a little way off. We put on more incense. Then Mme. Blavatsky commanded the spirit to appear of the person to whom the monument was reared. Soon a cloud of vapour arose and obscured the little moonlight there was. We put on more incense. The cloud took the indistinct shape of an old man with a beard, and a voice came, as it seemed, from a great distance, through the image. He said the monument was once the altar of a temple that had long disappeared. It was reared to a god that had long since gone to another world. "Who are you?" asked Mme. Blavatsky. "I am Hiero, one of the priests of the temple," said the voice. Then Mme.

Blavatsky ordered him to show us the place as it was when the temple stood. He bowed, and for one instant we had a glimpse of the temple and of a vast city filling the plain as far as the eye could reach. Then it was gone, and the image faded away."*

About the end of 1877, or beginning of 1878, we were visited by the Hon. John L. O'Sullivan, an American diplomat and an ardent Spiritualist, who was passing through New York on his way from London to San Francisco. He was kindly received by H. P. B. and stoutly defended his beliefs against her attacks. Some instructive phenomena were done for him, which he subsequently described in the *Spiritualist* for February 8, 1878, in the following terms:

"She had been toying with an oriental chaplet, in a lacquer cup or bowl, the aromatic wooden beads of which, strung together, were of about the size of a large marble, and copiously carved all round. A gentleman present took the chaplet in his hands, admired the beads, and asked if she would not give him one of them. 'Oh, I hardly like to break it,' she observed. But she took it presently, and resumed her playing with it in the lacquer bowl. My eyes were fixed upon them, under the full blaze of a large lamp just above her table. It soon became manifest that they were growing in number under her fingers as she handled them, till the bowl became nearly full. She presently lifted out of it the chaplet, leaving a considerable number of loose beads, of which she said he might take what he wanted. I have ever since regretted that I had not the presence of mind, or the venturesomeness, to ask

---

* *N. Y. World* of 21st of April, 1878, article entitled "Ghost Stories Galore."

for some for myself. I am sure she would have given them freely, for she is all kindness, as well as, apparently, a woman of all knowledge. My presumption about the beads thus created under our eyes was that they were '*apports*,' brought in by spirits, in compliance with her wish or will. I believe (though not quite certain) that her idea, and Olcott's is that these phenomena are produced in some way by a great brother '*adept*' in Thibet—the same one from whose old spinnet I was made to hear in the air overhead (as I have before mentioned, and as many other friends had done before) the faint but clear tinkling music which I was told came, borne on a current of 'astral fluid,' from Thibet; to which home of her heart Madame Blavatsky said she was going back (never again to leave it), after she should have completed her mission, task, and business which was chiefly that of publishing her book.

"Another case of fabrication of material objects out of apparently nothing. Coming in late one afternoon to her little parlour, where she usually spent seventeen hours out of the twenty-four at her writing-table, I found Colonel Olcott with her, occupied in correcting her earlier proof-sheets. I had by this time become somewhat intimate with her and Olcott, for both of whom I shall always retain a strong attachment as well as profound respect. He told me how there had taken place that afternoon one of those '*little incidents*' (as he calls them) which were of constant occurrence there. There had been a group of visitors, and an animated discussion on the comparative civilisation of the ancient Orient and the modern West.

"The subject came up of the tissues fabricated in the one and the other. Madame Blavatsky is an enthusiast on the

Orient side of this dispute. She suddenly put her hand to her neck and drew forth from her ample bosom (from beneath the old dressing-gown, which is the only garb in which I have seen her), a handkerchief of silk crape, with a striped border, very like what is called 'carton crape,' and asked whether occidental looms produced anything superior to that. They assured me (and I have ample warrant for believing them) that it had not been there before that moment. It was in smooth, fresh folds, and the conversation had arisen accidentally. I admired it, recognised in time the peculiar sickly sweet and pungent odour which attends all these *'apports'* from Far Cathay (including the beads above mentioned), and observed the peculiar signature on one edge of the handkerchief, which I had seen on various objects, and which I was told was the name (in pre-Sanskrit characters) of a great brother 'Adept' in Thibet to whom, by the way, she says she is very far inferior. When we were afterwards summoned to their very simple repast (to which had been added a hospitable bottle of wine for me, though they never touch it), she remarked to Olcott: 'Give me that handkerchief.' He gave it to her, out of the sheet of letter-paper in which he had carefully folded it in its smooth unruffled condition. She at once made a careless twist of it and tied it round her neck. When we returned from the dining-room to her warmer snuggery of a parlour, she took it off and threw it on the table by her side. I remarked, 'You treat it in a very unceremonious fashion. Will you give that one to me?'—'Oh, certainly if you would like to have it'; and she tossed it over to me. I smoothed out its creases as well as I could, again wrapped it in a sheet of paper, and put it in my breast pocket. Later on, as I was taking my departure, and we were all on foot, she said: 'Oh, just give me that handkerchief for a moment.' Of course I obeyed. She turned her back to me for an instant or two, and then, turning again to me, she held out two handkerchiefs, one in each hand, saying: 'Take which ever you please; I thought that perhaps you might prefer this one (handing me the new one) since you have seen it come.' Of course I did so, and after travelling about fifteen miles by rail that night, I gave it to the lady best entitled to receive a favour thus conferred upon me by another lady, which latter lady, by the way, claims to be a septuagenarian, though looking only about forty. When I left America, a few days afterwards, the handkerchief had not yet melted away, nor wafted back to Thibet, on a 'current of astral fluid,' I should add that the second handkerchief was a perfect facsimile of the first, down to every detail of the name in ancient oriental characters; which, by the way, was evidently written or painted in some black pigment or ink, not stamped mechanically."

My recollection of the handkerchief incident differs slightly from Mr. O'Sullivan's narrative. The original specimen was made out of nothing—to use the faulty common expression, for something never was nor could be made out of nothing, theologists to the contrary notwithstanding—during a conversation between H. P. B. and our friend Monsieur Herrisse of the Haytian Legation. He had said that a relative of his had brought back from China some fine crape handkerchiefs which Western looms had not yet equalled. She thereupon produced a handkerchief of the same description and asked M. Herrisse if that was what he meant, to which he assented. I took possession of it, and, at the interview with Mr. O'Sullivan, mentioned the incident and showed him the article, whereupon he asked H. P. B. to give it him. She did so, and when I humorously said she had no right to give away my property without my consent, she said I was not to mind, as she would give me another. At that moment we were called to dinner and were moving towards the door, when she bade Mr. O'Sullivan lend her the handkerchief for a moment. Standing as we were together, she turned her back for an instant, wheeled back again with a duplicate handkerchief in each hand, one of which she gave Mr. O'Sullivan, the other myself. Returning from the dining-room and resuming our former seats, she felt a cold draft from the partly opened window behind her chair and asked me for something to put on her neck. I gave her my magic handkerchief, which she loosely put about her neck and went on talking. Observing that the ends were not long enough to be properly twisted, I got a pin and wanted her to let me fasten them; but she exclaimed, "Bother you and your pins; here take back your handkerchief!" at the same time jerking it from her neck and throwing it at me. At the same instant we saw a second copy of the original still about her neck, and O'Sullivan starting forward and reaching out his hand, said: "That one—please give me that one, for I saw it formed under my own eyes!" She good-naturedly gave it him, and the one he had was restored to her and the conversation proceeded. The original one made in Herrisse's presence I have still in my possession, the second one my sister has.

I have thought it worth while to tell this story and others still to come, to show the nature of proofs she constantly afforded us of her wonder-working power in those early New York days, before there were missionaries encamped across her path, and it was worth their while to invent, purchase, or honestly come by evidence or enlist witnesses to cast doubt upon her personal character. If nothing else had subsequently been given me, those early phenomena would have fixed forever my belief in her possession of certain of the *Siddhis*, and made me very wary about discrediting her teachings on the psycho-dynamical laws behind them. It was not at long intervals, but frequently, that her friends and other visitors had this cumulative evidence that the psychically-endowed child of Sarotow had grown into the mysterious woman of 1875, without losing one of the supernormal faculties of her youth, but, on the contrary, had expanded and infinitely strengthened and augmented them. These incidents gave to her *salon* a fascinating attractiveness that was offered by no other in New York. Her personality, not the Theosophical Society, was the magnet of attraction, and she revelled in the excitement of the *entourage*. So miscellaneous was it, such a mixture of music, metaphysics, Orientalism, and local gossip, that I cannot give a better idea of it than by saying it was like the contents of *Isis Unveiled*, than which no literary product is a greater conglomerate.

Chapter XXII.

VARIOUS PHENOMENA
DESCRIBED

Although sad experience has taught us that psychical phenomena are weak things to build a great spiritual movement upon, yet they have a distinct value in their proper place when strictly controlled. That place is within the limits of the third of the Declared Objects of our Society. They have a paramount importance as elementary proofs of the power of the trained human will over the brute forces of nature. In this respect they bear upon the problem of the intelligence behind mediumistic phenomena. I think that the early phenomena of H. P. B. dealt a distinct blow at the theory, until then generally held, that the messages received through mediums must of necessity be from the dead. For here were things done in the absence of presumably necessary conditions, sometimes apparently in defiance of them. The records of them now survive only in clippings from contemporary newspapers, and in the memory of witnesses who have not yet put their experiences into print, but who, being still alive, are able to corroborate or correct my stories of phenomena that we saw together in her presence.

While highly suggestive in themselves, H. P. B.'s wonders were not usually led up to in conversation. When we were alone, she might produce some phenomenon to illustrate a teaching; or they might happen as if in answer to a query arising in my own mind as to the agency of some particular force in a given physical operation. Usually they were made, as it were, on the spur of the moment and independently of any prefatory suggestion by anybody present. Let me give an instance or two out of many that might be cited, to make my meaning clear.

One day an English Spiritualist and his friend called, and with the former his little son, a lad of 10 or 12 years. The boy amused himself for awhile by going about the room, rummaging among our books, examining our curios, trying the piano, and indulging in other freaks of curiosity. He then began fretting to go, pulling his father's sleeve and trying to make him break off a very interesting conversation with H. P. B. The father could not stop his importunities and was about to leave, when H. P. B. said: "Oh, don't mind him, he merely wants something to amuse him; let me see if I can find him a toy." Thereupon she rose from her chair, reached her hand around one of the sliding doors just behind her, and *pulled out a large toy sheep mounted on wheels*, which, to my positive knowledge, had not been there the moment before!

On a Christmas eve my sister came down from her flat, on the floor above the "Lamasery," to ask us to step up and see the Christmas-tree she had prepared for her children—then asleep in their beds. We looked the presents all over, and H. P. B. expressed her regret that she had not had any money to buy something for the tree herself. She asked my sister what one of the lads, a favourite of hers, would like, and being told a loud whistle, said: "Well, wait a minute." Taking her bunch of keys from her pocket, she clutched three of them together in one hand, and a moment later showed us a large iron whistle hanging in their stead on the key-ring. To make it she had used up the iron of the three keys and had to get duplicates made the next day by a locksmith. Again. For a year or so after we took up housekeeping at the "Lamasery," my family silver was used for the table, but at last it had to be sent away, and H. P. B. helped me to pack it up. That day after dinner, when we were to have coffee, we noticed that there were no sugar tongs, and in handing her the sugar basin I put in it a teaspoon instead. She asked where were our sugar tongs, and upon my replying that we had packed it up to send away with the other silver, she said: "Well, we must have another one, mustn't we?" and, reaching her hand down beside her chair, brought up a nonde-script tongs, the like of which one would scarcely find in a jeweller's shop. It had the legs much longer than usual, and the two claws slit like the prongs of a pickle-fork; while inside the shoulder of one of the legs was engraved the cryptograph of Máhátma "M." I have the curio now at Adyar.

An important law is illustrated here. To create anything objective out of the diffused matter of space, the first step is to *think* of the desired object—its form, pattern, colour, material, weight, and other characteristics: the picture of it must be sharp and distinct as to every detail; the next step is to put the trained Will in action, employ one's knowledge of the laws of matter and the process of its conglomeration, and compel the elemental spirits to form and fashion what one wishes made. If the operator fails in either of these details, his results will be imperfect. In this case before us it is evident that H. P. B. had confused in her memory the two different shapes of sugar-tongs and a pickle-fork and combined them together into this nondescript or hybrid table implement. Of course, the result was to give stronger proof of the genuineness of her phenomenon than if she had made perfect sugar-tongs: for such may be bought in shops anywhere.

One evening, when our writing-room was full of visitors, she and I sitting at opposite sides of the room, she motioned to me to lend her a large signet *intaglio* that I was wearing that evening as a scarf-ring. She took it between her closed hands, without saying anything to anybody or attracting any one's attention save mine, and rubbed the hands together for a minute or two, when I presently heard the clink of metal upon metal. Catching my eye, she smiled, and, opening her hands, showed me my ring and along with it another, equally large but of a different pattern: the seal-tablet also being of dark green bloodstone, whereas mine was of red carnelian. That ring she wore until her death, and it is now worn by Mrs. Annie Besant and is familiar to thousands. The stone was broken on our voyage out to India, and if I remember aright, the present one was engraved and set at Bombay. Here, again, not a word of the passing conversation led up to the phenomenon; on the contrary, nobody save myself knew of its occurring until afterwards.

Another instance. I had to go to Albany as special counsel to the Mutual Life Insurance Company of New York, to argue in Committee of the Legislature against a bill then under consideration. H. P. B. profited by the chance of an escort to go with me and make a long-promised visit to Dr. and Mrs. Ditson, of Albany. She was an unpractical creature as to common affairs, and a good deal dependent upon the kind offices of friends, for her packings and unpackings of trunks, among other things. Her former friend, Dr. L. M. Marquette, on this occasion packed the Gladstone bag she was to take, and it lay open in her room at the moment when the carriage drove up to take us to the Albany train. The bag was very full, and I had to repack some of the things on top and employ some strength to close the bag and lock it. I then carried it myself to the carriage, from the carriage to the railway carriage, and our train sped on its way. My reason for mentioning these details will presently be seen. Half way to Albany, a large bottle of sticky cough-medicine in her pocket got broken and made a mess of her tobacco, cigarette-papers, handkerchief, and the other contents of the pocket. This necessitated the re-opening of the bag and the taking out of a lot of things, to search for other smoking materials, etc. I did this myself, re-packed, closed, and re-locked the bag, and on reaching Albany I again carried it to the carriage and, at Dr. Ditson's house, took it up a flight of stairs and set it down on the landing outside the drawing-room door. The hostess at once began an animated conversation with H. P. B., whom she was seeing for the first time. Mrs. Ditson's little daughter was in the room and made friends with H. P. B., standing at her knee and petting her hand. The mysterious lady in question did not too highly appreciate this interruption of her talk with the mother, and finally said: "There, there, my child, keep quiet a few moments and I'll give you a nice present." "Where is it? Please give it me now," the child replied. I, believing that the alleged present was still in some Albany toy-shop from which I should be asked to presently fetch it, maliciously whispered the little one to ask Madame where she was hiding the present, and she did. H. P. B. said: "Now don't bother, my dear, I have it in my bag." That was enough for me: I asked her for her keys, went outside and opened the bag and—found packed most artistically among the clothing, and right before one's eyes upon the bag being opened, a harmonicon, or glass piano, of say 15 in. × 4 in. in size, with its cork mallet lying beside it! Now, H. P. B. did not pack her bag at New York; had not handled it up to that moment; I had closed and locked it before starting, reopened, unpacked, re-packed, and re-locked it midway on the journey; and besides that bag, H. P. B. had no other luggage. Whence the harmonicon came, and how in the world it could have been packed into a bag that was previously full to bursting, I do not know. Perhaps some S. P. R. will suggest that the engine driver of the train had been bribed and rendered invisible by H. P. B., had opened the bag on the floor at my feet by a ghostly picklock, and had made room for the musical toy by throwing some of H. P. B.'s clothes out of the car-window! Or—perhaps it was a genuine phenomenon and she was not an absolute trickster, after all. If Dr. Marquette still lives, she can testify to seeing us and our luggage aboard the train; and if Dr. Ditson is alive, he can affirm that he took us and the veritable

Gladstone bag from the station at Albany to his house. My part, to tell the story as truthfully as I can, and leave it on record as an instance of the way in which my dear old colleague sometimes did a wonder merely to gratify a child, who had not the least idea of the importance of what had occurred.

In my friend, Dr. Upham's *History of Salem Witchcraft*, he tells us that in the case of one of the poor victims of that terrible, fanatical persecution of 1695, it was brought against her as proof of her compact with Satan, that she had walked with spotless skirts through mud and rain to a certain meeting. Upon which, the learned author suggests that the probability rather is that the accused was a tidy woman and so could keep her garments unspotted along the muddy road. Throughout his book he takes up the attitude of incredulity as to any spiritual agency having been at work behind the phenomena of obsession, without, it must be confessed, making good his case. Once, H. P. B. and I being in Boston, on a very rainy and muddy day, she walked through the streets in a pelting rain and reached her lodgings without a drop of rain or splash of mud soiling her dress; and once, I remember, we had been talking on the balcony outside her drawing-room window in Irving Place, New York, and being driven indoors by a heavy rain which lasted through the greater part of the night, I carelessly left outside a handsome velvet or brocade-covered chair. In the morning, when I called as usual on H. P. B. before going to my office, I recollected the chair and went and brought it in, expecting to find it sodden and spoilt by the rain. It was as dry as possible, on the contrary; why or how I cannot explain.

Mr. O'Sullivan's story of the duplicated China crape

handkerchiefs in the preceding chapter will be fresh in the reader's memory. I saw her do a notable thing one evening for Wong Chin Fu, a Chinese lecturer, since well known in the United States. We three were chatting about the pictures of his country as lacking the elements of perspective, whereupon he said how admirable were the figure-paintings of their artists, how rich in colour and bold in drawing. H. P. B. concurred and, in the most casual way, as it seemed, opened the drawer where she kept her writing-paper, and drew forth a finely-executed painting of a Chinese lady dressed in full Court robes. I am sure as I can be that it was not there before, but as Wong Chin Fu was not specially interested in the occult science which for us had so great a charm, I made no remark. Our visitor took the picture in his hand, looked at it, remarked upon its beauty, but said: "This is not Chinese, Madam; it has no Chinese writing in the corner. It is probably Japanese." H. P. B. looked at me with an amused expression, returned the picture to the drawer, shut it for a moment, and then re-opening it, drew forth a second picture of a Chinese lady, but wearing different coloured robes, and handed it to Wong Chin Fu. This he recognised as unmistakably from his country, for it bore Chinese lettering in the left-hand lower corner, and he at once read it!

Here is an incident by which certain information about three members of my family was phenomenally communicated to me. H. P. B. and I were alone in the house, conversing about these persons, when a crash was suddenly heard in the next room. I hurried in there to ascertain the cause, and found that the photographic portrait of one of them, which stood on the mantel-shelf, had been turned face inward towards the wall, the large water-colour portrait of another had been pulled from the nail and lay on the floor with the glass smashed, and the photo of the third stood on the mantel-shelf undisturbed. My questions were answered. An incorrect and fabulous version of this story having been circulated, I give the facts exactly as they occurred. Not a person save us two was in the flat at the time, and nobody save myself was interested in the questions at issue.

What a strange woman she was, and what a great variety in her psychical phenomena! We have seen her duplicating tissues, let me recall incidents where letters were doubled. I received one day a letter from a certain person who had done me a great wrong, and read it aloud to H. P. B. "We must have a copy of that," she exclaimed, and, taking the sheet of note-paper from me, held it daintily by one corner and actually peeled off a duplicate, paper and all, before my very eyes! It was as though she had split the sheet between its two surfaces. Another example, perhaps even more interesting, is the following: Under date of December 22, 1887, Stainton Moses wrote her a five-paged letter of a rather controversial, or, at any rate, critical, character. The paper was of square, full letter size, and bore the embossed heading "University College, London," and near the left-hand upper corner his monogram—a W and M interlaced and crossed by the name "STAINTON" in small capitals. She said we must have a duplicate of this too, so I took from the desk five half-sheets of foreign letter-paper of the same size as Oxon's and gave her them. She laid them against the five pages of his letter, and then placed the whole in a drawer of the desk just in front of me as I sat. We went on with our conversation for some time, until she said she thought the copy was made and I had better look and see if that were so. I opened the drawer, took out the papers, and found that one page of each of my five pieces had received from the page with which it was in contact the impression of that page. So nearly alike were the original and copies that I thought them—as the reader recollects I did the copy of the Britten-Louis portrait—exact duplicates. I had been thinking so all these subsequent sixteen years, but since I hunted up the documents for description in this chapter, I see that this is not the case. The writings are almost duplicates, yet not quite so. They are rather like two original writings by the same hand. If H. P. B. had had time to prepare this surprise for me, the explanation of forgery would suffice to cover the case; but she had not. The whole thing occurred as described, and I submit that it has an unquestionable evidential value as to the problem of her possessing psychical powers. I have tried the test of placing one page over the other to see how the letters and marks correspond. I find they do not, and that is proof, at any rate, that the transfer was not made by the absorption of the ink by the blank sheet from the other; moreover, the inks are different, and Oxon's is not copying-ink. The time occupied by the whole phenomenon might have been five or ten minutes, and the papers lay the whole time in the drawer in front of my breast, so there was no trick of taking it out and substituting other sheets for the blank ones I had just then handed her. Let it pass to the credit of her good name, and help to make the case which her friends would offset against the intemperate slanders circulated against her by her enemies.

Mr. Sinnett prints in his *Incidents in the Life of Madame Blavatsky* (p. 199), a story given him by Mr. Judge about the production by her of some water colours for him to use in making an Egyptian drawing. I was present at the time and will add my testimony to his as an eye-witness. It happened one afternoon at the "Lamasery." Judge was sketching for her—I think—the figure of a god forming man on a potter's wheel, but for lack of colours could not finish it. H. P. B. asked him which shades he needed, and on being told, stepped over to the cottage piano just behind Judge's chair, and facing towards the corner made by the end of the piano and the wall, held her dress as an apron to receive something. She presently poured from the dress upon the table before Judge thirteen bottles of Winsor and Newton's dry colours, among which were those he had asked for. A little while after he said he would like some gold paint, whereupon she told him to fetch a saucer from the dining-room, which he did. She then asked him to hand her the brass door-key and, holding the two under the edge of the table, rubbed the key smartly upon the bottom of the saucer. In another moment she brought them into view again, and the flat part of the saucer bottom was found covered with a layer of gold-paint of the purest quality. To my question as to the function of the door-key in the experiment, she said that the soul of the metal was needed as a nucleus in which to collect together from the *dkds'a* the atoms of any other metal she meant to precipitate. For the same reason she had needed my signet ring as a help to form the other one that she made for her own use on the occasion above described. Is no hint given here of the principal at work when the alleged transmutation of metals is accomplished by the alchemist? Is, I say, for it is pretended that this art is known to various living fakirs and sanyâsis of modern India. And, moreover, do not the discoveries of Prof. Crookes as to the genesis of the elements* bring us to a point where, if science is to advance and not retrogress, she must move on to the Aryan hypothesis of Purusha and Prakriti? And does not this latter theory show us the possibility of shifting the elements of one metal into fresh combinations which would result in the development of another metal by employing the irresistible power of the Will? To do this by physical methods means—as Professor Crookes says—the carrying back of the elements of a given metal to that extreme point where they might be shunted off on the line which would develop and bring into aggregation the elements of the other desired metal; a thing not yet reached by physical science, even by employing the enormous resources of electricity. But what is so monstrously difficult for the chemist and electrician, who depends entirely upon the help of brute forces, may be quite easy to the Adept, whose active agent is the power of spirit, which he has learnt to bring into function: the power, in fact, which builds the Cosmos.

Between the point at which Crookes stood on the evening of January 15, 1891, when he delivered his Inaugural Address, as President of the Institution of Electrical Engineers, and made

---

* *Viz.*, that the atom is not a unity, but a composite of the world-stuff of space, resulting from the play of electricity.

the brilliant experiments which proved the truth of his immortal hypothesis, and that occupied by European science only a quarter century before, there is a distance immeasurably greater than there is between it and the Gupta Vidyâ of our Aryan ancestors. Crookes, hero-like, while recognising the obstacles ahead and noting that "a formidable amount of hard work remains to be completed," is not in the least degree discouraged. "As for myself," he says,* "I hold the firm conviction that unflagging research will be rewarded by an insight into natural mysteries, such as now can scarcely be conceived. Difficulties, said a keen old statesman, are *things to be overcome;* and to my thinking Science should disdain the notion of finality."

To have got so far as that is the harbinger of the brighter day, when men of science will see that their inductive method multiplies an hundredfold the difficulties of learning "natural mysteries"; that the key to all mysteries is the knowledge of spirit; and that the way to that knowledge leads, not through the laboratory fire, but through that fiercer flame which is fed by egoism, kept alight by the fuel of passion and fanned by the blast of desires.

When spirit is once more recognised as the supreme factor in the genesis of the elements and the building of the Cosmos, psychical phenomena like those of our lamented H. P. B. will acquire transcendent importance as elementary scientific facts, and no longer be looked on by one party as tricks of conjuring, by the other as miracles for the surfeiting of the *gobe-mouches.*

---

* *Vide Four. Inst. Elec. Engineers,* No. Vol. XX., p. 49.

Chapter XXIII.

PRECIPITATION OF
PICTURES

Readers of Lane's *Modern Egyptians,* will recall the story of a young man who, upon visiting a certain wonder-working sheikh, obtained some marvellous proofs of his occult powers. His father, then at a distant place, being somewhat ailing, the son asked that he might have news of his condition. The sheikh consenting, told him to write the father a note of enquiry; which was done, handed him by the anxious son, and by the sheikh placed under the back-pillow against which he was leaning. Presently, the sheikh drew from the same place a letter answering the young man's enquiries. It was written by the father's own hand, and, if my memory serves—for I am trusting to recollection only—stamped with his seal. At his request, also, coffee was served to the company in the father's own cups (*fingán*), which he had every reason to believe had been at the moment of asking in the paternal house in that far-off village. H. P. B. gave me one evening, without fuss or parade, a fact of the first of these two orders. I wished to hear from a certain Adept upon a certain subject.

She bade me write my questions, put them in a sealed envelope, and place the letter where I could watch it for the time being. This was even better than the Egyptian sheikh incident, for in that case the letter was hidden from the enquirer by the back-pillow. As I was sitting at the moment before the grate, I put my letter behind the clock on the mantel, leaving just one edge of the envelope projecting far enough for me to see it. My colleague and I went on talking about a variety of things for perhaps an hour, when she said my answer had come. I drew out the letter, found my own envelope with its seal unbroken, inside it my own letter, and inside that the answer in the Adept's familiar manuscript, written upon a sheet of green paper of peculiar make, the like of which—I have every reason to believe—was not in the house. We were in New York, the Adept in Asia. This phenomenon was, I submit, of a class to which the theory of trickery could not apply, and therefore has much weight. There is just one explanation possible—a very lame one—besides that which I conceive to be the true theory. Granting H. P. B. to be possessed of extraordinary hypnotic power, she might have instantaneously benumbed my waking faculties, so as to prevent my seeing her rise from her chair, take my letter from behind the clock, steam the gum, open the cover, read my letter, write the reply in forged handwriting, replace the contents of the envelope, refasten it, place it back again on the mantel-shelf, and then restore me to the waking state without leaving in my memory the least trace of my experiences! But I had and still preserve a perfect consciousness of having carried on the hour's conversation, of her moving about hither and thither, of her making and smoking a number of cigarettes, of my filling, smoking, and refilling my pipe, and, generally, doing what any waking person might do when his senses were alert as to a psychical phenomenon then in progress. If some forty years of familiarity with hypnotic and mesmeric phenomena and their laws go for anything, then I can positively declare that I was fully conscious of what was going on, and that I have accurately stated the facts. Perhaps even twice forty years' experience on the plane of physical Máyá would not qualify one to grasp the possibilities in Oriental hypnotic science. Perhaps I am no more capable than the tyro of knowing what really passed between the times of writing my note and getting the answer. That is quite possible. But in such case what infinitesimally little weight should be given to the aspersions of H. P. B.'s several hostile critics, learned and lay, who have judged her an unmitigated trickster, without having had even a fourth of my own familiarity with the laws of psychical phenomena! In the (London) *Spiritualist* for January 28, 1876, I described this incident with other psychical matters, and the reader is referred to my letter for the particulars.

I am not aware of there being a special class of hirsute phenomena, but if there is, then the following incident may be included in it, along with that of the sudden elongation of H. B. P.'s hair at Philadelphia, described in one of my earlier chapters. After having shaved my chin for many years I began to grow a full beard, under medical advice, as a protection to a naturally delicate throat, and at the time I speak of, it was about four inches long. One morning, when making my toilet after my bath, I discovered a tangle of long hair under my chin next to the throat. Not knowing what to make of it, I very carefully undid the mass at the expense of almost an hour's trouble, and found, to my great amazement, that I had a lock of beard, fourteen inches long, coming down as far as the pit of the stomach! Whence or why it had come no reading or experience helped me to guess; but there it was, a palpable fact and permanent phenomenon. Upon my showing it to H. P. B., she said it had been purposely done by our Guru while I slept, and advised me to take care of it as it would serve me as a reservoir of his helpful aura. I showed it to many friends, but none could venture any better theory to account for it, while all agreed that I ought not to cut it back to its former length. So I used to tuck it away inside my collar to hide it, and did so for years, until the rest of the beard had grown to match it. This accounts for the "Rishi beard," so often mentioned in friendly allusions to my personal appearance, and explains why I have not yielded to my long-felt wish to clip it into a more convenient and less conspicuous shape. Whatever the fact may be called, it assuredly is not a Máyá, but a very real and tangible verity.

In the department of "precipitation"* of writings and pictures, H. P. B. was exceptionally strong, as will have been inferred from all that has preceded. It was one of M. A. Oxon's strong points likewise. On an evening of 1875 I sat at the house of the President of the Photographic Section of the American Institute, Mr. H. J. Newton, with a private medium named

---

* A term, originally of my own invention, which seems to convey best of all an idea of the method employed.

Cozine, to witness his slate-writings, which were far more wonderful than Dr. Slade's. The communications came upon the slate in bright blue and red colours; no pencil or crayon was used in the experiment, and I myself held one end of the slate. Upon mentioning this to H. P. B., she said: "I think I could do that; at any rate, I will try." So I went out and bought a slate and brought it home; she took it, without crayons or pencil, into a small, pitch-dark closet bed-room and lay upon the couch, while I went out, closed the door, and waited outside. After a very few minutes she reappeared with the slate in her hand, her forehead damp with perspiration, and she seeming very tired. "By Jove!" she exclaimed, "that took it out of me, but I've done it; see!" On the slate was writing in red and blue crayons, in handwritings not her own. M. A. Oxon once wrote me an account of a similar experience of his own, save that in his case Imperator was the agent and he the passive medium, which is quite another affair. At his request Imperator wrote messages to him in various coloured inks, one after the other, inside the pocket-book he had in the breast pocket of his coat at the time. Imperator being still the x of Oxon's psychic life, perhaps it was the ethereal body of my friend which precipitated the coloured writings to appease the clamorous scepticism of his physical brain-consciousness, in which case his phenomenon and H. P. B.'s would be somewhat akin.

Elsewhere I have mentioned H. P. B.'s having done for me a precipitated picture on satin, which showed me the stage that Oxon had reached in his attempt to gain the power of projecting his Double by force of concentrated will-power. I had better now give the details:

One evening, in the autumn of 1876, she and I were work-ing, as usual, upon *Isis*, at opposite sides of our writing-table, and dropped into a discussion of the principles involved in the conscious projection of the Double. Through lack of early familiarity with those subjects, she was not good then at explaining scientific matters, and I found it difficult to grasp her meaning. Her fiery temperament made her prone to abuse me for an idiot in such cases, and this time she did not spare her expressions of impatience at my alleged obtuseness. Fi-nally, she did the very best thing by offering to show me in a picture how Oxon's evolution was proceeding, and at once made good her promise. Rising from the table, she went and opened a drawer from which she took a small roll of white satin—the remnant, I believe, of a piece she had given her at Philadelphia—and laying it on the table before me, pro-ceeded to cut off a piece of the size she wanted; after which she returned the roll to its place and sat down. She laid the piece of satin, face down, before her, almost covered it with a sheet of clean blotting-paper, and rested her elbows on it while she rolled for herself and lighted a fresh cigarette. Presently she asked me to fetch her a glass of water. I said I would, but first put her some question which involved an answer and some delay. Meanwhile I kept my eye upon an exposed edge of the satin, determined not to lose sight of it. Soon noticing that I made no sign of moving, she asked me if I did not mean to fetch her the water. I said: "Oh, certainly." "Then what do you wait for?" she asked. "I only wait to see what you are about to do with that satin," I replied. She gave me one angry glance, as though seeing that I did not mean to trust her alone with the satin, and then brought down her clenched fist upon the blotting-paper, saying: "I shall have it now—this minute!" Then, raising the paper and *turning over the satin*, she tossed it over to me. Imagine, if you can, my surprise! On the sheeny side I found a picture, in colours, of a most extraordinary character.* There was an excellent portrait, of the head only, of Stainton Moses as he looked at that age, the almost duplicate of one of his photographs that hung "above the line" on the wall of the room, over the mantel-shelf. From the crown of the head shot out spikes of golden flame; at the places of the heart and the solar plexus were red and golden fires, as it might be bursting forth from little craters; the head and the place of the thorax were involved in rolling clouds of pure blue aura, bespeckled throughout with flecks of gold; and the lower half of the space where the body should be was enwrapped in similarly rolling clouds of pinkish and greyish vapour, that is, of auras of a meaner quality than the superior cumuli.

At that stage of my occult education I had heard nothing about the six *chakrams*, or psychical evolutionary centres in the human body, which are mentioned in Yoga S'ástras, and are familiar to every student of Patanjali. I therefore did not grasp the significance of the two flaming vortices over the cardiac and umbilical regions; but my later acquaintance with the subject gives this satin picture an enhanced value, as showing that the practical occultist who made it apparently knew that, in the process of disentangling the astral from the

---

* The photo-engraving process not having as yet advanced to the point of photographing in colours, our cut but very poorly represents the original picture on satin.

physical body, the will must be focussed in succession at the several nerve-centres, and the disengagement completed at each in turn before moving on to the next centre in the order of sequence. I take the picture to mean that Stainton Moses' experiment was being conducted as an intellectual rather than as a spiritual process, wherefore he had completely formed and got ready for projection his head, while the other parts of his astral body were in a state of nebulous disturbance, but had not yet settled into the stage of *rûpa*, or form. The blue clouds would represent the pure but not most luminous quality of the human aura—described as shining, or radiant; a silvery nimbus. The flecks of gold, however, that are seen floating in the blue, typify sparks of the spirit, the "silvery spark in the brain," that Bulwer so beautifully describes in his *Strange Story;* while the greyish and pinkish vapours of the inferior portions show the auras of our animalistic, corporeal qualities. This grey becomes darker and darker as a man's animalism preponderates over his intellect, his moral and spiritual qualities, until in the wholly depraved, as the clairvoyants tell us, it is inky black. The aura of adeptship is described as a blended tint of silver and gold, as some of my readers, I am sure, must know from personal observation, and as the poets and painters of all ages have depicted in their sublimer flights of spiritual perception. This Téjas or soul-light, shines out through the mystic's face, lighting it up with a glow which, once seen, can never thereafter be mistaken. It is the "shining countenance" of the Biblical angels, the "glory of the Lord," the light that beamed in the face of Moses when descending from the Mount with such splendour that men could not bear to look upon his countenance; a radiance that even transfigures the wearer's robes into "shining garments." The Hebrews call it *shekinah*, and I once heard the term used by some Bagdad Jews to describe the face of a spiritual-minded visitor on that occasion. So, too, the word "shining" is applied similarly by various other nations; the pure spirits and pure men glow with the white light, the vicious and evil ones are veiled in blackness.

In the case of another precipitated portrait, made by H. P. B., there was no aura shown: I refer to that of an Indian yogi, which is described in Sinnett's *Occult World* and *Incidents in the Life of Mme. Blavatsky;* the documents respecting which were originally published in the *Spiritualist* shortly after the occurrence of the incident. It happened in this wise: On my way home to "The Lamasery" one day, I stopped at the Lotos Club and got some of the club note-paper and envelopes to use at home as occasion might require. It was late when I reached the house, and H. P. B. was at the dinner table already, with Mr. Judge and Dr. Marquette as guests. I laid the package of stationery on my desk in the writing-room (between which and the dining-room there was a dead wall, by the way), made a hurried toilet, and went to my seat at the table. At the close of the dinner we had drifted into talk about precipitations, and Judge asked H. P. B. if she would not make somebody's portrait for us. As we were moving towards the writing-room, she asked him whose portrait he wished made, and he chose that of this particular yogi, whom we knew by name as one held in great respect by the Masters. She crossed to my table, took a sheet of my crested club-paper, tore it in halves, kept the half which had no imprint, and laid it down on her own blotting-paper. She then scraped perhaps a grain of the plumbago of a Faber lead pencil on it, and then rubbed the surface for a minute or so with a circular motion of the palm of her right hand; after which she handed us the result. On the paper had come the desired portrait and, setting wholly aside the question of its phenomenal character, it is an artistic production of power and genius. Le Clear, the noted American portrait painter, declared it unique, distinctly an "individual" in the technical sense; one that no living artist within his knowledge could have produced. The yogi is depicted in *Samâdhi*, the head drawn partly aside, the eyes profoundly introspective and dead to external things, the body seemingly that of an absent tenant. There is a beard and hair of moderate length, the latter drawn with such skill that one sees through the upstanding locks, as it were—an effect obtained in good photographs, but hard to imitate with pencil or crayon. The portrait is in a medium not easy to distinguish: it might be black crayon, without stumping, or black lead; but there is neither dust nor gloss on the surface to indicate which, nor any marks of the stump or the point used: hold the paper horizontally towards the light and you might fancy the pigment was below the surface, combined with the fibres. This incomparable picture was subjected in India later to the outrage of being rubbed with india-rubber to satisfy the curiosity of one of our Indian members, who had borrowed it as a special favour "to show his mother," and who wished to see if the pigment was really on or under the surface! The effect of his vandal-like experiment is now seen in the obliteration of a part of the beard, and my sorrow over the disaster is not in the least mitigated by the knowledge that it was not due to malice but to ignorance and the spirit of childish curiosity. The yogi's name was always pronounced by H. P. B. "Tiraválá," but since coming to live in Madras Presidency, I can very well imagine that she meant Tiruvalluvar, and that the portrait, now hanging in the Picture Annex of the Adyar Library, is really that of the revered philosopher of ancient Mylapur, the friend and teacher of the poor Pariahs. As to the question whether he is still in the body or not I can venture no assertion, but from what H. P. B. used to say about him I always inferred that he was. And yet to all save Hindus that would seem incredible, since he is said to have written his immortal "Kural" something like a thousand years ago! He is classed in Southern India as one of the Siddhas, and like the other seventeen, is said to be still living in the Tirupati and Nilgiri Hills; keeping watch and ward over the Hindu religion. Themselves unseen, these Great Souls help, by their potent willpower, its friends and promoters and all lovers of mankind. May their benediction be with us!

In recalling the incidents for the present narrative, I note the fact that no aura or spiritual glow is depicted around the yogi's head, although H. P. B.'s account of him confirms that of his Indian admirers, that he was a person of the highest spirituality of aspiration and purest character.

The same remark applies to the first portrait of my Guru, the one done in black and white crayons at New York by M. Harrisse: there is no nimbus. In this case at least, I can testify to the likeness, along with others who have had the happiness of seeing him. Its production was, like that done in oils at London in 1884 by Herr Schmiechen, an example of thought-transference. I think I have never published the facts before, but in any case they should have a place in this historical retrospect.

One naturally likes to possess the portrait of a distant correspondent with whom one has had important relations; how much more, then, that of a spiritual teacher, the beginning of relations with whom has substituted a nobler for a commonplace ideal of life in one's consciousness. I most earnestly wished to be able to have in my room at least the likeness of my reverend teacher, if I might not see him in life; had long importuned H. P. B. to procure it for me; and had been promised it at a favourable time. In this case my colleague was not permitted to precipitate it for me, but a simpler yet most instructive method was resorted to: a non-medium and non-occultist was made to draw it for me without knowing what he was doing. M. Harrisse, our French friend, was a bit of an artist, and one evening when the conversation turned upon India and Rajput bravery, H. P. B. whispered to me that she would try to get him to draw our Master's portrait if I could supply the materials. There were none in the house, but I went to a shop close by and purchased a sheet of suitable paper and black and white crayons. The shopkeeper did up the parcel, handed it to me across the counter, took the *half-dollar coin* I gave him, and I left the shop. On reaching home I unrolled my parcel and, as I finished doing it, the sum of half a dollar, *in two silver pieces of a quarter-dollar each* dropped on the floor! The Master, it will be seen, meant to give me his portrait without cost to myself. Harrisse was then asked by H. P. B. to draw us the head of a Hindu chieftain, as he should conceive one might look. He said he had no clear idea in his mind to go upon, and wanted to sketch us something else; but to gratify my importunity went to drawing a Hindu head. H. P. B. motioned me to remain quiet at the other side of the room, and herself went and sat down near the artist and quietly smoked. From time to time she went softly behind him as if to watch the progress of his work, but did not speak until it was finished, say an hour later. I thankfully received it, had it framed, and hung it in my little bed-room. But a strange thing had happened. After we gave the picture a last glance as it lay before the artist, and while H. P. B. was taking it from him and handing it to me, the cryptograph signature of my Guru came upon the paper; thus affixing, as it were, his imprimatur upon, and largely enhancing the value of his gift. But at that time I did not know if it resembled the Guru or not, as I had not yet seen him. When I did, later on, I found it a true likeness and, moreover, was presented by him with the turban which the amateur artist had drawn in the picture as his head-covering. Here was a genuine case of thought-transference, the transfer of the likeness of an absent person to the brain-consciousness of a perfect stranger. Was it or was it not passed through the thought of H. P. B.? I think so. I think it was effected in the identical way in which the thought-images of geometrical and other figures were transferred to third parties in the convincing experiments recorded by the S. P. R. in its earlier published reports. With the difference, however, that H. P. B.'s own memory supplied the portrait to be transferred to Harrisse's mind, and her trained occult powers

enabled her to effect the transfer direct, *viz.*, without an intermediary; that is to say, without the necessity of having the
drawing first made on a card, for her to visualise it in her own
mind and then pass it on to the recipient brain. The painting
by Schmiechen, of the magnificent portraits in oils of the
same and another Master, which now hang in the Adyar
Library, was an even more interesting circumstance, for the
likenesses are so perfect and so striking as to seem endowed
with life. Their eyes speak to one and search one to the bottom of his heart; their glance follows on everywhere as he
moves about; their lips seem about to utter, as one may de-
serve, words of kindness or of reproach. They are an inspiration rather than an illustration of thought-transference.
The artist has made two or three copies of them, but not one
has the soul in it that is in the originals. They were not done
in the divine mood of inspiration, and the Masters' will-power
is not focussed in them. The originals are the palladium of
our headquarters; the copies, like images seen in a mirror,
possess the details of form and colour, but are devoid of the
energising spirit.

Chapter XXIV.

PROJECTION OF
THE DOUBLE

All theories and speculations upon the duplex corporeity of man, *i.e.*, of his possession of an astral, or phantasmal, body as well as a physical body, only lead up to the point where one demands proof before going further. It is so incredible to the materialistic mind as transcending common experience, that it is most likely to be pushed aside as a dream than accepted as even a working hypothesis. This, in fact, has been its handling by the average scientist, and when a braver investigator than the ordinary affirms it as his belief, he risks that reputation for cold caution which is presumed, with laughable inconsistency nevertheless, to be the mark of the true scientific discoverer. Yet many books as precise and suggestive as D'Assier's* have been published at different times, chief among them being the *Phantasms of the Living*, by Messrs. Gurney, Myers, and Podmore, and present a solid

---

* *Posthumous Humanity: a Study of Phantoms.*

front of facts impossible to deny, however difficult to believe. The case seems now to have been amply proved by the compilation of several thousand observed phenomena of this class; and the time seems to have come when the metaphysician who ignores them has no right to claim to be regarded as a trustworthy teacher of men. Yet, while the reason may be convinced by this array of facts, the real existence of the astral body, and the possibility of its separation from the physical "sheath" during life can only be known in one of two ways— by one's seeing the astral body of another person, or by projecting one's own and viewing one's physical body *ab extrâ*. With either of these experiences, one can say he KNOWS; with both, his knowledge becomes absolute and unshakable. I have had both. I take the witness-stand, and testify to the truth for the helping of my fellow-workers. I pass over with a bare mention the incidents of my seeing H. P. B. in her astral body in a New York street, while her physical body was in Philadelphia; of my seeing similarly a friend who was then in body in a Southern State, several hundred miles away; of seeing in an American railway train and on an American steamboat, a certain adept then physically in Asia; of receiving from the hand of another, at Jummu, a telegram sent me there by H. P. B. from Madras, and delivered to me by the adept under the guise of the Kashmiri telegraph-peon, whose appearance he borrowed momentarily for the purpose, and dissolved a moment later in full moonlight when I stepped to the door to watch him; of being saluted on Worli Bridge, Bombay, by another of these majestic men on another tropical evening as

H. P. B., Damodar, and I sat in our phaeton enjoying the heat lightning and the cooling breeze off the sea; of seeing him moving towards us from a little distance, advance to the very carriage side, lay his hand on H. P. B.'s, walk fifty yards away, and suddenly disappear from our sight on the causeway, bare of trees, shrubs, or other places of concealment, in the full sheen of the lightning: I pass these and other such experiences, and come to the one which of all was the most momentous in its consequences upon the course of my life. The story has been told before, but it had its place in the present retrospect, for it was the chief among the causes of my abandonment of the world and my coming out to my Indian home. Hence it was one of the chief factors in the upbuilding of the Theosophical Society. I do not mean to say that without it I should not have come to India, for my heart had been leaping within me to come, from the time when I learned what India had been to the world, what she might be made again. An insatiable longing had possessed me to come to the land of the Rishis and the Buddhas, the Sacred Land among lands; but I could not see my way clear to breaking the ties of circumstance which bound me to America, and I might have felt compelled to put it off to that "convenient season" which so often never comes to the procrastinator and waiter upon the turn of events. This experience in question, however, settled my fate; in an instant doubts melted away, the clear foresight of a fixed will showed the way, and before the dawn of that sleepless night came, I began to devise the means and to bend all things to that end. The happening was thus:

Our evening's work on *Isis* was finished, I had bade

good-night to H. P. B., retired to my own room, closed the door as usual, sat me down to read and smoke, and was soon absorbed in my book; which, if I remember aright, was Stephens' *Travels in Yucatan;* at all events, not a book on ghosts, nor one calculated in the least to stimulate one's imagination to the seeing of spectres. My chair and table were to the left in front of the door, my camp-cot to the right, the window facing the door, and over the table a wall gas-jet. The following simple ground plan will convey the correct idea of the premises of the "Lamasery," although not accurate as to the measurements.

EXPLANATION.—A, our working and only reception room; B, bed-room of H. P. B.; C, my bed-room; D, a small, dark bed-room; E, passage; F, kitchen; G, dining-room; H, bath-room; I, hanging closet; J, exterior door of the flat opening upon the house staircase; always closed with a spring-latch and locked at night. In my room, *a* is the chair where I sat reading; *b* the table; *c* the chair where my visitor seated himself during the interview; *d* my camp-cot. In our work-room *e* is where the cuckoo clock hung, and *f* the place of the hanging shelves against which I bruised myself. In B, *g* represents the place of H. P. B.'s bed. The door of my room, it will be seen, was to my right as I sat, and any opening of it would have at once been noticed; the more so, since it was locked, to the best of my present recollection. That I am not more positive will not seem strange in view of the mental excitement into which the passing events threw me; events so astonishing as to make me forget various minor details which, under a cooler frame of mind, would perhaps have been retained in my memory.

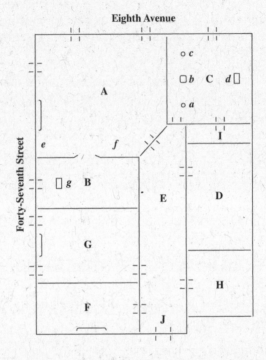

I was quietly reading, with all my attention centered on my book. Nothing in the evening's incidents had prepared me for seeing an adept in his astral body; I had not wished for it, tried to conjure it up in my fancy, nor in the least expected it. All at once, as I read with my shoulder a little turned from the door, there came a gleam of something white in the right-hand corner of my right eye; I turned my head, dropped my book in astonishment, and saw towering above me in his great stature an Oriental clad in white garments, and wearing a head-cloth or turban of amber-striped fabric, hand-embroidered in yellow floss-silk. Long raven hair hung from under his turban to the shoulders; his black beard, parted vertically on the chin in the Rajput fashion, was twisted up at the ends and carried over the ears; his eyes were alive with soul-fire; eyes which were at once benignant and piercing in glance; the eyes of a mentor and a judge, but softened by the love of a father who gazes on a son needing counsel and guidance. He was so grand a man, so imbued with the majesty of moral strength, so luminously spiritual, so evidently above average humanity, that I felt abashed in his presence, and bowed my head and bent my knee as one does before a god or a god-like personage. A hand was lightly laid on my head, a sweet though strong voice bade me be seated, and when I raised my eyes, the Presence was seated in the other chair beyond the table. He told me he had come at the crisis when I needed him; that my actions had brought me to this point; that it lay with me alone whether he and I should meet often in this life as co-workers for the good of mankind; that a great work was to be done for humanity, and I had the right to share in it if I wished; that a mysterious tie, not now to be explained to me, had drawn my colleague and myself together; a tie which could not be broken, however strained it might be at times. He told me things about H. P. B. that I may not repeat, as well as things about myself, that do not concern third parties. How long he was there I cannot tell: it might have been a half-hour or an hour; it seemed but a minute, so little did I take note of the flight of time. At last he rose, I wondering at his great height and observing the sort of splendour in his countenance—not an external shining, but the soft gleam, as it were, of an inner light—that of the spirit. Suddenly the thought came into my mind: "What if this be but hallucination; what if H. P. B. has cast a hypnotic glamour over me? I wish I had some tangible object to prove to me that he has really been here; something that I might handle after he is gone!" The Master smiled kindly as if reading my thought, untwisted the *fehtâ* from his head, benignantly saluted me in farewell and—was gone: his chair was empty; I was alone with my emotions! Not quite alone, though, for on the table lay the embroidered head-cloth; a tangible and enduring proof that I had not been "over-looked," or psychically befooled, but had been face to face with one of the Elder Brothers of Humanity, one of the Masters of our dull pupil-race. To run and beat at H. P. B.'s door and tell her my experience, was the first natural impulse, and she was as glad to hear my story as I was to tell it. I returned to my room to think, and the gray morning found me still thinking and resolving. Out of those thoughts and those resolves developed all my subsequent theosophical activities, and that loyalty to the Masters behind our movement which the rudest shocks and the cruelest disillusioning have never shaken. I have been blessed with meetings with this Master and others since then, but little profit is to be reaped in repeating tales of experiences of which the foregoing is a sufficient example. However others less fortunate may doubt, I know.

As due to my ideal of candour, I must recall a circum-stance which threw a doubt once upon my competency as a witness as to the above incident. While in London in 1884, I was examined as a witness before a Special Committee of the Society for Psychical Research, and told the above story among others. A member of the committee in cross-examination, so to say, put to me the question how I could be

sure that Madame Blavatsky had not employed some tall
Hindu to play this farce on me, and that as to the supposed
mysterious details my fancy might not have played me false. I
was thereupon seized with such a disgust for their cruel suspicion of H. P. B., and their seemingly dishonourable shirking
of palpable spiritual facts under cover of assumed astuteness,
that I hastily answered, among other things, that I had never
until that moment seen a Hindu in my life. The circumstance
of my having actually made in 1870 the voyage across the
Atlantic with two Hindu gentlemen, one of whom was later
our close friend at Bombay—Mooljee Thackersey—entirely
slipped out of my mind. This was a clear case of amnesia (loss
of memory) for I had not the least intention or interest in con-
cealing so commonplace a circumstance; the meeting of 1870,
fourteen years before the examination of me by the S. P. R.,
had left no such mark in my memory as to be recalled in my
moment of anger, and so the force of my testimony was weakened to that extent. A meeting with Hindus five years or so
before I knew H. P. B., and, through her, the real India, would
not have been of paramount importance to a man of such
multifarious acquaintanceships and adventures as myself.
Yes, it was amnesia; but amnesia is not lying, and my story is
true, even though some may doubt it. And this is the fitting
place for me to say that, as some of my chapters were written
while travelling, away from my books and papers, and especially as much of it is written from memory only of the long-
past events, I beg indulgence for any unintentional mistakes
that may be discovered. I try my best to be accurate and certainly shall be truthful.

I now pass on to my personal experiences in projections of the Double. In connection with this phenomenon let me give a word of caution to the less advanced student of practical psychology; the power of withdrawing the astral body from the physical *is no necessary proof of high spiritual development*. The contrary is believed, by perhaps the majority of dabblers in occultism, but they are wrong. A first and sufficient proof is that the emergence of the astral body happens very often with men and women who have given little or no time to occult research, have followed no yogic system, have made no attempts to do the thing, have usually been frightened or much ashamed and vexed when convicted of it, and have not been in the least remarkable above the average of persons for purity of life and thought, spirituality of ideal, or the "gifts of the spirit" of which the Scripture speaks; often the very opposite. Then, again, the annals of the Black Art teem with numberless instances of the visible, and invisible (save clairvoyantly), projection of the Double by wicked persons bent on mischief; of bilocations, hauntings of hated victims, lycanthropical masqueradings, and other "damnable witchcrafts." Then, again, there are the three or four or more thousand cases of projections of the Double by all sorts and conditions of men, some no better than they should be, if not a good deal worse occasionally, that have been recorded and winnowed down by the S. P. R., and the yet more thousands not garnered into their cast-iron granary; all combining to prove the truth of my warning, that one must not in the least take the mere fact that a certain person can travel—whether consciously or unconsciously it matters not—in the astral body as evidence that that person is either better, wiser, more spiritually advanced, or better qualified to serve as Guru, than any other person not so endowed. It is simply the sign that the subject of the experience has, either congenitally or by subsequent effort, loosened the astral body in its sheath, and so made it easier for it to go out and return again, when the outer body is naturally or hypnotically asleep, hence unobstructive. The reader will recall, in this connection, the satin picture of M. A. Oxon's experiments in this direction which H. P. B. made for me. Somehow or other, I have never found the time for self-training in yoga since I took up my line of practical work in our theosophical movement. I never seemed to care whether I acquired any psychical powers or not, never aspired to guruship, nor cared whether I could or could not attain Liberation during this life. To serve mankind always seemed to me the best of yogas, and the ability to do even a little towards spreading knowledge and diminishing ignorance, an ample reward. So it never entered my mind in the early days that I might train myself as a seer or a wonder-worker, a metaphysician or an adept; but I have been going on all these years on the hint given me by a Master, that *the best way to seek them was through the Theosophical Society*: a humble sphere, perhaps, yet one well within my limited capabilities, thoroughly congenial and at the same time useful. In telling about my early goings out of the body, I must not be thought, therefore, to be pluming myself upon my supposed high spiritual development, nor intending to boast of special cleverness as a psychic. The fact is, I presume, I was helped to get this, along with many other psychical experiences, as a basis of the special education needed by one who had such work as mine cut out for him.

Here is one of my facts: H. P. B. and I had one evening in 1876, while we were living in West 34th St.,* finished writing a chapter of the original draft of *Isis Unveiled*, and on parting for the night, laid away the great pile of "copy" in a pasteboard box, with the first page on top, the last at the bottom of the heap. She occupied the flat directly under my own, in the second story of the apartment-house, and both of us, of course, locked our outer doors to keep out thieves. While undressing it occurred to me that if I had added certain three words to the final sentence of the last paragraph, the sense of the whole paragraph would have been strengthened. I was afraid I might forget them in the morning, so the whim came to me that I might try to go down to the writing-room below stairs in my Double and perhaps write them phenomenally. Consciously, I had never travelled thus before, but I knew how it must be attempted, *viz.*, by fixing the intention to do it firmly in the mind when falling asleep, and I did so. I knew nothing more until the next morning, when, after dressing and taking my breakfast, I stopped in at H. P. B.'s flat to bid her good-bye on my way to my office. "Well," she said, "pray tell me what the deuce you were doing here last night after you went to bed?" "Doing," I replied, "what do you mean?" "Why," she rejoined, "I had got into bed and was lying there quietly, when lo! I saw my Olcott's astral body oozing through the wall. And stupid and sleepy enough you

---

* Not the "Lamasery," but the place we occupied before going there.

seemed, too! I spoke to you, but you did not reply. You went to the writing-room and I heard you fumbling with the papers; and that's all. What were you about?" I then told her of my intended experiment: we went together into the other room, emptied out the pile of MS., and on the last page, at the end of the concluding paragraph, found two of the intended three words fully written out in my own handwriting and the third begun, but not finished: the power of concentration seeming to have become exhausted, and the word ending in a scrawl! How I handled the pencil, if I did handle it, or how I wrote the words without handling it, I cannot say: perhaps I was able just that once to precipitate the writing with the help of one of H. P. B.'s benevolent elementals, by utilising molecules of the plumbago from either of the lead pencils lying on the table along with the manuscript. Be it as it may, the experience was useful.

The reader should take note of the fact that my writing in the phenomenal way stopped at the point where, from inexperience, I let my will wander away from the work in hand. To fix it immovably is the one thing indispensable, just as it is the necessary concomitant of good work on the normal intellectual plane. In the *Theosophist* for July, 1888 (Art. "Precipitated Pictures at New York"), I explained the connection between the concentration of trained will-power and the permanency of precipitated writings, pictures, and other similar proofs of the creative power of the mind. I instanced the very interesting and suggestive details of the projection of the Double and the precipitation of writing, given by Wilkie Collins in his novel, *The Two Destinies*—a book, in its way, as well worth reading by any student of occultism,* as *Zanoni, A Strange Story,* or *The Coming Race.* I cited, further, the case of the Louis portrait precipitated for Mlle. Liebert and myself, which faded out by the next morning, but was caused by H. P. B. to subsequently reappear at Mr. Judge's request, and to be so "fixed" as to be still as sharp and fresh after the lapse of many years as when first made. But no amount of reading or experimentation at second hand can compare with even one little original experience, like the one of mine above described, in its power to make one realise the truth of the universal cosmic operation of *thought* creating *form.* The s'loka *Bahúsyam Prajdyeyaiti,* etc. (VIth Anuváka, and Valli, Taittiryîaka-Upanishad), "He (Brahmâ) *wished,* may I be many, may I grow forth. He *brooded* over himself. *After* he had thus brooded, he sent forth all, whatever there is. Having sent forth, he entered it"; is to me profoundly instructive. It has a meaning immeasurably deeper, truer, more suggestive to one who has himself *meditated* and then *created* form, than to him whose eyes have but read the words on the page, without the echoing assent coming from within one's being.

I recall another case of my projecting my Double, which illustrates the law known as "repercussion." The reader may find the amplest materials for forming a correct opinion on this subject in the literature of Witchcraft, Sorcery, and Magic. The word "repercussion" means, in this connection,

---

* It was this article which caused Mr. Collins to write me that, among the incidents of his life, none had more surprised him than his finding from my notice of his book that he had by the *mere exercise of the imagination,* apparently stumbled on one of the mysterious laws of occult science.

the reacting upon one's physical body of a blow, stab, or other injury, inflicted upon the Double while it is projected and moving about as a separate entity: "bilocation" is the simultaneous appearance of a person in two places; one appearance that of the physical, the other that of the astral body, or Double. M. d'Assier discusses both in his *Posthumous Humanity*, and in my English version of that excellent work, I add remarks of my own upon the subject. Speaking of the infliction of injuries upon their victims by sorcerers who could duplicate their bodies and visit them in the Double, the author says (p. 224): "The sorceress entered into the house of him against whom she had a revenge to gratify, and vexed him in a thousand ways. If the latter were resolute, and had a weapon available, it would often happen that he would strike the phantom, and upon recovering from her trance, the sorceress *would find upon her own body* the wounds she had received in the phantasmal struggle."

Des Mousseaux, the Catholic writer against Sorcery and other "black arts," quotes from the judicial archives of England, the case of Jane Brooks, who persecuted a child named Richard Jones after a very malicious fashion. At one of her visitations, the child screamed out that the phantom of Jane was present and pretended to touch it with the point of his finger. A witness named Gilson, springing to the place indicated, slashed at it with a knife, although the phantom was visible only to the child. The house of Jane Brooks was at once visited by Gilson, with the child's father and a constable, and she was found sitting on her stool holding one of her hands with the other. She denied that anything had happened to her hand, but the other being snatched away, the concealed one was found covered with blood, and bearing just such a wound as the child had said had been inflicted on the hand of the phantom by Gilson's knife. A great number of similar cases are on record, all going to prove that any accident or injury to the projected Double reacts and reproduces itself upon the physical body in the identical spot.* This brings me to my own experience.

In our writing-room at the "Lamasery" there hung upon the wall, beside the chimney, a Swiss cuckoo-clock, which it was my methodical custom to wind up nightly before retiring to my own room. One morning, on going to my toilet-glass after my bath, I noticed that my right eye was black and blue, as though I had received a blow from a fist. I could not account for it in the least, and I was the more puzzled on finding that I had no pain in the injured part. In vain I racked my brain for an explanation. In my bed-room there was no post, pillar, projecting corner, or other obstruction from which I could have received injury, supposing that I had been walking about in my sleep—a habit I had never acquired, by the way. Then, again, a shock, rude enough to have blackened my eye like this, must,

---

* The exact duplexity of the astral and physical bodies in man has been affirmed from the remotest ages. It is the Eastern theory that the astral man is the product of his past Karma, and that it moulds the outer encasement according to its own innate qualities, making it a visible representation of the same. This idea is succinctly embodied in the verse in Spenser's *Faerie Queene*:

"For of the soul the body form doth take,
    For soul is form, and doth the body make."

of necessity, have wakened me instantaneously at the time, whereas I had slept the night through as quietly as usual. So my bewilderment continued, until I met H. P. B. and a lady friend, who had shared her bed that night, at the breakfast table. The lady friend gave me the clue to the enigma. She said: "Why, Colonel, you must have hit yourself last night when you came in to wind the cuckoo clock!" "Wind the clock," I replied, "what do you mean by that? Did you not lock the door when I went to my room?" "Yes," she said, "I locked it myself; and how ever *could* you have come in? Yet both Madame and I saw you pass the sliding-doors of our bed-room and heard you pulling the chain to wind the clock. I called, but you did not answer, and I saw nothing more." Well, then, I thought, if I did enter the room in my Double and wind the clock, two things are inevitable, (*a*) the clock must show that it was wound last night and not have run down; (*b*) there must be some obstacle on my path between the door and the opposite chimney against which I could have hit my eye. We examined the premises and found:

1. That the clock was going and had apparently been wound up at the usual time.
2. Just near the door hung a small hanging bookshelf, the farthest front corner of one of whose shelves was of the exact height to catch my eye if I had run against it. Then there came back to me the dim recollection of myself moving towards the door from the far side of the room, with my right hand outstretched as if to feel for the door, a sudden shock, "the seeing of stars"—as it is commonly expressed—and then oblivion until morning.

That is curious, it seems to me; very curious that a blow which, received upon the physical head, must almost inevitably have at once awakened one, should, when falling upon the projected Double, have left its substantial mark behind it by repercussion upon the physical body, without bringing me to consciousness. And the case is instructive in other aspects, as well. It shows that, provided the conditions are favourable for the slipping of the Double out of the physical body, the "duplication" is likely to occur under the stimulus of a thought-prepossession, for instance, that of a daily habit of doing any certain thing at a fixed hour. Supposing the conditions unfavourable for "projection" or "duplication," the subject would, under another set of conditions, become somnambulistic, rise from bed, go and do what was on his or her mind, and return to bed and to deep slumber without remembering anything that had occurred. The editors of the English version of the *Dabistan* say: "It is impossible to fix the epoch at which particular opinions and practices originated... particularly the belief that a man may attain the faculty to quit and to reassume his body, or to consider it as a loose garment, which he may put off at pleasure for ascending to the world of light, and on his return be reunited with the material elements. All these matters are considered very ancient" (*Dabistan*, Preface, lxxix). One of my most interesting experiences has been to encounter persons in different parts of the world, until then strangers, who have averred that they had seen me in public places, that I had visited them in the astral body, sometimes talked on occult matters with them, sometimes healed them of diseases, sometimes even gone with them on the astral plane to visit our Masters; yet without my keeping any remembrance of the several incidents. Yet, when one comes to think of it, it is not so improbable, after all, that one whose whole life and every waking thought and wish is bound up in this great movement of ours; who has no desire save for its success, no ambition save to push it forward to its ultimate goal, should carry his prepossession into the realms of sleep, and float through the currents of the Astral Light towards the kindred beings who are held by the same magnet to the same attractive centre of wish and aspiration. In its truest sense—

"It is the secret sympathy,
   The silver link, the silver tie,
   Which heart to heart, and mind to mind,
   In body and in soul can bind."

Chapter XXV.

SWAMI DYÁNAND

If I should fail to introduce the episode of our brief and upleasant connection with Swami Dyánand Sarasvati and his Arya Samaj, this could not be called a true history of the beginnings of our Society. I should prefer to omit it altogether if I could, for it is not agreeable to record the details of vanished hopes, bitter misunderstandings, and faded illusions. Now that both H. P. B. and the Swami are dead, and that sixteen years have passed since we voted for a blending of the two societies together, I feel at liberty to give the clue to what has been hitherto a sort of mystery as regards the incident, and to explain the hidden causes of the union and subsequent quarrel between the great Pandit and ourselves.

I have told all that concerns the formation of the Theosophical Society; how it originated; what were its avowed aims and objects; and how it gradually faded into a small, compact body, of which the two Founders were the dual energy: a mere nucleus of the present organisation. I make bold to say that not a line can be produced which goes to show that our religious opinions were ever concealed or misrepresented, to whatsoever exoteric creed our correspondents may have belonged. If, therefore, Swami Dyánand and his followers ever misunderstood our position and that of the Theosophical Society, the fault was theirs, not ours. Our two hearts drew us towards the Orient, our dreams were of India, our chief desire to get into relations with the Asiatic people. No way, however, had yet opened on the physical plane, and our chance of getting out to our Holy Land seemed very slight, until one evening in the year 1877 an American traveller, who had recently been in India, called. He happened to sit so that, in looking that way I noticed on the wall above him the framed photograph of the two Hindú gentlemen with whom I had made the Atlantic passage in 1870. I took it down, showed it to him, and asked if he knew either of the two. He did know Moolji Thackersey and had quite recently met him in Bombay. I got the address, and by the next mail wrote to Moolji about our Society, our love for India and what caused it. In due course he replied in quite enthusiastic terms, accepted the offered diploma of membership, and told me about a great Hindú pandit and reformer, who had begun a powerful movement for the resuscitation of pure Vedic religion. At the same time he introduced to my notice, in complimentary terms, one Hurrychund Chintamon, President of the Bombay Arya Samaj, with whom I chiefly corresponded thereafter; and whose evil treatment of us on arrival at Bombay is a matter of history. The latter nominated several Hindú gentlemen of Bombay for membership, spoke most flatteringly of Swami Dyánand, and brought about an exchange of letters between the latter and myself as chiefs of our respective societies. Mr. Hurrychund wrote to me, on reading my explanations of our views as to the impersonality of God—an Eternal and Omnipresent Principle which, under many different names, was the same in all religions—that the principles of the Arya Samaj were identical with our own, and suggested that, in that case, it was useless to keep up two societies, when by amalgamating we would increase our powers of usefulness and our chances of success.* Neither then nor ever since have I cared for the empty honour of leadership, and so I was but too glad to take second place under the Swami, whom I was made to look up to as immeasurably my superior in every respect. The letters of my Bombay correspondents, my own views about Vedic philosophy, the fact of his being a great Sanskrit pandit and actually playing the part of a Hindú Luther, prepared me to believe without difficulty what H. P. B. told me later about him. This was neither more nor less than that he was an adept of the Himalayan Brotherhood inhabiting the Swami's body; well known to our own teachers, and in relations with them for the accomplishment of the work he had in hand. What wonder that I was as ready as possible to fall in with Hurrychund's scheme to amalgamate the T. S. with the Arya Samaj, and to sit at the Swami's feet as pupil under a master! To make such a connection I should have been ready, if required, to be his servant and to have rendered him glad service for years to come, without hope of reward. So, the matter being explained

---

* For a full statement of the case, with documentary proofs, see Extra Supplement, *Theosophist*, July, 1882.

to my colleagues in New York, our Council, in May, 1878, passed a vote to unite the two societies and change the title of ours to "The Theosophical Society of the Arya Samaj." This was notified to the Swami, and in due time he returned to me the draft of a new Diploma (now before me as I write) which I had sent him, signed, as requested, with his name and stamped with his own seal. I had this engraved, issued it to a few members who wished to enlist under the new scheme, and put forth a circular reciting the principles under which we intended to work.

So far all went well, but, in due course, I received from India an English translation of the rules and doctrines of the Arya Samaj, made by Pandit Shyamji Krishnavarma, a protégé of the Swami's, which gave us a great shock—gave me, at least. Nothing could have been clearer than that the Swami's views had radically changed since the preceding August, when the Lahore Arya Samaj published his defence of his *Veda Bhâshya* against the attacks of his critics, in the course of which he quoted approvingly the opinions of Prof. Max Müller, Messrs. Colebrooke, Garrett, and others, that the God of the Vedas was an impersonality. It was evident that the Samaj was *not* identical in character with our Society, but rather a new sect of Hinduism—a Vedic sect accepting Swami Dyánand's authority as supreme judge as to which portions of the Vedas and Shâstras were and were not infallible. The impossibility of carrying out the intended amalgamation became manifest, and we immediately reported that fact to our Indian colleagues. The Theosophical Society resumed its *status quo ante;* and H. P. B. and I drafted and the Council put out two circulars, one defining what the Theosophical Society was, the other (dated September, 1878), defining a new body, the "Theosophical Society of the Arya Samaj of Aryavart," as a bridge between the two mother societies, giving in detail the translation of the A. S. rules, etc., and leaving our members perfectly free to join the "link-society," as I called it, and comply with its bylaws, or not.

Our London Branch, which after more than two years of preliminary *pourparlers*, had formally organised on the 27th June, 1878, under the title of the "British Theosophical Society,"* issued its first public circular as "The British Theosophical Society of the Arya Samaj of Aryavart." If the digression may be excused, I will quote here, for their historical interest, some passages out of my copy of this circular, *viz.*:

"1. The British Theosophical Society is founded for the purpose of discovering the nature and powers of the human soul and spirit by investigation and experiment.

"2. The object of the Society is to increase the amount of human health, goodness, knowledge, wisdom, and happiness.

"3. The Fellows pledge themselves to endeavour, to the best of their powers, to live a life of temperance, purity, and brotherly love. They believe in a Great First Intelligent Cause, and in the Divine Sonship of the spirit of

---

* Under the presidency of the late Dr. Anna Kingsford, the Branch name was changed in the year 1884 to that of the "London Lodge of the Theosophical Society," which it still bears.

man, and hence in the immortality of that spirit, and in the universal brotherhood of the human race.

"4. The Society is in connection and sympathy with the Arya Samaj of Aryavart, one object of which Society is to elevate, by a true spiritual education, mankind out of degenerate, idolatrous, and impure forms of worship, wherever prevalent."

This was a clear, frank, and unobjectionable programme, the reflection of the tone, though not of the actual letter, of my New York T. S. circular of the same year. In both, the aspiration for the attainment of spiritual knowledge through the study of natural, especially of occult, phenomena is declared, as well as the brotherhood of mankind. In drafting the New York circular it occurred to me that the membership of, and supervising entities behind, the Society would be naturally grouped in three divisions, *viz.*, new members not detached from worldly interests; pupils, like myself, who had withdrawn from the same or were ready to do so; and the adepts themselves, who, without being actually members, were at least connected with us and concerned in our work as a potential agency for the doing of spiritual good to the world. With H. P. B.'s concurrence I defined these three groups, calling them sections, and sub-dividing each into three degrees. This, of course, was in the hope and expectation that we should have more practical guidance in adjusting the several grades of members than we had had—or have since had, I may add. In the New York circular, Clause VI. said:

"The objects of the Society are various. It influences its

fellows to acquire an intimate knowledge of natural law, especially its occult manifestations."

Then follow these sentences written by H. P. B.:

"As the highest development, physically and spiritually, on earth of the creative cause, man should aim to solve the mystery of his being. He is the procreator of his species, physically, and having inherited the nature of the unknown but palpable cause of his own creation, must possess in his inner, psychical self, this creative power in lesser degree. He should, therefore, study to develop his latent powers, and inform himself respecting the laws of magnetism, electricity, and all other forms of force, whether of the seen or unseen universes."

I then proceed as follows:

"The Society teaches and expects its fellows to personally exemplify the highest morality and religious aspirations; to oppose the materialism of science and every form of dogmatic theology . . . ; to make known, among Western nations the long-suppressed *facts* about Oriental religious philosophies, their ethics, chronology, esoterism, symbolism . . . ; to disseminate a knowledge of the sublime teachings of that pure esoteric system of the archaic period which are mirrored in the oldest Vedas, and in the philosophy of Gautama Buddha, Zoroaster, and Confucius; finally, and chiefly, to aid in the institution of a Brotherhood of Humanity, wherein all good and pure men of every race shall recognise each other as the equal effects (upon this planet) of one Un-Create, Universal, Infinite and Everlasting Cause."

The parenthesis (upon this planet) was written in by H. P. B.

The step we were taking in resuming the Society's auton-
omy upon discovering the sectarian character of the Arya
Samaj, thus drew from us the above categorical declaration of
principles, in which, the reader will observe, were embraced—

1. The study of occult science;
2. The formation of a nucleus of universal brotherhood; and
3. The revival of Oriental literature and philosophy. In
   short, all the three Declared Objects upon which the
   Theosophical Society has been building itself up during
   the subsequent seventeen years.

If our Bombay friends had previously been under the least
misapprehension as regards the aims and principles of our
Society, the above circular removed the last excuse for its
continuance.

The preamble to the Arya Samaj circular issued by us in
September, 1878—three months only before our departure
for India—called attention to Pandit Shyamji's translation of
the Samaj rules, embodied in the circular, and said: "The
observance of these rules is obligatory only upon such fellows
as may voluntarily apply for admission to the Arya Samaj; the
rest will continue to be, as heretofore, unconnected with the
special work of the Samaj." It went on to say that our Society,
with the design of aiding "in the establishment of a Brotherhood of Humanity, had organised sections (meaning groups)
in which room is provided for persons born in the most varied
religious faiths, requiring only that applicants shall sincerely

wish to learn the sublime truths first written by the Aryans in the Vedas and in different epochs promulgated by sages and seers, and to order their lives accordingly. And also, should they so desire, labour to acquire that control over certain forces of nature which a knowledge of her mysteries imparts to its possessor." The occult training and developments of H. P. B. and her grade of pupils were here hinted at. The phrase shows that the chief original motive of the Founders of the Society was to promote this kind of study; it being their firm conviction that with the development of the psychical powers and spiritual insight, all religious knowledge was attainable, and all ignorant religious dogmatism must vanish. The circular adds that "the Society has thus welcomed, and its members dwell in harmony with Buddhists, Lamaists, Brahmanists, Parsis, Confucianists, and Jews," etc., which was strictly true, applicants from all these religious bodies having already been enrolled as fellows. The incongruity of this platform with that of the Arya Samajis unmistakable and seen at a glance. For Rule 2 in Shyamji's version reads:

"The four texts of the Vedas shall be received and regarded as containing within themselves all that is necessary to constitute them an extraordinary authority in all matters relating to human conduct."

Nothing is said here about any other religious scripture being an authority in human conduct, nor any benevolent interest expressed in the religious welfare of non-Vedic peoples; in short, it is a sectarian body, not eclectic. In saying which I pronounce no opinion as to whether the Samaj is a good or a bad sect, a conservative or a progressive one, or whether its establishment by the Swami was a blessing or the reverse to India. I simply mean that it is a sect, and that, our Society not being one and standing upon a quite different platform, could not properly be merged by us into the Samaj, although we could be and wished to be friends.

As further showing the arbitrary authority which the Swami claimed and exercised in prescribing which of the S'ástras were and were not "authoritative," I quote, from the same Rule 2 of the Arya Samaj, the following:

"The Brâhmanas beginning with the Shatapatka; the six Angas or limbs of the Vedas, beginning with the Shikshâ; the four Upvedas; the six Darshanas or Schools of Philosophy; and the 1,127 Lectures on the Vedas, called *Shâkhâs*, or the branches—these shall be accepted as exponents of the meaning of the Vedas, as well as of the history of the Aryas. So far as these shall concur with the views of the Vedas, they shall be considered as ordinary authority."

Here is defined a sect, a sect of Hinduism, a sect based on the lines traced by its founder. The Swami, it will be seen, in passing, puts himself in opposition to the whole body of orthodox pandits, since he excludes from his list of inspirational books many that are held by them as sacred.

For instance, Smritis are omitted by the Swami, as not being conclusive authorities. But Manu, Chap. II., 10, holds that "Vedas" are "revelations" and "Smritis" (Dharma S'ástras) are "traditions"; these two are irrefutable in all matters, for by these two virtues arose. It is therefore maintained that Smritis must be respected as *"authority."*

Things remained thus until the arrival of the Founders in

India and their meeting, soon after, with Swami Dyánand at Saharanpur. The chances for our entanglement in a series of misunderstandings were, of course, greatly enhanced by the necessity for the Swami and ourselves having to talk with each other through interpreters, who, however well up in ordinary English, lacked the fluency which would enable them to render correctly our views upon the abstruse questions of philosophy, metaphysics, and occult science which had to be discussed. We certainly were made to understand that Swami Dyánand's conception of God was that of the Vedântic Parabrahman, hence in accord with our own. Under this mistake—as it afterwards was declared by him to be—I lectured at Meerut to the Arya Samaj in his presence, and declared that now all causes of misunderstanding had been removed and the two societies were really twins. Yet it was not so: they were no more akin than our Society was with the Brahmo Samaj or any Christian or other sect. Disruption was inevitable, and in due time it came. The Swami, losing his temper, tried to repudiate his own words and acts, and finally turned upon us with abuse and denunciations, and put forth a circular to the public and posted handbills in Bombay to call us charlatans and I do not know what else. This forced us in self-defence to state our case and produce our proofs, and this was done in an extra Supplement to the *Theosophist*, of date July, 1882, in which all the evidence is cited in full and engraved facsimiles are given of an important document bearing the Swami's signature and the certificate of Mr. Seervai, then our Recording Secretary. Thus, after a disturbed relationship of about three years, the two societies were wrenched apart and each went on its own way.

The inherent disruptive elements were (1) My discovery that the Swami was simply that—*i.e.,* a pandit ascetic—and not an adept at all; (2) The fact that the Samaj was not standing upon the eclectic platform of the Theosophical Society; (3) The Swami's disappointment at our receding from our first consent to accept Harischandra's bid for the amalgamation; (4) His vexation—expressed to me in very strong terms—that I should be helping the Ceylon Buddhists and the Bombay Parsis to know and love their religions better than heretofore, while, as he said, both were false religions. I have also doubted whether his and our intermediary correspondent, Hurrychund Chintamon, had ever explained to him just what our views and the real platform of our Society were. The subsequent discovery of the fact that he (Hurrychund) had pocketed the Rs. 600-odd sent him by us for the Arya Samaj, and his restitution of the money at Bombay under H. P. B.'s compulsion, incline me to the opinion that he deceived both the Swami and ourselves in this respect, and that, but for my getting Shyamji's translation of the Samaj Rules, we should have gone on under the same misapprehension until coming out to India.

It is quite useless and waste of room for me to proceed further in this affair, since those who care for details can find them given at length in the extra Supplement to the *Theosophist* above mentioned. The Swami was undoubtedly a great man, a learned Sanskrit Pandit, with immense pluck, force of will and self-reliance—a leader of men. When we first met him, in 1879, he had recently recovered from an attack of cholera and his physique was more refined and delicate than usual. I thought him strikingly handsome; tall, dignified in carriage, and gracious in manner towards us, he made a very strong impression upon our imaginations. But when I next saw him—at Benares, I believe, some few years later—he was quite changed, and not for the better. He had grown obese, the fat stood in rolls on his half-nude body, and hung in "double-chin" masses from his under jaw. His breadth detracted from his height, so that he actually seemed to me shorter, and the poetical expression had left his Dantesque face. I have, fortunately, a souvenir of his earlier self in a copy in oils of a photograph, which was given me in Northern India. He is dead and gone now, but his Samaj survives and has spread throughout Northern India to the extent of two or three hundred branches. Annie Besant and I enjoyed a visit to the chief Samaj—at Lahore—during our recent visit to the Punjâb and helped a little, I hope, to mollify the hard feelings which the Samajists have, to my great regret, long held towards us.

The world is wide enough for us all, and it is better that we all should try to live together as brethren.

Chapter XXVI

MME. BLAVATSKY
AT HOME

H. P. B. has been mainly dealt with above in her public capacity; let us now see how she appeared in the home.

But first, does any one know why she so much preferred to be called "H. P. B.," and so abhorred the title of "Madame"? That she should not like to be addressed by the surname Blavatsky, is not so strange when one remembers the facts of that wretched marriage, as given by Mr. Sinnett in his *Incidents, etc.* It brought neither credit nor happiness to her, nor peace to the consort whom she, for a wager, tied to herself, for better for worse. Yet before she would marry the other Mr. B., at Philadelphia, she stipulated that she should not change her surname, and did not, save in the subsequent divorce papers, wherein she styles herself by her second husband's name. The title "Madame" she had a sort of loathing for, as she associated it with a female dog of that name that an acquaintance of hers owned in Paris, and which was specially disliked by her. I think the apparent eccentricity of calling herself by her three initials had a deeper significance than has been generally suspected. It meant that the personality of our friend was so blended with those of several of her Masters that, in point of fact, the name she bore but seldom applied to whatever intelligence was momentarily controlling it; and the Asiatic personage who was speaking to you through her lips was certainly neither Helena, nor the widow of Genl. Blavatsky, nor a woman at all. But each of these shifting personalities contributed towards the making of a composite entity, the sum of them all and of Helena Petrovna herself, which might as well be designated "H. P. B." as anything else. The case recalls to my mind that of the composite photograph—an apparently real entity, yet but a blending of a dozen or more—which Sir Francis Galton first brought to our notice in his *Inquiry into Human Faculty*. My theory may seem untenable, at first sight, by those who did not know her so intimately as myself, yet I incline to the belief that it is the correct one.

The routine of our life at the "Lamasery" was the following. We breakfasted at about 8, dined at 6, and retired at some small hour in the morning, according to our work and its interruption by visitors. H. P. B. lunched at home and I in town, somewhere near my law-office. When we first met I was a very active member of the Lotos Club, but the writing of *Isis* put an end, once for all, to my connection with clubs and worldly entanglements in general. After breakfast I left for my office and H. P. B. set herself for work at the desk. At dinner, more often than not, we had guests, and we had few evenings alone; for even if no visitors dropped in, we usually had somebody stopping with us in our apartment. Our house-keeping was of the simplest; we drank no wine or spirits, and ate but plain food. We had one maid-of-all-work, or rather a procession of them coming and going, for we did not keep one very long. The girl went to her home after clearing away the dinner things, and thenceforward we had to answer the door ourselves. That was not much; but a more serious affair was to supply tea, with milk and sugar, for a roomful of guests at, say, 1 A.M., when H. P. B., with lofty disregard of domestic possibilities, would invite herself to take a cup, and in a large way exclaim: "Let's all have some: what do you say?" It was useless for me to make gestures of dissent, she would pay no attention. So after sundry fruitless midnight searches for milk or sugar in the neighbourhood, the worm turned, and I put up a notice to this effect:

"TEA."

"Guests will find boiling water and tea in the kitchen, perhaps milk and sugar, and will kindly help themselves."

This was so akin to the Bohemian tone of the whole establishment that nothing was thought of it, and it was most amusing later on to see the habitués getting up quietly and going off to the kitchen to brew tea for themselves. Fine ladies, learned professors, famous artists and journalists, all jocosely became members of our "Kitchen Cabinet," as we called it.

H. P. B. had not even a rudimentary notion of housekeeping. Once, wishing boiled eggs, she laid the raw eggs on the live coals! Sometimes our maid would walk off on a Saturday evening and leave us to shift as we might for the day's meals.

Then was it H. P. B. who catered and cooked? Nay, verily, but her poor colleague. She would either sit and write and smoke cigarettes, or come into the kitchen and bother. In my Diary for 1878, I find this in the entry for April 12: "The servant 'vamosed the ranch' without preparing dinner; so the Countess L. P. turned in and helped me by making an excellent salad. Besides her, we had O'Donovan to dinner." He was a rare chap, that Irishman; a sculptor of marked talent, an excellent companion, with a dry humour that was irresistible. H. P. B. was very fond of him and he of her. He modelled her portrait from life in a medallion, which was cast in bronze, and which is in my possession. What he may be now I know not, but at that time he was fond of a glass of good whiskey (if any whiskey may be called good), and once made a roomful roar with laughter by a repartee he gave to one of the company present. They were drinking together, and the person in question after tasting his glass, put it down with the exclamation, "Pah! what bad whiskey that is!" O'Donovan, turning to him with solemn gravity, laid a hand upon his arm and said: "Don't, don't say that. There is no *bad* whiskey, but some is better than other." He was a Roman Catholic by birth, though nothing in particular, it appeared, in actual belief. But, seeing how hot and angry H. P. B. would always get when Roman Catholicism was mentioned, he used to pretend that he believed that that creed would eventually sweep Buddhism, Hinduism, and Zoroastrianism from the face of the earth. Although he played this trick on her twenty times, H. P. B. was invariably caught again in the trap whenever O'Donovan set it for her. She would fume and swear, and call him an incurable idiot and other pet names, but to no purpose: he would sit and smoke in dignified silence, without changing face, as if he were listening to a dramatic recitation in which the speaker's own feelings had no share. When she had talked and shouted herself out of breath, he would slowly turn his head towards some neighbour and say: "She speaks well, doesn't she; but she don't believe that; it is only her repartee. She will be a good Catholic some day." And then, when H. P. B. exploded at this crowning audacity, and made as if to throw something at him, he would slip away to the kitchen and make himself a cup of tea! I have known him bring friends there just to enjoy this species of bear-baiting; but H. P. B. never nourished malice, and after relieving herself of a certain number of objurgations, would be as friendly as ever with her inveterate teazer.

One of our frequent and most appreciated visitors was Prof. Alexander Wilder, a quaint personality, the type of the very large class of self-educated American yeomanry; men of the forceful quality of the Puritan Fathers; men of brain and thought, intensely independent, very versatile, very honest, very plucky and patriotic. Prof. Wilder and I have been friends since before the Rebellion, and I have always held him in the highest esteem. His head is full of knowledge, which he readily imparts to appreciative listeners. He is not a college-bred or city-bred man, I fancy, but if one wants sound ideas upon the migration of races and symbols, the esoteric meaning of Greek philosophy, the value of Hebrew or Greek texts, or the merits and demerits of various schools of medicine, he can give them as well as the most finished graduate. A tall, lank man of the Lincoln type, with a noble, dome-like head, thin jaws, grey hair, and language filled with quaint Saxon-Americanisms. He used to come and talk by the hour with H. P. B., often lying recumbent on the sofa, with—as she used to say—"one long leg resting on the chandelier, the other on the mantel-piece." And she, as stout as he was thin, as voluble as he was sententious and epigrammatic, smoking innumerable cigarettes and brilliantly sustaining her share of the conversation. She got him to write out many of his ideas to use in *Isis,* and they will be found there quoted. The hours would slip by without notice until he sometimes found himself too late for the last train to Newark, and would have to stop in town all night. I think that, of all our visitors, he cared about the least of all for H. P. B.'s psychical phenomena: he believed in their scientific possibility and did not doubt her possession of them, but philosophy was his idol, and the wonders of mediumship and adeptship interested him only in the abstract.

Yet some of H. P. B.'s phenomena were strange enough, in all conscience. Besides those heretofore described, I find mention of others in my Diary, among them this curious one:

I met one day in the lower part of the city (New York) an acquaintance with whom I stopped for a few moments to chat. He was very prejudiced against H. P. B., and spoke very harshly against her, keeping to his opinion despite all I could say. At last he used such objectionable language that, in sheer disgust, I hastily left him and went on my way. I got home as usual in time for dinner, and went to my room—the one marked "G" on the plan given in Chapter XXIV. was then my sleeping apartment—to make my toilet. H. P. B. came along the passage to the open door, and from thence bade me good evening.

The washing-stand was in the N. W. corner, opposite the door, and the "hard-finished" white wall above it uncovered with pictures or anything. After finishing my washing I turned toward the shaving-stand, behind me and just in front of the window, to brush my hair, when I saw something of a green colour reflected in the glass. A second glance showed it to be a sheet of green paper with writing upon it, and to be attached to the wall just over the washing-stand where I had the moment before been occupied without seeing anything save the blank wall before my eyes. I found the paper attached to the plastering by pins at the four corners, and the writing to be a number of Oriental texts from Dhammapâda and Sûtras, written in a peculiar style and signed at the lower corner by one of the Masters. The verses were reproaches to my address for having allowed H. P. B. to be reviled without defending her; unmistakably referring to my encounter down town with the person I had met, although no names were mentioned. I had not been five minutes in the house since my return, had spoken to nobody about the incident, nor exchanged with any one in the house more than the few words of greeting with H. P. B. from the door of my room. In fact, the incident had passed out of my mind. This is one of those phenomena of the higher class which involve the power of thought-reading, or clairaudience at a distance, and either that of producing written documents without contact, or of writing them in the ordinary way, attaching them to the wall before my return home, and then inhibiting my sight so as to make them invisible for the moment, but visible the next instant by the restoration to me of my normal vision. This seems the more probable

explanation of the two, yet, even then see how fine is the phenomenon, first, in the clairaudience at the distance of three
miles, and then in the inhibition of my sight without arousing
the slightest suspicion in my mind of the trick being played
upon me. I had carefully kept this green paper until 1891,
when it was with me on my round-the-world tour, and was
appropriated by somebody without my permission. I should
be glad to recover it. Another production of H. P. B.'s has disappeared along with it. It is a caricature representing my supposed ordeal of initiation into the school of adepts, and a most
comical picture it is. In the lower foreground I stand with a
Hindu *fehta* (turban) as my only article of dress, undergoing a
catechetical examination by Master K. H. In the lower right-
hand corner a detached hand holds in space a bottle of spirits,
and a bony bayadere, who looks like a starved Irish peasant in
a time of potato-blight, is dancing a *pas de fascination*. In the
upper corner H. P. B., wearing a New Jersey sunhood and
Deccanee men's turn-up shoes, and carrying a bell-shaped
umbrella with a flag marked "Jack" streaming from its point,
bestrides an elephant and holds out a mammoth hand to "control the elements" for my helping, while another Master stands
beside the elephant watching my ordeal. A funny little elemental in a cotton night cap and holding a lighted candle, says,
"My stars! what's that?" from a perch on K. H.'s shoulder, and
a series of absurd questions and answers written below my
Interrogator's book, complete the nonsensical satire. From
this description the reader may judge of the joviality of
H. P. B.'s temperament at that period, and of the kindly license
allowed us in our dealings with the Teachers. The mere

thought of such irreverence will doubtless make cold chills to run down the spines of some of H. P. B.'s latest pupils. I do not know how I could better illustrate this joyous exhuberance of hers than by quoting the expression used by a Hartford reporter in writing to his paper. "Madame laughed," he writes. "When we write Madame laughed, we feel as if we were saying Laughter was present! for of all clear, mirthful, rollicking laughter that we ever heard, hers is the very essence. She seems, indeed, the *Genius* of the mood she displays at all times so intense is her vitality." This was the tone of our household; and her mirthfulness, epigrammatic wit, briliance of conversation, caressing friendliness to those she liked or wanted to have like her, fund of anecdote and, chiefest attraction to most of her callers, her amazing psychical phenomena—made the "Lamasery" the most attractive *salon* of the metropolis from 1876 to the close of 1878.

A very interesting phenomenon is that of duplication of objects, the making of two or more out of one. I have given some instances above, and here is another which was described in the New York correspondence of the *Hartford Daily Times* of December 2, 1878. The correspondent passes an evening with us and meets a number of other visitors, from one of whom, an English artist, he gets the following story of what he saw H. P. B. do:

"I know it will seem incredible to you, my dear fellow," said my friend, "for it does to me as I look back upon it; yet, at the same time, I know my senses could not have deceived me.

Besides, another gentleman was with me at the time. I have seen Madame create things." "Create things!" I cried. "Yes, create things—produce them from nothing. I can tell you of two instances.

"Madame, my friend, and myself were out one day looking about the stores, when she said she desired some of these illuminated alphabets which come in sheets, like the painted sheets of little birds, flowers, animals, and other figures, so popular for decorating pottery and vases. She was making a scrap-book, and wished to arrange her title page in these pretty colored letters. Well, we hunted everywhere but could not find any, until at last we found just one sheet, containing the twenty-six letters, somewhere on Sixth Avenue. Madame bought that one and we went home. She wanted several, of course, but not finding them proceeded to use what she could of this. My friend and I sat down beside her little table, while she got out her scrap-book and busily began to paste her letters in. By and by she exclaimed, petulantly, 'I want two S's, two P's, and two A's.' I said, 'Madame, I will go and search for them down town. I presume I can find them somewhere.'

"'No you need not,' she answered. Then, suddenly looking up, said, 'Do you wish to see me make some?'

"'Make some? How? Paint some?'

"'No, make some exactly like these.'

"'But how is that possible? These are printed by machinery.'

"'It is possible—see!'

"She put her finger upon the S and looked upon it. She looked at it with infinite intensity. Her brow ridged out.

She seemed the very spirit of will. In about half a minute she smiled, lifted her finger, took up two S's exactly alike, exclaiming, 'It is done!' She did the same with the P's.

"Then my friend thought: 'If this is trickery, it can be detected. In one alphabet can be but one letter of a kind. I will try her.' So he said: 'Madame, supposing this time, instead of making two letters separately, you join them together, thus A—A—?'

"'It makes no difference to me how I do it,' she replied indifferently, and placing her finger on the A, in a few seconds she took it up, and handed him two A's, joined together as he desired. *They were as if stamped from the same piece of paper.* There were no seams or (artificial) joinings of any kind. She had to cut them apart to use them. This was in broad daylight, in the presence of no one but myself and friend, and done simply for her own convenience.

"We were both astounded and lost in admiration. We examined these with the utmost care. They seemed as much alike as two peas. But if you wish, I can show you the letters this moment. 'Madame, may we take your scrap-book to look at?'

"'Certainly, with pleasure,' returned Madame, courteously. We waited impatiently until Mr. P. could open the volume. The page was beautifully arranged, and read thus, in brilliant letters:

"THIRD VOLUME, SCRAP-BOOK OF
THE THEOSOPHICAL SOCIETY.
New York, 1878.
THEIR TRIBULATIONS AND TRIUMPHS.

"'There,' said he, pointing to the S in Scrap and the S in Society, 'those are the letters she used, and this is the one she made.' There was no difference in them."*

There was nothing out of the common in the furnishing and decoration of our apartment save in the dining-room and work-room—which was at the same time our reception-room and library all in one—and they were certainly quaint enough. The dead wall of the dining-room which separated it from H. P. B.'s bed-room was entirely covered with a picture *in dried forest leaves,* representing a tropical jungle scene. An elephant stood, ruminating beside a pool of water, a tiger was springing at him from the back-ground, and a huge serpent was coiled around the trunk of a palm tree. A very good representation of it is given on p. 205 of *Frank Leslie's Popular Monthly* for February, 1892; although the picture of the room, the Hindu servant bringing in the roast, and the dining party at table *drinking wine,* is ridiculously inaccurate. The room was not like the picture; we had no Hindu servant; we did not have a drop of wine or spirits in the house; our furniture was totally different from the artist's sketch of it. I have never heard of another wall-picture of the sort mentioned, and it

---

* The reporter, it seems, trusted to his memory, and omitted copying down at the time the words of the inscription which—being before me at this moment—I find to read as follows: "Ante and post natal history of the Theosophical Society, and of the mortifications, tribulations and triumphs of its Fellows." The letters H. P. B. duplicated are the S's in "History," "Theosophical" and "Society," two of them having been made out of the third; the P's are in "Post" and "Triumphs," and of a smaller size than the S's. She seems to have quietly duplicated several other letters, for I find no less than eight A's besides other duplicates.

seemed to strike all our guests as entirely appropriate in such a home as the "Lamasery." The whole forest scene grew out of the covering with autumn leaves, of a figure of an elephant cut from brown paper. I made another similar invention in the work-room. The entrance-door was in an angle made by cutting off a corner, and above it the wall formed a square of perhaps 4 × 5 ft. One day I found at a curiosity-shop a splendidly mounted lioness-head; the eyes glaring, the jaws wide open, the tongue retracted, the teeth white and menacing. On getting it home and looking around for a place to put it, this square of wall struck my eye, and there I hung my trophy. By an arrangement of long, dried grasses, I made it seem as though an angry lioness were creeping through the jungle and ready to spring upon the visitors who chanced to look up at her. It was one of our jokes to have new-comers seated in an easy chair that faced the door, and enjoy their start when their eyes wandered from H. P. B. to glance around the room. If the visitor chanced to be a hysterical old maid who screamed on seeing the trophy, H. P. B. would laugh heartily. In two corners of the room I stood palm-fronds that touched the ceiling and bent over their tips in graceful curves; little stuffed monkeys peered out over the curtain cornices; a fine stuffed snake lay on top of the mantel mirror, hanging its head over one corner; a large stuffed baboon, decked out with a collar, white cravat and pair of my spectacles, carrying under one arm the manuscript of a lecture on "Decent of Species," and dubbed "Professor Fiske," stood upright in a corner; a fine large grey owl sat perched on a bookcase; a toy lizard or two crawled up the wall; a Swiss cuckoo clock hung to the left of the chimney

breast; small Japanese cabinets, carved wooden images of
Lord Buddha and a Siamese talapoin, curios of sorts and
kinds, occupied the top of the cottage piano, wall brackets,
corner étagères and other convenient spaces; a long writing
table took up the centre of the room; some book shelves with
our scanty library rose above its farther end, between the two
Eighth Avenue windows; and chairs and a divan or two filled
up the floor space, so that one had to pick one's way to get to
the farther end of the chamber. A hanging four-light gas
chandelier with a drop-light over the table gave us the necessary physical illumination; the other, H. P. B. supplied. A pair
of sliding glass doors (seldom closed) divided the work-room
from her little bed-room, and on the wall over the doors we
constructed a huge double triangle of thin punched steel
sheets. Altogether the room was very artistic and pleasing to
its occupants and guests, the theme of many a description in
newspapers and talk among our friends. No frame could have
been more appropriate for setting off the bizarre personality
of its mysterious occupant, H. P. B. Many were the pen
sketches of the room that appeared in the American papers of
the day; among them the following by the same correspondent of the Hartford paper, from whose interesting letters the
above extracts were copied:

"Madame was seated in her little work-room and parlor,
all in one, and we may add her curiosity-shop as well, for
never was apartment more crammed with odd, elegant, old,
beautiful, costly, and apparently worthless things, than this.
She had cigarette in mouth, and scissors in hand, and was
hard at work clipping paragraphs, articles, items, criticisms,

and other matter, from heaps of journals from all parts of the world, relating to herself, to her book, to the Theosophical Society, to any and everything connected with her life-work and aims. She waved us to a seat, and while she intently read some article we had a chance to observe the walls and furniture of this NEW YORK LAMASERY. Directly in the centre stood a stuffed ape, with a white 'dickey' and necktie around his throat, manuscript in paw, and spectacles on nose. Could it be a mute satire on the clergy?* Over the door was the stuffed head of a lioness, with open jaws and threatening aspect; the eyes glaring with an almost natural ferocity. A god in gold occupied the centre of the mantelpiece; Chinese and Japanese cabinets, fans, pipes, implements, and rugs, low divans and couches, a large desk, a mechanical bird which sang as mechanically, albums, scrap-books, and the inevitable cigarette-holders, papers, and ash-pots, made the loose rich robe in which the Madame was apparelled seem in perfect harmony with her surroundings. A rare, strange countenance is hers. A combination of moods seems to constantly play over her features. She never seems quite absorbed by one subject. There is a keen, alert, subtle undercurrent of feeling and perception perceivable in the expression of her eyes. It impressed us then, and has invariably, with the idea of a double personality: as if she were here, and not here; talking and yet thinking, or acting far away. Her hair, light, very thick, and naturally waved, has not a grey thread in it. Her skin, evidently somewhat browned by exposure to sea and sun, has no wrinkles;

---

* No, on the materialistic scientists.—H. S. O.

her hands and arms are as delicate as a girl's. Her whole personality is expressive of self-possession, command, and a certain *sangfroid* which borders on masculine indifference,
without for a moment overstepping the bounds of womanly
delicacy."

It has been remarked above, if I remember, that what made
a visit to the Lamasery so piquant, was the chance that on any
given occasion the visitor might see H. P. B. do some wonder
in addition to amusing, delighting, or edifying him or her
with her witty and vivacious talk. In a pause in the conversation, perhaps a guest would hold up a finger, say "Hush!" and
then, all listening in breathless silence, musical notes would
be heard in the air. Sometimes they would sound faintly far
away in the distance, then coming nearer and gaining volume
until the elfin music would float around the room, near the
ceiling, and finally die away again in a lost chord and be succeeded by silence. Or it might be that H. P. B. would fling out
her hand with an imperious gesture and *ping! ping!* would
come, in the air whither she pointed, the silvery tones of a
bell. Some people fancy that she must have had a concealed
bell under her dress for playing her tricks; but the answer to
that is that, not only I but others, have, after dinner, before
rising from the table, arranged a series of finger-glasses and
tumblers, with various depths of water in them to cause them
to give out different notes when struck, and then tapping their
edges with a lead-pencil, a knife-blade, or some other thing,
have had her duplicate in space every note drawn from the
"musical glasses." No trick bell worked beneath a woman's
skirts would do that. Then, again, how often have people been

present when she would lay her hand on a tree-trunk, a house wall, a clock case, a man's head, or wherever else she might be asked to try it, and cause the fairy bell to ring within the substance of the solid body she had her hands in contact with. I was with her at Mr. Sinnett's house at Simla when, all of us standing on the veranda, she made the musical sounds to come towards us on the air of the starlit night, from across the dark valley into which descended the hill-slope on which the house was built. And I was present when she made a bell to ring inside the head of one of the greatest of the Anglo-Indian civilians, and another to sound inside the coat pocket of another very high civilian at the other side of the room from where she sat.

She never could give any satisfactory scientific explanation of the *modus operandi*. One day when she and I were alone and talking of it, she said: "Now, see here; you are a great whistler; how do you form instantaneously any given note you wish to produce?" I replied that I could not exactly say how I did it, except that a certain arrangement of the lips and compression of air within the mouth, the knack of which had been acquired by many years of practice, caused each note to sound simultaneously with the act of my thinking of it. "Well now, tell me: when you would sound a note do you think that, to produce it, you must put your lips, compress your breath, and work your throat-muscles in certain prescribed ways, and then proceed to do it?" "Not at all," I said; "long habit had made the muscular and pneumatic actions automatic." "Well, then, that's just the thing: I think of a note; automatically or instinctively I work the astral currents by my trained will; I send a sort of cross-current out from my brain to a certain point in space, where a vortex is formed between this current and the great current flowing in the astral light according to the earth's motion, and in that vortex sounds out the note I think. Just, you see, as the note you mean to whistle sounds in the air-tube formed by your lips, when you put them into the right position, work your lip and throat-muscles in the right way, and force your breath to rush out of this channel or lip-orifice. It is impossible for me to explain any better. I can do it, but can't tell you how I do it. Now try any notes you please and see if I cannot imitate them." I struck a note out of one of the tumblers at random, and instantly its echo, as if the soul of it ringing in Fairyland, would sound in the air; sometimes just overhead, now in this corner, now in that. She some-times missed the exact note, but when I told her so she would ask me to sound it again, and then the note would be exactly reflected back to us out of the A'kásha.

In connection with the above read what Mrs. Speer says (*Light,* January 28, 1893) about the musical sounds that used to accompany M. A., Oxon.

"*September 19th*—Before meeting this evening we heard the 'fairy bells' playing in different parts of the garden where we were walking; at times they sounded far off, seemingly playing at the top of some high elm trees, music and stars mingling together, then they would approach nearer to us, eventually following us into the séance-room, which opened on to the lawn. After we were seated the music still lingered with us, playing in the corners of the room, and then over the table round which we were sitting. They played scales and chords by request, with the greatest rapidity, and copied notes Dr. S. made with his voice. After Mr. S. M. was entranced the music became louder and sounded like brilliant playing on the piano. There was no instrument in that room."

The musical phenomena were evidently identical with those of H. P. B., but with the radical difference that she produced the sounds at will, while in Stainton Moseyn's case they were beyond his control and most brilliant when his body was entranced. The Speer Circle had a great deal of these "fairy bells" first and last, and, some very unconvincing theories given by the spirits to account for them. For instance, Benjamin Franklin's alleged spirit told them (*Light,* March 18, 1893, p. 130) that "the sound you call fairy bells represents a spirit instrument, one used in the spheres." Yet he adds: "We could do much more for you had our medium a musical organisation, but it is a bad one for music." Why, if it were to be drawn from an instrument? That is almost like saying that Thalberg or Paderevsky could play their instrument better if the gasman of the building were not deaf in one ear! We may safely deny the "spirit-instrument" theory, for we have the explanation in the fact that the more musical the temperament of the medium naturally, the more melodious the fairy bells can be made to jingle in his presence. Moreover, in the case of a medium, the more deeply he is plunged into trance, the nearer and clearer may be the tintinnabulation of the bells, bells, bells!

Chapter XXVII.

ILLUSIONS

The elemental messenger of H. P. B. once rang the fairy bell with pathetic effect, at the moment when her pet canary died. It is fixed indelibly in my memory from the fact that it is associated with the recollection of H. P. B.'s feeling of genuine sorrow. It was just an ordinary little hen canary, not much to look at for beauty, but an amazingly industrious housewife; lovable because so evidently honest. I forget where we got her, but think H. P. B. brought her from Philadelphia and that I bought her mate—a splendid singer—in New York. No matter; we had them a long time and they came to be almost like children, as it were. We used to let them fly about the room at their pleasure, and the male bird would reward us by perching on a picture-frame near our work-table and singing most melodiously. The hen would light upon our table in the most fearless way, walk, chirping, right under our noses, and pick up and carry away for nest-building near the ceiling, up in the bronze ornament on the chandelier pipe, any ends of twine or other likely materials. She seemed especially to value

the long thin snippings of paper cut off by H. P. B. when pasting and readjusting her foolscap MSS. sheets. Little "Jenny"
would sometimes wait until her mistress had cut off a piece of
paper and dropped it on the table or floor, and then hop to it
and carry it off, to the approving song of her handsome husband, "Pip." There was a Turkish carpet with fringed ends on
the floor, and this gave Jenny all she could do. The little creature would take one of the strands in her beak, brace herself
square upon her feet, and then lean back and tug and jerk
with all her might, trying in vain to get it loose.

The nest-building was finished at last, and then Jenny
began sitting up aloft over our table, her little head showing
beyond the edge of the bronze cup, or ornament, on the gas-
pipe. Pip sang his sweetest, and we waited for the hatching out
of the eggs with pleasurable interest. The weeks passed on and
Jenny still sat and we waited, but no young birds twittered,
and we wondered what could be up. At last one day when the
bird was away after seed and water, I placed a chair on our
writing-table, H. P. B. held it, and I mounted for a peep. The
nest was absolutely empty, neither fledgling there nor shell,
whether full or broken: we had been fooled by our busy little
canary-hen. H. P. B. gave the only possible explanation by saying that "Jenny had been sitting on her illusions": that is, she
had persuaded herself that she had laid eggs, and that it was
her duty to hatch them out!

All went well with us and the birds for many months, but
at last our quartette was broken up by the death of Jenny. She
was found lying at her last gasp on her back in her cage. I took
her out and placed her in H. P. B.'s hand, and we mourned

together over our pet. H. P. B. kissed her, gently stroked her plumage, tried to restore her vitality by magnetic breathing, but nothing availed; the bird's gasps grew feebler and feebler, until we saw it could only be a question of minutes. Then the stern, granite-faced H. P. B. melted into tenderness, opened her dress, and laid little Jenny in her bosom; as if to give her life by placing her near the heart that was beating in pity for her. But it was useless; there came a last gasp, a last flutter of the birdie's heart, and then? Then, sharp and sweet and clear in the A'kásha near us, rang out a fairy bell, the requiem of the passing life; and H. P. B. wept for her dead bird.

Speaking of the possibilities of *Máya,* shall we classify in that category the following phenomenon? One day, in moving about at the table, H. P. B. sent a huge splotch of ink over a light lawn wrapper that she was wearing. There must have been a teaspoonful of the fluid and it ran in a dozen streams down the front of the skirt to the floor. The dress was ruined. I shall drop a veil over the remarks that were elicited from her, merely saying that they were strong rather than poetical. Yet she soon showed me that the evil was not remediless, for, stepping towards her bedroom, but without crossing the threshold, she turned her back to me and went to passing her hands over the whole dress, or so much of it as she could reach; and in another moment turning towards me, lo! the light spotted wrapper had disappeared and she stood there clothed in one of a chocolate colour. Was this a Máya? If so, when will a Máya wear out? For she wore the brown dress until it had had its turn of use, and I never saw the light one again.

She told me once in great glee of a Máya that had been put

off on herself. She was travelling in the desert, she said, with a certain Coptic white magician who shall be nameless, and, camping one evening, expressed the ardent wish for a cup of good French *café au lait*. "Well, certainly, if you wish it so much," said the guardian guide. He went to the baggage-camel, drew water from the skin, and after awhile returned, bringing in his hand a cup of smoking, fragrant coffee mixed with milk. H. P. B. thought this, of course, was a phenomenal production, since her companion was a high adept and possessed of very great powers. So she thanked him gratefully, and drank, and was delighted, and declared she had never tasted better coffee at the Café de Paris. The magician said nothing, but merely bowed pleasantly and stood as if waiting to receive back the cup. H. P. B. sipped the smoking beverage, and chatted merrily, and—but what is this? The coffee has disappeared and naught but plain water remains in her cup! It never was anything else; she had been drinking and smelling and sipping the Máya of hot, fragrant Mocha. Of course, it will be said that such an illusion as that may be seen at any travelling mesmeriser's show, where parafine oil is made to taste like chocolate and vinegar like honey. But there is the difference that the illusion in the case of H. P. B. was produced in silence, by simple thought-transference, and upon a subject who herself had the power of casting glamours over third persons. From the crude mesmeric experimentation in a village hall, for pay, to the highest example of mayâvic glamour thrown silently upon one person or a crowd by an Eastern juggler, fakir, sanyâsi, or adept, it is but a difference in degree. One principle runs throughout all these and all other phenomena, the observation of which is the function of the bodily senses. Whether the Máya be induced from without by the spoken word, the suggestive gesture, or the silent will of another, or it be self-engendered by the deceived imagination acting through the will upon the senses, it is all one, and he who thoroughly masters the rationale of the show of the village showman and the naked Indian juggler, will be able to grasp the theory of Máya on a cosmic scale. When one is living in daily association with a person who possesses this power of casting glamour at will over one, the thought becomes most burdensome after awhile, for one never knows whether what is apparently spoken or seen is really so or not. Not even such a visit as the one made me by the Mahátma, with the concomitants of his touching me and speaking to me, and my feeling him as a man of substantial body like myself, would really be proof that I was not under a glamour at the time. It will be remembered that this train of thought came up in my mind during the course of our conversation, and when we were about to part, and that the Mahátma smilingly gave me the test I wanted by leaving his turban, a tangible cotton cloth with his cryptograph worked on it, on my table.

How much we read in folk-lore tales about "fairy gold" and "fairy jewels" which by the next dawn are found turned into bits of twigs, leaves, straw, or other rubbish! Such stories one finds current in almost every land and among every people. I have heard them in India. In such cases the principle of Máya is illustrated; but it would seem, from the instance I gave of the Mahátma refunding the half-dollar I had spent for the drawing materials with which his portrait was to be made for me, that the same person who could make the Máya of money at will, might also be able to either create real coin, or by the law of *apport,* bring it to one from some distant place where it lay at the moment.

The production of the two Chinese or Japanese pictures of ladies was glamour, and so was the following case. The Hon. J. L. O'Sullivan, formerly U. S. Minister to Portugal, of whom mention has been made above, was calling one day, when the conversation turned upon the phenomenon of duplication. I had brought home that afternoon a bank-note for $1,000 and had given it to H. P. B. to keep for me. She produced this note from her drawer, gave it to Mr. O'Sullivan to hold, rolled up, in his hand. Presently she told him to open his hand and see what he would find. He did so, and unrolling the bank-note found inside it another, its exact duplicate in paper, serial number, and face and back plate-printing. "Well," he exclaimed, "this is a famous way to become rich!" "No, indeed," answered H. P. B., "'t is but a psychological trick. We, who have the power of doing this, dare not use it for our own or any other's interest, any more than you would dare to commit the forgery by the methods of the counterfeiter. It would be stealing from the Government in either case." She refused to satisfy our curiosity as to how she effected the duplication, telling us with a laugh to find out if we could. The two notes were laid away in the drawer, and when our visitor had departed, she showed me that but the original one remained; the duplicate had dissolved again.

Shortly before we left New York, H. P. B. went out with me

one evening to shop for herself. The purchases amounted to fifty dollars, and as she had no money at all at the time, I paid the bills and took charge of the receipts. As we were about entering the door of our house, she let go my arm, took my hand, and thrust some bank-notes in it saying, "There are your fifty dollars!" I repeat, that she had no money of her own, and no visitor coming to the house from whom she could have borrowed it: nor, when we left the house, did she know what she would buy nor how much she would spend. She simply had money when she actually needed it and when it was right that she should have it. For example: I was once asked to go to a certain city and undertake some work for the Mahátmas, which had very important possibilities hanging upon its doing. I estimated that it would take me at least one or two months, and, as I was paying the "Lamasery" expenses and had other large demands upon my purse, I told H. P. B. frankly that I could not afford to spend the time away from New York. "Very well," she said, "do as you think right; you are not yet a pledged neophyte and the Brothers have not the smallest right to take you away from your business." Still, I could not bear the idea of refusing the least thing that the Teachers should ask me, and although I could not see how I would have enough coming in for my wants while absent, I finally said that I would go, at any cost. H. P. B. asked me what I should probably lose by going, and I told her that at the very lowest calculation it would be not less than $500 a month. I went, and did not return until well into the second month. On going to the bank to see what money I had to my credit, I was astounded on being told that the sum was just a thousand dollars more than I could account for. Was not the book-keeper mistaken? No, it was so and so much. Then I asked him if he could recollect the appearance of the person who had, it seemed, made two deposits of $500 each to the credit on my account. He fortunately could, because the man was of so strange an appearance: he was very tall, with long black hair rolling on his shoulders, piercing black eyes, and brown complexion: an Asiatic, in short. The same man had made both the deposits, merely handing in the money and asking that it might be placed to my credit. He did not have my pass-book, and he asked the Receiving Teller to fill up the deposit ticket himself as "he could not write English." Supposing H. P. B. to have had the friends she had years later in India and Europe, it would not have been at all remarkable if she had got one of them to lend her the money to make good my deficit, but at that time there was not a person of her acquaintance but myself, from whom she could have borrowed even one hundred dollars, much less one thousand.

Then, again, at Bombay, she always had money given her when it was badly needed. When we landed there was barely enough to pay our current household expenses a few months ahead, let alone to squander on luxuries or superfluities; yet she and I started off to the Punjáb, with Moolji and Baboola, on that memorable journey which she expanded into her vivid romance, *Caves and Fungles of Hindustan*, and spent about two thousand rupees without being the worse for it. The cruse of oil and measure of meal were never exhausted, because we were given what we required by the Masters whose work we were doing. When I asked how it was possible for this to be when the Masters were living outside the world of money-making and money-getting H. P. B. told me that they were the guardians over untold wealth of mines and buried treasure and jewels which, according to the Karma attaching to them, could be employed for the good of mankind through many different agencies. Some of these treasures were, however, so befouled with the aura of crime that if suffered to be dug up and circulated before the details of the law of Karma had worked themselves out, they would breed fresh crimes and more direful human misery. Again, the Karma of some individuals required that they should, as if by the merest accident, discover buried pots of money or other valuables, or attract to themselves in the way of business, fortunes greater or less. These effects of compensation were worked out by the elementals of the mineral kingdom with whom—according to Eastern belief—the apparent pets of fortune were closely allied through the elementals preponderating in their own temperaments.

This question of the existence of elemental spirits has always been the crux with the Spiritualists, yet Mrs. Britten, one of their chiefs, declares (see *Banner of Light*) that "SHE KNOWS of the existence of other than human spirits, and has seen apparitions of spiritual or elementary existence, evoked by cabalistic words and practices." The Hon. A. Aksakof, moreover, states that "Prince A. Dolgorouki, the great authority on Mesmerism, has written me that he has ascertained that spirits which play the most prominent part at séances are elementaries—gnomes, etc. His clairvoyants have seen them and describe them thus." *Spi. Sci.*, December, 1875. (T. S. Scrap-Book, I, 92.)

To resume, then, the hand of such an individual, having in him a preponderance of the elementals belonging to the natural kingdom of minerals and metals, like that of Midas, King of Phrygia, would have that magic property that "everything he touches turns to gold"; and no matter how stupid he might be as to general affairs, his "luck" would be constant and irresistible. So, too, with a preponderance of the watery elementals, he would be attracted to the life of a sailor and stick to it despite all hardships and sufferings. So, also, the preponderance of the elementals of the air in a man's temperament would set him, as a child, to climbing trees and house-roofs, as a man, to mountaineering, ballooning, walking the tightrope at dizzy heights, and otherwise trying to get above the earth's surface. H. P. B. told me various stories to illustrate this principle, which need not be quoted here, since human life teems with examples that may be comprehended upon testing them with the key above given. As regards the Theosophical Society, I may say that, while neither H. P. B. nor I were ever allowed to have a superfluity, we were never left to suffer for the necessaries of our life and work. Over and over again, twenty, fifty times have I seen our cash-box nearly emptied and the prospects ahead very discouraging in the pecuniary sense, yet as invariably have I received in remittances from some quarter or another, what was needed, and our work has never been stopped for a single day for lack of means to carry on the Headquarters.

Yet the agent of the unseen Masters is often disqualified for judging whether it is or is not necessary for the success of his public work that he should have money coming in to himself. When H. P. B. was ordered from Paris to New York in 1873, she soon found herself in the most dismal want, having, as stated in a previous chapter, to boil her coffee-dregs over and over again for lack of pence for buying a fresh supply; and to keep off starvation, at last had to work with her needle for a maker of cravats. She got no presents from unexpected sources, found no fairy-gold on her mattress on waking in the morning. The time was not yet. But, although she was in such stark poverty herself, she had lying in her trunk for some time after her arrival a large sum of money (I think something like 23,000 francs) which had been confided to her by the Master, to await orders. The order finally came to her to go to Buffalo. Where that was or how to reach it, she had not the remotest idea until she enquired: What to do at Buffalo? "No matter what: take the money with you." On reaching her destination she was told to take a hack and drive to such an address, and give the money to such and such a person; to make no explanations, but to take his receipt and come away. She did so: the man was found at the address given, and found in peculiar conditions. He was writing a farewell letter to his family, with a loaded pistol on the table with which he would have shot himself in another half hour if H. P. B. had not come. It seems—as she told me subsequently—that this was a most worthy man who had been robbed of the 23,000 francs in some peculiar way that made it necessary, for the sake of events that would subsequently happen as a consequence—events of importance to the world—that he should have the money restored to him at a particular crisis, and H. P. B. was the agent deputed to this act of beneficence. When we met she had entirely forgotten the man's name, his street and number. Here we have a case where the very agent chosen to carry the money to the beneficiary was herself in most necessitous circumstances, yet not permitted to use one franc of the trust fund to buy herself a pound of fresh coffee.

I recollect still another case where H. P. B. had the dispensing of "fairy-gold"—to use the popular term. Fortunately the beneficiary has left us the story in printer's ink.

It seems that at a meeting of certain well-known Spiritualists of Boston (Mass.) something was said as to the probability of the *Spiritual Scientist* dying out for lack of patronage. The late C. H. Foster, a famous medium who was present, gave as from a controlling spirit, the positive declaration that the calamity in question was impending; as, in fact, it was, since its Editor, Mr. Gerry Brown, had a rather large note to pay very soon and no means to meet it with. These introductory facts were published in the *Spiritual Scientist,* together with the following sequel, quoted from a clipping from that journal which I find in one of our scrap-books:

"A few days ago the manager of the *Scientist* received a notice to call at the Western Union Telegraph Office and receipt for money sent by telegraph. He went with the following experience:

"Scene—Western Union Telegraph Office. Time, noon. To the left, receiver at desk. Enter on the right an individual who presents a money-order notice.

"*Clerk.* Are you expecting money?

"*Individual.* Well, that's my name and address on the order, and that's your notice to me. I have no one in mind however.

"*Clerk.* Do you know of one Sir Henry de Morgan?

"*Individual.* (Smiling broadly.) Well, I have heard it said that the spirit of the gentleman you mention, who lived on earth 250 years ago, takes a kind interest in my welfare. I'll receipt for the money.

"*Clerk.* (Drawing back and changing tone.) Do you know any one about here who can identify you?

"*Individual.* Yes.

"Here a member of the company is called who knows Individual and the money is paid.

"An hour later a telegram came saying:

"'I contribute——dollars to pay——note, due June 19th, and defy Charles Foster to make his prophecy good. The challenge to be published. Go to Western Union Telegraph Office, get money, and acknowledge receipt by telegraph.

"'Sir Henry de Morgan.'

"The money was sent from a far distant city. As the telegram asks us to publish, we do so willingly. We advance no opinion in this case. We have already shown the telegram to several prominent spiritualists, one of whom suggests that a member of the circle is guying us. Well and good. We are willing to be guyed as often as any one wishes to *guy* us in this manner."

Of course, the "distant city" was Philadelphia, and the sender, H. P. B., who—as above mentioned—was, with myself, interested in helping the Editor to pull his paper through a pecuniary crisis. Now, I am fully acquainted with the extent of H. P. B.'s own resources at that time, and I absolutely know that she was not in a position to send sums, either large or small, to impecunious third parties, and that her second husband was as poor as herself and without credit to borrow upon. She must have got the money as she got that for her purchases in New York and for travelling expenses in India, *viz.*, from the Lodge. The Sir Henry Morgan of the telegram was John King, the alleged spirit control, in whose name H. P. B.'s first phenomena were done in New York and Philadelphia.

By an interesting coincidence, while correcting these proofs, I found in our Library a book about Morgan, of which I had lost sight for some years. Its title is *The History of the Bucaniers of America; from their First Original down to this Time;* written in several languages; and now collected into one volume. Containing: The Exploits and Adventures of Le Grand, Lolonois, Roche Brasiliano, Bat the Portuguese, Sir Henry Morgan, etc. Written in Dutch by Jo. Esquemeling, one of the Bucaniers, and thence translated into Spanish, etc., etc. [London, 1699. The Original Edition.]

It is a queer, quaint, blood-curdling old book, that I picked up in New York, I think, and we had it early in our acquaintance. The thing that gives it an especial interest to us is that the intelligence which masqueraded for my edification as John King phenomenally precipitated on the three blank leaves preceding the Title-page, the following doggerel verses:

"To my fast friend Harry Olcott.

"Hark ye o gents—to Captain Morgan's pedigree
Herein furnished by lying Esquemeling;
The latter but a truant, and in some degree
The Spaniard's spy—Dutch Jew—who pennance sought
    and sailing
Back to his foggy land, and took to book-selling.
Ye lying cur! Though Captain Morgan bucaniered
He natheless knew well I trow—the wrong from right,
From face of ennemie the Captain never steered,
And never tacked about to show his heels in fight,
Though he loved wenches, wine, and gold—he was a
    goodly knight.
He passed away for noble virtue praised round,
Encompast by his friends who shov'd him underground
And settled *Above*—disguising for a change—
His title, and name so famous once—that may seem
    strange—
But aint, and called himself *John King*—the King of
    Sprites
Protector to weak wench—defender of her rights. . . . .
Peace to the bones of both—the Pirat and the Knight—
For both have rotten away the good and wicked spright
And both of them have met—forwith when disembodied.

The Dutch biographer met with a tristful case
Sir Henry Morgan's spirit who had long uphoarded
The wrongs made by the Jew chased his foe's Sprite apace
And never Spirit world before or after witnessed
A more sound thrashing or more mirthful race."

"*Moralitey*

"Know—O friend Harry, that a Sprite's affray
In Summer Land is common any day,
That all thy evil deeds on earth begotten
Can never *there* be easily forgotten.

"Yer benevolent friend,

"John king."

The quaint diction and spelling of these verses will command attention, and I submit that they are much more characteristic of such an intelligence as presumably was the buccaneer knight's than the mass of sloppy communications we have got through mediums.

Besides the open book-shelves between the windows in our work-room at the Lamasery, there was a smaller one with glass doors, which stood in the N. E. window. On the day when I purchased the lioness head, above mentioned, I also bought a fine specimen of the large American grey owl, which was very well mounted. I first put it on a small stand in one of the corners, but later transferred it to the top of this smaller book-case, putting a box inside the cornice to raise the bird up to the proper height for display. I mention the circumstance because of an instructive phenomenon that happened between the time of my putting the box inside the cornice, and taking the stuffed bird from the writing table behind me to lift it to its place. In that instant of time there came upon the flat part of the cornice and the frames of the two glass doors, some large Tibetan writings in letters of gold; and of so permanent a character that they remained there until we left New York Observe the procedure: I face the book-case to put the empty box on top, and this brings my face in actual contact with the exposed front of the book-case, and I see nothing whatever written or painted on the plain wood surfaces. I turn about in my tracks, pick up the bird, turn back to lift it to its place, and—there are the gold-lettered Tibetan messages before my eyes. Was this a positive or a negative Máyá, the precipitation at that instant of a writing by thought-force, from the distance across the room where H. P. B. sat? or was it an inhibition on the sight of myself and the several others in the room, until the right moment came for removing the temporary and special blindness, and allowing us to see what H. P. B. had probably written in gold-ink during the daytime, and then had hidden under her "veil of Máyá"? I think the latter.

Mr. Judge tells Mr. Sinnett (*vide Incidents in the Life of Madame Blavatsky,* p. 191) of a phenomenon of precipitation, of which I also was witness. The facts are as follows: One evening H. P. B., Mr. Judge, and I were together and a letter had to be written to Mr. M. D. Evans, of Philadelphia, an insurance-broker. Neither of us could at the moment recollect his address; there was no place near by where a Philadelphia Directory could be consulted; and we were at our wit's end.

H. P. B. and I both recollected that in Philadelphia she had had on her table a slip of blotting paper with Mr. Evans' address printed on it, in a wave-line along with that of an insurance company, but neither of us could recall it. Finally, she did this: she took from the table before us a japanned tin paper-cutter, stroked it gently, laid a piece of blotting paper over it, passed her hand over the surface, lifted the paper, and there, on the black japanned surface of the paper-cutter was printed in bronze ink the facsimile of the inscription on the Philadelphia blotting slip that Evans had given her in that city. Her physical brain could not recollect the inscription, but when she focussed her will-power upon the (physically speaking) vague memory of her astral brain, the hidden image was dragged to light again and precipitated upon the determined surface. This was a case of a "subliminal" being converted into a supraliminal consciousness; and a most interesting one, it will be conceded.

I leave the reader to decide whether the following phenomenon was a Máyá, an *apport*, a trick, or a creation. She and I were as usual one evening smoking while at work; she her cigarette, I my pipe. It was a new one, I remember, and the tobacco was as good as one could wish, but she suddenly sniffed and exclaimed, "Pah! what horrid tobacco you are smoking, Olcott!" I said she was very much mistaken, as both pipe and tobacco were unexceptionable. "Well," she said, "I don't like it this evening; take a cigarette." "No," I replied, "I'll not smoke since it annoys you." "Why don't you use those nice Turkish pipes that come from Constantinople?" said she. "Because I have none—a very good reason." "Well, then, here's one for you," she exclaimed, dropping her hand down beside her arm-chair, and bringing it up again with a pipe in it, which she handed me. It had a red clay, flaring bowl, set in filagree gilt, and a stem covered with purple velvet and ornamented with a slight gilt chain with imitation coins attached. I took it with a simple "Thank you," filled and lit it, and went on with my work. "How do you like it?" she asked. "Well enough," I said, "although instead of purple I wish the velvet had been blue." "Oh well, have a blue one then," she remarked; again putting down her hand and lifting it again with a blue-stemmed pipe in it. I thanked her and continued my work. The manœuvre was again repeated, and she said, "Here's a baby pipe," and she gave me a miniature edition of the larger sort. Being apparently in the mood for surprises, she then successively produced a Turkish cigarette mouth-piece in gilt and amber, a Turkish coffee-pot and sugar-bowl, and finally a gilt tray in repoussé with imitation enamel ornamentation. "Any more?" I asked. "Has any Turkish shop been afire?" She laughed, and said that would do for that evening; but some time she might take the fancy of giving me by magic an Arab horse fully caparisoned, to ride down Broadway in a procession of the Theosophical Society and astonish the natives! Many, very many persons, saw the pipes and coffee equipage in our rooms thereafter, and when we left New York all were given away to friends, save the gilt tray and sugar-basin which I brought out to India and have still.

Chapter XXVIII.

CHARACTER SKETCH OF MME. BLAVATSKY

A few words more to complete the character sketch of H. P. B. She was, even in her youth—to judge from her early portraits—a plump person, and later in life became very corpulent. It seems to have been a family peculiarity. In her case the tendency was aggravated by the manner of life she led, taking next to no physical exercise whatever, and eating much unless seriously out of health. Even then she partook largely of fatty meats and used to pour melted butter by the quantity over her fried eggs at breakfast. Wines and spirits she never touched, her beverages being tea and coffee, preferably the latter. Her appetite, while I knew her, was extremely capricious, and she was most rebellious to all fixed hours for meals, hence a terror to all cooks and the despair of her colleague.

I remember an instance at Philadelphia which shows this peculiarity in an especial degree. She had one maid-of-all-work, and on this particular day a leg of mutton was boiling for dinner. Suddenly H. P. B. bethought her to write a note to a lady friend who lived at the other end of the city, an hour's

journey each way, as there were no trams or other public con-
veyances going direct from the one house to the other. She
called in trumpet tones for the maid, and ordered her to set
off instantly with the note and bring the answer. The poor girl
told her that the dinner would be spoilt, and she could not
possibly get back until an hour beyond the usual time. H. P. B.
would not listen and told her to begone at once. Three-
quarters of an hour later H. P. B. began complaining that the
stupid idiot of a girl had not returned; she was hungry and
wanted her dinner, and sent all Philadelphia servants to the
devil *en masse*. In another quarter of an hour she had grown
desperate, and so we went down to the kitchen for a look. Of
course, the pots of meat and vegetables were set back on the
range, the fire was banked, and the prospect of dinner was
extremely small. H. P. B.'s wrath was vehement, and so there
was nothing for us but to turn to and cook for ourselves.
When the maid returned she was scolded so roundly that she
burst into tears and gave warning! At New York, if any nice
visitor chanced to be there, either the dinner would have to
wait indefinitely, or he or she or they—for it made no
difference—would be asked to come in and dine, and the portions provided for us two had to be divided and sub-divided
for perhaps four people. At Bombay it was worse: one day the
dinner would be put off two hours and another H. P. B. would
demand to be served an hour before the time; and then
frighten the wretched Goanese servants into fits, because the
vegetables were half-boiled and the meat half-cooked. So
when we removed to Adyar I determined to put a stop to this
bother, and built a kitchen on the terrace near H. P. B.'s

bed-room, gave her a set of servants to herself, and let her eat or go without as she pleased.

I found on visiting her in London after her removal there, that the same old system was in vogue, H. P. B.'s appetite having become more capricious than ever because of the progress of disease, although every possible delicacy was provided by her friends to tempt her. Poor thing! it was not her fault, although her ill health had been largely caused by her almost life-long neglect of the rules of digestion. She was never an ascetic, not even a vegetarian while I knew her, flesh diet seeming to be indispensable for her health and comfort; as it is to so many others in our Society, including myself. I know many who have tried their best to get on with vegetable diet, and some, myself for example, who have followed up the experiment for several years together, yet have been forced finally to revert to their old diet against their will. Some, on the contrary, like Mrs. Besant and other prominent Theosophists I could name, have found themselves much healthier, stronger, and better on non-flesh food, and gradually acquire a positive loathing for meat in any of its forms. All which verifies the old proverb, "What is one man's meat is another man's poison." I think that neither blame is warranted in one case nor praise in the other, because of the regimen one chooses by preference. It is not what goes into the mouth that defiles a man, but what lies in his heart. A wise old saying, worth remembering by the self-righteous.

H. P. B. was, all the world knows, an inveterate smoker. She consumed an immense number of cigarettes daily, for the rolling of which she possessed the greatest deftness. She could even roll them with her left hand while she was writing "copy" with her right. Her devoted London physician, Dr. Mennell, has the most unique present she could have given any person: a box, with his monogram neatly carved on the lid, which contains several hundred cigarettes that she rolled for him with her own hands. She sent it to him just before her death, and the Doctor has it laid by as a souvenir of, doubtless, his most interesting and illustrious patient.

While she was writing *Isis Unveiled,* at New York, she would not leave her apartment for six months at a stretch. From early morning until very late at night she would sit at her table working. It was not an uncommon thing for her to be seventeen hours out of the twenty-four at her writing. Her only exercise was to go to the dining-room or bath-room and back again to her table. As she was then a large eater, the fat accumulated in great masses on her body: her chin doubled and trebled; a watery fat formed in her limbs and hung in masses over her ankles; her arms developed great bags of adipose, which she often showed visitors and laughed at as a great joke—a bitter one as it proved in after years. When *Isis* was finished and we began to see ahead the certainty of our departure, she went one day with my sister and got herself weighed: she turned the scales at 245 pounds (17 stone 7), and then announced that she meant to reduce herself to the proper weight for travelling, which she fixed at 156 pounds (11 stone 2). Her method was simple: every day, ten minutes after each meal, she had a wineglass of plain water brought her; she would hold one palm over it, look at it mesmerically, and then drink it off. I forget just how many weeks she continued this treatment, but finally she asked my sister to go again with her to be weighed. They brought and showed me the certificate of the shopkeeper who owned the scales, to the effect that "The weight of Madame Blavatsky this day is 156 pounds!" So she continued until long after we reached India, when the obesity reappeared and persisted, aggravated with dropsy, until her death.

There was one aspect of her character which amazed strangers, and made her very attractive to those who loved her. I mean a sort of childish delight that she exhibited when certain things pleased her very much. She was sent once into transports of joy on receipt of a box of caviare, sweet cakes, and other delicacies from Russia, while we were at New York. She was for having us all taste them, and when I protested that the fish-roes had the flavour of salted shoe-leather, she was almost ready to annihilate me. A crumb of black bread that chanced to be in a home newspaper she had had sent her, suggested the entire home life at Odessa. She described to me her beloved aunt Nadjeda, sitting late at night in her room, reading the papers while nibbling one of these very crusts; and then the different rooms in the house, the occupants, their habits and doings. She actually wrapped the crumb in a bit of the newspaper and laid it under her pillow to dream upon.

In my Diary of 1878, I find an entry for Sunday, July 14, 1878, about a seaside trip we took with Wimbridge. It says:

"A superb day, bright sun, cool, pleasant air, everything charming. We three took a carriage, drove to the beach and all bathed. H. P. B. presented a most amusing appearance; paddling about in the surf, with her bare legs, and showing an almost infantile glee to be in such a 'splendid magnetism.'"

At Madras she received the present of several toys in scroll-saw fret-work, from her aunt. Some of comical design she brought out to show all visitors until the novelty had worn off. One, a wall-pocket in ebony and calamander wood, hangs in her old bed-room at Adyar, where I am now writing.

On her table in New York stood an iron savings-box, modelled like a Gothic tomb or temple—one cannot say which—which was to her the source of constant delight. It had a slit in the dome inside, and an innocent-looking round table-top on a pillar. This was connected with a crank on the outside, and if a coin were placed on it and the crank turned, the coin would presently be swept off through a slot and fall inside, from whence it could only be removed by unscrewing a certain small plate at the bottom. We made this our collection-box for the Arya Samaj, and H. P. B.—but I shall let the reporter of the *N. Y. Star* speak for himself on this point. In that paper for December 8, 1878, it is written:

"Madame Blavatsky, or, as she prefers to be called, H. P. B. (she having sent the title of 'Madame' to look for that of 'Countess,' which she threw away before) was enraptured with the idea. 'I will fill my little temple with dollars,' she cried, 'and I shall not be ashamed to take it to India.' The temple she referred to is a small, but intricate structure, with an entrance, but no exit, for money contributed to the Arya Samaj. It is solidly constructed of cast-iron, and is surmounted by a small 'Dev.' H. P. B. kindly explained to the reporter that 'Dev' was a Sanskrit word, differently interpreted as god, or devil, or genie by different nations of the East. The casual visitor to the Lamasery is frequently invited to place a small coin on the top of the temple, and to turn a crank. The result is invariably the great glee of the Theosophs, the discomfiture of the casual visitor, and the enrichment of the Arya Samaj, for the coin disappears in the process."

The same writer, I find, says something nice about the mural picture in dried leaves, of a tropical jungle, that was made in our dining-room, and described in a recent chapter. We thought of making a lottery among our friends of the furniture of the Lamasery, and this was to be one of the prizes. The *Star* reporter says:

"Perhaps one of the most remarkable things in all the collection of unique prizes is one which has no claim to be considered magical. It is a mural ornament, so elaborately beautiful and yet so simple, that it seems strange that it is not fashionable. On one of the walls of the dining-room of the now famous flat is the representation of a tropical scene, in which appear an elephant, a tiger, a huge serpent, a fallen tree, monkeys, birds and butterflies, and two or three sheets of water. It is neither painted nor drawn, but the design was first cut out in paper and then autumn leaves of various hues were pasted on, while the water was represented by small pieces of broken mirror. The effect is remarkably beautiful, but the winner of the prize will probably need magical art to remove it in good condition, for it has been in its place so long that the leaves are dry and brittle."

The jocund side of H. P. B.'s character was one of her greatest charms. She liked to say witty things herself and to hear others say them. As above remarked, her *salon* was never dull save, of course, to those who had no knowledge of Eastern literature and understood nothing of Eastern philosophy, and to them time might have dragged heavily when H. P. B. and Wilder, or Dr. Weisse, or some other *savant* were discussing these deeper depths and loftier heights of thought by hours together. Yet even then she spoke so unconventionally, and formulated her views with so much *verve* and startling paradox, that even if the listener could not follow the thread of her thought, he must admire it; as one may the Crystal Palace pyrotechnics, although he does not know the chemical processes employed to manufacture the pieces. She caught up and made her own any quaint phrase or word as, for instance, "flapdoodle," "whistle-breeches," and several others which have come to be regarded as her own invention. In our playtimes, *i.e.*, after finishing our nightwork, or when visitors came or, rarely, when she wanted to have a little rest, she would tell me tales of magic, mystery, and adventure, and in return, get me to whistle, or sing comic songs, or tell droll stories. One of the latter became, by two years' increment added on to the original, a sort of mock Odyssey of the Moloney family, whose innumerable descents into matter, returns to the state of cosmic force, intermarriages, changes of creed, skin, and capabilities, made up an extravaganza of which H. P. B. seemed never to have enough. She would set me going in presence of third parties, much to my disgust sometimes, and enjoy their surprise at this rough and ready improvisation. It was all recited in an Irish brogue, and was a mere fanfaronade of every kind of nonsense; dealing extravagantly with the problems of macrocosmic and microcosmic evolution: the gist of the whole thing being that the Moloneys were related by marriage to the Molecules, and that the two together generated the supreme potency of Irish force, which controlled the vicissitudes of all worlds, suns, and galaxies. It was, as compared with the trifling story from which it developed, like the giant Banyan tree as compared with its tiny seed-germ. She got at last to call me Moloney, both in speaking and writing, and I retaliated by calling her Mulligan. Both nicknames were caught up by our friends, and my old boxes of archives contain many letters to her and myself, under those Hibernian pseudonyms.

She was a splendid pianist, playing with a touch and expression that were simply superb. Her hands were models—ideal and actual—for a sculptor and never seen to such advantage as when flying over the keyboard to find its magical melodies. She was a pupil of Moscheles, and when in London as a young girl, with her father, played at a charity concert with Madame Clara Schumann and Madame Arabella Goddard in a piece of Schumann's for three pianos.* During the time of our relationship she played scarcely at all. Once a cottage piano was bought and she played on it for a few weeks, but then it remained closed ever after until sold, and served as a double book-shelf. There were times when she was occupied by one of the Mahâtmas, when her playing was indescribably grand. She would sit in the dusk sometimes, with nobody else in the room beside myself, and strike from the sweet-toned

---

* Some weeks after the above was published I learned from a member of her family that shortly before coming to America, H. P. B. had made some concert tours in Italy and Russia under the pseudonym of "Madame Laura."

instrument improvisations that might well make one fancy he was listing to the Gandhâvas, or heavenly choristers. It was the harmony of heaven.

She had a bad eye for colours and proportions in her normal state, and very little of that fine æsthetic taste which makes a woman dress herself becomingly. I have gone to the theatre with her when I expected the house to rise at us. She, a stout and remarkable looking woman, wearing a perky hat with plumes, a *grand toilette* satin dress with much trimming, a long, heavy gold chain about her neck, attached to a blue-enamelled watch, with a monogram on the back in cheap diamonds, and on her lovely hands a dozen or fifteen rings, large and small. People might laugh at her aside, but if they caught her stern eye and looked into her massive Calmuck face, their laugh soon died away and a sense of awe and wonder possessed them.

She was at times generous to the extreme, lavishly so; at others the very opposite. When she had money she seemed to regard it as something to be got rid of soon. She told me that she spent within two years a legacy of 85,000 roubles (about 170,000 rupees) left her by her grandmother, in desultory wandering over the world. A good part of the time she had with her a huge Newfoundland dog, which she led by a heavy golden chain!

She was a most downright, plain-spoken person, when not exchanging politenesses with a new acquaintance, at which times she was *grande-dame* to her finger-tips. No matter how untidy she might be in appearance, she bore the ineffaceable stamp of high birth; and if she chose, could be as dignified as a

French duchesse. But in her ordinary, everyday life, she was as sharp as a knife in her sarcasm and like an exploding bomb in her moments of anger. The one unpardonable sin, for her, was hypocrisy and society airs. Then, she was merciless, and the sources of various languages were exhausted to cover the victim with contumely. She frequently saw as in a mirror, clairvoyantly, the secret sins of men and women whom she encountered; and if they happened to be particularly prone to speak of Theosophy with disdain or of herself with contempt, she would pour the vials of wrathful candour upon their heads. The "ower guid" folk were her abhorrence, but for a poor, ignorant but frank person, whether reputable or the opposite, she had always a kind word and often a gift. Unconventionality was with her almost a cult, and nothing pleased her more than to do and say things to shock the prudish. For example, I find an entry in my diary to the effect that, on a certain evening, she put on her night-dress, went to bed, and received a mixed company of ladies and gentlemen. This was after the fashion of royal and noble dames of pre-revolutionary days in Europe. Her palpable sexlessness of feeling carried all this off without challenge. No woman visitor would ever see in her a possible rival, no man imagine that she could be cajoled by him into committing indiscretions. She swore like the army in Flanders but meant no harm, and if her uncommon predilection in this respect had not been so much noticed and denounced by the sticklers for propriety—themselves, as she clairvoyantly saw, sometimes smug sinners behind closed doors—she would doubtless have given it up. It is in human-nature, and was in her nature, superlatively, to keep doing forbidden things just out of a spirit of revolt. I knew a lady once whose child caught from the farm servants the habit of saying wicked words. The mother, a most exemplary lady in every respect, was heart-broken about it. Whipping and other punishments only made matters worse, and no better result was obtained from the last expedient of *washing out the child's mouth with bar soap* after he had been heard swearing. At last some sensible friend advised the parents to try what would come of paying no atten-tion whatever to the bad language. The plan was a complete success, and within a few months the culprit swore no more. H. P. B. felt herself in revolt to every conventional idea of soci-ety, being in beliefs, tastes, dress, ideals, and behaviour a social helot; so she revenged herself by showing her own command-ing talents and accomplishments, and causing society to fear her. Secretly smarting for her lack of physical beauty, she con-tinually harped upon her "potatoe nose," as though she defied criticism. The world was to her an empty sham, its prizes but dross, her waking life a lugubrious existence, her real life that of the night when, leaving the body, she would go and sit at the feet of her Masters. So she felt little else than scorn and pro-found contempt for the blind bigots and narrow-thinking men of science, who had not even a stray glimpse of the truth, yet who would judge her with unrighteous judgment, and con-spire to silence her by a conspiracy of calumny. For clergymen as a body she felt hatred, because, being themselves absolutely ignorant of the truths of the spirit, they assumed the right to lead the spiritually blind, to keep the lay conscience under con-trol, to enjoy revenues they had not earned, and to damn the heretic, who was often the sage, the illuminatus, the adept. We had one scrap-book into which we used to paste paragraphs from the newspapers telling of the crimes of clergymen and priests who had been brought to justice, and before we left for India there was a large collection of them.

H. P. B. made numberless friends, but often lost them again and saw them turned into personal enemies. No one could be more fascinating than she when she chose, and she chose it when she wanted to draw persons to her public work. She would be caressing in tone and manner, and make the person feel that she regarded him as her best, if not her only friend. She would even write in the same tone, and I think I could name a number of women who hold her letters saying that they are to be her successors in the T. S., and twice as many men whom she declared her "only *real* friends and accepted chélas." I have a number of such certificates, and used to think them treasures until, after comparing notes with third parties, I found that they had been similarly encouraged, and I saw that all her eulogies were valueless. With ordinary persons like myself and her other intimate associates, I should not say she was either loyal or staunch. We were to her, I believe, nothing more than pawns in a game of chess, for whom she had no heart-deep love. She repeated to me the secrets of people of both sexes—even the most compromising ones—that had been confided to her, and she treated mine, such as they are, I am convinced, in the same fashion. But she was loyal to the last degree to her aunt, her other relatives, and to the Masters; for whose work she would have sacrificed not only one, but twenty lives, and calmly seen the whole human race consumed with fire, if needs be.

Chapter XXIX.

MADAME BLAVATSKY BECOMES AN AMERICAN CITIZEN. FORMATION OF THE BRITISH THEOSOPHICAL SOCIETY. LAST DAYS IN NEW YORK.

It was but natural that the Queen of our little Bohemia should have been asked for sittings by the Bohemian artists who clustered around her; and so it happens that she sat to Thos. Le Clear for her portrait in oils, and to O'Donovan for a bronze portrait-medallion. The Diary entry for 24th February (1878) shows that we two spent the evening at Walter Paris's studio, and had a jolly time of it with some of the best artists of New York. Most of them belonged to the famous Tile Club, whose members meet monthly at each other's studios, and paint designs on tiles supplied by the host of the evening, whose property they become, and who has them baked and glazed at his own expense. A charming arrangement, by which each member of the Club becomes in his turn, at trifling cost, the owner of a set of signed paintings by good artists.

H. P. B. was inexpressibly amused by an incident connected with my farcical improvisations, alluded to above. One of the things she frequently called for was a burlesque of "speaking mediumship," in which the mannerisms and platitudes of a certain class of platform speakers were travestied. On the evening in question we had as a visitor a London *litterateur,* a former editor of the *Spectator* and a University man. He had gone in for a good deal of investigation of Spiritualism and was a believer. I pretended to be controlled by the spirit of a deceased High Church clergyman and, with closed eyes and solemn tone, launched out into a tirade against the demoralising influences of the day, among which I accorded first place to the Theosophical Society. The promoters of this nefarious body, I made the pseudo-spirit denounce in an especial degree, while upon H. P. B., its high priestess and head devil, I launched the thunderbolts of the major and minor excommunication. The old lady laughed until she cried, but our guest sat staring at me (as I noticed from time to time when I took a hasty glance at him between my almost closed lids), and at last broke out with the exclamation: "It's terrible, it's awfully real; you really should not let him do it, Madame!" "Do what?" she asked. "Give way to this mediumship when his whole self is obsessed by so strong and so vindictive a personality of the spirit-world!" This was too much for my mirth-loving colleague, and she exploded with laughter. Finally, catching her breath, she cried out: "Stop! For goodness' sake, stop, Olcott, or you will kill me!" Just then I was at the middle of a fine burst of scorn over the pretended erudition and altruism of this "Russian schemer," but I stopped short and, turning to Mr. L., asked him in the quietest, most common-place tone, for a match for my pipe. I almost lost my gravity on seeing his sudden start of amazement, and the sharp look of enquiry he shot into my face, telling as though he had spoken the words, his belief that I was either mad, or the most extra-ordinary of mediums since I could so instantaneously "pass out of control." The sequel almost finished off H. P. B. The next morning, at eight o'clock, Mr. L. called, to walk down town with me and try his persuasive powers to make me throw up this mediumship which, he assured me, would de-stroy my hope of useful public work in the future! The medium, he explained—as though I had not then known it for at least twenty years—was a veritable slave in the degree of his real mediumship; the passive agent of disincarnate forces whose nature he had no means of testing, and as to whose domina-tion he had no selective power. Say what I might, he would not be persuaded that the whole affair of last evening was nothing but a joke, one of the various divertisements employed by H. P. B. and myself to relieve the strain of our serious work; he would have it that I was a medium, and so we had to let it rest. But to us it was a standing joke, and H. P. B. told it number-less times to visitors.

On the 5th April, T. A. Edison sent me his signed applica-tion for membership. I had had to see him about exhibiting his electrical inventions at the Paris Exposition of that year; I being the honorary secretary to a Citizens' National Commit-tee, which was formed at the request of the French Govern-ment, to induce the United States Congress to pass a bill providing for our country taking part in the first international exposition of the world's industries since the fall of the Empire and the foundation of the French Republic. Edison and I got to talking about occult forces, and he interested me greatly by the remark that he had done some experimenting in that direction. His aim was to try whether a pendulum, suspended on the wall of his private laboratory, could be made to move by will-force. To test this he had used as conductors, wire of various metals, simple and compound, and tubes containing different fluids, one end of the conductor being applied to his forehead, the other connected with the pendulum. As no results have since been published, I presume that the experiments did not succeed. It may interest him, if he should chance to see this record, to know that in 1852 I met in Ohio a young man named Macallister, an ex-Shaker, who told me that he had discovered a certain fluid, by bathing his forehead with which he could transmit thought to another person employing the same fluid at an agreed time, however distant the two might be apart. I remember writing an article on the subject under the title of "Mental Telegraphing" to the old *Spirituai Telegraph* newspaper, of the late Mr. S. B. Britten. Having been acquainted with several noted American inventors, and learnt from them the psychological processes by which they severally got the first ideas of their inventions, I described these to Edison and asked him how his discoveries came to him. He said that often, perhaps while walking on Broadway with an acquaintance, and talking about quite other matters, amid the din and roar of the street, the thought would suddenly flash into his mind that such a desired thing might be accomplished in a certain way. He would hasten home, set to work on the idea, and not give it up until he had either succeeded or found the thing impracticable.

On the 17th April we began to talk with Sotheran, General T., and one or two other high Masons about constituting our Society into a Masonic body with a Ritual and Degrees; the idea being that it would form a natural complement to the higher degrees of the craft, restoring to it the vital element of Oriental mysticism which it lacked or had lost. At the same time, such an arrangement would give strength and permanency to the Society, by allying it to the ancient Brotherhood whose lodges are established throughout the whole world. Now that I come to look back at it, we were in reality but planning to repeat the work of Cagliostro, whose Egyptian Lodge was in his days so powerful a centre for the propagation of Eastern occult thought. We did not abandon the idea until long after removing to Bombay, and the last mention of it in my Diary is an entry to the effect that Swami Dyánand Sarasvati had promised me to compile a Ritual for the use of our New York and London members. Some old colleagues have denied the above facts, but, although they knew it not, the plan was seriously entertained by H. P. B. and myself, and we relinquished it only when we found the Society growing rapidly by its own inherent impetus and making it impolitic for us to merge it into the Masonic body.

One evening H. P. B. made a pretty phenomenon of duplication. A French physician, Dr. B., was one of a party of nine visitors at our rooms, and sat near H. P. B.'s writing-table, so that the standing gas-light shone upon a large gold sleeve-button, bearing his initials, that he wore. H. P. B.'s eye being caught by its glitter, she reached across the table, touched the button, and then opening her hand, showed him and the rest of us a duplicate of the same. We all saw it, but she would not give it to either of us, and presently re-opening her hand, the *Máyá* had disappeared. One much more interesting thing she did for me, one evening when we two were alone. From time to time she had told me tales of adventure and doings about a number of persons; some in India, others in Western countries. This evening she was shuffling a pack of cards in her hands in an aimless sort of way, when suddenly she held the pack open towards me and showed me the *visiting card* of a certain British officer's wife, who had chanced to see a Mahâtma in Northern India and fallen offensively in love with his splendid face. The card bore her name, and, in a lower corner, that of her husband's regiment, *partly scratched out as with a knife,* so that I might not be able to identify the lady if I should ever meet her in India. The shuffling went on, and every minute or two she would open the pack and show me the visiting cards of other persons known to us by name; some were glazed, some plain; some with names engraved in script, others in square lettering; some type-printed, some black-bordered, some large, and others small. It was a marvellous and quite unique phenomenon. Yet how queer it was that precious psychic force—so hard to generate, so easy to lose—should have been wasted to objectify, for a brief moment in each case, these astral phantoms of common visiting cards, when the same volume of force might have been employed to compel some great scientist to believe in the existence of the records of the A'kas'a and devote his energies to spiritual research. My respected sister, Mrs.

Mitchell, who, with her husband and children, occupied a flat in the same apartment-house with us, was one day shown by H. P. B. a collection of gems and jewelry which, she says, must have represented a value of at least £10,000, and which she thought were part of her family inheritance. So little did she suspect that they were merely illusionary, that she was even incredulous when I told her that H. P. B. owned no such property. If she had, I am sure she would never have allowed herself to be put to such straits as she was.

The nearer we approached the time for our change of base, the more vehement became H. P. B.'s praise of India, the Hindus, the entire Orient and Orientals as a whole, and her disparagement of Western people as a whole, their social customs, religious tyranny, and ideals. There were stormy evenings at the Lamasery, among which stands out one episode very distinctly. Walter Paris, the artist, and one of the best of fellows, had lived at Bombay some years as Government Architect, and was glad to talk with us about India. But not having our excessive reverence for the country and sympathy for the people, he would often offend H. P. B.'s sensitiveness by remarks on what I now know to be Anglo-Indian lines. One evening he was talking about an old servant of his who had committed some stupidity in harnessing or saddling a horse, and quietly remarked that he had slashed the man with his whip. Instantly, as if she had received the blow across her own face, H. P. B. sprang up, stood before him, and in a speech of about five minutes gave him such a scathing rebuke as to make him sit speechless. She stigmatised the act as one of cowardice, and made it serve as a text for a neat discourse on the treatment of the Oriental races by the Anglo-Indian ruling class. This was not a mere casual outburst adapted to the Western market; she preserved the same tone from first to last, and I have often heard her at Allahabad, Simla, Bombay, Madras, and elsewhere, use the same boldness of speech to the highest Anglo-Indian officials.

One way H. P. B. had of beguiling tedious hours after *Isis Unveiled* was off our hands, was to draw caricatures on playing-cards, bringing the pips into the pictures. Several of these clever productions were very laughable. One, made out of the Ten of Clubs, was a minstrel performance; the grotesque contortions of the "end men," the solemn caddishness of the "Interrogator," and the amiable vacuity of the intermediates being admirably delineated. Another was a Spiritualistic séance, with banjo, accordeons, and tambourines flying through the air, a bucket inverted over one "investigator's" head, and an impish little elemental grinning from a lady's lap as she holds his forked tail in her hand under the impression that it is part of the body of some departed friend. A third card—made out of a Seven of Hearts, I think—shows two fat monks at a table laden with turkey, ham, and other delicacies, while bottles of wine stand ready at hand, and others are cooling in an ice vase on the floor. One of the reverend fathers, who has a most animal cast of features, is putting his hand behind him to receive a *billet-doux* from a prim servant-maid in cap and apron. Still another represents a policeman catching a runaway thief by the foot; another, a couple of swell Tommies walking with their sweethearts; a third, a patriarchal negro, running with his black grandchild in his arms, etc., etc. Quite recently I have learnt that her late father had a special talent in this same direction, so it was quite easy to account for her cleverness. I told her I thought it a pity that she should not make up an entire pack in this fashion, as it would surely yield her a goodly sum as copyright. She said she should, but the mood did not last long enough to bring the desired result.

On the 8th July she took out her naturalisation papers, went with me to the Superior Court, and was duly sworn in as a citizen of the United States of America. She describes it thus in my Diary: "H. P. B. was made to swear eternal affection, devotion and defence to and of the U. S. Constitution, forswear every particle of allegiance to the Russian Emperor, and was made a 'Citizen of the U. S. of America.' Received her naturalisation papers and went home happy." Of course, the next day's American papers were full of accounts of the event, and reporters were sent to interview the new citizen, who made them all laugh with her *naïve* opinions upon politics and politicians.

The formation of the British Theosophical Society, in London (now called the London Lodge T. S.), occupied a good deal of my attention during the early summer months of 1878. This, our first Branch, was finally organised on June 27, by Dr. J. Storer Cobb, LL.D., Treasurer of the T. S., whose visit to London at the time was availed of to make him my official agent for this purpose. Mr. Sinnett has kindly favoured me with the following copy of the record of the proceedings, from the Minute Book of the Lodge in his official custody; which I publish, because of its historical interest:

Meeting of Fellows

Held at 38 *Great Russell Street, London, June* 27, 1878. Present: Fellows, J. Storer Cobb, *Treasurer* (New York Society), C. C. Massey, Dr. C. Carter Blake, Dr. George Wyld, Dr. H. J. Billing, and E. Kislingbury.

Fellow J. Storer Cobb in the chair, read letters from Mr. Yarker, Dr. K. Mackenzie, Captain Irwin, and Mr. R. P. Thomas, expressing regret at their unavoidable absence, and sympathy with the objects of the meeting; also a letter from Rev. W. Stainton Moses, stating that he was unable to take part in the meeting, having resigned his Fellowship in the New York Society.

Mr. Treasurer Cobb having stated President Olcott's instructions as to the basis of an English branch society, as communicated since a former meeting of Fellows in this place, proposed to retire, as it was not his intention to become a member of the new branch. On his being invited to remain as a listener, an informal discussion ensued, and it was finally *Resolved,* on the motion of Fellow Massey, seconded by Dr. H. J. Billing, "that, in the opinion of the English Fellows of the Theosophical Society of New York, present at this meeting, it is desirable to form a Society in England, in connection and in sympathy with that body."

In accordance with the paper of instructions received from the President, the meeting proceeded to discuss the question of a President of the Branch Society, and on the ballot being taken, C. C. Massey was found to be chosen President.

Mr. Massey, in accepting the office, made a few remarks

and took the chair. It was proposed by him, and seconded by
Dr. Carter Blake, that Miss Kislingbury be Secretary to the
Branch Society. This was carried and accepted by Miss K.,
pro tem.

The meeting was adjourned until further advices from
New York, and the Secretary was requested to furnish a copy
of these minutes to Col. Olcott (President) and a copy of the
Resolution, above recorded, to the absent English members.

The following memorandum was then drawn up and
signed, and given to the Secretary to forward to Col. Olcott,
viz.:

"London, *June 27, 1878.*

"To
"Col. Henry s. Olcott,
        President of the T. S., New York.
    "I hereby certify that this day has been held a
meeting at which has been formed an English branch
of the above Society, of which Branch, Fellow Charles
Carleton Massey has been, by ballot of the Fellows
present, elected President.

(Signed) "John Storer Cobb,
            Treasurer, N. Y. Society.
(Signed) C. C. Massey."

My official letters recognising the British Theosophical
Society and ratifying the proceedings at the above reported

meeting, were written July 12, 1878, and sent to Mr. C. C. Massey and Miss E. Kislingbury, the President and the Secretary.

There is an entry in my Diary for October 25th which is interesting as showing the faculty of clairvoyance that H. P. B. sometimes exercised. It says:

"O'Donovan, Wimbridge, H. P. B., and I were at dinner when the servant brought in a letter from Massey left at the moment by the postman. Before it came, H. P. B. announced its coming and nature, and when I received it and before the seal was broken, she said it contained a letter from Dr. Wyld, and read that also without looking at it."

I recollect taking the cover from the hand of the servant and laying it beside my plate, intending to defer reading it until we rose from the table. Between it and H. P. B. stood a large earthenware water-pitcher, yet while it lay there she first read the contents of Massey's letter and then those of the enclosure from Dr. Wyld. I find, moreover, that the covering letter had Mahátmic writing on one of the pages, and that I returned it to the sender with a statement of the facts, signed by myself and Mr. Wimbridge.

It is a rather notable coincidence that several astrologers, clairvoyants, and Indian ascetics should have prophesied that H. P. B. would die at sea. I find one of the sort noted on the page for November 2, 1878. A gentleman psychic, a friend of Wimbridge's, "foretold H. P. B.'s death at sea—a sudden death. Doubted that she would even reach Bombay." Majji, the Benares *Yogíni*, made the same prognostic as to the place of H. P. B.'s death and even the time, but neither proved correct. No more did a card-reader at New York who predicted H. P. B.'s death by murder before 1886. In entering the affair H. P. B. very naturally put two points of exclamation after the word murder, and cynically added the remark: "Nothing like clairvoyance!"

One of our visitors was more successful as a prophet, but he did not try his faculty on H. P. B. Here is the description I wrote of him in the Diary:

"A mystical Hebrew physician. A strange, very strange man. Has prescience as to visitors, deaths, and a spiritual insight as to their maladies. Old, thin, stooping; his hair thin, fine, grizzled and stands out in all directions from his noble head. Rouges his cheeks to correct their unnatural pallor. Has a habit of throwing his head far back and looking up into space as he listens or converses. His complexion is waxen, his skin transparent and extremely thin. He wears summer clothing in the depth of winter. He has the peculiar habit of saying when about to answer: 'Vell, see he-ere, tee-ar!'"

For thirty years he had studied the Kabbalah, and his conversations with H. P. B. were largely confined to its mysteries. He said one evening in my hearing that despite his thirty years' researches he had not discovered the true meanings that she read into certain texts, and that illumined them with a holy light.

Our departure having been finally decided upon, I began in the autumn of 1878 to get my worldly affairs into order. An active correspondence was kept up with our Bombay and Ceylon friends (a number of Buddhists and Hindus joined the T. S. by letter), our small library was shipped, and little by little our household goods were sold or given away. We made no parade of intentions, but our rooms were thronged more than ever by the friends and acquaintances to whom they became known. H. P. B.'s entries in my Diary during my frequent absences from New York in the last weeks, testify to the nervous eagerness she felt to get away, and her fears that my plans might miscarry. In the entry of October 22d she writes—speaking of the urgency of our Mahâtmas: "N—went off watch and in came S—with orders from—to complete all by the early part of December. Well, H. S. O. is playing his great final stake." There is reference here to the change of personalities in the Intelligences controlling the H. P. B. body, and the entries in different handwritings support this idea. A similar entry occurs on November 14th, where it is said that we must use every exertion to get away by the 20th December at latest. There is a final paragraph on that page to this effect: "O gods, O India of the golden face, is this really the beginning of the end!" On November 21st other urgent orders came through the same channel, and we were bidden to begin packing our trunks. Various persons wished to accompany us to India, and some made efforts to do so, but the party finally comprised but four—H. P. B., Miss Bates, an English governess, Mr. Wimbridge, an artist and architect, and myself. On the 24th we were at it, and the following day the first of our intended party of four, Miss Bates, sailed for Liverpool, taking two of H. P. B.'s trunks with her. Again and again came the orders to hasten our departure. Writing about the unexpected resignation of a member, H. P. B. exclaims: "Oh! this wretched brood; when shall we be rid of it!" The next day's entry (in red pencil and large letters) says, *à propos* of my being ready soon: "His fate depends on that": our remaining furniture *must* be disposed of at auction before December 12th; and the sale actually came off on the 9th. That day she writes: "Went to bed at four and was roused again at six, thanks to M—who locked the door and Jenny (the servant) could not get in. Got up, breakfasted and went off to the Battery to meet—(an occultist connected with the Lodge of the White Brotherhood). Came back at two and found an infernal row and hullabaloo at the auction. All our things went for a song, as they say in America...5 P.M.—*Everything gone: Baron de Palm adieu! Supped on a board three inches wide!*"

Then there was a skurry and a rush of visitors, articles appearing in the papers, replies written by H. P. B. On the 13th I received from the President of the United States an autograph letter of recommendation to all U. S. Ministers and Consuls; and from the Department of State a special passport such as is issued to American diplomats, and a commission to report to Government upon the practicability of extending the commercial interests of our country in Asia. Those documents proved useful later on in India, when H. P. B. and I were under suspicion of being Russian spies! The particulars of which farcical episode will be told in their proper place.

I find entries in the Diary showing that I got scarcely any rest during these latter days, sitting up all night to write letters, rushing away to Philadelphia and other towns, snatching a morsel of food as I could get it: while throughout the whole narrative sounds the boom of the orders to depart before the fixed day of grace—the 17th—should pass away. H. P. B.'s writing grows scratchy, and on the page for December 15th I notice two of the above-mentioned variants of her script, which show that her body was occupied by two of the Mahâtmas on that same evening. I had bought an Edison phonograph of the original pattern, and on that evening quite a number of our members and friends, among them a Mr. Johnston, whom Edison had sent as his personal representative (he being unavoidably absent), talked into the voice-receiver messages to our then known and unknown brothers in India. The several tinfoil sheets, properly marked for identification, were carefully removed from the cylinder, packed up, and they are still kept in the Adyar Library, for the edification of future times.* Among the voices kept are those of H. P. B.—a very sharp and clear record—myself, Mr. Judge and his brother John, Prof. Alex. Wilder, Miss Sarah Cowell, two Messrs. Laffan, Mr. Clough, Mr. D. A. Curtis, Mr. Griggs, Mrs. S. R. Wells, Mrs. and Miss Amer, Dr. J. A. Weisse, Mr. Shinn, Mr. Terriss, Mr. Maynard, Mr. E. H. Johnston, Mr. O'Donovan, etc., of whom all were clever, and some very well known as authors, journalists, painters, sculptors, musicians, and in other ways.

The 17th December was our last day on American soil.

---

* Quite recently—*viz.*, in May, 1895—I sent these tinfoil records to Edison's London office, to see if they might not be received on one of the modern wax cylinders and so saved for posterity. Unfortunately, nothing could be done with them, the indentations made by the voices having become almost flattened out. It is a great pity, for otherwise we might have had duplicates taken off the original, and thus have had H. P. B.'s strong voice speaking audibly at our local meetings all over the world on "White Lotus Day," the anniversary of her death.

H. P. B.'s entry says: "Great day! Olcott packed up.... what next? All dark—but tranquil." And then comes, written in large letters, the heart-cry of joy, CONSUMMATUM EST! The closing paragraph reads thus: "Olcott returned at 7 P.M. with the tickets for the British Steamboat, the *Canada,* and wrote letters until 11:30. Curtis and Judge passed the evening. Maynard took H. P. B. [See the writers always speaking of her in the third person] to dine at his house. She returned home at 9. He made her a present of a tobacco-pouch. Charles (our big cat) lost!! At near 12, midnight, H. S. O. and H. P. B. took leave of the chandelier and drove off in a carriage to the steamer." So closes the first volume of the history of the Theosphical Society with the departure of its Founders from America.

Behind them lay three years of struggles; of obstacles surmounted; of crude plans partly worked out; of literary labour; of desertions of friends; of encounters with adversaries; of the laying of broad foundations for the structure that in time was destined to arise for the gathering in of the nations, but the possibility of which was then unsuspected by them. For they had builded better than they knew—better, at any rate, than I knew. What lay in the future we foresaw not. The words of H. P. B. show that: "All dark, but tranquil." The marvellous extension of our Society had not entered even into our dreams. An ex-officer of ours has published the statement that the Society had died a natural death before we left for India. The diagram opposite will show that, while it had dwindled to almost nothing, it began to revive from the moment its executive centre was shifted to India.

We passed a wretched night on the ship, what with the

bitter cold, damp bedding, no heating apparatus working, and the banging of tackle and rub-a-dub-dub of the winches getting in cargo. Instead of leaving early, the steamer did not get away from her wharf until 2.30 P.M. on the 18th. Then, having lost the tide, she had to anchor off Coney Island and crossed the Sandy Hook bar only at noon on the 19th. At last we were crossing the blue water towards our Land of Promise; and, so full was my heart with the prospect, that I did not wait on deck to see the Navesink Highlands melt out of view, but descended to my cabin and searched for Bombay on my Map of India.

HENRY STEEL OLCOTT: THE TIMELINE OF A SPIRITUAL PIONEER

By Mitch Horowitz

Colonel Henry Steel Olcott (1832–1907) cofounded the Theosophical Society with Madame Helena Petrovna Blavatsky in New York City in 1875. In its early years, the Theosophical Society ignited new interest in occult and esoteric philosophy  throughout much of the West, inspiring the wave of alternative spirituality that soon swept the modern world.

Olcott's influence spread in other significant ways, as well: He brought Westerners some of their first exposure to Vedic and Buddhist religious ideas, and in 1876 he presided over America's first public cremation service, at a time when cremation was considered an exotic oddity.

Olcott and Blavatsky relocated to India in late 1878, taking the nucleus of the Theosophical Society with them. In marathon speaking tours throughout the East, Olcott helped inspire Hindu and Buddhist religious revivals in the colonial-dominated societies of India and Sri Lanka. In the late nineteenth century, members of the Theosophical Society brought vigor and early leadership to India's nascent independence movement. Mohandas Gandhi cited Theosophy as a major influence on his earliest ideas about human equality and religious universality. Without Blavatsky, Olcott, and the Theosophical Society, the political and religious landscape of today's world would look markedly different.

Even before becoming Theosophy's roving ambassador, Olcott led a notable career. While still in his twenties, he was considered a wunderkind of scientific and experimental agriculture. As a staff colonel for the Union Army, he investigated and exposed fraud among military contractors during the Civil War. After the war, Olcott became one of the early investigators of the Lincoln assassination, and made some of the first arrests and interrogations of suspected coconspirators.

For anyone curious about the life of this remarkable (and under-recognized) American, this timeline highlights the key dates and events of his life.

1832

Henry Steel Olcott is born on August 2 to Presbyterian parents Henry Wyckoff and Emily in Orange, New Jersey. He is the first of six children.

1847

At age fifteen, he enters the University of the City of New York, later called New York University. A downturn in his father's finances forces Olcott to quit after one year.

1848

At sixteen, he works on a relative's farm near Elyria, Ohio. Maternal uncles expose him to séances, table-rapping, and Spiritualism.

Circa 1853

Olcott returns East to study experimental agricultural at a research farm near Newark, New Jersey. (The farm's owner shares his interest in Spiritualism.) He also works on the staff of an agricultural magazine.

Circa 1855

A relative leaves Olcott a bequest, which he and a friend use to open a school of scientific agriculture near Mount Vernon, New York.

1856

Mother Emily dies. Olcott attracts wide attention with his lectures and agricultural research on the highly adaptable foreign sugarcane crops called sorgho and imphee.

1857

Olcott publishes an influential monograph, *Sorgho and Imphee, the Chinese and African Sugar Canes.* The book attracts widespread interest on the eve of the Civil War, when Northerners are looking for alternatives to the South's sugar-cane crop.

1858

Olcott publishes his *Yale Agricultural Lectures* and embarks upon a European tour to lecture on scientific agriculture. His farm school closes. He is offered the chair of agriculture at the University of Athens in Greece, but instead accepts a job as the agricultural editor at the *New York Tribune*.

1859

As a journalist for the *New York Tribune*, Olcott covers the December 2 hanging of abolitionist John Brown.

1860

On April 26, he marries Mary Epplee Morgan, the daughter of an Episcopal minister.

1861

In January, his first son, Richard Morgan, is born. When Civil War breaks out in April, Olcott joins the Union Army and receives a commission as a signals officer.

1862

In June his second son, William Topping, is born. Around September Olcott enters a military hospital with malaria and dysentery. In November he is reassigned to an investigations unit to uncover fraudulent billing practices among military contractors. He is named a staff colonel to lend weight to his investigative authority and is placed in command of a team of detectives and stenographers.

1864

Secretary of War Edwin M. Stanton commends Olcott for his success in routing out contractor fraud. Olcott's third son, Henry Steel, is born and dies in infancy.

1865

On April 14, Lincoln is assassinated and Olcott volunteers to assist the investigation. Stanton summons him to bring his staff of detectives from New York to Washington, D.C., to help search for the assassin. Olcott is appointed to a three-man commission to review evidence of a conspiracy and to identify possible coconspirators. He makes the first major arrest of a suspected conspirator, Edmund Spangler. He also interrogates Mary Surratt who ran boardinghouses where assassin John Wilkes Booth and his confederates met. Olcott and his detectives are ordered to raid the Surratt boardinghouse to search for conspirators. Surratt is hanged in a questionable trial, though Olcott's interrogation of her is never introduced into evidence.

Olcott resigns his commission at the end of the year.

1866

Olcott obtains a job at a New York law office and starts to study for the bar.

1868

He is admitted to the New York Bar and appointed secretary and managing director of the National Insurance Convention, where he helps draft laws governing the insurance industry. His first daughter, Bessie, is born; she dies before age two.

1870

Olcott visits London where he frequents Spiritualist mediums. He continues his work in journalism.

1873

The world-traveled Russian noblewoman and occult seeker Madame Helena Petrovna Blavatsky arrives in New York. She has journeyed to America, she writes, to visit the "cradle of Modern Spiritualism." Blavatsky and Olcott do not meet until the following year.

1874

By midyear, Olcott is divorced from his wife—but records do not survive. (Olcott's contemporary and fellow Theosophist William Quan Judge says Olcott's ex-wife remarried in 1881.) While reasons for the divorce are unknown, Olcott's contemporaries speculate that part of the cause was Olcott's avant-garde spiritual interests.

In July, Olcott reads in the Spiritualist newspaper *Banner of Light* about the Eddy brothers, a pair of spirit mediums who conjure ghostly figures at their farmhouse in Chittenden,

Vermont. In the late summer/early fall Olcott begins covering events at the "ghost-farm," first for the *New York Sun* and later for the *New York Daily Graphic*. On October 14, he meets Blavatsky at the farmhouse. They strike up a close (but not amorous) friendship. In November Olcott returns to New York City.

1875

Olcott publishes his Spiritualist investigations as the book *People from the Other World*.

In May, Olcott receives his first letter from one of Madame Blavatsky's "Masters," or hidden spiritual mentors. The letter is signed by a Tuitit Bey identified as hailing from the "Brotherhood of Luxor." Olcott soon installs Blavatsky in a Manhattan apartment at 46 Irving Place.

Also in May, Olcott makes a failed attempt to form a "Miracle Club" dedicated to investigating the esoteric and paranormal.

A September 17 gathering at Irving Place attracts Spiritualist thinker Emma Hardinge Britten and others to hear a lecture on Egyptian geometry. Olcott proposes to form another organization to study ancient and contemporary spiritual mysteries.

On November 17, Olcott, Blavatsky, and others inaugurate the Theosophical Society. Olcott is named president. Later that month, Olcott rents separate apartments for himself and Blavatsky at 433 West 34th Street. They work together on her book *Isis Unveiled*.

1876

In May, Olcott organizes the nation's first public cremation service at New York's Masonic Hall, eulogizing a European-American nobleman named Baron de Palm and announcing plans to cremate his body. The press calls the controversial event a "pagan funeral." The deceased subject is not actually cremated until December at a private crematorium in Pennsylvania in the presence of Olcott and Blavatsky.

In summer-fall, Olcott and Blavatsky move to a small suite of apartments on Manhattan's West Side at the corner of Eighth Avenue and 47th Street. Their home becomes an occult salon and a gathering spot where Thomas Edison, Major General Abner Doubleday, and other notable figures congregate to discuss mystical religious ideas. The place is considered such a hotbed of avant-garde religion that the New York press calls it the Lamasery, after the monastic retreats of Tibet.

1877

One winter night, Olcott reports being visited at the Lamasery by Master Morya, one of the hidden Masters, or Mahatmas, spoken of by Blavatsky. Olcott said the figure materialized before him while he was reading late one night—and the experience sealed his decision to later travel with Blavatsky to India. (The precise date of the visitation is unclear, though it seems to follow the events of 1876, and Olcott cites its having occurred during their writing of *Isis Unveiled*, which was published in the fall. Hence, the encounter is likely to have taken place in winter.)

In September, Madame Blavatsky publishes her sprawling study of occult subjects, *Isis Unveiled*.

1878

In April, Thomas Edison joins the near-dormant Theosophical Society.

On December 17, Olcott and Blavatsky depart for India, uprooting the nucleus of the Theosophical Society.

1879

Olcott and Blavatsky reach Bombay in February.

1880

Olcott makes his first visit to Ceylon (later Sri Lanka). He and Blavatsky become the first Westerners to publicly take formal Buddhist vows.

1881

Against Blavatsky's wishes, Olcott leaves her side to return to Ceylon for a speaking tour. He crisscrosses the island nation via oxcart, calling for a Buddhist revival. Olcott starts a National Education Fund for Buddhist schools and publishes his influential *Buddhist Catechism*.

1882

Olcott begins practicing magnetic, or Mesmeric, healings in Ceylon. In November, he returns to Blavatsky at Theosophical headquarters at a suburb of Madras in Adyar, India.

1884

In May, Olcott travels to London to lobby for the rights of Ceylon's Buddhists to worship publicly. He responds to questions about Blavatsky's mediumistic abilities before the Society for Psychical Research, which includes notable scientist Frederic Myers.

In the fall, British colonial officials agree to lighten regulations of public Buddhist worship and to officially recognize the holiday of Wesak, the birthday/passing of Buddha.

In September, a disgruntled married couple formerly affiliated with the Theosophical Society circulates a series of public letters impugning Blavatsky as a fake conjuror and fraud. In December, psychical investigator Richard Hodgson arrives in Adyar to investigate these and other charges for the Society for Psychical Research.

1885

Olcott makes his first visit to the Buddhist communities of Burma (later Myanmar).

In March, Blavatsky departs India in the wake of scandals arising from the letters and investigations over her activities.

In April, Olcott codesigns the international Buddhist flag in Ceylon.

In June, researcher Hodgson issues his initial findings through the Society for Psychical Research. The controversial "Hodgson Report" appears in December, impugning Blavatsky, and writing off Olcott as her dupe.

1885–1886

Blavatsky resides in different parts of Western Europe and begins writing her epic study of occult cosmology, *The Secret Doctrine*.

Circa 1888

Blavatsky settles in London. *The Secret Doctrine* is published.

1889

Olcott takes a four-month tour of Japan and its Buddhist temples; he delivers seventy-five lectures in 107 days. He attempts to start a unifying International Buddhist League.

In November Blavatsky meets with a young Mohandas Gandhi in London.

1891

Blavatsky dies in London.

1894–1895

Olcott becomes embroiled in internal Theosophical Society controversies with William Q. Judge, who maintained he received his own guidance from Blavatsky and Olcott's Masters. Olcott disputes Judge's claims, leading to splits within the society.

1895

Olcott publishes the first installment of his six-book memoir, *Old Diary Leaves* (which is issued through 1935, including in posthumous volumes). He writes numerous articles in the years ahead.

1906
In October, Olcott suffers a severe fall on a passenger ship en route from New York to Italy.

1907
Olcott dies on February 17 at Adyar. He leaves behind hundreds of Buddhist schools in Ceylon, a sign of his success at reigniting Buddhist practice there and in other nations.

INDEX

If you enjoyed this book, visit

www.tarcherbooks.com

and sign up for Tarcher's e-newsletter to receive
special offers, giveaway promotions, and
information on hot upcoming releases.

TARCHER
PENGUIN

Great Lives Begin with Great Ideas

Connect with the Tarcher Community

• • •

Stay in touch with favorite authors!
Enter weekly contests!
Read exclusive excerpts!
Voice your opinions!

Follow us

 Tarcher Books

 @TarcherBooks

If you would like to place a bulk order
of this book, call 1-800-847-5515.